THE SANDBURG RANGE

BY CARL SANDBURG

Abraham Lincoln: The Prairie Years (*Two Volumes*)

Abraham Lincoln: The War Years (*Four Volumes*)

Abraham Lincoln: The Prairie Years and The War Years (*One-Volume Edition*)

The Chicago Race Riots

The American Songbag

Steichen the Photographer

Potato Face

Mary Lincoln: Wife and Widow (*documented by Paul M. Angle*)

Storm over the Land

Home Front Memo

The Photographs of Abraham Lincoln (*with Frederick H. Meserve*)

Lincoln Collector: The Story of the Oliver R. Barrett Lincoln Collection

Always the Young Strangers

NOVEL

Remembrance Rock

POETRY

Chicago Poems

Cornhuskers

Smoke and Steel

Slabs of the Sunburnt West

Selected Poems (*edited by Rebecca West*)

Good Morning, America

The People, Yes

Complete Poems

FOR YOUNG FOLKS

Rootabaga Stories

Rootabaga Pigeons

Abe Lincoln Grows Up

Early Moon

Prairie-Town Boy

CARL SANDBURG

The
Sandburg
Range

HARCOURT, BRACE AND COMPANY

New York

Thanks are due the following for the introductory notes used throughout: The Boston *Globe* for the Foreword; Appleton-Century-Crofts for the selection from *Spokesmen;* Willard Thorp and the Macmillan Company for the comment from *Literary History of the United States;* Frank Lloyd Wright and Duell, Sloan and Pearce for the letter from Mr. Wright's *Autobiography;* Kathryn Lloyd Lewis and Harcourt, Brace and Company for the essay from *It Takes All Kinds* by Lloyd Lewis; Irita Van Doren for her remarks on *Remembrance Rock* at a New York *Herald Tribune* Book and Author Luncheon; John K. Hutchens and the New York *Herald Tribune Book Review* for the excerpt from his review of *Always the Young Strangers* and the New York *Times Book Review* for the excerpt from the Robert E. Sherwood review of the same volume; David C. Mearns and the New York *Herald Tribune* for the excerpt from his review of *Lincoln Collector;* the New York *World-Telegram and Sun* for the excerpt from the William Allen White review of *Abraham Lincoln: The Prairie Years;* Fanny Butcher and the Chicago *Tribune* for her comment on *Mary Lincoln: Wife and Widow;* and the *Virginia Quarterly Review* for the Charles A. Beard review of *Abraham Lincoln: The War Years.*

Library of Congress Catalog Card Number: 57-12373

Printed in the United States of America
ISBN 0-15-601408-4 (pbk)

Publisher's Note

"Like other towering figures in the great tradition of letters, he has been not one man but many: poet and biographer, essayist and critic, historian and novelist, teller of prose tales for children, and indefatigable bearer of song to the nation as a traveling minstrel." So the Boston Globe *editorialized in 1952 when Carl Sandburg was awarded the Gold Medal for History and Biography by the American Academy of Arts and Letters. This tribute suggests the nature and intent of the present volume.*

Heretofore a reader hoping to assess the full measure of Carl Sandburg has had to make his way through a library of published works. We have long felt that a volume such as The Sandburg Range *would serve a twofold purpose: it would present every aspect of a notable literary career, in relatively brief compass, to the reader already familiar with one or more phases of Sandburg's writing; and it would enable the new reader of Sandburg to discover at once the remarkable scope of a major writer of our time.*

The general scheme for the book was suggested by Carl Sandburg's editor, Catherine McCarthy, who worked in close collaboration with the author and the author's wife, Paula Sandburg, in compiling the selections from his works.

Foreword*

"He was a dreamer and a man of reverie, as all poets are, while at the same time he had the practicality of an Edison—a combination you don't often find. Besides, he was endowed with a New Testament patience and an Old Testament stubbornness."

The speaker was the poet, Carl Sandburg. The time—nearly a generation ago. The theme was Abraham Lincoln, whose life he had just finished writing in six massive volumes quite unlike any other biography known to American letters before or since, for in them was spread the panorama of an epoch as only a poet could unfold it: the prairie years, the land of blossom and storm, the thunder and cruelty of battlefields, the swarming procession of figures from a vanished world, and the gaunt, humorous, resolute, sad faced, humble, brooding Midwesterner, who dominated the drama.

Nearly 35 years had passed since the idea of writing that life story first possessed Carl Sandburg. Twenty had gone into translating that idea into reality from mountains of documents and tireless journeyings. Now it was finished. The poet, characteristically relaxed, was afoot once more on the endless wanderings that began in boyhood and have not yet ended.

"He was a dreamer and a man of reverie . . ." The vignette, though seemingly he was unaware of it, was, to a considerable extent, a picture of himself.

In another week or two, the American Academy of Arts and Letters is to bestow upon Carl Sandburg the highest honor in that illustrious society's gift: its gold medal. The award, strangely enough, will not be for Sandburg's poems but for his "Lincoln." It is this work, completed a decade and a half ago, that they have

---

* An editorial in the Boston *Globe* signed "Uncle Dudley" and published five years ago, when Carl Sandburg was awarded the Gold Medal for History and Biography by the American Academy of Arts and Letters.

singled out, not the songs into whose torrent stream he has
poured the tumult and faith, the failure and strength, the bitter-
ness and glory, the meanness, heroism, ambition and beauty of
our life as a people in these past 50 changing years.

Perhaps the decision is wise. For what indeed is Sandburg's
"Lincoln" if not an epitome and summation of the America
which preceded his own; the America to which, in a score of
other volumes, he has added his own supplement? Today, in
his 75th year, he towers above a generation of lesser, more fear-
ful bards who flinch before a life he began to encounter in all
its brawling contrasts of mediocrity and beauty as a boy in his
teens. They all too often seem to lose the vision and sureness of
faith in the humble, still his, as they were Whitman's before
him.

"The people, undependable as prairie rivers in flood time,
The people, uncertain as lights on the face of the sea . . .
The people is a plucked goose and a shorn sheep of legalized
        fraud . . .
The people will live on . . .
This reality is alive . . ."

At the three-quarter century mark, Carl Sandburg is a symbol
of the abiding virility of an America whose continuity from the
past binds it to the present. His words bite and sting with inde-
pendence of judgment. They also erupt into beauty and surge
with power. His earliest volume, *Chicago Poems*, jarred the
genteel tradition down to earth. His latest insists upon pitiless
confrontation of good and evil alike.

He is of the high tradition of creative letters, a figure which,
in times of timidity, cautious specialization, and poetic obscu-
rantism, is rare enough, but which will find its successors. A
volunteer in the Spanish War, a hobo, a Mayor's secretary, a
newspaper editor and writer, a roving troubadour through
prairie villages, a war correspondent, lecturer and chanter of
folk tales—all this is but part of the story. Even as he has sought
the hearts and minds of the anonymous multitudes, exploring
their dreams and scourging mediocrity with the lash of a prophet,
so he has lashed with caustic phrase those who would crib and
cabin men's minds.

Like other towering figures in the great tradition of letters, he has been not one man but many: poet and biographer, essayist and critic, historian and novelist, teller of prose tales for children, and indefatigable bearer of song to the nation as a traveling minstrel.

To the many honors he has already received, this latest is a fitting climax.

Contents

STORYTELLER AND POET FOR CHILDREN

SINGER AND SONG-SEEKER

NOVELIST

AUTOBIOGRAPHER

Poet

In his book Spokesmen, *T. K. Whipple writes of Carl Sandburg:*

The best term that I can find for Sandburg is that of psalmist—not in form only, although his predilection for the form of the Psalms may be significant, but in deeper ways. His feeling for the sky, the ocean, the winds, for all the more grandiose aspects of nature, for vastness in time and space, is like that of the Psalms. He is given to wondering how the foundations of the hills were laid and how the sea was poured forth. *Slabs of the Sunburnt West* in its theme and mood and even its conclusions as to human impotence affords strange parallels to passages in the Book of Job. Sandburg's poetry is in truth a veritable Psalm of Life—for he is essentially an accepting, yea-saying psalmist.

In contemporary verse, Sandburg's work stands out for its breadth, volume, and body. Many of our poets are far more perfect, have rid themselves more successfully of alloy; but not one of them has Sandburg's massive bulk. No doubt his work suffers both in material and in form from the peculiarities of his environment, but at least he is not at all undernourished; he has derived ample sustenance from his surroundings. If discipline in taste is the more important for the individual's achievement and reputation, yet the nourishment provided the artist's imagination is the more important for national literature—and that is where Sandburg excels, and for the historian of national literature is most significant. He proves that it is possible for a man endowed with the poetic temper to lead the life of realization to good purpose among us. Furthermore, Sandburg has extraordinary social value in that only Whitman has done more in the arduous labor of opening up the country and subjecting it to artistic treatment. He has made the way easier not only for all other artists, but also for all who are inclined to follow the life of realization.

Chicago Poems

CHICAGO

Hog Butcher for the World,
Tool Maker, Stacker of Wheat,
Player with Railroads and the Nation's Freight Handler;
Stormy, husky, brawling,
City of the Big Shoulders:

They tell me you are wicked and I believe them, for I have seen your
    painted women under the gas lamps luring the farm boys.
And they tell me you are crooked and I answer: Yes, it is true I have
    seen the gunman kill and go free to kill again.
And they tell me you are brutal and my reply is: On the faces of
    women and children I have seen the marks of wanton hunger.
And having answered so I turn once more to those who sneer at this
    my city, and I give them back the sneer and say to them:
Come and show me another city with lifted head singing so proud to
    be alive and coarse and strong and cunning.
Flinging magnetic curses amid the toil of piling job on job, here is a
    tall bold slugger set vivid against the little soft cities;
Fierce as a dog with tongue lapping for action, cunning as a savage
    pitted against the wilderness,
        Bareheaded,
        Shoveling,
        Wrecking,
        Planning,
        Building, breaking, rebuilding,
Under the smoke, dust all over his mouth, laughing with white teeth,
Under the terrible burden of destiny laughing as a young man laughs,
Laughing even as an ignorant fighter laughs who has never lost a battle,
Bragging and laughing that under his wrist is the pulse, and under his
    ribs the heart of the people,
        Laughing!

4

Laughing the stormy, husky, brawling laughter of Youth, half-naked,
    sweating, proud to be Hog Butcher, Tool Maker, Stacker of
    Wheat, Player with Railroads and Freight Handler to the Nation.

HAPPINESS

I asked professors who teach the meaning of life to tell me what is hap-
    piness.
And I went to famous executives who boss the work of thousands of
    men.
They all shook their heads and gave me a smile as though I was trying
    to fool with them.
And then one Sunday afternoon I wandered out along the Desplaines
    river
And I saw a crowd of Hungarians under the trees with their women
    and children and a keg of beer and an accordion.

MAG

I wish to God I never saw you, Mag.
I wish you never quit your job and came along with me.
I wish we never bought a license and a white dress
For you to get married in the day we ran off to a minister
And told him we would love each other and take care of each other
Always and always long as the sun and the rain lasts anywhere.
Yes, I'm wishing now you lived somewhere away from here
And I was a bum on the bumpers a thousand miles away dead broke.
    I wish the kids had never come
    And rent and coal and clothes to pay for
    And a grocery man calling for cash,
    Every day cash for beans and prunes.
    I wish to God I never saw you, Mag.
    I wish to God the kids had never come.

PERSONALITY
Musings of a Police Reporter in the Identification Bureau

You have loved forty women, but you have only one thumb.
You have led a hundred secret lives, but you mark only one thumb.

You go round the world and fight in a thousand wars and win all the
   world's honors, but when you come back home the print of the
   one thumb your mother gave you is the same print of thumb you
   had in the old home when your mother kissed you and said
   good-by.
Out of the whirling womb of time come millions of men and their feet
   crowd the earth and they cut one another's throats for room to
   stand and among them all are not two thumbs alike.
Somewhere is a Great God of Thumbs who can tell the inside story of
   this.

SKYSCRAPER

By day the skyscraper looms in the smoke and sun and has a soul.
Prairie and valley, streets of the city, pour people into it and they
   mingle among its twenty floors and are poured out again back to
   the streets, prairies and valleys.
It is the men and women, boys and girls so poured in and out all day
   that give the building a soul of dreams and thoughts and memories.
(Dumped in the sea or fixed in a desert, who would care for the build-
   ing or speak its name or ask a policeman the way to it?)

Elevators slide on their cables and tubes catch letters and parcels and
   iron pipes carry gas and water in and sewage out.
Wires climb with secrets, carry light and carry words, and tell terrors
   and profits and loves—curses of men grappling plans of business
   and questions of women in plots of love.

Hour by hour the caissons reach down to the rock of the earth and
   hold the building to a turning planet.
Hour by hour the girders play as ribs and reach out and hold together
   the stone walls and floors.
Hour by hour the hand of the mason and the stuff of the mortar clinch
   the pieces and parts to the shape an architect voted.
Hour by hour the sun and the rain, the air and the rust, and the press
   of time running into centuries, play on the building inside and
   out and use it.

Men who sunk the pilings and mixed the mortar are laid in graves
   where the wind whistles a wild song without words

And so are men who strung the wires and fixed the pipes and tubes and those who saw it rise floor by floor.

Souls of them all are here, even the hod carrier begging at back doors hundreds of miles away and the bricklayer who went to state's prison for shooting another man while drunk.

(One man fell from a girder and broke his neck at the end of a straight plunge—he is here—his soul has gone into the stones of the building.)

On the office doors from tier to tier—hundreds of names and each name standing for a face written across with a dead child, a passionate lover, a driving ambition for a million dollar business or a lobster's ease of life.

Behind the signs on the doors they work and the walls tell nothing from room to room.

Ten-dollar-a-week stenographers take letters from corporation officers, lawyers, efficiency engineers, and tons of letters go bundled from the building to all ends of the earth.

Smiles and tears of each office girl go into the soul of the building just the same as the master-men who rule the building.

Hands of clocks turn to noon hours and each floor empties its men and women who go away and eat and come back to work.

Toward the end of the afternoon all work slackens and all jobs go slower as the people feel day closing on them.

One by one the floors are emptied. . . . The uniformed elevator men are gone. Pails clang. . . . Scrubbers work, talking in foreign tongues. Broom and water and mop clean from the floors human dust and spit, and machine grime of the day.

Spelled in electric fire on the roof are words telling miles of houses and people where to buy a thing for money. The sign speaks till midnight.

Darkness on the hallways. Voices echo. Silence holds. . . . Watchmen walk slow from floor to floor and try the doors. Revolvers bulge from their hip pockets. . . . Steel safes stand in corners. Money is stacked in them.

A young watchman leans at a window and sees the lights of barges butting their way across a harbor, nets of red and white lanterns

in a railroad yard, and a span of glooms splashed with lines of
white and blurs of crosses and clusters over the sleeping city.
By night the skyscraper looms in the smoke and the stars and has a soul.

GONE

Everybody loved Chick Lorimer in our town.
        Far off
        Everybody loved her.
So we all love a wild girl keeping a hold
        On a dream she wants.
Nobody knows now where Chick Lorimer went.
Nobody knows why she packed her trunk . . . a few old things
And is gone,
        Gone with her little chin
        Thrust ahead of her
        And her soft hair blowing careless
        From under a wide hat,
Dancer, singer, a laughing passionate lover.

Were there ten men or a hundred hunting Chick?
Were there five men or fifty with aching hearts?
        Everybody loved Chick Lorimer.
        Nobody knows where she's gone.

Cornhuskers

PRAIRIE

I was born on the prairie and the milk of its wheat, the red of its clover,
the eyes of its women, gave me a song and a slogan.

Here the water went down, the icebergs slid with gravel, the gaps and
the valleys hissed, and the black loam came, and the yellow sandy
loam.
Here between the sheds of the Rocky Mountains and the Appalach-
ians, here now a morning star fixes a fire sign over the timber
claims and cow pastures, the corn belt, the cotton belt, the cattle
ranches.
Here the gray geese go five hundred miles and back with a wind under
their wings honking the cry for a new home.
Here I know I will hanker after nothing so much as one more sunrise
or a sky moon of fire doubled to a river moon of water.

The prairie sings to me in the forenoon and I know in the night I rest
easy in the prairie arms, on the prairie heart.

.   .   .

After the sunburn of the day
handling a pitchfork at a hayrack,
after the eggs and biscuit and coffee,
the pearl-gray haystacks
in the gloaming
are cool prayers
to the harvest hands.

In the city among the walls the overland passenger train is choked and
the pistons hiss and the wheels curse.
On the prairie the overland flits on phantom wheels and the sky and
the soil between them muffle the pistons and cheer the wheels.

. . .

I am here when the cities are gone.
I am here before the cities come.
I nourished the lonely men on horses.
I will keep the laughing men who ride iron.
I am dust of men.

The running water babbled to the deer, the cottontail, the gopher.
You came in wagons, making streets and schools,
Kin of the ax and rifle, kin of the plow and horse,
Singing *Yankee Doodle, Old Dan Tucker, Turkey in the Straw,*
You in the coonskin cap at a log house door hearing a lone wolf howl,
You at a sod house door reading the blizzards and chinooks let loose
     from Medicine Hat,
I am dust of your dust, as I am brother and mother
To the copper faces, the worker in flint and clay,
The singing women and their sons a thousand years ago
Marching single file the timber and the plain.

I hold the dust of these amid changing stars.
I last while old wars are fought, while peace broods mother-like,
While new wars arise and the fresh killings of young men.
I fed the boys who went to France in great dark days.
Appomattox is a beautiful word to me and so is Valley Forge and the
     Marne and Verdun,
I who have seen the red births and the red deaths
Of sons and daughters, I take peace or war, I say nothing and wait.

Have you seen a red sunset drip over one of my cornfields, the shore
     of night stars, the wave lines of dawn up a wheat valley?
Have you heard my threshing crews yelling in the chaff of a straw-
     pile and the running wheat of the wagonboards, my cornhuskers,
     my harvest hands hauling crops, singing dreams of women,
     worlds, horizons?

. . .

Rivers cut a path on flat lands.
The mountains stand up.
The salt oceans press in
And push on the coast lines.

The sun, the wind, bring rain
And I know what the rainbow writes across the east or
  west in a half-circle:
A love-letter pledge to come again.

. . .

Towns on the Soo Line,
Towns on the Big Muddy,
Laugh at each other for cubs
And tease as children.

Omaha and Kansas City, Minneapolis and St. Paul, sisters in a house
  together, throwing slang, growing up.
Towns in the Ozarks, Dakota wheat towns, Wichita, Peoria, Buffalo,
  sisters throwing slang, growing up.

. . .

Out of prairie-brown grass crossed with a streamer of wigwam smoke
  —out of a smoke pillar, a blue promise—out of wild ducks woven
  in greens and purples—
Here I saw a city rise and say to the peoples round the world: Listen,
  I am strong, I know what I want.
Out of log houses and stumps—canoes stripped from tree-sides—flat-
  boats coaxed with an ax from the timber claims—in the years
  when the red and the white men met—the houses and streets rose.

A thousand red men cried and went away to new places for corn and
  women: a million white men came and put up skyscrapers, threw
  out rails and wires, feelers to the salt sea: now the smokestacks
  bite the skyline with stub teeth.

In an early year the call of a wild duck woven in greens and purples:
  now the riveter's chatter, the police patrol, the song-whistle of
  the steamboat.

To a man across a thousand years I offer a handshake.
I say to him: Brother, make the story short, for the stretch of a thou-
  sand years is short.

. . .

What brothers these in the dark?
What eaves of skyscrapers against a smoke moon?

These chimneys shaking on the lumber shanties
When the coal boats plow by on the river—
The hunched shoulders of the grain elevators—
The flame sprockets of the sheet steel mills
And the men in the rolling mills with their shirts off
Playing their flesh arms against the twisting wrists of steel:
          what brothers these
          in the dark
          of a thousand years?

                    .   .   .

A headlight searches a snowstorm.
A funnel of white light shoots from over the pilot of the Pioneer
     Limited crossing Wisconsin.

In the morning hours, in the dawn,
The sun puts out the stars of the sky
And the headlight of the Limited train.

The fireman waves his hand to a country school teacher on a bobsled.
A boy, yellow hair, red scarf and mittens, on the bobsled, in his lunch
     box a pork chop sandwich and a V of gooseberry pie.

The horses fathom a snow to their knees.
Snow hats are on the rolling prairie hills.
The Mississippi bluffs wear snow hats.

Keep your hogs on changing corn and mashes of grain,
     O farmerman.
     Cram their insides till they waddle on short legs
     Under the drums of bellies, hams of fat.
     Kill your hogs with a knife slit under the ear.
     Hack them with cleavers.
     Hang them with hooks in the hind legs.

                    .   .   .

     A wagonload of radishes on a summer morning.
     Sprinkles of dew on the crimson-purple balls.
The farmer on the seat dangles the reins on the rumps of dapple-gray
     horses.

The farmer's daughter with a basket of eggs dreams of a new hat to
wear to the county fair.

. . .

On the left- and right-hand side of the road,
          Marching corn—
I saw it knee high weeks ago—now it is head high—tassels of red silk
creep at the ends of the ears.

. . .

I am the prairie, mother of men, waiting.
They are mine, the threshing crews eating beefsteak, the farmboys
driving steers to the railroad cattle pens.
They are mine, the crowds of people at a Fourth of July basket picnic,
listening to a lawyer read the Declaration of Independence,
watching the pinwheels and Roman candles at night, the young
men and women two by two hunting the bypaths and kissing-
bridges.
They are mine, the horses looking over a fence in the frost of late
October saying good morning to the horses hauling wagons of
rutabaga to market.
They are mine, the old zigzag rail fences, the new barbwire.

. . .

The cornhuskers wear leather on their hands.
There is no let-up to the wind.
Blue bandanas are knotted at the ruddy chins.

Falltime and winter apples take on the smolder of the five-o'clock No-
vember sunset: falltime, leaves, bonfires, stubble, the old things
go, and the earth is grizzled.
The land and the people hold memories, even among the anthills and
the angleworms, among the toads and woodroaches—among
gravestone writings rubbed out by the rain—they keep old things
that never grow old.

       The frost loosens cornhusks.
       The sun, the rain, the wind
            loosen cornhusks.
       The men and women are helpers.

They are all cornhuskers together.
I see them late in the western evening
in a smoke-red dust.

. . .

The phantom of a yellow rooster flaunting a scarlet comb, on top of a
dung pile crying hallelujah to the streaks of daylight,
The phantom of an old hunting dog nosing in the underbrush for
muskrats, barking at a coon in a treetop at midnight, chewing a
bone, chasing his tail round a corncrib,
The phantom of an old workhorse taking the steel point of a plow
across a forty-acre field in spring, hitched to a harrow in summer,
hitched to a wagon among cornshocks in fall,
These phantoms come into the talk and wonder of people on the front
porch of a farmhouse late summer nights.
"The shapes that are gone are here," said an old man with a cob pipe
in his teeth one night in Kansas with a hot wind on the alfalfa.

. . .

Look at six eggs
In a mockingbird's nest.

Listen to six mockingbirds
Flinging follies of O-be-joyful
Over the marshes and uplands.

Look at songs
Hidden in eggs.

. . .

When the morning sun is on the trumpet-vine blossoms, sing at the
kitchen pans: Shout All Over God's Heaven.
When the rain slants on the potato hills and the sun plays a silver shaft
on the last shower, sing to the bush at the backyard fence: Mighty
Lak a Rose.
When the icy sleet pounds on the storm windows and the house lifts
to a great breath, sing for the outside hills: The Ole Sheep Done
Know the Road, the Young Lambs Must Find the Way.

. . .

Spring slips back with a girl face calling always: "Any new songs for
me? Any new songs?"

O prairie girl, be lonely, singing, dreaming, waiting—your lover
    comes—your child comes—the years creep with toes of April
    rain on new-turned sod.
O prairie girl, whoever leaves you only crimson poppies to talk with,
    whoever puts a good-by kiss on your lips and never comes back—
There is a song deep as the falltime redhaws, long as the layer of black
    loam we go to, the shine of the morning star over the corn belt,
    the wave line of dawn up a wheat valley.

. . .

O prairie mother, I am one of your boys.
I have loved the prairie as a man with a heart shot full of pain over
    love.
Here I know I will hanker after nothing so much as one more sunrise
    or a sky moon of fire doubled to a river moon of water.

. . .

I speak of new cities and new people.
I tell you the past is a bucket of ashes.
I tell you yesterday is a wind gone down,
    a sun dropped in the west.
I tell you there is nothing in the world
    only an ocean of tomorrows,
    a sky of tomorrows.

I am a brother of the cornhuskers who say
    at sundown:
        Tomorrow is a day.

ILLINOIS FARMER

Bury this old Illinois farmer with respect.
He slept the Illinois nights of his life after days of work in Illinois
    cornfields.
Now he goes on a long sleep.
The wind he listened to in the cornsilk and the tassels, the wind that
    combed his red beard zero mornings when the snow lay white on
    the yellow ears in the bushel basket at the corncrib,
The same wind will now blow over the place here where his hands
    must dream of Illinois corn.

WILDERNESS

There is a wolf in me . . . fangs pointed for tearing gashes . . . a
red tongue for raw meat . . . and the hot lapping of blood—I
keep this wolf because the wilderness gave it to me and the wil-
derness will not let it go.

There is a fox in me . . . a silver-gray fox . . . I sniff and guess . . .
I pick things out of the wind and air . . . I nose in the dark night
and take sleepers and eat them and hide the feathers . . . I circle
and loop and double-cross.

There is a hog in me . . . a snout and a belly . . . a machinery for
eating and grunting . . . a machinery for sleeping satisfied in the
sun—I got this too from the wilderness and the wilderness will
not let it go.

There is a fish in me . . . I know I came from salt-blue water-gates
. . . I scurried with shoals of herring . . . I blew waterspouts
with porpoises . . . before land was . . . before the water went
down . . . before Noah . . . before the first chapter of Genesis.

There is a baboon in me . . . clambering-clawed . . . dog-faced
. . . yawping a galoot's hunger . . . hairy under the armpits
. . . here are the hawk-eyed hankering men . . . here are the
blonde and blue-eyed women . . . here they hide curled asleep
waiting . . . ready to snarl and kill . . . ready to sing and give
milk . . . waiting—I keep the baboon because the wilderness
says so.

There is an eagle in me and a mockingbird . . . and the eagle flies
among the Rocky Mountains of my dreams and fights among the
Sierra crags of what I want . . . and the mockingbird warbles in
the early forenoon before the dew is gone, warbles in the under-
brush of my Chattanoogas of hope, gushes over the blue Ozark
foothills of my wishes—And I got the eagle and the mockingbird
from the wilderness.

O, I got a zoo, I got a menagerie, inside my ribs, under my bony head,
under my red-valve heart—and I got something else: it is a man-

child heart, a woman-child heart: it is a father and mother and lover: it came from God-Knows-Where: it is going to God-Knows-Where—For I am the keeper of the zoo: I say yes and no: I sing and kill and work: I am a pal of the world: I came from the wilderness.

BILBEA
(From tablet writing, Babylonian excavations of 4th millennium B.C.)

Bilbea, I was in Babylon on Saturday night.
I saw nothing of you anywhere.
I was at the old place and the other girls were there, but no Bilbea.

Have you gone to another house? or city?
Why don't you write?
I was sorry. I walked home half-sick.

Tell me how it goes.
Send me some kind of a letter.
And take care of yourself.

COOL TOMBS

When Abraham Lincoln was shoveled into the tombs, he forgot the copperheads and the assassin . . . in the dust, in the cool tombs.

And Ulysses Grant lost all thought of con men and Wall Street, cash and collateral turned ashes . . . in the dust, in the cool tombs.

Pocahontas' body, lovely as a poplar, sweet as a red haw in November or a pawpaw in May, did she wonder? does she remember? . . . in the dust, in the cool tombs?

Take any streetful of people buying clothes and groceries, cheering a hero or throwing confetti and blowing tin horns . . . tell me if the lovers are losers . . . tell me if any get more than the lovers . . . in the dust . . . in the cool tombs.

Smoke and Steel

JAZZ FANTASIA

Drum on your drums, batter on your banjoes,
sob on the long cool winding saxophones.
Go to it, O jazzmen.

Sling your knuckles on the bottoms of the happy
tin pans, let your trombones ooze, and go husha-
husha-hush with the slippery sand-paper.

Moan like an autumn wind high in the lonesome treetops, moan soft
like you wanted somebody terrible, cry like a racing car slipping away
from a motorcycle cop, bang-bang! you jazzmen, bang altogether
drums, traps, banjoes, horns, tin cans—make two people fight on the
top of a stairway and scratch each other's eyes in a clinch tumbling
down the stairs.

Can the rough stuff . . . now a Mississippi steamboat pushes up the
night river with a hoo-hoo-hoo-oo . . . and the green lanterns calling
to the high soft stars . . . a red moon rides on the humps of the low
river hills . . . go to it, O jazzmen.

CALLS

Because I have called to you
as the flame flamingo calls,
or the want of a spotted hawk
is called—
        because in the dusk
the warblers shoot the running
waters of short songs to the

18

homecoming warblers—
                            because
the cry here is wing to wing
and song to song—

   I am waiting,
waiting with the flame flamingo,
the spotted hawk, the running water
warbler—
            waiting for you.

EVENING WATERFALL

What was the name you called me?—
And why did you go so soon?

The crows lift their caw on the wind,
And the wind changed and was lonely.

The warblers cry their sleepy-songs
Across the valley gloaming,
Across the cattle-horns of early stars.

Feathers and people in the crotch of a treetop
Throw an evening waterfall of sleepy-songs.

What was the name you called me?—
And why did you go so soon?

PAULA

Nothing else in this song—only your face.
Nothing else here—only your drinking, night-gray eyes.

The pier runs into the lake straight as a rifle barrel.
I stand on the pier and sing how I know you mornings.
It is not your eyes, your face, I remember.
It is not your dancing, race-horse feet.
It is something else I remember you for on the pier mornings.

Your hands are sweeter than nut-brown bread when you touch me.
Your shoulder brushes my arm—a south-west wind crosses the pier.
I forget your hands and your shoulder and I say again:

Nothing else in this song—only your face.
Nothing else here—only your drinking, night-gray eyes.

HOW MUCH?

How much do you love me, a million bushels?
Oh, a lot more than that, Oh a lot more.

And tomorrow maybe only half a bushel?
Tomorrow maybe not even a half a bushel.

And is this your heart arithmetic?
This is the way the wind measures the weather.

WIND SONG

Long ago I learned how to sleep,
In an old apple orchard where the wind swept by counting its money
 and throwing it away,
In a wind-gaunt orchard where the limbs forked out and listened or
 never listened at all,
In a passel of trees where the branches trapped the wind into whistling,
 "Who, who are you?"
I slept with my head in an elbow on a summer afternoon and there I
 took a sleep lesson.
There I went away saying: I know why they sleep, I know how they
 trap the tricky winds.
Long ago I learned how to listen to the singing wind and how to for-
 get and how to hear the deep whine,
Slapping and lapsing under the day blue and the night stars:
        Who, who are you?

        Who can ever forget
        listening to the wind go by
        counting its money
        and throwing it away?

NIGHT STUFF

Listen a while, the moon is a lovely woman, a lonely woman, lost in a silver dress, lost in a circus rider's silver dress.

Listen a while, the lake by night is a lonely woman, a lovely woman, circled with birches and pines mixing their green and white among stars shattered in spray clear nights.

I know the moon and the lake have twisted the roots under my heart the same as a lonely woman, a lovely woman, in a silver dress, in a circus rider's silver dress.

WHITE ASH

There is a woman on Michigan Boulevard keeps a parrot and goldfish and two white mice.

She used to keep a houseful of girls in kimonos and three pushbuttons on the front door.

Now she is alone with a parrot and goldfish and two white mice . . . but these are some of her thoughts:

The love of a soldier on furlough or a sailor on shore leave burns with a bonfire red and saffron.

The love of an emigrant workman whose wife is a thousand miles away burns with a blue smoke.

The love of a young man whose sweetheart married an older man for money burns with a sputtering uncertain flame.

And there is a love . . . one in a thousand . . . burns clean and is gone leaving a white ash. . . .

And this is a thought she never explains to the parrot and goldfish and two white mice.

FOR YOU

The peace of great doors be for you.
Wait at the knobs, at the panel oblongs.
Wait for the great hinges.

The peace of great churches be for you,
Where the players of loft pipe organs
Practice old lovely fragments, alone.

The peace of great books be for you,
Stains of pressed clover leaves on pages,
Bleach of the light of years held in leather.

The peace of great prairies be for you.
Listen among windplayers in cornfields,
The wind learning over its oldest music.

The peace of great seas be for you.
Wait on a hook of land, a rock footing
For you, wait in the salt wash.

The peace of great mountains be for you,
The sleep and the eyesight of eagles,
Sheet mist shadows and the long look across.

The peace of great hearts be for you,
Valves of the blood of the sun,
Pumps of the strongest wants we cry.

The peace of great silhouettes be for you,
Shadow dancers alive in your blood now,
Alive and crying, "Let us out, let us out."

The peace of great changes be for you.
Whisper, Oh beginners in the hills.
Tumble, Oh cubs—tomorrow belongs to you.

The peace of great loves be for you.
Rain, soak these roots; wind, shatter the dry rot.

Bars of sunlight, grips of the earth, hug these.

The peace of great ghosts be for you,
Phantoms of night-gray eyes, ready to go
To the fog-star dumps, to the fire-white doors.

Yes, the peace of great phantoms be for you,
Phantom iron men, mothers of bronze,
Keepers of the lean clean breeds.

Slabs of the Sunburnt West

THE WINDY CITY

I

The lean hands of wagon men
put out pointing fingers here,
picked this crossway, put it on a map,
set up their sawbucks, fixed their shotguns,
found a hitching place for the pony express,
made a hitching place for the iron horse,
the one-eyed horse with the fire-spit head,
found a homelike spot and said, "Make a home,"
saw this corner with a mesh of rails, shuttling
     people, shunting cars, shaping the junk of
     the earth to a new city.

The hands of men took hold and tugged
And the breaths of men went into the junk
And the junk stood up into skyscrapers and asked:
Who am I? Am I a city? And if I am what is my name?
And once while the time whistles blew and blew again
The men answered: Long ago we gave you a name,
Long ago we laughed and said: You? Your name is Chicago.

       Early the red men gave a name to a river,
         the place of the skunk,
         the river of the wild onion smell,
         Shee-caw-go.

Out of the payday songs of steam shovels,
Out of the wages of structural iron rivets,
The living lighted skyscrapers tell it now as a name,
Tell it across miles of sea blue water, gray blue land:

I am Chicago, I am a name given out by the breaths of working men,
   laughing men, a child, a belonging.

So between the Great Lakes,
The Grand De Tour, and the Grand Prairie,
The living lighted skyscrapers stand,
Spotting the blue dusk with checkers of yellow,
   streamers of smoke and silver,
   parallelograms of night-gray watchmen,
Singing a soft moaning song: I am a child, a belonging.

2

How should the wind songs of a windy city go?
Singing in a high wind the dirty chatter gets blown
      away on the wind—the clean shovel,
                  the clean pickax,
                  lasts.

It is easy for a child to get breakfast and pack off
      to school with a pair of roller skates,
      buns for lunch, and a geography.
Riding through a tunnel under a river running backward,
      to school to listen . . . how the Pottawatomies . . .
      and the Blackhawks . . . ran on moccasins . . .
      between Kaskaskia, Peoria, Kankakee, and Chicago.

It is easy to sit listening to a boy babbling
      of the Pottawatomie moccasins in Illinois,
      how now the roofs and smokestacks cover miles
      where the deerfoot left its writing
      and the foxpaw put its initials
      in the snow . . . for the early moccasins . . . to read.

It is easy for the respectable taxpayers to sit in the
      streetcars and read the papers, faces of burglars,
      the prison escapes, the hunger strikes, the cost of
      living, the price of dying, the shop gate battles of
      strikers and strikebreakers, the strikers killing
      scabs and the police killing strikers—the strongest,
      the strongest, always the strongest.

It is easy to listen to the haberdasher customers hand each other their
    easy chatter—it is easy to die
    alive—to register a living thumbprint and be dead
    from the neck up.
And there are sidewalks polished with the footfalls of
    undertakers' stiffs, greased mannikins, wearing up-to-
    the-minute sox, lifting heels across doorsills,
    shoving their faces ahead of them—dead from the
    neck up—proud of their sox—their sox are the last
    word—dead from the neck up—it is easy.

3

Lash yourself to the bastion of a bridge
and listen while the black cataracts of people go by,
        baggage, bundles, balloons,
        listen while they jazz the classics:

        "Since when did you kiss yourself in
        And who do you think you are?
        Come across, kick in, loosen up.
        Where do you get that chatter?"

        "Beat up the short-change artists.
        They never did nothin' for you.
        How do you get that way?
        Tell me and I'll tell the world.
        I'll say so, I'll say it is."

        "You're trying to crab my act.
        You poor fish, you mackerel,
        You ain't got the sense God
        Gave an oyster—it's raining—
        What you want is an umbrella."

          "Hush baby—
        I don't know a thing.
        I don't know a thing.
          Hush baby."

          "Hush baby,
        It ain't how old you are,

It's how old you look.
It ain't what you got,
It's what you can get away with."

　"Bring home the bacon.
Put it over, shoot it across.
　Send 'em to the cleaners.
What we want is results, re-sults
　And damn the consequences.
　　Sh . . . sh. . . .
You can fix anything
If you got the right fixers."

"Kid each other, you cheap skates.
Tell each other you're all to the mustard—
You're the gravy."

　"Tell 'em, honey.
Ain't it the truth, sweetheart?
　Watch your step.
　You said it.
　You said a mouthful.
We're all a lot of damn fourflushers."

"Hush baby!
　Shoot it,
　Shoot it all!
　Coo coo, coo coo"—
This is one song of Chicago.

4

It is easy to come here a stranger and show the whole works, write a
　book, fix it all up—it is easy to come and go away a muddle-
　headed pig, a bum and a bag of wind.

Go to it and remember this city fished from its
　depths a text: "independent as a hog on ice."
Venice is a dream of soft waters, Vienna and Bagdad recollections of
　dark spears and wild turbans; Paris is a thought in Monet gray on
　scabbards, fabrics, façades; London is a fact in a fog filled with
　the moaning of transatlantic whistles; Berlin sits amid white

scrubbed quadrangles and torn arithmetics and testaments; Moscow brandishes a flag and repeats a dance figure of a man who walks like a bear.
Chicago fished from its depths a text: Independent
   as a hog on ice.

5

Forgive us if the monotonous houses go mile on mile
Along monotonous streets out to the prairies—
If the faces of the houses mumble hard words
At the streets—and the street voices only say:
"Dust and a bitter wind shall come."
Forgive us if the lumber porches and doorsteps
Snarl at each other—
And the brick chimneys cough in a close-up of
Each other's faces—
And the ramshackle stairways watch each other
As thieves watch—
And dooryard lilacs near a malleable iron works
Long ago languished
In a short whispering purple.

        And if the alley ash cans
        Tell the garbage-wagon drivers
        The children play the alley is Heaven
        And the streets of Heaven shine
        With a grand dazzle of stones of gold
        And there are no policemen in Heaven—
        Let the rag-tags have it their way.

        And if the geraniums
        In the tin cans on the window sills
        Ask questions not worth answering—
        And if a boy and a girl hunt the sun
        With a sieve for sifting smoke—
        Let it pass—let the answer be—
        "Dust and a bitter wind shall come."

        Forgive us if the jazz timebeats
        Of these clumsy mass shadows
        Moan in saxophone undertones,

And the footsteps of the jungle,
The fang cry, the rip claw hiss,
The sneak-up and the still watch,
The slant of the slit eyes waiting—
If these bother respectable people
        with the right crimp in their napkins
        reading breakfast menu cards—
        forgive us—let it pass—let be.

If cripples sit on their stumps
And joke with the newsies bawling,
"Many lives lost! many lives lost!
Ter-ri-ble ac-ci-dent! many lives lost!"—
If again twelve men let a woman go,
"He done me wrong; I shot him" —
Or the blood of a child's head
Spatters on the hub of a motor truck—
Or a 44-gat cracks and lets the skylights
Into one more bank messenger—
Or if boys steal coal in a railroad yard
And run with humped gunnysacks
While a bull picks off one of the kids
And the kid wriggles with an ear in cinders
And a mother comes to carry home
A bundle, a limp bundle,
To have his face washed, for the last time,
Forgive us if it happens—and happens again—
And happens again.

    Forgive the jazz timebeat
    of clumsy mass shadows,
    footsteps of the jungle,
    the fang cry, the rip claw hiss,
    the slant of the slit eyes waiting.

Forgive us if we work so hard
And the muscles bunch clumsy on us
And we never know why we work so hard—
If the big houses with little families
And the little houses with big families
Sneer at each other's bars of misunderstanding;

Pity us when we shackle and kill each other
And believe at first we understand
And later say we wonder why.

Take home the monotonous patter
Of the elevated railroad guard in the rush hours:
"Watch your step. Watch your step. Watch your step."
Or write on a pocket pad what a pauper said
To a patch of purple asters at a whitewashed wall:
"Let every man be his own Jesus—that's enough."

6

The wheelbarrows grin, the shovels and the mortar
        hoist an exploit.
The stone shanks of the Monadnock, the Transportation,
        the People's Gas Building, stand up and scrape
        at the sky.
The wheelbarrows sing, the bevels and the blueprints
        whisper.
The library building named after Crerar, naked
        as a stock farm silo, light as a single eagle
        feather, stripped like an airplane propeller,
        takes a path up.
Two cool new rivets say, "Maybe it is morning,"
        "God knows."

                Put the city up; tear the city down;
                        put it up again; let us find a city.
                Let us remember the little violet-eyed
                        man who gave all, praying, "Dig and
                        dream, dream and hammer, till your
                        city comes."

                Every day the people sleep and the city dies;
                        every day the people shake loose, awake and
                        build the city again.

                The city is a tool chest opened every day,
                        a time clock punched every morning,
                        a shop door, bunkers and overalls
                        counting every day.

The city is a balloon and a bubble plaything
        shot to the sky every evening, whistled in
        a ragtime jig down the sunset.

The city is made, forgotten, and made again,
        trucks hauling it away haul it back
        steered by drivers whistling ragtime
        against the sunsets.

Every day the people get up and carry the city,
        carry the bunkers and balloons of the city,
        lift it and put it down.

"I will die as many times
as you make me over again,
says the city to the people,
I am the woman, the home, the family,
I get breakfast and pay the rent;
I telephone the doctor, the milkman, the undertaker;
        I fix the streets
        for your first and your last ride—
Come clean with me, come clean or dirty,
I am stone and steel of your sleeping numbers;
        I remember all you forget.
        I will die as many times
        as you make me over again."

Under the foundations,
Over the roofs,
The bevels and the blueprints talk it over.
The wind of the lake shore waits and wanders.
The heave of the shore wind hunches the sand piles.
The winkers of the morning stars count out cities
And forget the numbers.

7

At the white clock-tower
lighted in night purples

over the boulevard link bridge
only the blind get by without acknowledgments.

The passers-by, factory punch-clock numbers,
    hotel girls out for the air, teameoes,
    coal passers, taxi drivers, window washers,
    paperhangers, floorwalkers, bill collectors,
    burglar alarm salesmen, massage students,
    manicure girls, chiropodists, bath rubbers,
    booze runners, hat cleaners, armhole basters,
    delicatessen clerks, shovel stiffs, work plugs—
They all pass over the bridge, they all look up
    at the white clock-tower
    lighted in night purples
    over the boulevard link bridge—
    And sometimes one says, "Well, we hand it to 'em."

Mention proud things, catalogue them.
The jack-knife bridge opening, the ore boats,
    the wheat barges passing through.
Three overland trains arriving the same hour,
    one from Memphis and the cotton belt,
    one from Omaha and the corn belt,
    one from Duluth, the lumberjack and the iron range.
Mention a carload of shorthorns taken off the valleys of Wyoming
    last week, arriving yesterday, knocked in the head, stripped,
    quartered, hung in ice boxes today, mention the daily melodrama
    of this humdrum, rhythms of heads, hides, heels, hoofs hung up.

8

It is wisdom to think the people are the city.
It is wisdom to think the city would fall to pieces
    and die and be dust in the wind
If the people of the city all move away and leave no people at all to
    watch and keep the city.
It is wisdom to think no city stood here at all until the working men,
    the laughing men, came.
It is wisdom to think tomorrow new working men, new laughing
    men, may come and put up a new city—
Living lighted skyscrapers and a night lingo of lanterns testify
    tomorrow shall have its own say-so.

9

Night gathers itself into a ball of dark yarn.
Night loosens the ball and it spreads.
The lookouts from the shores of Lake Michigan
     find night follows day, and ping! ping! across
     sheet gray the boat lights put their signals.
Night lets the dark yarn unravel, Night speaks and the yarns change
     to fog and blue strands.

The lookouts turn to the city.
The canyons swarm with red sand lights
     of the sunset.
The atoms drop and sift, blues cross over,
     yellows plunge.
Mixed light shafts stack their bayonets,
     pledge with crossed handles.
So, when the canyons swarm, it is then the
     lookouts speak
Of the high spots over a street . . . mountain language
Of skyscrapers in dusk, the Railway Exchange,
The People's Gas, the Monadnock, the Transportation,
Gone to the gloaming.

The river turns in a half circle.
The Goose Island bridges curve
     over the river curve.
     Then the river panorama
     performs for the bridge,
     dots . . . lights . . . dots . . . lights,
     sixes and sevens of dots and lights,
     a lingo of lanterns and searchlights,
     circling sprays of gray and yellow.

10

A man came as a witness saying:
"I listened to the Great Lakes
And I listened to the Grand Prairie,
And they had little to say to each other,
A whisper or so in a thousand years.
'Some of the cities are big,' said one.

'And some not so big,' said another.
'And sometimes the cities are all gone,'
Said a black knob bluff to a light green sea."

Winds of the Windy City, come out of the prairie,
     all the way from Medicine Hat.
Come out of the inland sea blue water, come where
     they nickname a city for you.

Corn wind in the fall, come off the black lands,
     come off the whisper of the silk hangers,
     the lap of the flat spear leaves.

Blue water wind in summer, come off the blue miles
     of lake, carry your inland sea blue fingers,
     carry us cool, carry your blue to our homes.

White spring winds, come off the bag wool clouds,
     come off the running melted snow, come white
     as the arms of snow-born children.

Gray fighting winter winds, come, come along on the tear-
     ing blizzard tails, the snouts of the hungry
     hunting storms, come fighting gray in winter.

Winds of the Windy City,
Winds of corn and sea blue,
Spring wind white and fighting winter gray,
Come home here—they nickname a city for you.

The wind of the lake shore waits and wanders.
The heave of the shore wind hunches the sand piles.
The winkers of the morning stars count out cities
And forget the numbers.

UPSTREAM

The strong men keep coming on.
They go down shot, hanged, sick,
    broken.
They live on fighting, singing,
    lucky as plungers.
The strong mothers pulling them
    on . . .
The strong mothers pulling them
    from a dark sea, a great prairie,
    a long mountain.
Call hallelujah, call amen, call
    deep thanks.
The strong men keep coming on.

Good Morning, America

NINE TENTATIVE (FIRST MODEL)
DEFINITIONS OF POETRY

1 *Poetry is a projection across silence of cadences arranged to break that silence with definite intentions of echoes, syllables, wave lengths.*

2 *Poetry is an art practised with the terribly plastic material of human language.*

3 *Poetry is an echo asking a shadow dancer to be a partner.*

4 *Poetry is a dance music measuring buck-and-wing follies along with the gravest and stateliest dead-marches.*

5 *Poetry is a mock of a cry at finding a million dollars and a mock of a laugh at losing it.*

6 *Poetry is a packsack of invisible keepsakes.*

7 *Poetry is the achievement of the synthesis of hyacinths and biscuits.*

8 *Poetry is a mystic, sensuous mathematics of fire, smoke-stacks, waffles, pansies, people, and purple sunsets.*

9 *Poetry is the capture of a picture, a song, or a flair, in a deliberate prism of words.*

BABY SONG OF THE FOUR WINDS

Let me be your baby, south wind.
Rock me, let me rock, rock me now.

Rock me low, rock me warm.
Let me be your baby.

Comb my hair, west wind.
Comb me with a cowlick.
Or let me go with a pompadour.
Come on, west wind, make me your baby.

North wind, shake me where I'm foolish.
Shake me loose and change my ways.
Cool my ears with a blue sea wind.
I'm your baby, make me behave.

And you, east wind, what can I ask?
A fog comfort? A fog to tuck me in?
Fix me so and let me sleep.
I'm your baby—and I always was.

A COUPLE

He was in Cincinnati, she in Burlington.
He was in a gang of Postal Telegraph linemen.
She was a pot rassler in a boarding house.
"The crying is lonely," she wrote him.
"The same here," he answered.
The winter went by and he came back and they married
And he went away again where rainstorms knocked down telegraph
     poles and wires dropped with frozen sleet.
And again she wrote him, "The crying is lonely."
And again he answered, "The same here."
Their five children are in the public schools.
He votes the Republican ticket and is a taxpayer.
They are known among those who know them
As honest American citizens living honest lives.
Many things that bother other people never bother them.
They have their five children and they are a couple,
A pair of birds that call to each other and satisfy.
As sure as he goes away she writes him, "The crying is
     lonely."
And he flashes back the old answer, "The same here."

It is a long time since he was a gang lineman at Cincinnati
And she was a pot rassler in a Burlington boarding house;
Yet they never get tired of each other; they are a couple.

EARLY HOURS
(*To A. W. F.*)

Since you packed your rubber bottom boots
And took the night train for northern Wisconsin
To hunt deer in the ten days allowed by law,
I have remembered your saying the hunters
Get up out of bed and dress for shooting,
For reading snow tracks, circling, waiting, firing,
At the hour of half past four in the morning;
Now this has been in my mind sometimes
When after a long day's work and more than half a night
I opened the east window before going to bed
At half past three o'clock in the morning
And there were deer feet and horns of stars on the sky.
I listened to the chiming of a watch and said,
"A couple of hours and Jim'll kill a deer, maybe."
There are different kinds of early hours.

BETWEEN WORLDS

And he said to himself
in a sunken morning moon
between two pines,
between lost gold and lingering green:

I believe I will count up my worlds.
There seem to me to be three.
There is a world I came from which is Number One.
There is a world I am in now, which is Number Two.
There is a world I go to next, which is Number Three.

There was the seed pouch, the place I lay dark in, nursed and shaped
    in a warm, red, wet cuddling place; if I tugged at a latchstring

or doubled a dimpled fist or twitched a leg or a foot, only the
Mother knew.

There is the place I am in now, where I look back and
    look ahead, and dream and wonder.

There is the next place—
And he took a look out of a window
at a sunken morning moon
between two pines,
between lost gold and lingering green.

PHIZZOG

This face you got,
This here phizzog you carry around,
You never picked it out for yourself,
        at all, at all—did you?
This here phizzog—somebody handed it
        to you—am I right?
Somebody said, "Here's yours, now go see
        what you can do with it."
Somebody slipped it to you and it was like
        a package marked:
"No goods exchanged after being taken away"—
This face you got.

THEY ASK: IS GOD, TOO, LONELY?

When God scooped up a handful of dust,
And spit on it, and molded the shape of man,
And blew a breath into it and told it to walk—
That was a great day.

And did God do this because He was lonely?
Did God say to Himself He must have company
And therefore He would make man to walk the earth
And set apart churches for speech and song with God?

These are questions.
They are scrawled in old caves.
They are painted in tall cathedrals.
There are men and women so lonely they believe
    God, too, is lonely.

SEA CHEST

There was a woman loved a man
as the man loved the sea.
Her thoughts of him were the same
as his thoughts of the sea.
They made an old sea chest for their belongings
together.

WE HAVE GONE THROUGH GREAT
ROOMS TOGETHER

And when on the dark steel came the roads
Of a milky mist, and a spray of stars,
Bunches and squares and a spatter of stars,
We counted stars, one by one, a million and a million.
And we remembered those stars as fishermen remember fish,
As bees remember blossoms, as crops remember rains.
And these were rooms too; we can so reckon.
We can always say we have gone through great rooms together.

MAYBE

Maybe he believes me, maybe not.
Maybe I can marry him, maybe not.
Maybe the wind on the prairie,
The wind on the sea, maybe,
Somebody somewhere, maybe, can tell.
I will lay my head on his shoulder
And when he asks me I will say yes,
Maybe.

SNATCH OF SLIPHORN JAZZ

Are you happy? It's the only
way to be, kid.
Yes, be happy, it's a good nice
way to be.
But not happy-happy, kid, don't
be too doubled-up doggone happy.
It's the doubled-up doggone happy-
happy people . . . bust hard . . . they
do bust hard . . . when they bust.
Be happy, kid, go to it, but not too
doggone happy.

HELLS AND HEAVENS

Each man pictures his hell or heaven different.
Some have snug home-like heavens, suburban, well-kept.
Some have a wild, storm-swept heaven; their happiness has
    been in storms, heaven must have storms mixed with
    fair weather.
And hell for some is a jail, for others a factory, for others
    a kitchen, for others a place of many polite liars full
    of blah, all gah gah.

BUNDLES

I have thought of beaches, fields,
Tears, laughter.

I have thought of homes put up—
And blown away.

I have thought of meetings and for
Every meeting a good-by.

I have thought of stars going alone,
Orioles in pairs, sunsets in blundering
Wistful deaths.

I have wanted to let go and cross over
To a next star, a last star.

I have asked to be left a few tears
And some laughter.

MANY HATS

I

When the scrapers of the
deep winds were done, and
the haulers of the tall
waters had finished, this
was the accomplishment.

The drums of the sun never
get tired, and first off
every morning, the drums of
the sun perform an intro-
duction of the dawn here.

The moon goes down here
as a dark bellringer doing
once more what he has done
over and over already in
his young life.

Up on a long blue platform
comes a line of starprints.

If the wind has a song, it
is moaning; Good Lawd, I
done done what you told me
to do.

2

Whose three-ring circus is this? Who stipulated in a contract for this to be drunken, death-defying, colossal, mammoth, cyclopean, mystic as the light that never was on land or sea, bland, composed, and imperturbable as a cool phalanx of sphinxes? Why did one woman cry, The silence is terrible? Why did another smile, There is a sweet gravity here? Why do they come and go here and look as in a looking-glass?

The Grand Canyon of Arizona, said one, this is it, hacked out by the broadax of a big left-handed God and left forgotten, fixed over and embellished by a remembering right-handed God who always comes back.

If you ask me, said an old railroader, I'll never tell you who took the excavation contract for this blowout—it took a lot of shovels and a lot of dynamite—several large kegs, I would guess—and maybe they had a case or two of T N T.

Yes, he went on, the Grand Canyon, the daddy of 'em all—the undisputed champeen—that range rider sure was righto—the elements had a hell of a rassle here.

The Grand Canyon—a long ride from where Brigham Young stands in bronze gazing on the city he bade rise out of salt and alkali—a weary walk from Santa Fe and the Mountains of the Blood of Christ—a bitter hike from where the Sonora dove at Tucson mourns, No hope, no hope—a sweet distance from where Balboa stripped for his first swim in the Pacific—a mean cross-country journey to where Roy Bean told the muchacho, By the white light of a moon on the walls of an arroyo last Tuesday you killed a woman and next Tuesday we're going to hang you—a traveler's route of many days and sleeps to reach the place of the declaration, God reigns and the government at Washington lives.

Shovel into this cut of earth all past and present possessions, creations, belongings of man; shovel furioso, appassionata, pizzicato; shovel cities, wagons, ships, tools, jewels; the bottom isn't covered; the wild burros and the trail mules go haw-hee, haw-hee, haw-hee.

Turn it into a Hall of Fame, said a rambler, let it be a series of memorials to the Four Horsemen, to Napoleon, Carl the Twelfth, Caesar, Alexander the Great, Hannibal and Hasdrubal, and all who have rode in blood up to the bridles of the horses, calling, Hurrah for the next who goes—let each have his name on a truncated cyclops of rock—let passers-by say, He was pretty good but he didn't last long.

Now I wonder, I wonder, said another, can they all find room here? Elijah fed by the ravens, Jonah in the belly of the whale, Daniel in the lion's den, Lot's wife transmogrified into salt, Elijah riding up into the sky in a chariot of fire—can they all find room? Are the broken pieces of the Tower of Babel and the Walls of Jericho here? Should I look for the ram's horn Joshua blew?

3

A phantom runner runs on the rim. "I saw a moon man throw hats in, hats of kings, emperors, senators, presidents, plumed hats of knights, red hats of cardinals, five-gallon hats of cowboys, tasselled hats of Bavarian yodelers, mandarin hats, derbies, fedoras, chapeaus, straws, lady picture hats out of Gainsborough portraits—

"Hats many proud people handed over, dying and saying, Take this one too—hats furioso, appassionata, pizzicato—hats for remembrance, good-by, three strikes and out, fade me, there's no place to go but home—hats for man alone, God alone, the sky alone."

4

Think of the little birds, said another, the wee birdies—before God took a hunk of mud and made Man they were here, the birds, the robins, juncoes, nuthatches, bats, eagles, cedar birds, chickadees, bluejays, I saw a blackbird gleaming in satin, floating in the scrolls of his glamorous wings, stopping on an airpath and standing still with nothing under his feet, looking at the gray Mojave desert level interrupted by the Grand Canyon—the birds belong, don't they?

5

Comes along a hombre saying, Let it be dedicated to Time; this is what is left of the Big Procession when Time gets through with it; the sun loves its stubs; we will give a name to any torso broken and tumbled by Time; we will leave the vanished torsos with no names.

Comes along a hombre accidentally remarking, Let it be dedicated to Law and Order—the law of the Strong fighting the Strong, the Cunning outwitting the Less Cunning—and the Weak Ones ordered to their places by the Strong and Cunning—aye—and ai-ee—Law and Order.

Comes along another hombre giving his slant at it, Now this sure was the Gyarden of Eden, smooth, rich, nice, watered, fixed, no work till tomorrow, Adam and Eve satisfied and sitting pretty till the day of the Snake Dance and the First Sin; and God was disgusted and wrecked the works; he ordered club-foot angels with broken wings to shoot the job; now look at it.

Comes another hombre all wised up, This was the Devil's Brick-yard; here were the kilns to make the Kitchens of Hell; after bricks enough were made to last Hell a million years, the Devil said, "Shut 'er down"; they had a big payday night and left it busted from hell to breakfast; the Hopis looked it over and decided to live eighty miles away where there was water; then came Powell, Hance, the Santa Fe, the boys shooting the rapids, and Fred Harvey with El Tovar.

6

Now Hance had his points; they asked him how he come to find the Canyon and he told 'em, I was ridin' old Whitey and the Mojaves after me when we comes to this gap miles across; I told Whitey, It's you now for the longest jump you ever took; Whitey jumped and was half way across when I pulled on the bridle, turned him around, and we come back to the same place on the Canyon rim we started from.

Yes, Hance told 'em, if they asked, how he come to dig the Canyon. "But where did you put all the dirt?" "Took it away in wheel-barrows and made San Francisco Peaks."

Hance sleeping near a big rock, woke up and saw seven rattlesnakes circle seven times around the rock, each with the tail of the snake ahead in his mouth, and all of them swallowing, till after a while there wasn't a snake left. Hance's wife got her leg caught between two rocks; couldn't get her loose, said Hance, so I had to shoot her to save her from starving to death; look down there between those two rocks and you can see her bones, said Hance.

This is where we find the original knuckle snake; he breaks to pieces if you try to pick him up; and when you go away he knuckles himself together again; yes, and down here, is the original echo canyon; we holler, "Has Smith been here?" and the echo promulgates back, "Which Smith?"

7

Down at the darkest depths, miles down, the Colorado River grinds, toils, driving the channel deeper—is it free or convict?—tell me —will it end like a great writer crying, I die with my best books unwritten?

Smooth as glass run the streaming waters—then a break into rapids, into tumblers, into spray, into voices, roars, growls, into command- ing monotones that hunt far corners and jumping-off places.

And how should a beautiful, ignorant stream of water know it heads for an early release—out across the desert, running toward the Gulf, below sea level, to murmur its lullaby, and see the Imperial Valley rise out of burning sand with cotton blossoms, wheat, water- melons, roses, how should it know?

8

The hombres keep coming; here comes another; he says, says he, I met four people this morning, the poker face, the baby stare, the icy mitt, and the peace that passeth understanding—let this place be dedicated to X, the unknown factor, to the Missing Link, to Jo Jo the dog-faced boy, to the Sargossa Sea, to Humpty Dumpty, to Little Red Riding Hood crying for her mother, to those who never believe in Santa Klaus, to the man who turned himself inside out because he was so sleepy.

9

Steps on steps lift on into the sky; the lengths count up into stair- ways; let me go up for the Redeemer is up there; He died for me; so a Spanish Indian was speaking—and he asked, When the first French Jesuit looked from Yavapai four hundred years ago, did he murmur of a tall altar to go on a mile-long rock shelf down there on a mesa? did he whisper of an unspeakably tall altar there for the raising of the ostensorium and the swinging of censers and the calling up of the presence of the Heart of the Living Christ? And he went on, Where the Son of God is made known surely is a place for the removal of shoes and the renewal of feet for the journey—surely this is so.

10

Came a lean, hungry-looking hombre with Kansas, Nebraska, the Dakotas on his wind-bitten face, and he was saying, Sure my boy, sure my girl, and you're free to have any sweet bluebird fancies you please, any wild broncho thoughts you choose to have, when you stand before this grand scrap-pile of hats, hammers, haciendas, and hidalgos. He went on, Yes, let this be dedicated to Time and Ice; a memorial of the Human Family which came, was, and went; let it stand as a witness of the short miserable pilgrimage of mankind, of flame faiths, of blood and fire, and of Ice which was here first and will be here again—Faces once frozen you shall all be frozen again—the little clocks of Man shall all be frozen and nobody will be too late or too early ever again.

11

On the rim a quizzical gray-glinting hombre was telling himself how it looked to him—the sun and the air are endless with silver tricks— the light of the sun has crimson stratagems—the changes go on in stop-watch split seconds—the blues slide down a box of yellow and mix with reds that melt into gray and come back saffron clay and granite pink—a weaving gamble of color twists on and it is anybody's guess what is next.

A long sand-brown shawl shortens to a glimmering turquoise scarf—as the parapets and chimneys wash over and out in the baths of the sunset and the floats of the gloaming; one man says, There goes God with an army of banners, and another man, Who is God and why? who am I and why?

> He told himself, This may be
> something else than what I
> see when I look—how do I
> know? For each man sees him-
> self in the Grand Canyon—

each one makes his own Canyon
before he comes, each one brings
and carries away his own Canyon—
who knows? and how do I know?

12

If the wind has a song, it
is moaning: Good Lawd, I
done done what you told me
to do.

When the scrapers of the
deep winds were done, and
the haulers of the tall
waters had finished, this
was the accomplishment.

The moon goes down here
as a dark bellringer doing
once more what he has done
over and over already in
his young life.

Up on a long blue platform
comes a line of starprints.

The drums of the sun never
get tired, and first off
every morning, the drums of
the sun perform an intro-
duction of the dawn here.

Complete Poems

THE FIREBORN ARE AT HOME IN FIRE

Luck is a star.
Money is a plaything.
Time is a storyteller.
The sky goes high, big.
The sky goes wide and blue.
And the fireborn—they go far—
        being at home in fire.

Can you compose yourself
The same as a bright bandana,
A bandana folded blue and cool,
Whatever the high howling,
The accents of blam blam?
Can I, can John Smith, John Doe,
Whatever the awful accents,
Whatever the horst wessel hiss,
Whatever books be burnt and crisp,
Whatever hangmen bring their hemp,
Whatever horsemen sweep the sunsets,
Whatever hidden hovering candle
Sways as a wafer of light?

Can you compose yourself
The same as a bright bandana,
A bandana folded blue and cool?
Can I, too, drop deep down
In a pool of cool remembers,
In a float of fine smoke blue,
In a keeping of one pale moon,
Weaving our wrath in a pattern
Woven of wrath gone down,

49

Crossing our scarlet zigzags
With pools of cool blue,
With floats of smoke blue?

Can you, can I, compose ourselves
In wraps of personal cool blue,
In sheets of personal smoke blue?
        Bach did it, Johann Sebastian.
So did the one and only John Milton.
        And the old slave Epictetus
        And the other slave Spartacus
        And Brother Francis of Assisi.
So did General George Washington
        On a horse, in a saddle,
        On a boat, in heavy snow,
        In a loose cape overcoat
        And snow on his shoulders.
So did John Adams, Jackson, Jefferson.
So did Lincoln on a cavalry horse
At the Chancellorsville review
        With platoons right, platoons left,
In a wind nearly blowing the words away
        Asking the next man on a horse:
"What's going to become of all these
                boys when the war is over?"

The shape of your shadow
Comes from you—and you only?
Your personal fixed decisions
Out of you—and your mouth only?
        Your No, your Yes, your own?

Bronze old timers belong here.
Yes, they might be saying:
        Shade the flame
Back to final points
Of all sun and fog
In the moving frame
Of your personal eyes.
Then stand to the points.

Let hunger and hell come.
Or ashes and shame poured
On your personal head.
Let death shake its bones.
The teaching goes back far:
      Compose yourself.

    Luck is a star.
    Money is a plaything.
    Time is a storyteller.
And the sky goes blue with mornings.
And the sky goes bronze with sunsets.
And the fireborn—they go far—
      being at home in fire.

THE LONG SHADOW OF LINCOLN: A LITANY

(We can succeed only by concert. . . . The dogmas of the quiet past are in-
adequate to the stormy present. The occasion is piled high with difficulty,
and we must rise with the occasion. As our case is new so we must think
anew and act anew. We must disenthrall ourselves. . . . DECEMBER 1, 1862.
The President's Message to Congress.)

Be sad, be cool, be kind,
remembering those now dreamdust
hallowed in the ruts and gullies,
solemn bones under the smooth blue sea,
faces warblown in a falling rain.

Be a brother, if so can be,
to those beyond battle fatigue
each in his own corner of earth
    or forty fathoms undersea
    beyond all boom of guns,
    beyond any bong of a great bell,
    each with a bosom and number,
    each with a pack of secrets,
each with a personal dream and doorway
and over them now the long endless winds
    with the low healing song of time,
    the hush and sleep murmur of time.

Make your wit a guard and cover.
Sing low, sing high, sing wide.
Let your laughter come free
remembering looking toward peace:
"We must disenthrall ourselves."

Be a brother, if so can be,
to those thrown forward
for taking hardwon lines,
for holding hardwon points
        and their reward so-so,
little they care to talk about,
their pay held in a mute calm,
highspot memories going unspoken,
what they did being past words,
what they took being hardwon.
        Be sad, be kind, be cool.
            Weep if you must
        And weep open and shameless
            before these altars.

There are wounds past words.
There are cripples less broken
than many who walk whole.
        There are dead youths
        with wrists of silence
        who keep a vast music
        under their shut lips,
what they did being past words,
their dreams like their deaths
beyond any smooth and easy telling,
having given till no more to give.

        There is dust alive
with dreams of The Republic,
with dreams of the Family of Man
flung wide on a shrinking globe
        with old timetables,
        old maps, old guide-posts
        torn into shreds,
        shot into tatters,

burnt in a firewind,
lost in the shambles,
faded in rubble and ashes.

There is dust alive.
Out of a granite tomb,
Out of a bronze sarcophagus,
Loose from the stone and copper
Steps a whitesmoke ghost
Lifting an authoritative hand
In the name of dreams worth dying for,
In the name of men whose dust breathes
        of those dreams so worth dying for,
what they did being past words,
beyond all smooth and easy telling.

Be sad, be kind, be cool,
remembering, under God, a dreamdust
hallowed in the ruts and gullies,
solemn bones under the smooth blue sea,
faces warblown in a falling rain.

Sing low, sing high, sing wide.
Make your wit a guard and cover.
Let your laughter come free
like a help and a brace of comfort.

The earth laughs, the sun laughs
over every wise harvest of man,
over man looking toward peace
by the light of the hard old teaching:
        "We must disenthrall ourselves."

(Read as the Phi Beta Kappa poem at the Mother Chapter of William and
Mary College, Williamsburg, Virginia, December, 1944.)

WORMS AND THE WIND

Worms would rather be worms.
Ask a worm and he says, "Who knows what a worm knows?"
Worms go down and up and over and under.
Worms like tunnels.
When worms talk they talk about the worm world.
Worms like it in the dark.
Neither the sun nor the moon interests a worm.
Zigzag worms hate circle worms.
Curve worms never trust square worms.
Worms know what worms want.
Slide worms are suspicious of crawl worms.
One worm asks another, "How does your belly drag today?"
The shape of a crooked worm satisfies a crooked worm.
A straight worm says, "Why not be straight?"
Worms tired of crawling begin to slither.
Long worms slither farther than short worms.
Middle-sized worms say, "It is nice to be neither long nor short."
Old worms teach young worms to say, "Don't be sorry for me unless
    you have been a worm and lived in worm places and read worm
    books."
When worms go to war they dig in, come out and fight, dig in again,
    come out and fight again, dig in again, and so on.
Worms underground never hear the wind overground and sometimes
    they ask, "What is this wind we hear of?"

NUMBER MAN
(For the ghost of Johann Sebastian Bach)

He was born to wonder about numbers.

He balanced fives against tens
and made them sleep together
and love each other.

He took sixes and sevens
and set them wrangling and fighting
over raw bones.

He woke up twos and fours
out of baby sleep
and touched them back to sleep.

He managed eights and nines,
gave them prophet beards,
marched them into mists and mountains.

He added all the numbers he knew,
multiplied them by new-found numbers
and called it a prayer of Numbers.

For each of a million cipher silences
he dug up a mate number
for a candle light in the dark.

He knew love numbers, luck numbers,
how the sea and the stars
are made and held by numbers.
He died from the wonder of numbering.

He said good-by as if good-by is a number.

New Poems

BRAINWASHING

Repeat and repeat till they say what you
are saying.
Repeat and repeat till they are helpless
before your repetitions.
Say it over and over till their brains can
hold only what you are saying.
Speak it soft, yell it and yell it, change
to a whisper, always in repeats.
Come back to it day on day, hour after hour,
till they say what you tell them to say.
To wash A B C out of a brain and replace it
with X Y Z—this is it.

KISSES FORGOTTEN

We will weep
yet not weep together.
the harm is over
the blame is on both
the harm forgotten
the blame kissed away
with kisses forgotten.

SLEEP IMPRESSION

The dark blue wind
ran on the early autumn sky
in the fields of yellow moon harvest.
I slept, I almost slept,

I said listening:
Trees you have leaves rustling like rain
    when there is no rain.

THEOREM

There are prices and costs.
The price is what you are willing to pay.
The cost is what you put across as pay.
The circles of price and cost intersect
    in a kiss or a curse or a song.

MAN THE MOON SHOOTER

The shapes of change take their time
ai ai they take their time
moving hidden and deep
asking what the dawn asks
giving the answers evening gives
letting one tomorrow and another go by
till tomorrow comes saying,
"We are born of the yesterdays
and our unseen children wait to be born."

Where a thousand years is a clocktick,
where a hundred years is a split-second,
where a million miles is a moment of light,
the shapes go on working change
the same as forms once sea-hidden
crept to the land to become land forms,
    creeping in sun and rain,
    huddled in drizzle and fog,
    rising in mist and rainbow,
forgetful of time long or time too long,
murmuring in a music of mud and stars,
"We are born of the yesterdays
and our unseen children wait to be born.
    Take your time.
    We have all the time there is."

Where change tugs, feeds, grows,
where the-yet-to-be-born clutches and gropes
    in the folds of a womb ever weaving—
    this tells only there is to be a child,
    a shape beyond all guess and fathoming.
        Time and a womb of time tell only
    the child will have a face when it comes
    and a name given the begotten face.

    How could the Stone Age
    once born and given a name
see the Iron Age on the way to being born?
How could man carving the first wheel
    see the later labyrinths
of steel and brass wheels moving interlocked
    in a spun fabric of wheels?

How could the hairy Mesopotamian kings,
the hard-riding Persians, Jews, Greeks,
read it in the stars they were on their way out
and read too the next shapes of change to come?

Came the Romans and they did business,
likewise Moslems on horses, Vikings on ships,
barbarian strongarms riding wild horses,
saying to women or girls wanted,
hauled to the saddles by the hair,
"You belong to us by the right of capture"—
on their way to nowhere in the womb of time,
the Dark Ages given one name, Renascence another.
Magna Carta, Westphalia, Augsburg,
    names throwing shadows striped red and purple,
America, France, Russia, shaken with tramplings,
    declarations fireborn and sky-flaring,
    documents baptized and blood-dripping,
children and shapes, flags and forms—new names—
tomorrow breaking silence with fresh answers
    and the old questions hard and weather-worn:
        "Where to now? What next?"
How could Gutenberg or Caxton foretell
trucks hauling a million newspapers

roaring their banner headlines
and the desperate proverb
"Nothing is so dead as yesterday's newspaper"?

Ever the prophets are a dime a dozen
and man goes on a moon shooter
forgetful of time long or time too long,
    letting tomorrow come wool-shod
    making the noise a shadow makes,
    then a name given its face.

Machine Age given a name
went weaving into Power Age, another name—
Mass Production, Supermarkets, more names,
    Electrodynamics holding its own
till the cry "Atomic!" flashed world-wide
and "Global War" no careless bastard name,
each a child weaving in a time-hidden womb,
when it came saying, "Now I am here,"
    then having a face and a name.

The hammers of man from stone to steel,
the fire of man from pine flare to blowtorch,
the lights of man from burnt wood to flash bulb,
clew readings of man from hill bonfire to radar shadings,
the fights of man from club and sling
        to the pink mushroom of Hiroshima,
the words of men from spoken syllables
    to rushing rivers of books begetting books,
    to speech and image transmissions
    crowding the day and the night air
    for the looking and listening Family of Man—
the tools of man ever foretelling tools of new faces
        to be given new names—
        ever the prophets are a dime a dozen
        and man goes on a moon shooter.

The shapes of change
ai ai they take their time
asking what the dawn asks
giving the answers evening gives

till tomorrow moves in
saying to man the moon shooter,
"Now I am here—now read me—
    give me a name."

[*Holiday*, September 1953]

PSALM OF THE BLOODBANK

(*And hath made of one blood all nations of men for to dwell on all the face of the earth.*—The Acts XVII:26)

Scarlet the sunset, crimson the dawn,
    Rising moongold red curves
    through the night
    to sinking moongold red.
Poppy red a singing woman's lips.
Ruddy red the blush of true love's rose.
Fleeting the flash of a birdwing red.
    Red the cardinal's hat.
    Red the communist flag.
Token red the corpsman's right sleeve cross.
    Red the emblem cross
    of surgeon, nurse, ambulance,
    of hospital tent and ship—
    crimson blood streams poured
        together and together
        blended into one likeness,
        mingled in mute communions,
        Catholic in flow with Protestant,
        Nordic in flux with Negro.
Scoffers, sinners, deniers, in strength and rest
        from blood of Christian believers.
Help and quiet to Christian believers from blood
        of thieves, harlots, blasphemers.
                    Deep, oh deep, brother,
                    Deep, oh deep, sister,
                        The scarlet and crimson,
                        The human bloodbank red.

(Read at the Boston Arts Festival, June 1955. Published in *Collier's*,
                                            September 2, 1955)

ACQUAINTANCE WITH DEATH, SIR

Acquaintance with death, sir,
comes by ice and is slow, sir,
comes by fire and is fast, sir,
comes by the creep of clock-hands,
comes by the crash of split-seconds.

The dignity of man may be kept, sir,
where a man dies slow with witnesses
and loved ones gathered at clean sheets
with time to take note of the last words:
and the dignity of man may be kept, sir,
where a boy dies unseen in the frozen mud,
dies with his dogtag in Iwo Jima sulphur ash
        at the sping of a split-second doom
and days later is recorded as "missing"
and days still later officially, irrevocably
named on the books as forever "killed in action."

        So here are two kinds of the dignity of man,
        one far easier to look at than the other,
        one far easier to forget and leave forgotten:
                always a silence and content
                of evening bronze shadows
                and blue fog beyond fathoming
                goes with the unforgotten.

[*Collier's*, December 7, 1956]

SHENANDOAH JOURNEY
(*For Ralph McGill*)

I shall be in the Shenandoah some day.
(The time is not told in the almanacs.)
And I shall not go again to the tomb
of Robert E. Lee in white recumbent marble
Nor to the hill again where Sheridan counted
A circle of twenty-two burning barns

Nor repeat the days when any wise crow
Carried its own rations down that valley.
Yet I shall see apple blossoms on many hills,
Orchards slung with pink up the long slopes
And nearby the snowfall piles of petals
And farther off the hideouts of running waters
Always confidential in the slide over flat rocks . . .
In the telling what they know to the flat rocks . . .
And I shall know forgetful bells.
I shall no longer remember my own hard words,
Coming back only to the decent monosyllabics.
At Cherry Run or Harpers Ferry or Round Hill
I shall hear a veery thrush in an oak or chestnut
Some rainy April morning when the earth has sacraments
And the red scars are lost under a blue rain flute.

[The Atlanta *Journal and Constitution Magazine*, July 26, 1953]

STAR SILVER

The silver of one star
Plays cross-lights against pine green.

And the play of this silver
crosswise against the green
Is an old story . . .
                    thousands of years.

And sheep raisers on the hills by night
Watching the wooly four-footed ramblers,
Watching a single silver star—
Why does the story never wear out?

And a baby slung in a feed-box
Back in a barn in a Bethlehem slum,
A baby's first cry mixing with the crunch
Of a mule's teeth on Bethlehem Christmas corn,
Baby fists softer than snowflakes of Norway,
The vagabond Mother of Christ
And the vagabond men of wisdom,

All in a barn on a winter night,
And a baby there in swaddling clothes on hay—
Why does the story never wear out?

The sheen of it all
Is a star silver and a pine green
For the heart of a child asking a story,
The red and hungry, red and hankering heart
Calling for cross-lights of silver and green.

CONSOLATION SONATA

These poplars dream,
still or shaken they dream:
they never come out of it:
to this dreaminess they are born.

::

::
Consecration is a flower,
also it is many vegetables
or again it is neither,
not a flame of rose seen
nor a new potato eaten:
it is one tumbling moment
flowing over from a bowl
of many earlier moments.

::

::
In all prisons are keepsakes:
prisoners live on memories—
their forgottens are gone—
they let the forgottens go—
out and out they sift them,
pick, choose, save these those,
leaving keepsakes to count:
this happens in all prisons.

::

::
To live big is good:
to deny much is good too.
You would have a bag of gold:
you might ask a sack of peanuts.
Be full, not so full, go hungry,
Life is all time yes no yes no.
::

::
Kiss the faint bronze
of this garment of the sun.
Kiss the hem of this spun fire
brought from a smoldering,
leafed out in handspreads,
two four five handspreads.
::

::
The sun burns its gold
and this to you
is home and mother.

The night frames its stars
and this to you
is a book and prayers.

The People, Yes

Willard Thorp, in *Literary History of the United States*, calls this "one of the great American books. But," he says, "as so often happened in the history of our literature, its new matter required a new form, and the form is hard to name. Some of the one hundred and seven sections of the book are poems in the usual Sandburg manner, on such themes as the death of those who die for the people, or the common man as builder, wrecker, and builder again. Some sections merely assemble the collective wisdom of the people, on property, war, justice, and the law. One section puts together the best words of Lincoln, and it reads, as Sandburg knew it would, like the sections in which the people speak. Whatever may be the name you put to it, a foreigner will find more of America in *The People, Yes* than in any other book we can give him. But he will have to spell it out slowly."

More than ten per cent of this long poem is here represented, with rearrangement of some passages.

Being several stories and psalms nobody would want to laugh at
interspersed with memoranda variations worth a second look
along with sayings and yarns traveling on grief and laughter
running sometimes as a fugitive air in the classic manner
breaking into jig time and tap dancing nohow classical
and further broken by plain and irregular sounds and echoes from
the roar and whirl of street crowds, work gangs, sidewalk clamor,
with interludes of midnight cool blue and inviolable stars
over the phantom frames of skyscrapers.

From the four corners of the earth,
from corners lashed in wind
and bitten with rain and fire,
from places where the winds begin
and fogs are born with mist children,
tall men from tall rocky slopes came
and sleepy men from sleepy valleys,
their women tall, their women sleepy,
with bundles and belongings,
with little ones babbling, "Where to now?
    what next?"

The people of the earth, the family of man,
wanted to put up something proud to look at,
a tower from the flat land of earth
on up through the ceiling into the top of the sky.

    And the big job got going,
    the caissons and pilings sunk,
    floors, walls and winding staircases
    aimed at the stars high over,
    aimed to go beyond the ladders of the moon.

    And God Almighty could have struck them dead
    or smitten them deaf and dumb.

    And God was a whimsical fixer.
    God was an understanding Boss
    with another plan in mind,
    And suddenly shuffled all the languages,
        changed the tongues of men
        so they all talked different
And the masons couldn't get what the hodcarriers said,
The helpers handed the carpenters the wrong tools,
Five hundred ways to say, ''W h o a r e y o u?''
Changed ways of asking, "Where do we go from here?"
Or of saying, "Being born is only the beginning,"
Or, "Would you just as soon sing as make that noise?"
Or, "What you don't know won't hurt you."
And the material-and-supply men started disputes
With the hauling gangs and the building trades
And the architects tore their hair over the blueprints

And the brickmakers and the mule skinners talked back
To the straw bosses who talked back to the superintendents
And the signals got mixed; the men who shovelled the bucket
Hooted the hoisting men—and the job was wrecked.

Some called it the Tower of Babel job
And the people gave it many other names.
The wreck of it stood as a skull and a ghost,
a memorandum hardly begun,
swaying and sagging in tall hostile winds,
held up by slow friendly winds.

. . .

From Illinois and Indiana came a later myth
Of all the people in the world at Howdeehow
For the first time standing together:
From six continents, seven seas, and several archipelagoes,
From points of land moved by wind and water
Out of where they used to be to where they are,
The people of the earth marched and travelled
To gather on a great plain.

At a given signal they would join in a shout,
    So it was planned,
One grand hosannah, something worth listening to.
    And they all listened.
    The signal was given.
    And they all listened.
    And the silence was beyond words.
They had come to listen, not to make a noise.
    They wanted to hear.
So they all stood still and listened,
Everybody except a little old woman from Kalamazoo
Who gave out a long slow wail over what she was missing
    because she was stone deaf.

This is the tale of the Howdeehow powwow,
One of a thousand drolls the people tell of themselves,
Of tall corn, of wide rivers, of big snakes,
Of giants and dwarfs, heroes and clowns,
Grown in the soil of the mass of the people.

. . .

The people know what the land knows
the numbers odd and even of the land
the slow hot wind of summer and its withering
or again the crimp of the driving white blizzard
and neither of them to be stopped
neither saying anything else than:
          "I'm not arguing. I'm telling you."

The old timer on the desert was gray
and grizzled with ever seeing the sun:
          "For myself I don't care whether it rains.
          I've seen it rain.
          But I'd like to have it rain
          pretty soon sometime.
          Then my son could see it.
          He's never seen it rain."

                    .   .   .

The white man drew a small circle in the sand
and told the red man, "This is what the Indian
knows," and drawing a big circle around the
small one, "This is what the white man knows."
The Indian took the stick and swept an immense
ring around both circles: "This is where the
white man and the red man know nothing."

                    .   .   .

For sixty years the pine lumber barn
had held cows, horses, hay, harness, tools, junk,
amid the prairie winds of Knox County, Illinois
and the corn crops came and went, plows and wagons,
and hands milked, hands husked and harnessed
and held the leather reins of horse teams
in dust and dog days, in late fall sleet
till the work was done that fall.
And the barn was a witness, stood and saw it all.
     "That old barn on your place, Charlie,
     was nearly falling last time I saw it,
     how is it now?"
     "I got some poles to hold it on the east side
     and the wind holds it up on the west."

                    .   .   .

There are dreams stronger than death.
Men and women die holding these dreams.
Yes, "stronger than death": let the hammers beat on this slogan.
Let the sea wash its salt against it and the blizzards drive wind and
　　winter at it.
Let the undersea sharks try to break this bronze murmur.
Let the gentle bush dig its root deep and spread upward to split one
　　boulder.
Blame the frustrate? Some of them have lived stronger than death.
Blame only the smug and scrupulous beyond reproach.
Who made the guess Shakespeare died saying his best plays didn't get
　　written?
Who swindles himself more deeply than the one saying, "I am holier
　　than thou"?

　　　　　　　　"I love you,"
　　　　　said a great mother.
　　　　　"I love you for what you are
　　　　　knowing so well what you are.
　　　　　And I love you more yet, child,
　　　　　deeper yet than ever, child,
　　　　　for what you are going to be,
　　　　　knowing so well you are going far,
　　　　　knowing your great works are ahead,
　　　　　ahead and beyond,
　　　　　yonder and far over yet."

　　　　　　　　.　.　.

The sea moves always, the wind moves always.
They want and want and there is no end to their wanting.
What they sing is the song of the people.
Man will never arrive, man will be always on the way.
It is written he shall rest but never for long.
The sea and the wind tell him he shall be lonely, meet love, be shaken
　　with struggle, and go on wanting.

　　　　　　　　.　.　.

　　The people is Everyman, everybody.
　　Everybody is you and me and all others.
　　What everybody says is what we all say.
　　　　And what is it we all say?

Where did we get these languages?
Why is your baby-talk deep in your blood?
What is the cling of the tongue
To what it heard with its mother-milk?

They cross on the ether now.
They travel on high frequencies
Over the border-lines and barriers
Of mountain ranges and oceans.
When shall we all speak the same language?
And do we want to have all the same language?
Are we learning a few great signs and passwords?

Over the ether crash the languages.
                    And the people listen.
As on the plain of Howdeehow they listen.
                    They want to hear.

Two countries with two flags
are nevertheless one land, one blood, one people—
        can this be so?
And the earth belongs to the family of man?
        can this be so?

                        .   .   .

From the people the countries get their armies.
By the people the armies are fed, clothed, armed.
Out of the smoke and ashes of the war
The people build again their two countries with two flags
Even though sometimes it is one land, one blood, one people.

Hate is a vapor fixed and mixed.
Hate is a vapor blown and thrown.
And the war lasts till the hate dies down
And the crazy Four Horsemen have handed the people
Hunger and filth and a stink too heavy to stand.
Then the earth sends forth bright new grass
And the land begins to breathe easy again
Though the hate of the people dies slow and hard.
        Hate is a lingering heavy swamp mist.

And after the strife of war
begins the strife of peace.

. . .

You can drum on immense drums
the monotonous daily motions of the people
taking from earth and air
their morsels of bread and love,
a carryover from yesterday into tomorrow.

You can blow on great brass horns
the awful clamors of war and revolution
when swarming anonymous shadowshapes
obliterate old names Big Names
and cross out what *was*
and offer what *is* on a fresh blank page.

. . .

The scaffolding holds the arch in place
till the keystone is put in to stay.
Then the scaffolding comes out.
Then the arch stands strong as all the
massed pressing parts of the arch
and loose as any sag or spread
failing of the builders' intention, hope.
"The arch never sleeps."
Living in union it holds.
So long as each piece does it work
the arch is alive, singing, a restless choral.

. . .

Hope is a tattered flag and a dream out of time.
Hope is a heartspun word, the rainbow, the shadblow in white,
The evening star inviolable over the coal mines,
The shimmer of northern lights across a bitter winter night,
The blue hills beyond the smoke of the steel works,
The birds who go on singing to their mates in peace, war, peace,
The ten-cent crocus bulb blooming in a used-car salesroom,
The horseshoe over the door, the luckpiece in the pocket,

The kiss and the comforting laugh and resolve—
Hope is an echo, hope ties itself yonder, yonder.

.   .   .

The sacred legion of the justborn—
how many thousands born this minute?
how many fallen for soon burial?
what are these deaths and replacements?
what is this endless shuttling of shadowlands
where the spent and done go marching into one
and from another arrive those crying Mama Mama?

In the people is the eternal child,
the wandering gypsy, the pioneer homeseeker,
the singer of home sweet home.

The people say and unsay,
put up and tear down
and put together again—
a builder, wrecker, and builder again—
this is the people.

.   .   .

They have yarns
Of a skyscraper so tall they had to put hinges
On the two top stories so to let the moon go by,
Of one corn crop in Missouri when the roots
Went so deep and drew off so much water
The Mississippi riverbed that year was dry,
Of pancakes so thin they had only one side,
Of "a fog so thick we shingled the barn and six feet out on the fog,"
Of Pecos Pete straddling a cyclone in Texas and riding it to the west
    coast where "it rained out under him,"
Of the man who drove a swarm of bees across the Rocky Mountains
    and the Desert "and didn't lose a bee,"
Of a mountain railroad curve where the engineer in his cab can touch
    the caboose and spit in the conductor's eye,
Of the boy who climbed a cornstalk growing so fast he would have
    starved to death if they hadn't shot biscuits up to him,
Of the old man's whiskers: "When the wind was with him his whisk-
    ers arrived a day before he did,"

Of the hen laying a square egg and cackling, "Ouch!" and of hens laying eggs with the dates printed on them,

Of the ship captain's shadow: it froze to the deck one cold winter night,

Of mutineers on that same ship put to chipping rust with rubber hammers,

Of the sheep counter who was fast and accurate: "I just count their feet and divide by four,"

Of the man so tall he must climb a ladder to shave himself,

Of the runt so teeny-weeny it takes two men and a boy to see him,

Of mosquitoes: one can kill a dog, two of them a man,

Of a cyclone that sucked cookstoves out of the kitchen, up the chimney flue, and on to the next town,

Of the same cyclone picking up wagon-tracks in Nebraska and dropping them over in the Dakotas,

Of the hook-and-eye snake unlocking itself into forty pieces, each piece two inches long, then in nine seconds flat snapping itself together again,

Of the watch swallowed by the cow—when they butchered her a year later the watch was running and had the correct time,

Of horned snakes, hoop snakes that roll themselves where they want to go, and rattlesnakes carrying bells instead of rattles on their tails,

Of the herd of cattle in California getting lost in a giant redwood tree that had hollowed out,

Of the man who killed a snake by putting its tail in its mouth so it swallowed itself,

Of railroad trains whizzing along so fast they reach the station before the whistle,

Of pigs so thin the farmer had to tie knots in their tails to keep them from crawling through the cracks in their pens,

Of Paul Bunyan's big blue ox, Babe, measuring between the eyes forty-two ax-handles and a plug of Star tobacco exactly,

Of John Henry's hammer and the curve of its swing and his singing of it as "a rainbow round my shoulder."

> "Do tell!"
> "I want to know!"
> "You don't say so!"
> "For the land's sake!"

.   .   .

The sea rolls easy and smooth.
Or the sea roars and goes wild.
The smell of clams and fish comes
    out of the sea.
The sea is nothing to look at
    unless you want to know something
    unless you want to know
    where you came from.

.   .   .

Who was that early sodbuster in Kansas? He leaned at the gatepost
    and studied the horizon and figured what corn might do next year
    and tried to calculate why God ever made the grasshopper and
    why two days of hot winds smother the life out of a stand of
    wheat and why there was such a spread between what he got for
    grain and the price quoted in Chicago and New York. Drove up a
    newcomer in a covered wagon: "What kind of folks live around
    here?" "Well, stranger, what kind of folks was there in the coun-
    try you come from?" "Well, they was mostly a lowdown, lying,
    thieving, gossiping, backbiting lot of people." "Well, I guess,
    stranger, that's about the kind of folks you'll find around here."
    And the dusty gray stranger had just about blended into the dusty
    gray cottonwoods in a clump on the horizon when another new-
    comer drove up: "What kind of folks live around here?" "Well,
    stranger, what kind of folks was there in the country you come
    from?" "Well, they was mostly a decent, hardworking, lawabid-
    ing, friendly lot of people." "Well, I guess, stranger, that's about
    the kind of folks you'll find around here." And the second wagon
    moved off and blended with the dusty gray cottonwoods on the
    horizon while the early sodbuster leaned at his gatepost and tried
    to figure why two days of hot winds smother the life out of a nice
    stand of wheat.

.   .   .

The people, yes, the people,
Until the people are taken care of one way or another,
Until the people are solved somehow for the day and hour,
Until then one hears "Yes but the people what about the people?"
Sometimes as though the people is a child to be pleased or fed
Or again a hoodlum you have to be tough with

And seldom as though the people is a caldron and a reservoir
Of the human reserves that shape history,
The river of welcome wherein the broken First Families fade,
The great pool wherein wornout breeds and clans drop for restorative
    silence.

    Fire, chaos, shadows,
Events trickling from a thin line of flame
On into cries and combustions never expected.
The people have the element of surprise.
    Where are the kings today?
What has become of their solid and fastened thrones?
Who are the temporary puppets holding sway while anything, "God
    only knows what," waits around a corner, sits in the shadows and
    holds an ax, waiting for the appointed hour?

In hurricanes beyond foretelling of probabilities,
In the shove and whirl of unforeseen combustions
    The people, yes, the people,
Move eternally in the elements of surprise,
Changing from hammer to bayonet and back to hammer,
The hallelujah chorus forever shifting its star soloists.

       .   .   .

The free man willing to pay and struggle and die for the freedom for
    himself and others
Knowing how far to subject himself to discipline and obedience for
    the sake of an ordered society free from tyrants, exploiters and
    legalized frauds—
This free man is a rare bird and when you meet him take a good look
    at him and try to figure him out because
Some day when the United States of the Earth gets going and runs
    smooth and pretty there will be more of him than we have now.

       .   .   .

       The grass lives, goes to sleep, lives again,
       and has no name for it.
       The oaks and poplars know seasons while standing
       to take what comes.
       The grinding of the earth on its gnarled axis

touches many dumb brothers.
Time toils on translations of fire and rain into
air, into thin air.

In the casual drift of routine
in the day by day run of mine
in the play of careless circumstance
the anecdotes emerge
alive with people in words, errands,
motives and silhouettes
taller than the immediate moment:

"I remember," said the fond Irish mother to the white-headed boy,
   "I remember when you was nothing but a beautiful gleam
   in your father's eye."

In Vermont a shut-mouthed husband finally broke forth to his wife,
   "When I think of how much you have meant to me all these
   years it is almost more than I can do sometimes to keep from
   telling you so."

"Is you married?" the elder negro asked his son.
"I ain't sayin' I is and I ain't sayin' I ain't."
"I ain't askin' you is you ain't. Ise askin' you ain't you is."

They were ninety years old and of their seventeen children had just
   buried the firstborn son who died seventy-two years of age.
"I told you," said the old man as he and his hillborn wife sat on the
   cabin steps in the evening sunset, "I told you long ago we would
   never raise that boy."

. . .

The wheel turns.
The wheel comes to a standstill.
The wheel waits.
The wheel turns.

"Something began me
and it had no beginning:

something will end me
and it has no end."

The people is a long shadow
trembling around the earth,
stepping out of fog gray into smoke red
and back from smoke red into fog gray
and lost on parallels and meridians
learning by shock and wrangling,
by heartbreak so often and loneliness so raw
the laugh comes at least half true,
"My heart was made to be broken."

"Man will never write,"
they said before the alphabet came
and man at last began to write.
"Man will never fly,"
they said before the planes and blimps
zoomed and purred in arcs
winding their circles around the globe.

"Man will never make the United States of Europe
nor later yet the United States of the World,
"No, you are going too far when you talk about one
world flag for the great Family of Nations,"
they say that now.

And man the stumbler and finder goes on,
man the dreamer of deep dreams,
man the shaper and maker,
man the answerer.
The first wheel maker saw a wheel, carried
in his head a wheel, and one day found his
hands shaping a wheel, the first wheel.
The first wagon makers saw a wagon, joined
their hands and out of air, out of what
had lived in their minds, made the first
wagon.
One by one man alone and man joined
has made things with his hands

beginning in the fog wisp of a dim imagining
resulting in a tool, a plan, a working model,
        bones joined to breath being alive
in wheels within wheels, ignition, power,
transmission, reciprocals, beyond man alone,
alive only with man joined.
                        Where to? what next?

Man the toolmaker, tooluser,
son of the burning quests
fixed with roaming forearms,
hands attached to the forearms,
fingers put on those hands,
a thumb to face any finger—
hands cunning with knives, leather, wood,
        hands for twisting, weaving, shaping—
Man the flint grinder, iron and bronze welder,
        smoothing mud into hut walls,
        smoothing reinforced concrete into
        bridges, breakwaters, office buildings—
two hands projected into vast claws, giant hammers,
        into diggers, haulers, lifters.
The clamps of the big steam shovel? man's two hands:
the motor hurling man into high air? man's two hands:
        the screws of his skulled head
        joining the screws of his hands,
pink convolutions transmitting to white knuckles
        waves, signals, buttons, sparks—
        man with hands for loving and strangling,
        man with the open palm of living handshakes,
man with the closed nails of the fist of combat—
        these hands of man—where to? what next?

                        .   .   .

        We'll see what we'll see.
        Time is a great teacher.
        Today me and tomorrow maybe you.
This old anvil laughs at many broken hammers.
What is bitter to stand against today may be sweet to remember to-
        morrow.

Whether the stone bumps the jug or the jug bumps the stone it is bad
    for the jug.

We all belong to the same big family and have the same smell.

Handling honey, tar or dung some of it sticks to the fingers.

    The liar comes to believe his own lies.

He who burns himself must sit on the blisters.

    God alone understands fools.

To work hard, to live hard, to die hard, and then to go to hell after all
    would be too damned hard.

You can fool all the people some of the time and some of the people
    all the time but you can't fool all of the people all of the time.

    It takes all kinds of people to make a world.

        What is bred in the bone will tell.

        Between the inbreds and the cross-breeds the argument goes
           on.

        You can breed them up as easy as you can breed them down.

        "I don't know who my ancestors were," said a mongrel, "but
           we've been descending for a long time."

        "My ancestors," said the Cherokee-blooded Oklahoman,
           "didn't come over in the *Mayflower* but we was there to
           meet the boat."

        "Why," said the Denver Irish policeman as he arrested a
           Pawnee Indian I.W.W. soapboxer, "why don't you go
           back where you came from?"

An expert is only a damned fool a long ways from home.

You're either a thoroughbred, a scrub, or an in-between.

Speed is born with the foal—sometimes.

Always some dark horse never heard of before is coming under the
    wire a winner.

A thoroughbred always wins against a scrub, though you never know
    for sure: even thoroughbreds have their off days: new blood tells:
    the wornout thoroughbreds lose to the fast young scrubs.

        There is a luck of faces and bloods
        Comes to a child and touches it.
        It comes like a bird never seen.
        It goes like a bird never handled.
        There are little mothers hear the bird,

Feel the flitting of wings never seen,
And the touch of the givers of luck,
The bringers of faces and bloods.

.   .   .

The sea has fish for every man.
Every blade of grass has its share of dew.
The longest day must have its end.
Man's life? A candle in the wind, hoar-frost
          on stone.
Nothing more certain than death and nothing
          more uncertain than the hour.
Men live like birds together in a wood; when
          the time comes each takes his flight.
As wave follows wave, so new men take old
          men's places.

.   .   .

The mazuma, the jack, the shekels, the kale,
     The velvet, the you-know-what,
     The what-it-takes, a roll, a wad,
     Bring it home, boy.
     Bring home the bacon.
     Start on a shoestring if you have to.
     Then get your first million.
The second million is always easier than the first.

Now take some men, everything they touch turns into money: they
     know how the land lays: they can smell where the dollars grow.
Money withers if you don't know how to nurse it along: money flies
     away if you don't know where to put it.
The first question is, Where do we raise the money, where is the cash
     coming from?
A little horse sense helps: an idea and horse sense
     take you far: if you got a scheme ask yourself,
     Will it work?
And let me put one bug in your ear: inside information helps: how
     many fortunes came from a tip, from being on the ground first,
     from hearing a piece of news, from fast riding, early buying,
     quick selling, or plain dumb luck?
Yes, get Lady Luck with you and you're made: some fortunes were

tumbled into and the tumblers at first said, Who would have
believed it? and later, I knew just how to do it.

Yes, Lady Luck counts: before you're born pick the right papa and
mama and the newsreel boys will be on the premises early for a
shot of you with your big toe in your mouth.

> Money is power: so said one.
> Money is a cushion: so said another.
> Money is the root of evil: so said
>   still another.
> Money means freedom: so runs an old
>   saying.
>
> And money is all of these—and more.
> Money pays for whatever you want—if
>   you have the money.
> Money buys food, clothes, houses, land,
>   guns, jewels, men, women, time to be
>   lazy and listen to music.
> Money buys everything except love,
>   personality, freedom, immortality,
>   silence, peace.
>
> Therefore men fight for money.
> Therefore men steal, kill, swindle,
>   walk as hypocrites and whited
>   sepulchers.
> Therefore men speak softly carrying
>   plans, poisons, weapons, each in the
>   design: The words of his mouth were
>   as butter but war was in his heart.
>
> Money is power, freedom, a cushion, the
>   root of all evil, the sum of bless-
>   ings.
>
> Where the carcass is the buzzards gather.
> Where the treasure is the heart is also.
>   Money breeds money.
>   Money runs the world.
> Money talk is bigger than talk talk.
> No ear is deaf to the song that gold sings.

Money is welcome even when it stinks.
Money is the sinew of love and of war.
Money breaks men and ruins women.
     Money is a great comfort.
     Every man has his price.
There are men who can't be bought.
There are women beyond purchase.
When you buy judges someone sells justice.
You   can   buy   anything except day   and   night.

.   .   .

The people is the grand canyon of humanity
     and many many miles across.
The people is pandora's box, humpty dumpty,
     a clock of doom and an avalanche when it
     turns loose.
The people rest on land and weather, on time
     and the changing winds.
The people have come far and can look back
     and say, "We will go farther yet."
The people is a plucked goose and a shorn
     sheep of legalized fraud
And the people is one of those mountain slopes
     holding a volcano of retribution,
Slow in all things, slow in its gathered wrath,
     slow in its onward heave,
Slow in its asking: "Where are we now? what time
     is it?"

.   .   .

The sea only knows the bottom of the ship.
One grain of wheat holds all the stars.
The bosoms of the wise are the tombs of secrets.
When you must, walk as if on eggshells.
It looks good but is it foolproof?
Only a poor fisherman curses the river he fishes in.
I can read your writing but I can't read your mind.
     Threatened men live long.
     The glad hand became the icy mitt.
Applause is the beginning of abuse.
If born to be hanged you shall never be drowned.

Life without a friend is death without a witness.
      Sleep is the image of death.
Six feet of earth make us all of one size.
The oldest man that ever lived died at last.
The turnip looked big till the pumpkin walked in.
The dime looked different when the dollar arrived.
      Who said you are the superintendent?
      Spit on your hands and go to work.
Three generations from shirtsleeves to shirtsleeves.
We won't see it but our children will.

      Everything is in the books.
      Too many books overload the mind.
      Who knows the answers?
      Step by step one goes far.
The greatest cunning is to have none at all.
      Sow wind and you reap whirlwind.
A hundred years is not much but never is a long while.
A good blacksmith likes a snootful of smoke.
Fire is a good servant and a bad master.
You can fight fire with fire.
The fireborn are at home in fire.

      The stars make no noise.
You can't hinder the wind from blowing.
      Who could live without hope?

          .   .   .

Sayings, sentences, what of them?
Flashes, lullabies, are they worth remembering?
On the babbling tongues of the people have these been kept.
In the basic mulch of human culture are these grown.
Along with myths of rainbow gold where you shovel all you want
    and take it away,
Along with hopes of a promised land, a homestead farm, and a stake
    in the country,
Along with prayers for a steady job, a chicken in the pot and two
    cars in the garage, the life insurance paid, and a home your own.

    In sudden flash and in massive chaos
    the tunes and cries of the people
    rise in the scripts of Bach and Moussorgsky.

The people handle the food you eat, the clothes you wear,
        and stick by stick and stone by stone
        the houses you live in, roof and walls,
        and wheel by wheel, tire by tire,
        part by part your assembled car,
and the box car loadings of long and short hauls.

Those who have nothing stand in two pressures.
Either what they once had was taken away
Or they never had more than subsistence.
Long ago an easy category was provided for them:
    "They live from hand to mouth,"
Having the name of horny-handed sons of toil.
From these hands howsoever horny, from these sons,
Pours a living cargo of overwhelming plenty
From land and mill into the world markets.
    Their pay for this is what is handed them.
Or they take no pay at all if the labor market is glutted,
Losing out on pay if the word is: "NO HANDS WANTED
                    next month maybe
                    next year maybe
                    the works start."

· · ·

Three things you can't nurse: an old woman, a hen, and a sheep.
Three who have their own way: a mule, a pig, and a miser.
.Three to stay away from: a snake, a man with an oily tongue, and
    a loose woman.
Three things dear to have: fresh eggs, hickory smoked ham, and
    old women's praise.
Three things always pleasing: a cat's kittens, a goat's kid, and a
    young woman.
The three prettiest dead: a little child, a salmon, a black cock.
Three of the coldest things: a man's knee, a cow's horn, and a dog's
    nose.
Three who come unbidden: love, jealousy, fear.
Three soon passing away: the beauty of a woman, the rainbow, the
    echo of the woods.
Three worth wishing: knowledge, grain, and friendship.

· · ·

Always the storm of propaganda blows.
Buy a paper. Read a book. Start the radio.
Listen in the railroad car, in the bus,
Go to church, to a movie, to a saloon.
And always the breezes of personal opinion
are blowing mixed with the doctrines
of propaganda or the chatter of selling spiels.
Believe this, believe that. Buy these, buy them.
Love one-two-three, hate four-five-six.
Remember 7-8-9, forget 10-11-12.
Go now, don't wait, go now at once and buy
Dada Salts Incorporated, Crazy Horse Crystals,
for whatever ails you and if nothing ails you
it is good for that and we are telling you
for your own good. Whatever you are told,
you are told it is for your own good and not
for the special interest of those telling you.
Planned economy is forethought and care.
Planned economy is regimentation and tyranny.
What do you know about planned economy
and how did this argument get started and why?
Let the argument go on.

The storm of propaganda blows always.
In every air of today the germs float and hover.
The shock and contact of ideas goes on.
Planned economy will arrive, stand up,
and stay a long time—or planned economy will
take a beating and be smothered.
The people have the say-so.
Let the argument go on.
Let the people listen.
Tomorrow the people say Yes or No by one question:
"What else can be done?"
In the drive of faiths on the wind today the people know:
"We have come far and we are going farther yet."

. . .

Sleep is a suspension midway
and a conundrum of shadows

lost in meadows of the moon.
The people sleep.
Ai! ai! the people sleep.
Yet the sleepers toss in sleep
and an end comes of sleep
and the sleepers wake.
Ai! ai! the sleepers wake!

. . .

The people will live on.
The learning and blundering people will live on.
They will be tricked and sold and again sold
And go back to the nourishing earth for rootholds,
The people so peculiar in renewal and comeback,
You can't laugh off their capacity to take it.
The mammoth rests between his cyclonic dramas.

The people so often sleepy, weary, enigmatic,
is a vast huddle with many units saying:
"I earn my living.
I make enough to get by
and it takes all my time.
If I had more time
I could do more for myself
and maybe for others.
I could read and study
and talk things over
and find out about things.
It takes time.
I wish I had the time."

The people is a tragic and comic two-face:
hero and hoodlum: phantom and gorilla twist-
ing to moan with a gargoyle mouth: "They
buy me and sell me . . . it's a game . . .
sometime I'll break loose . . ."

Once having marched
Over the margins of animal necessity,
Over the grim line of sheer subsistence
Then man came

To the deeper rituals of his bones,
To the lights lighter than any bones,
To the time for thinking things over,
To the dance, the song, the story,
Or the hours given over to dreaming,
Once having so marched.

Between the finite limitations of the five senses
and the endless yearnings of man for the beyond
the people hold to the humdrum bidding of work and food
while reaching out when it comes their way
for lights beyond the prism of the five senses,
for keepsakes lasting beyond any hunger or death.
This reaching is alive.
The panderers and liars have violated and smutted it.
Yet this reaching is alive yet
for lights and keepsakes.

The people know the salt of the sea
and the strength of the winds
lashing the corners of the earth.
The people take the earth
as a tomb of rest and a cradle of hope.
Who else speaks for the Family of Man?
They are in tune and step
with constellations of universal law.

The people is a polychrome,
a spectrum and a prism
held in a moving monolith,
a console organ of changing themes,
a clavilux of color poems
wherein the sea offers fog
and the fog moves off in rain
and the labrador sunset shortens
to a nocturne of clear stars
serene over the shot spray
of northern lights.

The steel mill sky is alive.
The fire breaks white and zigzag

shot on a gun-metal gloaming.
Man is a long time coming.
Man will yet win.
Brother may yet line up with brother:

This old anvil laughs at many broken hammers.
    There are men who can't be bought.
    The fireborn are at home in fire.
    The stars make no noise.
    You can't hinder the wind from blowing.
    Time is a great teacher.
    Who can live without hope?

In the darkness with a great bundle of grief
    the people march.
In the night, and overhead a shovel of stars for
    keeps, the people march:
                    "Where to? what next?"

Storyteller
and
Poet for Children

Frank Lloyd Wright includes in his autobiography a letter to Carl Sandburg about Rootabaga Stories:

Dear Carl:

I read your fairy tales nearly every night before I go to bed. They fill a long-felt want—Poetry.

I'll soon know them all by heart.

Have you sent the books to Lord Dunsany? It would make him feel sorry he was born a Lord and so had to fool around with Gods and Goddesses.

I've tried so long to play the guitar with my mittens on that Henry Hagglyhoagly is mine—and O man! the beauty of the White Horse Girl and the Blue Wind Boy! And the fairies dancing on the wind-swept corn! The Wedding Procession of the Rag Doll and the Broom Handle! The Skyscrapers that Decided to have a Child!

All of the children that will be born into the Middle West during the next hundred years are peeping at you now, Carl— between little pink fingers—smiling, knowing in their hearts they have found a friend.

And Lucky Spink and Skabootch—to have a daddy—"fire-born" who understands blue. Blue is happy imagination. Something that wakes and sings no matter how much it hurts —or is it always singing?

Yes, Carl, only the Fire-born understand blue. You are the kind of artist for me. Stick this little posy in your hatband for a day. I fling it to you from where, as always, the tracks leave the ground for the sky and I'll be waiting for you at this station in the Rootabaga Country to bring Spink and Skabootch to play with their Uncle:

Frank

Rootabaga Stories

HOW THEY BROKE AWAY TO GO TO THE
ROOTABAGA COUNTRY

Gimme the Ax lived in a house where everything is the same as it always was.

"The chimney sits on top of the house and lets the smoke out," said Gimme the Ax. "The doorknobs open the doors. The windows are always either open or shut. We are always either upstairs or downstairs in this house. Everything is the same as it always was."

So he decided to let his children name themselves.

"The first words they speak as soon as they learn to make words shall be their names," he said. "They shall name themselves."

When the first boy came to the house of Gimme the Ax, he was named Please Gimme. When the first girl came she was named Ax Me No Questions.

And both of the children had the shadows of valleys by night in their eyes and the lights of early morning, when the sun is coming up, on their foreheads.

And the hair on top of their heads was a dark wild grass. And they loved to turn the doorknobs, open the doors, and run out to have the wind comb their hair and touch their eyes and put its six soft fingers on their foreheads.

And then because no more boys came and no more girls came, Gimme the Ax said to himself, "My first boy is my last and my last girl is my first and they picked their names themselves."

Please Gimme grew up and his ears got longer. Ax Me No Questions grew up and her ears got longer. And they kept on living in the house where everything is the same as it always was. They learned to say just as their father said, "The chimney sits on top of the house and lets the smoke out, the doorknobs open the doors, the windows are always either open or shut, we are always either upstairs or downstairs—everything is the same as it always was."

After a while they began asking each other in the cool of the evening after they had eggs for breakfast in the morning, "Who's who? How much? And what's the answer?"

"It is too much to be too long anywhere," said the tough old man, Gimme the Ax.

And Please Gimme and Ax Me No Questions, the tough son and the tough daughter of Gimme the Ax, answered their father, "It *is* too much to be too long anywhere."

So they sold everything they had, pigs, pastures, pepper pickers, pitchforks, everything except their ragbags and a few extras.

When their neighbors saw them selling everything they had, the different neighbors said, "They are going to Kansas, to Kokomo, to Canada, to Kankakee, to Kalamazoo, to Kamchatka, to the Chattahoochee."

One little sniffer with his eyes half shut and a mitten on his nose, laughed in his hat five ways and said, "They are going to the moon and when they get there they will find everything is the same as it always was."

All the spot cash money he got for selling everything, pigs, pastures, pepper pickers, pitchforks, Gimme the Ax put in a ragbag and slung on his back like a ragpicker going home.

Then he took Please Gimme, his oldest and youngest and only son, and Ax Me No Questions, his oldest and youngest and only daughter, and went to the railroad station.

The ticket agent was sitting at the window selling railroad tickets the same as always.

"Do you wish a ticket to go away and come back or do you wish a ticket to go away and *never* come back?" the ticket agent asked wiping sleep out of his eyes.

"We wish a ticket to ride where the railroad tracks run off into the sky and never come back—send us far as the railroad rails go and then forty ways farther yet," was the reply of Gimme the Ax.

"So far? So early? So soon?" asked the ticket agent wiping more sleep out of his eyes. "Then I will give you a new ticket. It blew in. It is a long slick yellow leather slab ticket with a blue spanch across it."

Gimme the Ax thanked the ticket agent once, thanked the ticket agent twice, and then instead of thanking the ticket agent three times he opened the ragbag and took out all the spot cash money he got for selling everything, pigs, pastures, pepper pickers, pitchforks, and paid the spot cash money to the ticket agent.

Before he put it in his pocket he looked once, twice, three times at the long yellow leather slab ticket with a blue spanch across it.

Then with Please Gimme and Ax Me No Questions he got on the railroad train, showed the conductor his ticket and they started to ride to where the railroad tracks run off into the blue sky and then forty ways farther yet.

The train ran on and on. It came to the place where the railroad tracks run off into the blue sky. And it ran on and on chick chick-a-chick chick-a-chick chick-a-chick.

Sometimes the engineer hooted and tooted the whistle. Sometimes the fireman rang the bell. Sometimes the open-and-shut of the steam hog's nose choked and spit pfisty-pfoost, pfisty-pfoost, pfisty-pfoost. But no matter what happened to the whistle and the bell and the steam hog, the train ran on and on to where the railroad tracks run off into the blue sky. And then it ran on and on more and more.

Sometimes Gimme the Ax looked in his pocket, put his fingers in and took out the long slick yellow leather slab ticket with a blue spanch across it.

"Not even the Kings of Egypt with all their climbing camels, and all their speedy, spotted, lucky lizards, ever had a ride like this," he said to his children.

Then something happened. They met another train running on the same track. One train was going one way. The other was going the other way. They met. They passed each other.

"What was it—what happened?" the children asked their father.

"One train went over, the other train went under," he answered. "This is the Over and Under country. Nobody gets out of the way of anybody else. They either go over or under."

Next they came to the country of the balloon pickers. Hanging down from the sky strung on strings so fine the eye could not see them at first, was the balloon crop of that summer. The sky was thick with balloons. Red, blue, yellow balloons, white, purple and orange balloons—peach, watermelon and potato balloons—rye loaf and wheat loaf balloons—link sausage and pork chop balloons—they floated and filled the sky.

The balloon pickers were walking on high stilts picking balloons. Each picker had his own stilts, long or short. For picking balloons near the ground he had short stilts. If he wanted to pick far and high he walked on a far and high pair of stilts.

Baby pickers on baby stilts were picking baby balloons. When they fell off the stilts the handful of balloons they were holding kept them in the air till they got their feet into the stilts again.

"Who is that away up there in the sky climbing like a bird in the morning?" Ax Me No Questions asked her father.

"He was singing too happy," replied the father. "The songs came out of his neck and made him so light the balloons pulled him off his stilts."

"Will he ever come down again back to his own people?"

"Yes, his heart will get heavy when his songs are all gone. Then he will drop down to his stilts again."

The train was running on and on. The engineer hooted and tooted the whistle when he felt like it. The fireman rang the bell when he felt that way. And sometimes the open-and-shut of the steam hog had to go pfisty-pfoost, pfisty-pfoost.

"Next is the country where the circus clowns come from," said Gimme the Ax to his son and daughter. "Keep your eyes open."

They did keep their eyes open. They saw cities with ovens, long and short ovens, fat stubby ovens, lean lank ovens, all for baking either long or short clowns, or fat and stubby or lean and lank clowns.

After each clown was baked in the oven it was taken out into the sunshine and put up to stand like a big white doll with a red mouth leaning against the fence.

Two men came along to each baked clown standing still like a doll. One man threw a bucket of white fire over it. The second man pumped a wind pump with a living red wind through the red mouth.

The clown rubbed his eyes, opened his mouth, twisted his neck, wiggled his ears, wriggled his toes, jumped away from the fence and began turning handsprings, cartwheels, somersaults and flipflops in the sawdust ring near the fence.

"The next we come to is the Rootabaga Country where the big city is the Village of Liver-and-Onions," said Gimme the Ax, looking again in his pocket to be sure he had the long slick yellow leather slab ticket with a blue spanch across it.

The train ran on and on till it stopped running straight and began running in zigzags like one letter Z put next to another Z and the next and the next.

The tracks and the rails and the ties and the spikes under the train all stopped being straight and changed to zigzags like one letter Z and another letter Z put next after the other.

"It seems like we go halfway and then back up," said Ax Me No Questions.

"Look out of the window and see if the pigs have bibs on," said Gimme the Ax. "If the pigs are wearing bibs then this is the Rootabaga country."

And they looked out of the zigzagging windows of the zigzagging cars and the first pigs they saw had bibs on. And the next pigs and the next pigs they saw all had bibs on.

The checker pigs had checker bibs on, the striped pigs had striped bibs on. And the polka dot pigs had polka dot bibs on.

"Who fixes it for the pigs to have bibs on?" Please Gimme asked his father.

"The fathers and mothers fix it," answered Gimme the Ax. "The checker pigs have checker fathers and mothers. The striped pigs have striped fathers and mothers. And the polka dot pigs have polka dot fathers and mothers."

And the train went zigzagging on and on running on the tracks and the rails and the spikes and the ties which were all zigzag like the letter Z and the letter Z.

And after a while the train zigzagged on into the Village of Liver-and-Onions, known as the biggest city in the big, big Rootabaga country.

And so if you are going to the Rootabaga country you will know when you get there because the railroad tracks change from straight to zigzag, the pigs have bibs on and it is the fathers and mothers who fix it.

And if you start to go to that country remember first you must sell everything you have, pigs, pastures, pepper pickers, pitchforks, put the spot cash money in a ragbag and go to the railroad station and ask the ticket agent for a long slick yellow leather slab ticket with a blue spanch across it.

And you mustn't be surprised if the ticket agent wipes sleep from his eyes and asks, "So far? So early? So soon?"

THE WEDDING PROCESSION OF THE RAG DOLL
AND THE BROOM HANDLE AND WHO WAS IN IT

The Rag Doll had many friends. The Whisk Broom, the Furnace Shovel, the Coffee Pot, they all liked the Rag Doll very much.

But when the Rag Doll married, it was the Broom Handle she picked because the Broom Handle fixed her eyes.

A proud child, proud but careless, banged the head of the Rag Doll against a door one day and knocked off both the glass eyes sewed on long ago. It was then the Broom Handle found two black California prunes, and fastened the two California prunes just where the eyes belonged. So then the Rag Doll had two fine black eyes brand new. She was even nicknamed Black Eyes by some people.

There was a wedding when the Rag Doll married the Broom Handle. It was a grand wedding with one of the grandest processions ever seen at a rag doll wedding. And we are sure no broom handle ever had a grander wedding procession when he got married.

Who marched in the procession? Well, first came the Spoon Lickers. Every one of them had a teaspoon, or a soupspoon, though most of them had a big tablespoon. On the spoons, what did they have? Oh, some had butterscotch, some had gravy, some had marshmallow fudge. Every one had something slickery sweet or fat to eat on the spoon. And as they marched in the wedding procession of the Rag Doll and the Broom Handle, they licked their spoons and looked around and licked their spoons again.

Next came the Tin Pan Bangers. Some had dishpans, some had frying pans, some had potato peeling pans. All the pans were tin with tight tin bottoms. And the Tin Pan Bangers banged with knives and forks and iron and wooden bangers on the bottoms of the tin pans. And as they marched in the wedding procession of the Rag Doll and the Broom Handle, they banged their pans and looked around and banged again.

Then came the Chocolate Chins. They were all eating chocolates. And the chocolate was slippery and slickered all over their chins. Some of them spattered the ends of their noses with black chocolate. Some of them spread the brown chocolate nearly up to their ears. And then as they marched in the wedding procession of the Rag Doll and the Broom Handle, they stuck their chins in the air and looked around and stuck their chins in the air again.

Then came the Dirty Bibs. They wore plain white bibs, checker bibs, stripe bibs, blue bibs and bibs with butterflies. But all the bibs were dirty. The plain white bibs were dirty, the checker bibs were dirty, the stripe bibs, the blue bibs and the bibs with butterflies on them, they were all dirty. And so in the wedding procession of the Rag Doll and the Broom Handle, the Dirty Bibs marched with their dirty fingers on the bibs and they looked around and laughed and looked around and laughed again.

Next came the Clean Ears. They were proud. How they got into the procession nobody knows. Their ears were all clean. They were clean not only on the outside but they were clean on the inside. There was not a speck of dirt or dust or muss or mess on the inside nor the outside of their ears. And so in the wedding procession of the Rag Doll and the Broom Handle, they wiggled their ears and looked around and wiggled their ears again.

The Easy Ticklers were next in the procession. Their faces were shining. Their cheeks were like bars of new soap. Their ribs were strong and the meat and the fat was thick on their ribs. It was plain to see they were saying, "Don't tickle me because I tickle so easy." And as they marched in the wedding procession of the Rag Doll and the Broom Handle, they tickled themselves and laughed and looked around and tickled themselves again.

The music was furnished mostly by the Musical Soup Eaters. They marched with big bowls of soup in front of them and big spoons for eating the soup. They whistled and chuzzled and snozzled the soup and the noise they made could be heard far up at the head of the procession where the Spoon Lickers were marching. So they dipped their soup and looked around and dipped their soup again.

The Chubby Chubs were next. They were roly-poly, round-faced smackers and snoozers. They were not fat babies—oh no, oh no—not fat but just chubby and easy to squeeze. They marched on their chubby legs and chubby feet and chubbed their chubbs and looked around and chubbed their chubbs again.

The last of all in the wedding procession of the Rag Doll and the Broom Handle were the Sleepyheads. They were smiling and glad to be marching but their heads were slimpsing down and their smiles were half fading away and their eyes were half shut or a little more than half shut. They staggered just a little as though their feet were not sure where they were going. They were the Sleepyheads, the last of all, in the wedding procession of the Rag Doll and the Broom Handle, and the Sleepyheads they never looked around at all.

It *was* a grand procession, don't you think so?

THE WHITE HORSE GIRL AND
THE BLUE WIND BOY

When the dishes are washed at nighttime and the cool of the evening has come in summer or the lamps and fires are lit for the night in winter, then the fathers and mothers in the Rootabaga Country sometimes tell the young people the story of the White Horse Girl and the Blue Wind Boy.

The White Horse Girl grew up far in the west of the Rootabaga Country. All the years she grew up as a girl she liked to ride horses. Best of all things for her was to be straddle of a white horse loping with a loose bridle among the hills and along the rivers of the west Rootabaga Country.

She rode one horse white as snow, another horse white as new-washed sheep wool, and another white as silver. And she could not tell because she did not know which of these three white horses she liked best.

"Snow is beautiful enough for me any time," she said, "new-washed sheep wool, or silver out of a ribbon of the new moon, any or either is white enough for me. I like the white manes, the white flanks, the white noses, the white feet of all my ponies. I like the forelocks hanging down between the white ears of all three—my ponies."

And living neighbor to the White Horse Girl in the same prairie country, with the same black crows flying over their places, was the Blue Wind Boy. All the years he grew up as a boy he liked to walk with his feet in the dirt and the grass listening to the winds. Best of all things for him was to put on strong shoes and go hiking among the hills and along the rivers of the west Rootabaga Country, listening to the winds.

There was a blue wind of daytime, starting sometimes six o'clock on a summer morning or eight o'clock on a winter morning. And there was a night wind with blue of summer stars in summer and blue of winter stars in winter. And there was yet another, a blue wind of the times between night and day, a blue dawn and evening wind. All three of these winds he liked so well he could not say which he liked best.

"The early morning wind is strong as the prairie and whatever I tell it I know it believes and remembers," he said, "and the night wind with the big dark curves of the night sky in it, the night wind gets inside of me and understands all my secrets. And the blue wind of the times between, in the dusk when it is neither night nor day, this is the wind that asks me questions and tells me to wait and it will bring me whatever I want."

Of course, it happened as it had to happen, the White Horse Girl and the Blue Wind Boy met. She, straddling one of her white horses, and he, wearing his strong hiking shoes in the dirt and the grass, it had to happen they should meet among the hills and along the rivers of the west Rootabaga Country where they lived neighbors.

And of course, she told him all about the snow-white horse and the horse white as new-washed sheep wool and the horse white as a silver ribbon of the new moon. And he told her all about the blue winds he liked listening to, the early morning wind, the night sky wind, and the wind of the dusk between, the wind that asked him questions and told him to wait.

One day the two of them were gone. On the same day of the week the White Horse Girl and the Blue Wind Boy went away. And their fathers and mothers and sisters and brothers and uncles and aunts wondered about them and talked about them, because they didn't tell anybody beforehand they were going. Nobody at all knew beforehand or afterward why they were going away, the real honest why of it.

They left a short letter. It read:

To All Our Sweethearts, Old Folks and Young Folks:
We have started to go where the white horses come from and where the blue winds begin. Keep a corner in your hearts for us while we are gone.

> *The White Horse Girl*
> *The Blue Wind Boy*

That was all they had to guess by in the west Rootabaga Country, to guess and guess where two darlings had gone.

Many years passed. One day there came riding across the Rootabaga Country a Gray Man on Horseback. He looked like he had come a long ways. So they asked him the question they always asked of any rider who looked like he had come a long ways, "Did you ever see the White Horse Girl and the Blue Wind Boy?"

"Yes," he answered, "I saw them."

"It was a long, long ways from here I saw them," he went on. "It would take years and years to ride to where they are. They were sitting together and talking to each other, sometimes singing, in a place where the land runs high and tough rocks reach up. And they were looking out across water, blue water as far as the eye could see. And away far off the blue waters met the blue sky.

" 'Look!' said the Boy, 'that's where the blue winds begin.'

"And far out on the blue waters, just a little this side of where the blue winds begin, there were white manes, white flanks, white noses, white galloping feet.

" 'Look!' said the Girl, 'that's where the white horses come from.'

"And then nearer to the land came thousands in an hour, millions in a day, white horses, some white as snow, some like new-washed sheep wool, some white as silver ribbons of the new moon.

"I asked them, 'Whose place is this?' They answered, 'It belongs to us; this is what we started for; this is where the white horses come from; this is where the blue winds begin.' "

And that was all the Gray Man on Horseback would tell the people of the west Rootabaga Country. That was all he knew, he said, and if there was any more he would tell it.

And the fathers and mothers and sisters and brothers and uncles and aunts of the White Horse Girl and the Blue Wind Boy wondered and talked often about whether the Gray Man on Horseback made up the story out of his head or whether it happened just like he told it.

Anyhow this is the story they tell sometimes to the young people of the west Rootabaga Country when the dishes are washed at night and the cool of the evening has come in summer or the lamps and fires are lit for the night in winter.

Rootabaga Pigeons

SLIPFOOT AND HOW HE NEARLY ALWAYS NEVER GETS WHAT HE GOES AFTER

Blixie Bimber flipped out of the kitchen one morning, first saying good-by to the dishpan, good-by to the dishrag, good-by to the dish towel for wiping dishes.

Under one arm she put a basket of peonies she picked, under the other arm she put a basket of jonquils she picked.

Then she flipped away up the street and downtown where she put the baskets of peonies and jonquils one on each side of the Potato Face Blind Man.

"I picked the pink and lavender peonies and I picked the yellow jonquils for you to be smelling one on each side of you this fine early summer morning," she said to the Potato Face. "Have you seen any-body good to see lately?"

"Slipfoot was here this morning," said the old man.

"And who is Slipfoot?" asked Blixie.

"I don't know. He says to me, 'I got a foot always slips. I used to wash windows—and my foot slips. I used to be king of the collar buttons, king of a million dollars—and my foot slips. I used to be king of the peanuts, king of a million dollars again. I used to be king of the oyster cans, selling a million cans a day. I used to be king of the peanut sacks, selling ten million sacks a day. And every time I was a king my foot slips. Every time I had a million dollars my foot slips. Every time I went high and put my foot higher my foot slips. Some-body gave me a slipfoot. I always slip.'"

"So you call him Slipfoot?" asked Blixie.

"Yes," said the old man.

"Has he been here before?"

"Yes, he was here a year ago, saying, 'I marry a woman and she runs away. I run after her—and my foot slips. I always get what I want—and then my foot slips.

" 'I ran up a stairway to the moon one night. I shoveled a big sack full of little gold beans, little gold bricks, little gold bugs, on the moon and I ran down the stairway from the moon. On the last step of the stairway, my foot slips—and all the little gold beans, all the little gold bricks, all the little gold bugs, spill out and spill away. When I get down the stairway I am holding the sack and the sack holds nothing. I am all right always till my foot slips.

" 'I jump on a trapeze and I go swinging, swinging, swinging out where I am going to take hold of the rainbow and bring it down where we can look at it close. And I hang by my feet on the trapeze and I am swinging out where I am just ready to take hold of the rainbow and bring it down. Then my foot slips.' "

"What is the matter with Slipfoot?" asks Blixie.

"He asks me that same question," answered the Potato Face Blind Man. "He asks me that every time he comes here. I tell him all he needs is to get his slipfoot fixed so it won't slip. Then he'll be all right."

"I understand you," said Blixie. "You make it easy. You always make it easy. And before I run away will you promise me to smell of the pink and lavender peonies and the yellow jonquils all day today?"

"I promise," said the Potato Face. "Promises are easy. I like promises."

"So do I," said the little girl. "It's promises pushing me back home to the dishpan, the dishrag, and the dish towel for wiping dishes."

"Look out you don't get a slipfoot," warned the old man as the girl flipped up the street going home.

HOW BOZO THE BUTTON BUSTER BUSTED ALL
HIS BUTTONS WHEN A MOUSE CAME

One summer evening the stars in the summer sky seemed to be moving with fishes, cats and rabbits.

It was that summer evening three girls came to the shanty of Hatrack the Horse. He asked each one, "What is your name?" And they answered, first, "Me? My name is Deep Red Roses"; second, "Me? My name is The Beans are Burning"; and last of all, "Me? My name is Sweeter than the Bees Humming."

And the old man fastened a yellow rose for luck in the hair of each one and said, "You ought to be home now."

"After you tell us a story," they reminded him.

"I can only tell you a sad story all mixed up tonight," he reminded them, "because all day today I have been thinking about Bozo the Button Buster."

"Tell us about Bozo the Button Buster," said the girls, feeling in their hair and fixing the yellow roses.

The old man sat down on the front steps. His eyes swept away off toward a corner of the sky heavy with mist where it seemed to be moving with firetails, fishes, cats, and rabbits of slow-changing stars.

"Bozo had buttons all over him," said the old man. "The buttons on Bozo fitted so tight, and there were so many buttons, that sometimes when he took his lungs full of new wind to go on talking a button would bust loose and fly into the face of whoever he was speaking to. Sometimes when he took new wind into his lungs two buttons would bust loose and fly into the faces of two people he was speaking to.

"So people said, 'Isn't it queer how buttons fly loose when Bozo fills his lungs with wind to go on speaking?' After a while everybody called him Bozo the Button Buster.

"Now, you must understand, Bozo was different from other people. He had a string tied to him. It was a long string hanging down with a knot in the end. He used to say, 'Sometimes I forget where I am; then I feel for the string tied to me, and I follow the string to where it is tied to me; then I know where I am again.'

"Sometimes when Bozo was speaking and a button busted loose, he would ask, 'Was that a mouse? Was that a mouse?' And sometimes he said to people, 'I'll talk with you—*if you haven't got a mouse in your pocket.*'

"The last day Bozo ever came to the Village of Cream Puffs, he stood on the public square and he was all covered with buttons, more buttons than ever before, and all the buttons fitting tight, and five, six buttons busting loose and flying into the air whenever he took his lungs full of wind to go on speaking.

" 'When the sky began to fall, who was it ran out and held up the sky?' he sang out. 'It was me, it was me ran out and held up the sky when the sky began to fall.

" 'When the blue came off the sky, where did they get the blue to put on the sky to make it blue again? It was me, it was me picked the bluebirds and the blue pigeons to get the blue to fix the sky.

" 'When it rains now it rains umbrellas first so everybody has an umbrella for the rain afterward. Who fixed that? I did—Bozo the Button Buster.

" 'Who took the rainbow off the sky and put it back again in a hurry? That was me.

" 'Who turned all the barns upside down and then put them right side up again? I did that.

" 'Who took the salt out of the sea and put it back again? Who took the fishes out of the sea and put them back again? That was me.

" 'Who started the catfish fighting the cats? Who made the slippery elms slippery? Who made the King of the Broken Bottles a wanderer wandering over the world mumbling, "Easy, easy"? Who opened the windows of the stars and threw fishes, cats and rabbits all over the frames of the sky? I did, I did, I did.'

"All the time Bozo kept on speaking the buttons kept on busting because he had to stop so often to fill his lungs with new wind to go on speaking. The public square was filled with piles of buttons that kept busting off from Bozo the Button Buster that day.

"And at last a mouse came, a sneaking, slippery, quick little mouse. He ran with a flash to the string tied to Bozo, the long string hanging down with a knot in the end. He bit the knot and cut it loose. He slit the string with his teeth as Bozo cried, 'Ai! Ai! Ai!'

"The last of all the buttons busted loose off Bozo. The clothes fell off. The people came up to see what was happening to Bozo. There was nothing in the clothes. The man inside the clothes was gone. All that was left was buttons and a few clothes.

"Since then whenever it rains umbrellas first so everybody has an umbrella for the rain afterward, or if the sky looks like it is falling, or if a barn turns upside down, or if the King of the Broken Bottles comes along mumbling, 'Easy, easy,' or if firetails, fishes, cats and rabbits come on the sky in the night, or if a button busts loose and flies into somebody's face, people remember Bozo the Button Buster."

When the three girls started home, each one said to Hatrack the Horse, "It looks dark and lonesome on the prairie, but you put a yellow rose in my hair for luck—and I won't be scared after I get home."

HOW DEEP RED ROSES GOES BACK AND FORTH BETWEEN THE CLOCK AND THE LOOKING GLASS

One morning when big white clouds were shouldering each other's shoulders, rolling on the rollers of a big blue sky, Blixie Bimber came along where the Potato Face Blind Man sat shining the brass bickerjiggers on his accordion.

"Do you like to shine up the brass bickerjiggers?" asked Blixie.

"Yes," he answered. "One time a long time ago the brass bickerjiggers were gold, but they stole the gold away when I wasn't looking."

He blinked the eyelids over his eyeballs and said, "I thank them because they took gold they wanted. Brass feels good to my fingers the same as gold." And he went on shining up the brass bickerjiggers on the accordion, humming a little line of an old song, "Tomorrow will never catch up with yesterday because yesterday started sooner."

"Seems like a nice morning with the sun spilling bushels of sunshine," he said to Blixie, who answered, "Big white clouds are shouldering each other's shoulders, rolling on the rollers of a big blue sky."

"Seems like it's April all over again," he murmured, almost like he wasn't talking at all.

"Seems just that way—April all over again," murmured Blixie, almost like she wasn't talking at all.

So they began drifting, the old man drifting his way, the girl drifting her way, till he drifted into a story. And the story he told was like this and in these words:

"Deep Red Roses was a lovely girl with blue skylights like the blue skylights of early April in her eyes. And her lips reminded people of deep red roses waiting in the cool of the summer evening.

"She met Shoulder Straps one day when she was young yet. He promised her. And she promised him. But he went away. One of the long wars between two short wars took him. In a faraway country, then, he married another girl. And he didn't come back to Deep Red Roses.

"Next came High High Over, one day when she was young yet. A dancer he was, going from one city to another city to dance, spending his afternoons and evenings and late nights dancing, and sleeping in the morning till noon. And when he promised she promised. But he went away to another city and after that another city. And he married one woman and then another woman. Every year there came a new story about one of the new wives of High High Over, the dancer. And while she was young yet, Deep Red Roses forgot all about her promise and the promise of High High Over, the dancer who ran away from her.

"Six Bits was the next to come along. And he was not a soldier or a dancer or anything special. He was a careless man, changing from one job to another, changing from paper hanging to plastering, from fixing shingle roofs where the shingles were ripped to opening cans with can openers.

"Six Bits gave Deep Red Roses his promise and she gave him her promise. But he was always late keeping his promise. When the wedding was to be Tuesday he didn't come till Wednesday. If it was Friday he came Saturday. And there wasn't any wedding.

"So Deep Red Roses said to herself, 'I am going away and learn. I am going away and talk with the wives of High High Over, the dancer, and maybe if I go far enough I will find the wife of Shoulder Straps, the soldier—and maybe the wives of the men who promised me will tell me how to keep promises kept.'

"She packed her baggage till her baggage was packed so full there was room for only one more thing. So she had to decide whether to put a *clock* or whether to put a *looking glass* in her baggage.

" 'My head tells me to carry the clock so I can always tell if I am early or late,' she said to herself. 'But my heart tells me to carry a looking glass so I can look at my face and tell if I am getting older or younger.'

"At last she decides to take the clock and leave the looking glass—because her head says so. She starts away. She goes through the door, she is out of the house, she goes to the street, she starts up the street.

"Then her heart tells her to go back and change the clock for the looking glass. She goes back up the street, through the door, into the house, into her room. Now she stands in front of the clock and the looking glass saying, 'Tonight I sleep home here one more night, and tomorrow morning I decide again.'

"And now every morning Deep Red Roses decides with her head to take the clock. She takes the clock and starts away and then comes back because her heart decides she must have the looking glass.

"If you go to her house this morning you will see her standing in the doorway with blue skylights like the blue sky of early April in her eyes, and lips that remind you of deep red roses in the cool of the evening in summer. You will see her leave the doorway and go out of the gate with the clock in her hands. Then if you wait you will see her come back through the gate, into the door, back to her room where she puts down the clock and takes up the looking glass.

"After that she decides to wait until tomorrow morning to decide again what to decide. Her head tells her one thing, her heart tells her another. Between the two she stays home. Sometimes she looks at her face in the looking glass and says to herself, 'I am young yet and while I am young I am going to do my own deciding.' "

Blixie Bimber fingered the end of her chain with her little finger and said, "It is a strange story. It has a stab in it. It would hurt me if I couldn't look up at the big white clouds shouldering their shoulders, rolling on the rollers of the big blue sky."

"It is a good story to tell when April is here all over again—and I am shining up the brass bickerjiggers on my accordion," said the Potato Face Blind Man.

New Stories

First told to children and then written, they are intended to be read aloud.

THE FIVE MARVELOUS PRETZELS

Five nights before Christmas, five pretzels sit looking out of a grocery window lighted by five candles. And outside they see snow falling, big white snowflakes coming down cool and quiet. And they see a man come along and stop in front of the window and he looks in while they look out. They see his right hand brush off snow from his left shoulder and his left hand brush off snow from his right shoulder. And they see him shake off snow from his hat and put his hat back on his head. But they don't hear the man saying, "Well, well, here are five pretzels. And how many children is it I have at home running around upstairs and downstairs, in and out of the corners? One, two, three, four, five, one for each pretzel."

Now early that afternoon they decide they will go with a circus and be trapeze actors. On billboards everywhere people will see in big letters THE FIVE MARVELOUS PRETZELS. And just before they run out of their dressing rooms in pink tights and bow to the audience and throw kisses to the audience, one kiss with the right hand and the other kiss with the left hand, a man with a big musical megaphone calls to the audience "THE FIVE MARVELOUS PRET-ZELS!" Then up in the air they go and two of them hang by their knees and throw the other three pretzels back and forth in the air, in the empty and circumambient air.

So far, so good. Then comes the argument, the fuss, the dispute. Which two shall hang by their knees and which three shall be thrown back and forth in the empty and circumambient air? All five want to be the two that hang by their knees. None of them wants to be one of the three thrown back and forth. So they say, "Let's forget it."

109

Now they decide instead they will ride on the heads of the first five elephants in the vast mammoth stupendous parade of the elephants. On billboards people will see five elephants and on the head of each mammoth stupendous elephant rides one dazzling glittering little pretzel, in pink tights, bowing and throwing kisses to the audience, one kiss with the right hand and the other kiss with the left hand. Yes, so they decide. And they will have it fixed that just before the first elephant comes out leading the parade a man with a big musical megaphone calls to the audience "THE FIVE MARVELOUS PRETZELS!"

So far, so good. Then comes the argument. Who should ride on the head of the first elephant? Who should be the first one to come out bowing and throwing kisses to the audience? They argue, they fuss, they dispute, they wrangle. And at last they decide that whoever rides the first elephant today rides the last elephant tomorrow.

Then they see the man who stands looking in where they are looking out, brushing snow off his right shoulder with his left hand, brushing snow off his left shoulder with his right hand, shaking snow off his hat and putting it back on his head. And the man walks into the store, pays ten cents and comes out with the five pretzels in a paper sack and walks along the street in the falling snow, big white snowflakes coming down cool and quiet on his shoulders, on his hat.

And does he know as he walks along in the falling snow what happens that afternoon and evening? No. Does he know he has in a paper sack THE FIVE MARVELOUS PRETZELS? No. Does he know they decide to go with a circus and be trapeze actors and then change their minds? No. Does he know they decide instead they will ride on the heads of five elephants and bow and throw kisses to the audience while thousands of people laugh and cheer and cry, "Look, look, look, here come the five marvelous pretzels"? No.

Then what does the man know about what the five pretzels want to be? Nothing, absolutely nothing. Which shows *how* ignorant some people are!

THE THREE NICE MICE

Mr. and Mrs. Cat sit in their house in nice easy chairs. And a fat little mouse comes out of a hole in a corner of the room and looks around looking for something.

Mr. Cat sits quiet and says to Mrs. Cat, "I notice Anaxagoras is paying us a call this evening." "Yes," replies Mrs. Cat. "It is very nice of Anaxagoras to call on us and I hope Anaxagoras will visit our home again."

While Mr. and Mrs. Cat are saying this the mouse stands on his hind legs and listens to every last word of it. Then he whisks himself back into his corner hole in a flick of a feather and a flish of a flash.

The next night again Mr. and Mrs. Cat sit quiet in nice easy chairs. And again a fat little mouse comes out of a corner hole and looks around looking for something.

And now Mr. Cat sits quiet and says to Mrs. Cat, "I notice Alcibiades is paying us a call this evening," Mrs. Cat replying, "Yes, it is nice of Alcibiades to call on us and I hope Alcibiades will visit our home often."

While Mr. and Mrs. Cat say this the mouse stands on his hind legs and listens to every last word of it. Then they hear him saying, "It was Alcibiades came here last night. It is me, it is I, it is whoever you are listening to now, who is Anaxagoras and I bid you good evening good evening good evening." Then he whisks himself back into his corner hole with a flick of a feather and a flish of a flash.

Now on the third night again Mr. and Mrs. Cat sit quiet in nice easy chairs. And again a fat little mouse comes out of a corner hole and looks around looking for something. And Mrs. Cat says to Mr. Cat, "I wonder whether it is Anaxagoras or Alcibiades who pays us the honor of a call this evening." "Well," says Mr. Cat, "it must be either Anaxagoras or Alcibiades."

And the mouse, of course, stands on his hind legs and listens to every last word of this. Then they hear him saying, "I am sorry I must tell you that you are both mistaken. For I am Anonymous, the youngest brother of Anaxagoras and Alcibiades. You were wrong about each of them and you are wrong about me. So I bid you good evening good evening good evening." Then he whisks himself back in the corner hole with a flick of a feather and a flish of a flash.

From then on, from that night on, Mr. and Mrs. Cat sit quiet in their nice easy chairs and when a fat little mouse comes out of a corner hole, they both say to it in a polite voice and with much respect, "Will you be so good and kind as to tell us your name so nobody makes a mistake and nobody is wrong when they call you either Anaxagoras, Alcibiades or Anonymous?"

And from then on, from that night on, the mouse stands on his hind legs and listens to every last word of this. Then he tells who he is, which one of the three mice brothers. Then he says good evening good evening good evening and whisks himself back into his corner hole with a flick of a feather and a flish of a flash.

And every morning at breakfast and every evening at supper Anaxagoras, Alcibiades and Anonymous—one mouse who has three names—says to himself as though he is three themselves, "We sure look alike."

Early Moon

In his preface to Early Moon, *a book of poems for young people, Carl Sandburg writes:*

Should children write poetry? Yes, whenever they feel like it. If nothing else happens they will find it a training for writing and speaking in other fields of human work and play. No novelist has been a worse writer for having practiced at poetry. Many a playwright, historian, essayist, editorial writer, could have improved his form by experimenting with poetry.

At what age should a child begin writing poetry? Any age. Poems are made of words and when a child is learning to talk, to shape words on its tongue, is a proper time for it to speak poetry —if it can.

Does it help a child poet to have praise for his poems? The child should be told that poetry is first of all for the poet, that great poets usually die saying their best work is not written. Perhaps it is wise for every child to be told that it is a mistake for either a child or a grown-up accomplished artist to be satisfied with any past performance.

The foremost American woman poet, Emily Dickinson, had scarcely any of her poetry published in her lifetime. What she wrote had to be. And it is doubtful if her poems would have had the same complete glory they have if she had been taken up and praised. On the other hand there have been poets saved to live and write beautiful pages because they found friends, an audience, and enough money to keep the wolf from sniffing round their little doorways.

Once a little girl showed to a friend a poem she had written. "Why didn't you make it longer?" asked the friend. "I could have," she answered, "but then it wouldn't have been a poem." She meant she left something in the air for the reader of the poem to linger over, as any of us do over a rose or a sunset or a face. Roses, sunsets, faces, have mystery.

If poems could be explained, then poets would have to leave out roses, sunsets, faces, from their poems. Yet it seems that for thousands of years poets have been writing about roses, sunsets, faces, because they have mystery, significance, and a heavy or a light beauty, an appeal, a lesson and a symbolism that stays with us long as we live. It was something like this in the heart of the philosopher who declared, "What can be explained is not poetry."

PRIMER LESSON

Look out how you use proud words.
When you let proud words go, it is
      not easy to call them back.
They wear long boots, hard boots; they
      walk off proud; they can't hear you
      calling—
Look out how you use proud words.

SPLINTER

The voice of the last cricket
across the first frost
is one kind of good-by.
It is so thin a splinter of singing.

THEME IN YELLOW

I spot the hills
With yellow balls in autumn.
I light the prairie cornfields
Orange and tawny gold clusters
And I am called pumpkins.
On the last of October
When dusk is fallen
Children join hands
And circle round me
Singing ghost songs
And love to the harvest moon;

I am a jack-o'-lantern
With terrible teeth
And the children know
I am fooling.

SEA-WASH

The sea-wash never ends.
The sea-wash repeats, repeats.
Only old songs? Is that all the sea knows?
Only the old strong songs?
Is that all?
The sea-wash repeats, repeats.

BUFFALO DUSK

The buffaloes are gone.
And those who saw the buffaloes are gone.
Those who saw the buffaloes by thousands and how they pawed the
prairie sod into dust with their hoofs, their great heads down paw-
ing on in a great pageant of dusk,
Those who saw the buffaloes are gone.
And the buffaloes are gone.

POTOMAC TOWN IN FEBRUARY

The bridge says: Come across, try me; see how good I
am.
The big rock in the river says: Look at me; learn how
to stand up.
The white water says: I go on; around, under, over, I
go on.
A kneeling, scraggly pine says: I am here yet; they
nearly got me last year.
A sliver of moon slides by on a high wind calling: I know
why; I'll see you tomorrow; I'll tell you everything
tomorrow.

CHILD MOON

The child's wonder
At the old moon
Comes back nightly.
She points her finger
To the far silent yellow thing
Shining through the branches
Filtering on the leaves a golden sand,
Crying with her little tongue, "See the moon!"
And in her bed fading to sleep
With babblings of the moon on her little mouth.

SMALL HOMES

The green bug sleeps in the white lily ear.
The red bug sleeps in the white magnolia.
Shiny wings, you are choosers of color.
You have taken your summer bungalows wisely.

SUMMER STARS

Bend low again, night of summer stars.
So near you are, sky of summer stars,
So near, a long arm man can pick off stars,
Pick off what he wants in the sky bowl,
So near you are, summer stars,
So near, strumming, strumming,
        So lazy and hum-strumming.

BABY TOES

There is a blue star, Janet,
Fifteen years' ride from us,
If we ride a hundred miles an hour.

There is a white star, Janet,
Forty years' ride from us,
If we ride a hundred miles an hour.

Shall we ride
To the blue star
Or the white star?

HELGA

The wishes on this child's mouth
Came like snow on marsh cranberries;
The tamarack kept something for her;
The wind is ready to help her shoes.
The north has loved her; she will be
A grandmother feeding geese on frosty
Mornings; she will understand
Early snow on the cranberries
Better and better then.

SLIPPERY

The six month child
Fresh from the tub
Wriggles in our hands.
This is our fish child.
Give her a nickname: Slippery.

Complete Poems

LITTLE GIRL, BE CAREFUL WHAT YOU SAY

Little girl, be careful what you say
when you make talk with words, words—
for words are made of syllables
and syllables, child, are made of air—
and air is so thin—air is the breath of God—
air is finer than fire or mist,
finer than water or moonlight,
finer than spider-webs in the moon,
finer than water-flowers in the morning:
    and words are strong, too,
    stronger than rocks or steel
stronger than potatoes, corn, fish, cattle,
and soft, too, soft as little pigeon-eggs,
soft as the music of hummingbird wings.
    So, little girl, when you speak greetings,
when you tell jokes, make wishes or prayers,
    be careful, be careless, be careful,
    be what you wish to be.

PAPER I

Paper is two kinds, to write on, to wrap with.
If you like to write, you write.
If you like to wrap, you wrap.
Some papers like writers, some like wrappers.
Are you a writer or a wrapper?

PAPER II

I write what I know on one side of the paper
    and what I don't know on the other.

Fire likes dry paper and wet paper laughs at
   fire.
Empty paper sacks say, "Put something in me,
   what are we waiting for?"
Paper sacks packed to the limit say, "We hope
   we don't bust."
Paper people like to meet other paper people.

DOORS

An open door says, "Come in."
A shut door says, "Who are you?"
Shadows and ghosts go through shut doors.
If a door is shut and you want it shut,
   why open it?
If a door is open and you want it open,
   why shut it?
Doors forget but only doors know what it is
   doors forget.

BOXES AND BAGS

The bigger the box the more it holds.
Empty boxes hold the same as empty heads.
Enough small empty boxes thrown into a big empty box fill it full.
A half-empty box says, "Put more in."
A big enough box could hold the world.
Elephants need big boxes to hold a dozen elephant handkerchiefs.
Fleas fold little handkerchiefs and fix them nice and neat in flea hand-
   kerchief-boxes.
Bags lean against each other and boxes stand independent.
Boxes are square with corners unless round with circles.
Box can be piled on box till the whole works comes tumbling.
Pile box on box and the bottom box says, "If you will kindly take
   notice you will see it all rests on me."
Pile box on box and the top one says, "Who falls farthest if or when
   we fall? I ask you."
Box people go looking for boxes and bag people go looking for bags.

ARITHMETIC

Arithmetic is where numbers fly like pigeons in and out of your head.

Arithmetic tells you how many you lose or win if you know how many you had before you lost or won.

Arithmetic is seven eleven all good children go to heaven—or five six bundle of sticks.

Arithmetic is numbers you squeeze from your head to your hand to your pencil to your paper till you get the answer.

Arithmetic is where the answer is right and everything is nice and you can look out of the window and see the blue sky—or the answer is wrong and you have to start all over and try again and see how it comes out this time.

If you take a number and double it and double it again and then double it a few more times, the number gets bigger and bigger and goes higher and higher and only arithmetic can tell you what the number is when you decide to quit doubling.

Arithmetic is where you have to multiply—and you carry the multiplication table in your head and hope you won't lose it.

If you have two animal crackers, one good and one bad, and you eat one and a striped zebra with streaks all over him eats the other, how many animal crackers will you have if somebody offers you five six seven and you say No no no and you say Nay nay nay and you say Nix nix nix?

If you ask your mother for one fried egg for breakfast and she gives you two fried eggs and you eat both of them, who is better in arithmetic, you or your mother?

Singer
and
Song-Seeker

In 1929 Lloyd Lewis wrote of Carl Sandburg, the troubadour:

The best singing Carl Sandburg ever did was at the dinner Morris Fishbein gave for Sinclair Lewis in 1925. Lewis had just come back from England, and Fishbein had assembled the local authors and critics to meet him—a score of guests or so—quite an affair.

Everybody but the distinguished guest was talking about the British baronetcy that Lewis had turned down, and Ben Hecht got to calling him "Sir Red" on account of that and his red hair. To add to the whoop-de-doodle, James Weber Linn, the University of Chicago English professor, got himself jumped on by Lewis for some things he had said about *Main Street*, and Hecht immediately sided with "Sir Red" and attacked Linn on the flank. Some of the other young rebels joined in, accusing Linn of conservatism in literature, and for a good hour Professor Weber was a verbal Doug Fairbanks, fencing with a dozen swordsmen all at once on a narrow stair, and doing a gallant job of it, too. The hullabaloo grew general.

Down at the very end of the table, opposite the host, sat Chicago's biggest literary figure, Carl Sandburg, behind his hair and his stogy. Every once in a while Carl would shoot in a remark like a Virginia sharpshooter in leather pants, stepping out from behind a hickory tree to plug a Tory, then stepping back to load his muzzle-loader again.

At length Fishbein, to keep his tablecloth from being bitten, asked Carl if he'd sing. Somebody brought a guitar and the iron-jawed Swede stood up and, in that soft, don't-give-a-damn way of his, sang "The Buffalo Skinners."

Everything got quiet as a church, for it's a great rough song, all about starvation, blood, fleas, hides, entrails, thirst, and Indian-devils, and men being cheated out of their wages and killing their employers to get even—a novel, an epic novel boiled down to simple words set to queer music that rises and falls like the winds on Western plains. I've heard the discoverer of the song, John Lomax, of Texas, sing it, but never like Carl sang it this

night. It was like a funeral song to the pioneer America that has
gone, and when Carl was done Sinclair Lewis spoke up, his face
streaked with tears, "That's the America I came home to. That's
it."

Most of the other guests were swallowing hard, too, and
everybody was sort of glad when Keith Preston, the Chicago
Daily News columnist and wit, piped up to break the spell.
Keith nodded his head at Lewis and said, "Kind hearts are more
than coronets." They all laughed at this—Lewis, too—and
Sandburg went on to livelier songs. It was the first time a lot
of supposedly well-informed men knew Carl as anything but
a poet and newspaperman. . . .

Sandburg may not be a great singer, but his singing is
great. . . . The man's voice is heavy and untrained—he has
never had but three vocal lessons and they were from a choir
singer in Galesburg, Illinois, long ago—and all his accomplish-
ments on the guitar sound alike, but for every song that he sings
there comes a mood, a character, an emotion. He just stands
there, swaying a little like a tree, and sings, and you see farm-
hands wailing their lonely ballads, hill-billies lamenting over
drowned girls, levee hands in the throes of the blues, cowboys
singing down their herds, barroom loafers howling for sweeter
women, Irish section hands wanting to go home, hoboes making
fun of Jay Gould's daughter. The characters are real as life,
only more lyric than life ever quite gets to be. . . .

Many listeners have asked him to teach them his vocal
method. Always he eludes them in his slow, knowing way,
understanding well enough that his method is not so much a
method as a philosophy of life, a solitary art evolved in loneli-
ness and in an eternal faith in democracy. . . .

With the fame of being a poet back in 1916, he began to
get calls to a new business, that of lecturing. "Come and read
your poems," he was told. At the end of one of these very first
readings, he laid aside *Chicago Poems*, dug out a guitar from
behind the rostrum, and said, "I will now sing a few folk-
songs that somehow tie into the folk-quality I have tried to
get into my verse. They are all authentic songs people have sung
for years. If you don't care for them and want to leave the hall,
it will be all right with me. I'll only be doing what I'd be doing
if I were home, anyway."

The audience stayed, liking the songs better than the poems, and since that day the singing has been half of every program. When the Republican Club of New York asked him, as the author of *Abraham Lincoln: The Prairie Years,* to address it, they added, "Bring along your guitar."

All through his roamings as a youth Sandburg listened to the songs people sang. He jotted them down, using a weird system of musical shorthand. And as he went about the country, in this later period of his career giving song-lectures, new folksongs rolled in on him.

There is nothing dearer to the average person than to give great people assistance. Sandburg reaped this harvest. Lecture-committees in towns where he came to read and sing soon learned that Sandburg is one of the de luxe guests of Our Times. Picturesque in his long, prematurely gray hair, his speech and his gentle roughness, he colors up a living room immoderately. When he feels at home, he will sing, tell anecdotes in tantalizing slowness, and make his hosts ecstatic. With such ability he has found himself, for years, swamped with proffers of folk-songs. Traveling as he has all over America, he had the chance to winnow out the best from a colossal number of songs. Of these he made *The American Songbag* of 300-odd selections. . . .

He is the last of the troubadors, is Sandburg, the last of the nomad artists who hunted out the songs people made up, and then sang them back to the people like a revelation. An American Ossian, a throwback to the days when songs passed from mouth to mouth. Both his singing and his search for songs are part of his belief in the essential merit of the common man. Like Whitman, his philosophy is that of a pioneer Quaker who has turned paradoxically to song. Rousseau, Goethe, and old Walt would have sat up at night to hear him sing. George Fox, for all his Quaker distrust of music, would have understood him perfectly.

However, that is speculation. All I know for sure is that you should have heard him sing the night he made Sinclair Lewis cry.

The American Songbag

THE COLORADO TRAIL

A hoss wrangler brought a car of ponies to Duluth, Minnesota. The next day, after brave stunt riding, he was laid in a hospital bed with "ruptures on both sides." He told the surgeon Dr. T. L. Chapman, in a soft, forgiving voice, "That was a terribly bad hoss—not only throwed me, but he trompled me." Out of past years this rider had, Dr. Chapman's examination disclosed, "bones of both upper and lower legs broken, fractures of collar bone on both sides, numerous fractures of both arms and wrists, and many scars from lacerations and tramplings, the bones knit any way that God and Nature let them heal." As his strength came back he sang across the hospital ward in a mellowed tenor voice. And they always called for more. One song was "The Colorado Trail" remembered by Dr. Chapman as here set down.

Arr. A. G. W.

126

1 Eyes like the morning star,
   Cheek like a rose,
   Laura was a pretty girl,
   God Almighty knows.

Weep, all ye little rains,
   Wail, winds, wail,
   All along, along, along
   The Colorado trail.

HELLO, GIRLS

Girls who are thinking about getting married find advice here. The third verse carries a laugh, with a slight mourning border of sober second thought. Movers from Kentucky, probably, took the tune to Kansas, gave it new verses, and called the song "Kansas Boys."

Arr. A. G. W.

Hel-lo girls, lis-ten to my voice, Don't you nev-er mar-ry no good-for-nothing boys.

If you do your doom shall be   Hoe-cake, ho-min-y and sass-a-fras tea.

1 Hello girls, listen to my voice,
Don't you never marry no good-for-nothing boys.
If you do your doom shall be
Hoe-cake, hominy, and sassafras tea.

2 Young boys walking down the street,
Young girls think they look mighty sweet.
Hands in their pockets not a dime can they find,
Oh, how tickled, poor girls mine.

3 When a young man falls in love,
First it's honey and then turtle dove.
After he's married no such thing,
"Get up and get my breakfast, you good-for-nothing thing!"

IN THE DAYS OF OLD RAMESES

In the years when Jack the Ripper was baffling the police of London with his murders of women, leaving mutilated victims in the Whitechapel district, there flourished in Chicago an organization of newspapermen known as the Whitechapel Club. Its rooms fronted on the alley at the rear of the Chicago *Daily News* office, between Wells Street and La Salle Street. George Ade says of the club, "It was a little group of thirsty intellectuals who were opposed to everything. The fact that Jack the Ripper was their patron saint will give a dim idea of the hard-boiledness of the organization. They had kind words and excuses for many of the anarchists who had been hanged for the bomb-throwing at the Haymarket riot. They were social revolutionists and single-taxers and haters of the rich. They scoffed at the conventional and orthodox and deplored the cheap futility of their own slave-tasks as contributors to the daily press. They were young men enjoying their first revolt." Ade, James Keeley, Finley Peter Dunne, Brand Whitlock, John T. McCutcheon, Ben King, Drury Underwood and others were members. It was about the time of the Chestnut Bell, an attachment for men's vests; when a story that had been told many times before was narrated, it was the custom to give a ring or two on the bells, signifying that the hearers had heard the story once or twice. At the Whitechapel Club, however, instead of ringing Chestnut Bells, they sang a song. The verses, as given below, are jointly from James Keeley and George Ade while the melody is a Keeley reminiscence. Ade tells us that Rudyard Kipling remembered his evening at their club because, later on, he tried to recall and write the words of the club song.

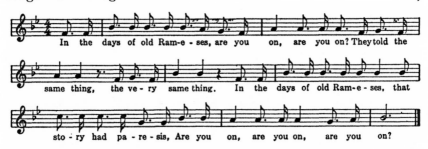

1 In the days of old Rameses, are you on, are you on?
   They told the same thing, the very same thing.
   In the days of old Rameses, that story had paresis,
   Are you on, are you on, are you on?

2 Adam told it to the beast before the fall, are you on?
   He told the same thing, the very same thing.
   When he told it to the creatures, it possessed redeeming features,
   But to tell it now requires a lot of gall.

3 Joshua told it to the boys before the wall, are you on?
   He told the same thing, the very same thing
   At the wall of Jericho before the wall began to fall,
   Are you on, are you on, are you on?

4 In the days of Sodom and Gomorrah, are you on?
   They told the same thing, the very same thing.
   In Sodom and Gomorrah, people told it to their sorrow,
   Are you on, are you on, are you on?

5 In the days of ancient Florence, are you on?
   They told the same thing, the very same thing
   In the days of ancient Florence, it was held in great abhorrence,
   Are you on, are you on, are you on?

WHEN THE CURTAINS OF NIGHT
ARE PINNED BACK

The cowboys of Colorado took a garrulous popular song of the
1870's, and kept a fragment, the heart's essence of it. It is impressive
when sung by a lone horseman silhouetted against a distant horizon.
Given anywhere with ease, feeling, control, it may leave echoes as
thin and air-hung as certain apparitions of a clear night's sky of

stars. That is, it holds an honest and independent poetry. . . . Text and tune are from Jane Ogle of Rock Island, Illinois.

1 When the curtains of night
  Are pinned back by the stars,
  And the beautiful moon
      sweeps the sky,
  I'll remember you,
  Love,
  In my prayers.

2 When the curtains of night
  Are pinned back by the stars,
  And the dew drops of heav'n
      kiss the rose,
  I'll remember you,
  Love,
  In my prayers.

BY'M BY

The stealth and mystery of the coming out of the stars one by one on the night sky . . . a fragment of a spiritual heard in Texas in the early 1880's by Charley Thorpe of Santa Fe.

Arr. M. L.

By'm by, by'm by,
Stahs shinin',
Numbah, numbah one,
Numbah two, numbah three,
Good Lawd, by'm by, by'm by,
Good Lawd, by'm by.

Novelist

*Irita Van Doren in introducing Carl Sandburg as guest
speaker at a New York* Herald Tribune Book and Author *lunch-
eon said of his newly published novel:*

Remembrance Rock he calls a novel. Actually it transcends
definition. It is an evocation of the meaning of America. Here
are our ancestors at Plymouth, growing up in the Puritan tra-
dition, or later, rebelling with Roger Williams. Here they are
in 1776 among the Tories and Patriots and neutrals of the
Revolution. In 1863 they fought on Cemetery Ridge in Gettys-
burg's three-day slaughter. In 1918 we ourselves, their de-
cendants, endured the German guns in the French Argonne; and
in 1944 and 1945 our sons braved the beaches of Normandy and
Okinawa.

This American story with all its rich variation is told in folk
song and proverb, in strong, slow-moving narrative, in emotion-
ally enthralling climaxes, and always with Carl Sandburg's un-
paralleled ear for the latent music of his country. An accomplish-
ment worthy to stand beside his great biography of Lincoln,
Remembrance Rock is Carl Sandburg's fullest, ripest tribute to
the American people whom he loves—"this swift and furious
people . . . the most original, inventive, unpredictable people
in the world."

*Unified passages have been excerpted to give the reader the
underlying theme of this 670,000-word novel.*

Remembrance Rock

PROLOGUE

A silence of a few seconds and he watched the face of the announcer at a microphone opposite him, in a smooth, quiet and perfect gravity, "It is a rare privilege and an honor that does not come often—to present for his first radio address to the American people one of the greatest of living Americans, former Justice of the United States Supreme Court, Orville Brand Windom."

He was surprised at how easy and natural he sent his voice into the disk before him. This was partly because he forgot about how many millions might be listening when his eyes could find the lovable face of his grandson's wife and the face bundled in her arms that was the Future, the boy not yet two years old who tried to say "Grandpa" and came out with "Bowbong." There was the thought too that his grandson in a hospital somewhere in the South Pacific might be hearing him tonight or soon would be hearing him in the rebroadcast.

"When we say a patriot is one who loves his country," ran the voice of Justice Windom, "what kind of love do we mean? A love we can throw on a scale and see how much it weighs? A love we can take apart to see how it ticks? A love where with a yardstick we record how long, high, wide it is? Or is a patriot's love of country a thing invisible, a quality, a human shade and breath, beyond all reckoning and measurement? These are questions old as the time of man. And the answers to them we know in part. For we know when a nation goes down and never comes back, when a society or a civilization perishes, one condition may always be found. They forgot where they came from. They lost sight of what brought them along. The hard beginnings were forgotten and the struggles farther along. They became satisfied with themselves. Unity and

136

common understanding there had been, enough to overcome rot and dissolution, enough to break through their obstacles. But the mockers came. And the deniers were heard. And vision and hope faded. And the custom of greeting became 'What's the use?' And men whose forefathers would go anywhere, holding nothing impossible in the genius of man, joined the mockers and deniers. They forgot where they came from. They lost sight of what had brought them along.

"When we say a patriot is one who loves his country, what kind of love is it we mean? That is a tremendous question. I could write a book trying to answer it. You have heard that the shroud has no pockets and the dead to whatever place they go carry nothing with them—you have heard that and you know its meaning is plain. Whatever cash or collateral a man may have, whatever bonds, securities, deeds and titles to land, real estate, buildings, leases and patents, whatever of jewels, medals, decorations, keepsakes or costly apparel, he leaves them all behind and goes out of the world naked and bare as he came. You have also heard the dead hold in their clenched hands only that which they have given away. In this we begin to approach the meaning of a patriot though we do not unlock the secret that hides in the bosom of a patriot. The dead hold in their clenched hands only that which they have given away. When men forget what is at the heart of that sentiment—and it is terribly sentimental—they are in danger of power being taken over by swine, or beasts of prey or men hollow with echoes and vanities. It has happened and the records and annals cry and moan with specific instances.

"As I speak to you from the seclusion of my home, I can see many of your faces. They are faces I have seen in our America, faces I have met from coast to coast, from the Great Lakes to the Gulf. They are the faces of today, of now, of this hour and this minute. Yet it is worth considering that many of those same faces have had their shining moments in our America of the past. We can go back fifty or a hundred years, two and three hundred years, and we meet these same faces of men, women and children. They shared in the making of America, in bringing this country on from the colonial wilderness days through one crisis after another. Their faces moved through shattering events and the heartbreak of war and revolution. Their faces gazed from the canvas slits of the covered wagon, from the glass windows of railway coaches, from the shatterproof glass of motorcars on concrete highways, from the

Plexiglas nose of the latest make of airplane curving in the sky. They saw years of startling change and dazzling invention, till America took her place among nations as one of the great world powers. In each time of storm, in each period of development, have been these faces—and I can see them out among you who are listening tonight.

"Now at this moment I wonder about two people. One of them happens to be my granddaughter-in-law. I love her very much. And there is her husband, my grandson, somewhere in the South Pacific, I don't know where. I know you people are troubled. I confess I am troubled, too. I'm selfish enough to admit I'm troubled about my own flesh and blood—my grandson and his wife and the little great-grandson sitting in front of me now.

"It is perfectly natural we should be troubled. Yet we must keep it in mind and press it home in our minds that something like what is happening to our dear ones now has happened before. This is one crisis, the latest one. There have been others in the making of this nation. The call to hardship, toil and combat runs like a blood-scarlet thread over and through the story of our people. It has cost to build this nation. Living men in struggle and risk, in self-denial and pain, in familiarity with sacrifice, wounds and death—those living men of the past paid that cost.

"I have reached the period of life when I am somewhat behind a cloud. Past, present and future become one. I know it is more reality than illusion when I look back and see my grandson and his wife three hundred years ago in the town of Plymouth—and in the next moment I see him in a place named Valley Forge and she is at home with their child wondering when the war will end—and again I see him in that tornado of action called Gettysburg and amid the suffering afterward he finds time to write her a letter.

"I see their faces the same in those days as now. From one spot of time to another the faces repeat. The mother of my great-grandson, seated here holding that child as I speak to you—she could have stood on the New England shore three hundred years ago. And her man who is away could have been there, too, in that time, hewing planks for a shelter, hoeing corn for their food, three hundred years ago. And so through the ups and downs and windings of the whole story of the American people there have been these people, these faces. My children and yours have been given this heritage, this land of ours, by their toil and struggle. And has it been worth the cost they paid? I think it has. To do it took men willing to throw in with all they had. And they did that. And we've got to let those who now are to shape the future know what the present time came from and what it's worth as a heritage.

"In a very real sense there is no such thing as a death of thought and energy. The will and vision that motivated people in Plymouth did not fade but moved on alive and written on faces at Valley Forge. It is still with us. Generations vanish, people disappear, the earth stays and the transmissions of energy. Life goes on.

"Long before this time of ours America saw the faces of her men and women torn and shaken in turmoil, chaos and storm. In each major crisis you could have seen despair written on the faces of the foremost strugglers. Yet there always arose enough of reserves of strength, balances of sanity, portions of wisdom, to carry the nation through to a fresh start with an ever-renewing vitality.

"You may bury the bones of men and later dig them up to find they have moldered into a thin white ash that crumbles in your fingers. But their ideas won. Their visions came through. Men and women who gave all they had and wished they had more to give— how can we say they are sunk and buried? They live in the sense that their dream is on the faces of living men and women today. In a rather real sense the pioneers, old settlers, First Comers as some called themselves—they go on, their faces here now, their lessons worth our seeing. They ought not to be forgotten—the dead who held in their clenched hands that which became the heritage of us, the living."

Justice Windom had finished. His face lighted, he stepped quickly over to where Mimah stood with the little one in her arms. Bowbong reached his long arms around the two of them, and in an eager whisper, "I hope Raymond was listening."

Telegrams came that night and the next morning. For a week the mail was heavy with letters from new-found friends and from old-timers he had lost track of.

He was haunted by what he termed "The American Dream," the tenacity and wonder of it. He had written Book I about the Pilgrim period, Book II the American Revolution, Book III the Civil War time. He lived to finish notes of counsel and commentary on World War II and in his will to say, "My dear ones—Mimah and Raymond— you will please me for the love I bear you—by reading this manuscript book by book—and may it be that as you live with these repeating faces that weave a blood-scarlet thread over and through the story of our country—may it be that you find tokens and values worth your time in living with them—a thousand deep prayers I speak for you."

BOOK ONE: THE FIRST COMERS

EYES ACROSS THE CHURCH AISLE

The new meetinghouse of Plymouth congregation was finished in 1683. Its steeple pointed upward with the lift of hands in prayer yearning for the Heavenly City of the faithful. The pews inside had plain hardwood benches, high straight backs to encourage the listless to keep awake through the two- and three-hour sermons. The preacher in the high pulpit could be seen with no effort.

On a Lord's Day in mid-November the prayer had been offered. All present had stood up to sing. Their voices carried a favorite from the book of psalms. The First Comers had sung it on land, on sea, on two continents.

At the singing of the line "his gates, his courtyards with praising," the large front door swung open and closed. Several heads turned, as they sang the familiar hymn, to see who was the late-comer. Remember Spong turned her head. She saw a tall young man in a leather doublet, his tall hat held by his two hands to his breast. He entered the pew across the middle aisle from her and two rows to the rear. She turned her head toward the pulpit to face the preacher again. But at the last line "& his faith unto all ages," she turned for another swift glance at the newcomer before resuming her seat. Her eyes met his, looking at her straight, cool and sure. She sank in her seat saying to herself she would not turn her head toward him again till the services were over.

She heard the preacher observe that it was a period of extreme misery and humiliation for the psalmist who had shortly before referred to his enemies and how "They have parted my garments among them, and cast lots upon my vesture."

This set a picture going in the mind of Remember—of a man fallen among robber gamblers who take his every stitch of clothing, leaving him to stand naked while they draw numbers to see who wins his cloak, his shirt, his hat and shoes. Suddenly while this picture held her mind she found her head turning and her eyes seeking the face of the late-comer. Again there were his eyes looking straight, cool and sure into hers. This time her will said she must turn from him; nevertheless she was held to a long strange gaze into the steady eyes of this man.

Her skin tingled and a rush of feeling ran through her. The preacher and his pulpit seemed a mile away, his face a floating spot of gray. Had others seen? Was Patience Goodman's right arm gently nudging her left elbow as a reproof? She sat fixed, wanting to turn her head again. Her ears caught the preacher's voice saying words drenched with meaning for her and she could hear no more after the words "Thou art he that took me out of my mother's womb; thou wast my hope when I hanged yet upon my mother's breasts." She sat rigid.

Suddenly she was going to turn her head again. Fatefully, help-lessly, as though she might be falling into a deep blue pool of icy waters turning hot and changing to ice again, her head pivoted slowly to meet a face and eyes. There he was. Like her, she could read it, he wished to conduct himself otherwise on the Lord's Day, but he was helpless as she.

So there began between them this conversation, without words, by means of short abrupt glances, of long deep looks of question and wonder. His eyes were large and dark blue, the deepest of sea-blue, danger-blue, Remember was saying. His wavy black hair came half-way down over his ears and at the back fell below his wide white linen collar. His nose was straight, his mouth not too large and the lips, she said, "dreamy sad, mayhap too sad." His chin jutted out a little too far, she thought, "but it may improve with better light."

His eyes roving her had noted her cheeks, "Not rose bloom, not spring wildflower, but what?" and answering himself, "The winter apple, the fruit better for the first frost and the earliest snow biting and chilling it and giving it a flush to keep and endure." The faint burnish of her chestnut hair falling below her immaculate wide white linen collar, the dim sea-blue of her sea-wind eyes, the compulsion of bony and gaunt strength in her face—these troubled and pleased him as he sat straight, looking toward the preacher, yet turning his head toward the left across the aisle at the exact moment her head and eyes turned seeking him.

Half the congregation took to watching Remember Spong and the late-come visitor. What was this to which they were witness? Could it be that one of their unmarried women and a new-come man not a member of their church were conducting an outrageous sensuous

affair of mortal and sinful flesh before their very eyes during Lord's
Day services? Remember saw their frowns, caught glowering faces
rebuking her, felt Patience Goodman's hand take hers and press it
till it stung with pain.

From new members came glances of righteous astonishment. To
these Remember could rise superior. When, however, elder First
Comers, *Mayflower* companions she respected, gave her their calm
forbidding stare, her face shrank from them and her eyes gazed
straight at the preacher.

In the second hour of the sermon she turned but twice to the
new face across the aisle. And each time he seemed to know the
instant her look was coming and turned to meet it.

The sermon ended. She heard her father in the aisle in low voice,
"You have given them a scandal. It was never thought a daughter
of mine would bring such shame."

"I am abashed. I would give my oath I do not know how it hap-
pened nor why. As my father you know your eyes have never seen
the like before this day. I beseech you to go to the visitor and make
the proper inquiries why he joined so freely with me in this pro-
ceeding on the Lord's Day."

The visitor had sought various faces, found them cold and forbid-
ding, and had moved toward the door. When John Spong reached
him he was outside standing quiet and looking at a fresh light snow-
fall. "I would have a word with you," said Spong. "What was the
meaning of your bold and scandalous misbehavior toward my
daughter on this Lord's Day?"

"I shall hope to clear myself of any evil intent, sir."

"He hath a face of brass," said a deacon to Spong. And another
of the elders forming a small circle, "In what house of sin was the
upbringing of this sojourner that he does not know conduct for
the House of God?"

Hard words then John Spong poured on the sojourner who stood
with face and eyes telling he was deeply moved. Yet there was no
sign of cringing or fear. He spoke as a man of education, and might
be of the upper classes by the quality of his doublet and linen,
perhaps a minister.

"I wish to present my apology for conduct on my part that I would
have desired to be otherwise than what you witnessed. It was a
breach of good behavior and I was seized by some force beyond
my understanding."

"The Evil One is ever present," came an elder's voice. "You should seek in yourself whether he cast his power over you."

"I have my shields of prayer and humility against the Evil One. Should there be any glint of high pride or vain desire or sensuous purpose in what I did this Lord's Day, the fault is in me to atone for it before my God and Creator, with no credit to a lurking Evil One having power over me."

They wondered a little at such a reply. William Bradford had joined the circle and his eyes lighted, for the answer had somewhat of John Robinson in it. "Your name and where from?"

"From a ship at Boston last month. I have heard much of you and I come among you as a sojourner. I may learn of you. I may go from here to Salem or Providence. My name is Resolved Wayfare and my last home in London, England. I was a Puritan, a Nonconformist. I am a pilgrim and a seeker."

"You are a pilgrim?"

"Should a pilgrim be one prepared to journey far seeking new light and ready to toil for his Master, for the Mediator sitting at the right hand of God, the Redeemer, then by such a reading I am a pilgrim."

They relented toward him. That was on their faces. His look and tone carried gravity, sorrow, reverence. He might yet be one of them.

"I seek lodging among you. I may stay the winter. My belongings are in a seabag at your wharf where a fishing vessel landed me this morning before I hastened to your Lord's Day meeting."

"Till we consider further," said Bradford, "you can manage a space for him in your house, can you not, John Spong? There are only you two." Bradford's glance shifted to Remember, who had joined the circle.

"He will demean himself as is proper," urged Remember.

"And what of you?" asked her father. "You were as flagrant as he. What of your demeanor?"

"I have a name in Plymouth. I am no wench of folly and sin."

So Resolved Wayfare lodged at the Spong house and at early twilight of that Lord's Day joined Remember and her father in a supper of boiled carrots and salt mackerel, warm corn bread with butter and cheese, and homemade beer.

"Why should men drink beyond refreshing?" asked Spong who explained that in Plymouth men were admonished for going beyond "refreshing" in wine, rum or brandy. And four classes or categories of Plymouth law carried the punishments heavy or light according to the category. They were: 1. Plain drunk; 2. beastly drunk; 3. filthy drunk; 4. unmentionable drunk.

Wayfare spoke for himself; a quart of beer a day was enough for him, a glass of wine would last him an afternoon or evening. He brought from a pouch his pipe and joined Spong in crushing dried tobacco leaves and filling the pipe. "This is of our own Plymouth raising and not so sweet as we import from Virginia," said Spong of the first pipe, and, "This hath a coolness good to taste," of the second pipe, from Wayfare's pouch. He warned Wayfare not to smoke on the streets or highways nor in the meetinghouse or he would be arrested and fined. In a house or place of refreshment or in the fields or woods, it was lawful to smoke. Dancing, at any time and anywhere, was forbidden. On the Lord's Day card-playing, indoors or out, was against the law. And on the Lord's Day one must rest and worship; the man who worked on that day, even in his own garden, was brought before the magistrates.

The three sat silent and the quiet of the room was broken only by the crackle and sputter of fire logs. After a time Remember spoke in a very low voice. "We are persuaded. The coming of thee is as a well-willer. Of that we know. Pride is not of your constitution. Of that, too, we know. The first work in the service of the Master, He has told us, is to deny thyself. We must be content to be underlings of Him in this worldly kingdom."

At the door was a sound Remember's ear caught at once. She stepped to the door and opened it for a cat to come running in and chuzzle at her feet. She stooped and rubbed its fur in a long stroke from head to tail's end. Then she picked it up and holding it in her arms came to her chair saying, "Tamia, you have been out among the field mice again. You are late coming home. You deserve a scolding. You harry the mice of the fields too hard, Tamia."

Resolved Wayfare straightened in his chair, sat tensed, his face struck with lights. "Tamia? Tamia?" He gave it as a loud cry.

They were startled. Wayfare saw his excitement troubling them. He lowered his voice, spoke so soft they could scarce hear him. "Tamia, did you say the name is Tamia?"

"Mesopotamia is the full name. Tamia for short."

"What can be happening this strange Lord's Day?" he asked. "Never since the morning my mother brought me to the light of day have I heard but once before of a cat named Mesopotamia and

Tamia for short and the cat bright yellow with black spots on its haunches."

Remember, whose face had broken into ripples of light, her eyes blazing, "At a wharf? At a shed at the end of the wharf?"

"In Plymouth, England, it was, and the year 1620 and a ship sailing—and you on that ship—for this new Plymouth."

He stepped from his chair and she rose from hers. He put his hands to her shoulders, stood searching her face slow and long, moving to print a kiss on her forehead. Standing back and keeping his hands to her shoulders, his eyes dwelt on her bony face with its changing blue sea-wind eyes and winter-apple skin. Then his words came, "Queer people! You come from the queer people," and with a slow sadlike smile, "What if I should spit in your face?"

And Remember thought back to the day she was thus taunted by ruffians on the wharf and was rescued by the boy swinging his ax handle. She murmured with dreaminess, "Where is your ax handle?" Remember felt her mother inside of her dancing and singing and she was certain she was the child of Mary Windling who said, "My feet may go to hell though my soul will not follow my feet. The good Lord should not have made my feet so glad."

John Spong went to bed. The two by the fire talked. Remember told of the early years at Plymouth, of her mother's death so soon after their arrival. But mostly it was Wayfare talking, Remember asking questions, telling him to go on and on.

He told of his stupidity in not learning the name of the ship she sailed on, how his mother asked him the name and he answered, "I don't remember." His mother and a younger brother were still on their farm near Plymouth, England, devoted to the Church of England and troubled about him. For he had gone to London, worked in several occupations, and read books, many books, never enough. "How many books?" Remember asked. He said more than five hundred. Remember looked at him with open eyes. "You have read more books than there are in all of this Plymouth town." He had met writers of books, one of them young John Milton. He had served as a lawyer's clerk, as a copyist for a Nonconformist minister, had become involved in the organizations of extremist Separatists, with more secret work than he cared for because he liked to be outspoken. Twice he had been jailed, held for questioning and released by authorities who assured him they knew he was guilty and though this time they did not have the evidence against him, they would have it next time. His decision to go to America came when he heard of the adventure of Roger Williams at Providence. It was what he himself would like to be doing. He must go to Providence and see for himself. It might be his lifework awaited him there in Providence.

WILDERNESS WINTER—AND WILD HEARTS

In the late evening twilight Remember Spong looked for the men to come home. Dark came on and she sat by candlelight with a bowl of mutton stew before her, a favorite dish she had cooked lovingly for the two men. Little of it did she eat. They would come later and she would eat with them. The hours passed. She stood at the window listening, through the heavy paper soaked with linseed oil, listening to the howl of the storm. She walked back and forth, from the fireplace to the door and back to the fireplace. She unlatched the door, stood on the step outside and saw a starless sky and a merciless wind driving the snow into curves and huddles. The cold had a wicked bite to it and she prayed for those who might not have shelter or fire this night. She stepped back into the house, fell on her knees in the middle of the room, held her clasped hands high and spoke a passionate prayer to the everliving God to guide home the lost ones. She slept in fitful snatches. At daybreak she opened the door and saw the snow knee-high and still coming, the fury of the wind giving no sign of going down. She swiftly fastened the door. Not since she was seasick on the *Mayflower* had she scorned breakfast and felt too low to wash her face and comb her hair. She drew a chair before the fire, piled on logs, sat stony-faced an hour, two hours, longer yet.

Near noon she came out of this black mood. She washed her face and hands. She combed her hair and studied herself in the polished steel looking-glass, bringing out every wave and gleam of her hair, murmuring, "So should it look framing my pale face on the day they gaze on me before carrying me to Burial Hill."

She put the mutton stew on to warm and ate a full bowl of it. A short sobbing wail came from her. She cursed herself for being so many hours witless. She ran to four neighbor houses, then to the Governor, and by midafternoon eight of the lustier young men were making a search that reached out and combed two miles and more in every landward direction. The wind had gone down to a light breeze, the snow was falling lighter, the cold less piercing.

Early twilight four of the searching crew brought to the Spong house the two men, John Spong able to stagger and lift heavy feet, Resolved Wayfare so far gone he had to be carried head first through the Spong doorway.

Remember could hardly believe her eyes as she saw the two men. Her father looked swollen and Wayfare too lean. Then her eyes took note of her father wearing Wayfare's leather doublet, a wool-wadded garment.

The days passed and it was seen that Spong's body and arms were only mildly touched by the cold though his feet would suffer and he would limp for a long time. Likewise the feet of Wayfare would suffer and he too would limp for a long time but worse yet was the condition of his arms. They had numbed to where he couldn't move them. Remember was awe-struck seeing him on a couch in a corner of the main living room, a man of strength and will, helpless to hold a spoon and take food. She must be of good cheer and hope every moment, she told herself as she saw his calm face suddenly twist when he writhed from streaks of flame zigzagging through his arms. Feeding him with a spoon she murmured, "I rejoice you are alive." When she repeated this, his eyes opened and he murmured, "Queer people! Queer people!"

Elders came, some of the First Comers, with advice from experience with frostbite, with cheer and choice victuals. Orton Wingate came and his quiet keen eyes made their observations. Plymouth had no physician and Remember inclined to follow the hermit's counsel: no rubbing with snow, no hot water, do not bring him near the fire, wait and let the health of the rest of the body coax, heal, restore. As the arms thawed and blisters came on the skin, Wingate with a needle opened the larger ones, and from day to day for longer periods lifted the arms vertical. Later yet, he rubbed the arms and soothed the muscles and coaxed the lagging blood circulation.

Day on day, after a long stretch of pain, sleep would come to Wayfare and Remember saw him in the rest that heals. Then he would come out of it with a sharp moan from another zigzag of fire in an arm. His few sentences giving his own thoughts were short; what he spoke most were Scripture lines that came as though he kept them for times of difficulty and they had become part of him. And Remember was haunted by the meaningful glance he gave her after having finished the last spoon of a savory rabbit stew, "O woman, great is thy faith; be it done unto thee even as thou wilt."

Hard it was for her to watch when Wingate took hold of the arms and commanded him to move them; at whatever cost he must learn to make use of them; they would languish and wither unless used. One day Remember laid between his two hands the cat Mesopotamia, saying in a soft clear undertone, "She is the great-granddaughter and the living image of the one I had on Plymouth wharf." His hands rested on Tamia's fur, his eyes closed, his lips pursed in silence.

The days of rambling and random utterance drew toward an end as the pain grew less and the blood vessels and muscles of the arms once more became obedient to their owner. Three weeks and John Spong was about, limping, crying out from a sudden jerk of pain, then smiling, "That one had a bite to it." Slower came the time of Resolved Wayfare moving about, stretching his arms toward the roof planks. And to Remember, "You never once wearied of finding my large sad mouth with spoon after spoon till the bowl or the plate was empty."

Neither of the men cared to tell hour by hour what had happened to them. "After Wednesday twilight it was one long horrible monotony," said Wayfare. Spong told of how they had picked an oak tree with a wide spread of branches, rounded by underbrush that gave slight protection from the wind, and there they had beaten a path and kept to the circle of that path, walking to keep the cold from numbing them. It was like to an hour before daybreak that Wayfare, only half alive and awake, was suddenly amazed that he had walked twice, yes, three times around without seeing his companion. He found Spong fallen near the path. He picked the older man up, slapped him awake, took off his doublet and made the older man get into it. Then they walked their path again. Each time around they must catch sight of one another. Whoever might fall, the other must pound him awake and set him on his feet.

At daybreak Spong made his guess of what direction to take. They dragged heavy feet for hours. About noon Spong came to ground he knew, three miles from Plymouth. Their numbing and stiffening feet moved at a slower pace, Wayfare walking ahead, crunching the snow down for Spong to follow. Less than two miles from Plymouth, meeting the searchers, taking a few bites of bread and cold meat with a few swallows of rum, they had enough new hope and strength to go on most of the route home though Wayfare had to be carried part of the way.

Shoes and sleeves had to be cut with a knife to get them off when they reached home. When Remember or Wingate mentioned to Wayfare that he had made a sacrifice or been heroic he demurred. "I was under compulsion. I could do no else than I did."

Eight weeks Resolved Wayfare lay bedfast that winter, five weeks spoon-fed by Remember Spong. Further weeks he was up limping, learning to stand and walk again, learning again what to do with arms and hands. Through all these weeks Remember kept a lightness and cheer in the presence of Wayfare. Alone in her room or outside the house she had at times heavy clutches at her heart. She was asking herself why she cared so for this man and why he took hold of her like nothing else ever entering her life. For him she knew she had the final abandon she lacked with Peter Ladd. Then she asked further, and this question pounded at her, "What is to come? What is written for the days to be?"

He had kissed her hand as she fed him and she knew it was more than thankfulness. On his feet again he had kissed her, gathered her in his restored arms and held her bosom to bosom and afterward in a low fierce crying asked why he had so taken her and whether there was harm done.

Happiness near to bursting she knew when he in his lighter moods talked of books, men, myths, odd stories of places and people, and then would depart from the impersonal into flowing little praises of her face and hair, her swift feet, her skilled and kindly hands. "For weeks they were a part of me, your hands mine when my hands had gone away from me." In these moods she was one with him.

Then there were the darker moods that would run for hours, occasionally for two or three days with no words from him, matters beyond her knowing revolving in his mind. She noticed that his grave talk in moving out of one of these moods always had some reference to Roger Williams. He seemed to be shaping for himself something stern and shadowy that related to Roger Williams and Providence. Neither he nor she nor her father had ever spoken about how Plymouth impressed him and whether he had any expectation of becoming a citizen and a member of their congregation.

All had run so pleasant that it was in a way accepted among them that he was their kind of a believer and as he joined with them and worked with them he might become one of the best and illustrious among them. This was partly because when he came among them he was not sure what in reality and deep down was their way of life and belief, what they had hold of in "things terrestrial and celestial." And of such things there could have been no talk in the long weeks when he hovered near the peril of being a tragic cripple for life. He had been powerless to dispel the impression that arose among the others that before long he would ask John Spong for the hand of his daughter. More than a trifle of guilt was in his mind about this after he had suddenly and irresistibly gathered Remember to his arms for a long deep kiss. But he could say that was no more to be helped or avoided than the way they had gazed at each other the first Lord's Day he came to Plymouth, no more to be foreseen than the storm change of weather that had struck him and her father in the woods.

His legs and arms were good as new again, spring and April a few weeks off. He began unfolding to Remember the sealed determinations that had come to him out of groping, weighing, resolving, in the shadowy moods that had baffled her. He felt now as he did at first the worth and merits of the Plymouth settlement. Their zeal, courage, tenacity, he admired, especially the heroic material of the First Comers, the Leydeners, those who had first proven what could be done so that other colonizers had followed. But his resolve was made that he must go to Providence and join the work of Roger Williams. "I hope this will not stand between thee and me." He was asking her to go with him.

Knowing how deep her roots, said Remember to herself, he was asking her to leave Plymouth and go with him. She said nothing. She sat thinking it over. She was near to saying Yes, though to break from Plymouth would be the hardest and loneliest step of her life. The two sat silent. Wayfare stepped to her, pulled her up from her chair, held her tight and looked in her face. She demurred to his will. He saw it in her sea-wind eyes. It was the first unkind moment they had known. Remember pushed at his shoulders, broke away from him, pulled her chair near the fireplace, sat looking into the burning logs, and began a flare of wrath at Roger Williams:

"The man was here. We know the man. Excellent in discourse, yea he is, and handsome, pleasing, yea he is. And again he is a fool, one of the proudest vain fools that ever walked the streets of Plymouth. Filled with delusions, this Roger Williams. Even a very child of the Evil One is this Roger Williams when you become aware of the snakes and worms that creep and writhe in the caverns of his mind and heart."

Wayfare walked back and forth. Remember sat stony-faced peering into the fire logs. Wayfare paused at her side, stood quietly, laid a hand on the chestnut hair, and it was as though he had touched an image of ice. He walked back and forth. He drew a chair alongside and sat beside her with no word.

The wind rattling at the door they could hear. And the sputter of the fire logs they could hear. Then Wayfare, "There is a time to

plant and a time to pull up that which is planted. What I could desire
might not be yet, but the Lord knoweth what is best and His will be
done."

"It is dangerous," and Remember stood up with blazing eyes. "It is
dangerous to gather flowers that grow on the brink of the pit of hell.
You might fall into the pit itself while you think to pick pretty
flowers." She waited. No word from him. Then a soft moan as though
to herself rather than to him, "A woman should be from her house
three times; when she is christened, married—and buried."

The wind rattling at the door they could hear. And the sizzle of
firewood with a snow damp on it they could hear. Then Remember
with a straight glance at him and in a meditative voice infinitely
gentle, "I remember long ago hearing my mother tell a bride, fresh in
her virgin bloom, overconfident and overbright in her gleaming white
linen, 'More belongs to marriage than four bare legs in a bed.' It is my
wish she were here to give me her precious counsel on whether to go
or stay, whether to put on my shoes of travel or be true to this house I
helped build, this house I have swept and garnished these fleeting years
of time, this house where I have tended the stricken and now am beset
with the torment of the plea of the stricken made whole again."

"Nothing happens for nothing and God works in moments," said
Resolved in a quiet tone. His eyes roved the ax sweeps of the hewn
planks of the ceiling, then roved down to meet hers. Hard it was to
say but now he was saying it. One day this week he must be going.
He cherished her so truly that he could not consider taking her with
him. Her doubts, the sincere shakings of her soul, would come again.
"You have your sacred rights to live by the roots you have struck so
deep in your beloved Plymouth."

Now a fear bit deep in her heart. This was the first time he had
spoken to her in a tone of deprecation, of belittlement, as though he
could be sorry for her, as though his sorrow at what must be done
moved with a purity above hers. She rose to her feet, dumping Tamia
without care.

"You that take your self-willed course, you too have your sacred
rights and what is the use you make of them? To speak taunts of the
roots I have struck in Plymouth that hold me here while you go root-
less over the earth wheresoever it pleases you to live rootless." The
words flashed from her, each word deliberate and each meant to re-
proach and sting, her head high, her impetuous hands making a talk
of their own. Now he knew he had been guilty, at least to the extent
that he had not seen the range of her passionate loveliness. She too

knew that things sleeping in her had come awake and she was the child of her mother dancing in the kitchen at Leyden. She went on. "I can take chaos in my bosom and I can eat it and drink it and smack my lips after it and dance it before a loved one. I know well those who marry with love and without money have sorry days but their nights shine with scarlet moons and the music of white sea horses calling. Yet every moon is pressed by a time guide and the sea would be silly and inconceivable without a bottom. So love must have roots and time tries every troth."

"You are two persons, Remember Spong—a natural storm bird and a born homebody and they will fight in your bosom long as you live."

"It is a bold mouse that nestles in a cat's ear, Resolved Wayfare. Deck yourself with borrowed feathers and see how cheap is your comeliness. Stand in the shadow of Roger Williams and ask yourself is it he or you makes the shadow. My own mother, on the *Mayflower*, weak and hearing another weak one spoken to harshly and no need for it, asked us, Why should those who puke into the sea together ever be enemies? She had her saying from the Song of Songs which is Solomon's, Love is a fire of God. Of a certainty love does teach eternity and is like a river that never dries up and has ever new water to succeed that which passeth. They who wear rings have an image of eternity on their fingers. They who handle a wheel have an emblem of eternity before them. For to what part soever of the ring or wheel one looks, one will still see another part beyond it."

Her first vehemence had gone down like a storm wind faded to whatever it is that moves in the spaces between quiet summer stars. Her speech amazed Wayfare. He saw new promptings at work in her. What he had seen and heard before were fragments and ripples alongside this relentless outpouring of wisdom and conjecture. Yet for all that might seem impersonal and abstract, the fear drove hard in him that she was clinging to the purpose of claiming her personal identity as an individual, the deep roots that fastened her life to Plymouth.

"You and I," he said, low-voiced with an utter anxiety and care, "before we give up hope, should search and scrutinize if there is a way for us to be buckled together as man and wife." He told her that if she went with him on the journey to Providence, their differences of belief would not trouble him, that he could never have aught but respect for her beliefs. "I would marry you, not your beliefs."

She was almost persuaded, saying she wondered if she could go with him and in time the two of them so weave their beliefs together that he could come back with her to Plymouth where was the grave of her mother whose last words were, "Stay with them, my love," where her father had toiled horny-handed, where she herself had planted and hoed and reaped corn and beans, where she had helped carry the hewn planks of their house. She mentioned the Great Sickness, trials past forgetting, her thorough inweaving with Plymouth congregation. She came to another plan for them to consider. Could he not stay for a time in Plymouth and throw in his strength and beneficence toward the end pleasing to him? Should he do so and after such a trial find it had not borne good fruit as he would like, then she would consider going elsewhere with him.

He had taken up a knife for polishing, and he heard her in a quiet finality. "You would then be my yokefellow. We would learn of each other. We would be better prepared if a day came there must be a going away."

He dropped his knife-polishing. He told her she did not know how deep ran his beliefs nor her own. A marriage and a later parting in Plymouth would be cruel. He could not let his mind dwell on it. Away from Plymouth, with both of them as seekers together, they would stand a good chance of finding, nay it would be certain they would together find, garments of faith adjusted and fitted for them. He begged her to go with him on the morrow.

"Again I say," came her fierce outburst, "you speak taunts of the roots I have struck in Plymouth that hold me here while you go rootless over the earth wheresoever it pleases you to live rootless."

The door had opened while she spoke and John Spong came in, to hear for the first time words of dispute between them. They told him what troubled them and asked for his judgment. He waited and considered, then, "I am beholden to you, Resolved Wayfare, for life, it is true." His voice rose: "Were it not for you I would be a carcass with the meat eaten off by the wolves, a sad pile of mere bones." He paused. "And yet—" He paused longer. Then with a low-spoken tenderness joined to absolute resolution, "And yet, what you teach and proclaim is from the Evil One and is the gospel of Satan as certainly as that of Roger Williams. Just as you saved my mortal and bodily life in the wilderness storm so we are giving our prayer and effort to rescue your spiritual life from destruction, your immortal soul from everlasting torment."

He finished saying this with composure. The three sat silent. Then Wayfare saw tears down the face of John Spong and the man's throat gulping. Wayfare looked toward Remember and her eyes were moist,

her hands folding and unfolding. He tried to speak his own heart as
he absently polished at a knife blade. "Tomorrow or the day after I
must go and with a hurt in my heart harder to carry than any in all of
my born days. Long hours in this room I studied it, long days I con-
sidered it, and I have infinite sorrow there should be between us this
chasm related to Roger Williams. I go to that man not as a subject or
a minion but one with him as a seeker, as one in fear of a faith that
does not hold toleration of all other faiths."

SO LONG AS GRASS GROWS AND RIVERS RUN

Resolved Wayfare was making ready his packsack for his walk to
Providence, to start the next day. A rain blew up that night and near
daybreak changed to snow, laid a cover of slush on the road toward
Providence. Wayfare would stay another day. By noon the sun came
out, the snow vanished and the sky arched blue and warm.

Remember busied herself with cleaning and tidying every part of
the house. Late afternoon she stood glancing about the living room,
satisfied there was nothing more to be done. Wayfare came in from
a walk, and seeing her sweeping glances, took his own look around,
said, "The house is swept and garnished as though it could go without
tending for a long time." Her quick answer in an undertone: "Do me
this help to say nothing till this night."

A spare supper the three ate, John Spong feeling bitter and going
to his bed. "Now I'll be telling you," said Remember to Wayfare, her
voice grave yet her bony face having bright sea lights in its frame of
plaited chestnut hair. She had made a bundle. She would go with him
tomorrow for the foot journey to Providence. She would tell her
father after breakfast in the morning. The shock, shame and pity of the
day before—the public whipping of the woman Dorothy Temple,
for the crime of "unlawful maternity"—had kept her awake nearly
the night through, had lessened her Plymouth for her. They would
have a civil marriage by the Governor and be two miles away before
noon.

All of this tumbled from her as though it could have no slips nor
flaws as a plan. Resolved Wayfare in the sweep of this new turn, in
the glow of the fresh blaze, let himself be whirled along in the rush
and warmth of it. He pulled her into his arms and held her close. They
lost themselves and talked bold and flaming compliments, shading into
brief mysterious whispers and drifting into a silence broken by a thin

music only they together could hear. They would see laurel and honeysuckle together, he was sure, and she added violets, the musk rose, the wild rose.

She went to her room dancing on stars. Resolved Wayfare in his corner couch of the living room slept deep and woke long before daybreak, puzzled, searching, praying.

Remember set warm porridge and milk, bread and butter, boiled eggs, cheese, beer, for breakfast. They ate with few words. Then she told her father of her preparations, of the civil marriage to be, of the foot journey to Providence. And John Spong waited while three friends and neighbors entered. "Tell them what you have told me," the father solemnly told his daughter. And briefly she did.

Then John Spong let loose with a wild tongue. A stranger had been taken in and given respect, affection, care, food, and drink, and repaid with mockery of their faith, had violated their ordinance that a man must speak to the father before proposal of marriage to the daughter —a man vile and unclean, a thief, betrayer, seducer, loose-tongued servant of Satan. Wayfare's face wore sorrow. He winced at hearing the questions shrieked at Remember, "How do you know where this man may leave you? What do you know of life in a strange town with a husband not at all proven?"

The father went into a recital of Leyden, the *Mayflower*, the landing, the Great Sickness, the words of her dying mother, "Stay with them, my love," the very house where she had helped with carrying and hewing planks, carrying stones for their fireplace, the fields they owned where she had planted, weeded, hoed, and reaped, their keepsakes and memories, her steadfast faith and works in their church they had come so far to build and cherish, the church that had made a name and commanded regard and praise for what it had done in a wilderness.

She clenched her hands before her bosom and held them tight-closed in a beseeching. She fell on her knees at the feet of Resolved Wayfare and, her hands and head on his knees, cried out, "I am too weak a vessel of the Lord to hold what is poured on me and what runs over without mercy. Stay longer here. Consider what may be done. Time will find a way."

Resolved looked in her face, stroked her hair, pulled her to her feet. "Tomorrow the Lord's Day—we go to meeting. We pray and worship together. We have one more talk. Then I go."

Then his two hands took the right hand of John Spong as he gazed into Spong's unrelenting, unforgiving, hard face. "In the days to come

I hope you will give me pardon. We have bonds. Did we for naught walk many hundred times around a tree in the blowing snow and bitter cold? Your kindness to me under your roof, your many thoughtfulnesses, will never be forgotten."

The others went away in twilight. The three ate little of supper. They were early to bed, wondering about tomorrow.

One more day Wayfare was waiting to start on his walk to Providence. He would go to the house of worship on the Lord's Day. He would show his face in public to Plymouth's men, women, children. They would see him—afraid of whom? "Ready to look any other man in the eye, I am," he said to himself. "The only danger is I might laugh in some faces."

After the morning services, ending at noon, he would have his one last talk with Remember. To this she had agreed, saying, "Our parting may be for a long time. It would be well we have no regrets over saying what we have said before. And if tomorrow we have only silence to share it may be a silence worth remembering over the long time."

And Wayfare soberly, "You say it well."

Spring rode the air that May morning, the Lord's Day, when the drum roll sounded for morning service. Spring had come again. The songbirds said so. The fresh flimmer of new grass peeping out, the whisper of buds on tree branches ready to soon leaf out, the stir of earth and air moving in the newborn—they all said: Listen and see. Give this Lord's Day to listening. And you may find a quiet mind and a singing heart.

Her father at her left and Resolved Wayfare at her right, Remember Spong walked from home to church. John Spong had the set, fixed face of a stopped clock. He cared to hear nothing and say nothing. Remember and Wayfare accommodated him. They saw the procession of soldiers, magistrates, elders, the preacher, file into the new meeting-house wherein they had pride.

The service began. The Scripture was read. The sermon came to its end, the dismissal benediction was intoned by the preacher. Only once in those three hours had Remember and Wayfare exchanged glances. He had kept his face and eyes straight toward the preacher, except for that swift instant when he knew her face and eyes were turned toward him. A long slow look, a deep look at each other they had at the end of the first hour. It was not lost on the congregation.

For a long time Remember's right hand, then her left hand, rested in calm on her bosom. Her fingers, while the preacher spoke on, could feel under her dress, at her bosom, the bronze plaque she had from her dying mother. Engraved on her mind were the Four Stumbling Blocks to Truth as written by Roger Bacon. She could say them forward and backward. Once she had talked over their meaning with her father and he was so suspicious and superior that she had never again brought them up before him. Elder Brewster had smiled, discussed each Block, rated the Four as worthy instruction.

She knew she was not through with her study of the Four Blocks. Year by year she had seen a little more to each one. Resolved Wayfare had written them out in a large bold script on a small narrow oblong of parchment. "A tough piece of parchment and it will wear and keep well," he smiled. She had come near asking him to let her keep it, his personal shaping of those momentous admonitions:

The Four Stumbling Blocks to Truth

1. The influence of fragile or unworthy authority.
2. Custom.
3. The imperfection of undisciplined senses.
4. Concealment of ignorance by ostentation of seeming wisdom.

Wayfare and Remember moved slow down the aisle and out the front door. Wayfare said good-by to certain ones he knew to be friendly, to some he had helped, to several who believed him queer and didn't hold it against him, to others who suspected him to be a menace to the church and community and were pleased they were to see no more of him.

Wayfare saw the sexton about to close the door and went inside to pick up from the corner where he had thrown them his pack, his musket and tall hat. He and Remember walked away in the soft May air over the smiling earth.

They left the Providence trail and their walk ended at a clump of pines with a tall solitary beech tree at its edge. They had been here before. A chapel, Wayfare had called it, their personal and private chapel. They seated themselves on an age-old moss-covered tree trunk, an oak predecessor of the circling pines.

"We have come in silence," gravely smiled Wayfare.

"Our silence becomes us this Lord's Day."

"Often I find I trust our silence more than I do our speech."

"Yet our speech has not been useless."

"I have valued many a thought that came in swift speech on your tongue. And other moments when your long dark eyelashes had sweeps of meaning over your flashing eyes. I have had to marvel at speeches that lie hidden in you and are yet to come out."

"Please say naught of how I look. A slattern I shall be, I believe, after you go. What shall I care who sees me and what I present to their eyes?"

A wren quarrel began and ended in the beech tree. A scarlet tanager flashed to the end of a pine branch and was off and away to leave the branch swaying.

"Why be so final in this decision that you cannot go with me to Providence so we can make a life of it together? Why so final?"

"And you—why must you be so final in your plan to go today, to go now with no further waiting, as though Plymouth had kept you a prisoner and now being no longer a prisoner you must use your freedom to rush away, to break all bonds that have held you here?" She implied if he truly loved her he would take his chances, stay near and see what would happen and not impose on her a decree that she must follow his will to go this day with no delay.

"Must we begin over?" His arms were around her. "Must we again at this parting dispute and argue and then return to dispute and argument? All words are a babbling and between lovers of no use." His hold of her was fierce.

"You would crush me?" She was mocking, merry, bitter, at once, and there was exultation in her tone. He caught it. She wanted him to hurt her with the fierce press of his body against hers. "If I must be broken, it is you, sir, should do the breaking."

"Here we are the two sweetest companions in the New World," he laughed—and then somberly, "So we must go away from each other. So you must stay here while I go. And the two of us parted from each other should eat our hearts out for loneliness."

"And why? It is your will to be leaving. It arises from your stubborn heart and mind."

"You wrong me. You wrong yourself. Your heart knows we are not so simple as that."

"Why do you go? You go because it is your wish to go. And your wish is to be leaving me to whatever fate awaits me here."

"I go away alone because you do not wish to join me in leaving. I go away alone and without you because it is your wish not to go with me. It is by your desire you stay here and by your desire I sleep alone under the stars tonight on the trail to Providence."

The words blazed from them. They stood up and he clutched her tighter, printed a long kiss on her mouth and gathered a wild answer from her lips. He pushed her from him and held her at the shoulders, at arm's length. They gazed at each other long, then Wayfare, "It means nothing and you may forget I ever said it here among these quiet pines this day of mild and holy May air." His hands loosened at her shoulders, took a tighter hold. "Forget I ever said I held in my arms here a pearl beyond price, the Rose of Sharon, the pool of Bethesda, the road to Jericho, the lily of the field whose natural array surpasses that of Solomon in all his glory. Forget that I drank nothing and yet I was drunk with the look of her face and her clean stark loveliness."

And the fingers of his right hand gentle and slow moved in feather-soft sweeping caresses of her eyes and cheeks, slid softly along her throat, her "white poem of a throat," he was saying.

And Remember knew she wanted him for all the days of her life. She was trying to murmur something like that without making a plain confession of it. The palm of his right hand pushed gently under her chin and pressed back her head. Then her husky, throaty words, "You are saying with that—you are saying I belong to you—I am yours to do with—as you please—and when you choose."

She shook loose from him. He took her by the elbows and pressed her to a seat again on the tree trunk. He seated himself alongside her. They turned, looked deep and unafraid into each other's faces, and said nothing.

Plymouth was having its midday food, its spare Lord's Day meal. Now and again came a rooster crow, a hen cackle, the moo of a cow, and bird calls, bird conversations, with fast repartee and nothing settled. They sat in quiet studying the serene sway of pines with flat branches dipping and rising in a deliberation. The carpet of pine needles, the brown and rusty undercarpet and the later cover of needles still green, the testamentary time sense of the place—each knew the other to be aware it was a sanctuary to them and they would again and again live over every moment spent here.

How long this mood lasted neither could have told afterward. It had low music, consolation, strengthening, a communion of preparation for ordeals to come.

Wayfare rose, stretched his arms high over his head as though to limber them. He walked to his pack, took his favorite knife from under a strap, the knife a foot long with a narrow thick blade, a silver hilt and an embellished mahogany handle. He stepped over to the beech tree. On the trunk at about the height of his shoulders he scraped off the bark, cleared clean a space wide as his two hands, swiftly carved two hearts entwined. He moved away counting one for each of ten steps, "one step for each of the Ten Commandments." Then he turned, his left foot far to the front, the knife in his right hand back of his shoulder held by blade point. The knife slipped away in a clean throw, turned one somersault, and the point of the blade landed spang in the exact area where the two hearts joined, the hilt trembling in a slowdown from shock and impact. This he did with the smooth and accomplished grace of a performance familiar and practiced to him.

"That was for luck." Remember heard him in an undertone meant to be just loud enough for her to hear. Again he stepped off ten paces, again the knife streaked with a bright low whizzing sound and again landed spang exactly where those two carved hearts joined.

"That was for love, deep divine love." Remember heard his somber undertone.

And now Resolved Wayfare stepped off ten paces, then ten paces more. She could see his face with care and eagerness on it though for all the depth of care on his face, he was cool. In the other throws he had been carefree, debonair, as though he couldn't miss. Now he was on his mettle. The last two were for luck and love. What would he say this was for? Slowly he took his position. Very deliberately he measured the distance of his feet apart, the hang and balance of his body.

Now he was all set. He drew back shoulders, twisted slow in hip and foot. His right hand holding the knife drew far back of the right shoulder, then the hand shot forward, let the knife go and it began its fearful streak, its little arc and trajectory of a glittering path toward that target of two intertwined hearts. As before it went spang and true, the blade driven deep, the haft and handle quivering long. Then Remember heard him, "That was a prayer, that was the intercession of two hearts, that was a manifest and a plea."

He turned to her, "To make it a joint prayer and a mutual plea you must come here and with your right hand draw it from where it has pierced."

She stood up, hesitated. "If this is of your own devising I will do it, if it is a form of pagan ceremonial I cannot have a hand in it."

"Spoken like your own father—your father is here telling you what to say, he has put his own fears and trembling into your blood and brain. Take that handle and hilt now and pull that knife out. And say with me the words, 'This is our joint prayer and mutual plea.'"

Slow, hesitant, Remember curled her fingers around the knife handle, pulled the blade out, her lips mumbling faintly after him the words, "This is our joint prayer and mutual plea."

They walked to their moss-wrought oak trunk and Remember, "Now you mock at me as though a mind of my own I have none, thoughts of my own I have none, as though I am a piece of baggage in my father's hands. I am not afraid to confront you. I am not scared by the skill you have which may be clever and yet betray you as being in league with an Evil Power, the Supreme Dark Power that never ceases its work against the ways of Light and the Supreme Genius of Light who is God Himself."

"Are you saying it is Satan, the Devil himself, who gave me lessons in throwing the knife? Do you believe it is the Devil's conjuration and not my own eyes and my own good right arm that guides the flying blade and sends it where I aim it, straight between our two hearts carved on that tree? Are you trying to say I could not have done this thing unless by covenant with the Devil?"

"It may be your own skill. Yet I am not sure but this and other gifts you have came to you by connivance beyond your own understanding. There have been handsome doers, sinners pleasant to look upon, who did not know in the smooth way they lived that the Evil One sought them for his own, and he bestowed his favors and charms on them without their knowing he was so doing. Before they were aware he was their friend and helper, he had seduced them into ways they could enjoy only by his consent and cunning."

"Remember Spong, you had better search farther in that dark tangled heart of yours. Joy came into your life, a strange new joy. And because it was joy it smote you with fear. And you have nursed that fear. You have let that fear guide your decision. You say No— Yes—No—Yes—No by the control of that fear always moving and stirring in your dark and tangled heart."

He reached out a hand as he stood before her, patted the gleaming waves of chestnut hair. She stood numb. Now she spoke clearly enough but her words seemed to her blurred as she handed him the knife. "This is your belonging. It is yours by right of use. You should have some pride in it. You endow it with cunning."

Wayfare took the knife, moved a step away from her and standing some twelve paces from the double heart carved on the tree trunk, whirled on his toes three times and let go the knife as if without aim. The blade streaked again to the center of the target. The zing it made echoed dimly, lingered in the air as the hilt quivered.

Then Wayfare laughed, a ringing mocking laugh. He turned his head up toward the blue sky and laughed long and loud. "And you believe the Devil has some hand in that innocent knife going exactly where my good right arm sends it. You think that Satan, the Prince of Darkness, has come here among these fragrance-of-balsam pines, on this sweet May day, a Sabbath Day, the Lord's Day; here on this afternoon has come the Head of Hell, the Chief of the Imps and Demons of Hades to help me throw a little innocent knife into a noble beech tree for his own dark purpose of seducing me into his ranks.

"When I first saw you on the wharf that day at Plymouth, England, we didn't see them carry hell and the Devil on board for cargo. We didn't see it. But they didn't leave that part of the cargo in England. They took it on board. The ship was crowded with cargo but they made space for hell and the Devil. And arriving at Cape Cod and finding the place where they would land, they unloaded hell and the Devil with the food, the tools and the remaining cargo. It pleased them to do so. Each one had a clear right to his personal hell and his personal Devil. But why must they say all others must accept their hell, their Devil? Why must they force their particular hell, their particular Devil, on others?"

Wayfare now turned and flashed, "If I want a hell I want it to be my personal hell, my invention, my fate. If I want a Devil I don't want one handed to me by others. I want my Devil to be personal. I can make for myself a more terrible hell than I have heard any of them teaching in Massachusetts Bay Colony or here in Plymouth Colony. I can make a Devil for myself more terrible than any they have tried to frighten me with here in Plymouth or in Massachusetts Bay Colony. So can you. You have visioned a Devil more cunning and oily and terrible than what they gave you to accept for a Prince of Darkness."

He turned to see Remember's face, a single tear coursing down each cheek, her eyes soft. Her lips twisted in a series of changes; she was laughing and crying at once—though crying more than laughing. She knew she had in her the same streak of gay mocking fantasy he had been talking. She knew she could wait the rest of her lifetime in Plymouth or she might roam the world over and she would not meet another man with such streaks that matched her own. What went on inside of him was like what went on inside of her.

At this she could laugh with joy. But the tears came because she knew there was a place where she left off, afraid to go farther, while he went on. He let himself have freedom she was afraid of. He went on and on. She was afraid to go on and on. And she was afraid both for him and for herself. She was afraid that if she let herself go farther it was the strength and lure of a Dark Power. In the end that Dark Power might come to possess her and ruin her life and slowly change her into a loose evil woman. She was afraid that Resolved's skill and cunning, his brightness that she marveled at, came to him from an outside Dark Power, the Prince of Darkness, the Evil One, Satan, the Archdemon, the Head of Hell—yes—the Devil.

Each of these two faces of Remember that kept shifting and mingling Wayfare had seen before, her joy face and her fear face. Not till this afternoon however had he seen the two of them on her at once. He saw her rise and stand before him.

He put his hands to her shoulders. "Your face is more than one face. Your sad mouth is trying to say things that fight and struggle in your blood and heart." Then with a low moan, "You will not believe it is I who can weep with your sorrow and shout laughter with your joy. You must go on believing I do nothing by myself—what I do comes by an Evil Conjurer, the Prince of Conjurers. And though I think I know what I do—it is not so at all—I have come into the possession of the Great Evil Shadow."

She saw his eyes moisten and his body shudder as the words came, "It is not I, Resolved Wayfare, you kissed with a long deep kiss today. It is not I at all. It is the Evil Shadow that has seduced me and brought me away from myself without my knowing I have sold myself for his price and charms."

Her face, released from its torment of changes and questionings, turned white and calm. Her eyes closed as her knees gave way and her body began to sink. He caught her, took her in his arms, seated himself on the ground holding her head in his lap. Her eyes soon opened; she said nothing, nor did he. His hands brushed her hair and forehead. The way he held her, the way his hands tried to talk to her of his care for her and his adoration of her, swept through her.

After a time she found words for him—and for herself. "I am strong yet. Believe me, I am strong yet. I have been sunk in darkness and have before this made my bed in thorns. I grope now. I grope in weariness. Believe me, it is a weariness. By the waters of Babylon we sat down and wept. Believe naught of what I say. Let me babble my nothings now of Babylon and the waters where we sat down and wept. The verses I say must have no meaning. My lips babble of what I must not lose. And what can I know of that which I must not lose? The verses are idle. If I forget thee, O Jerusalem: let my right hand forget her cunning. If I do not remember thee, let my tongue cleave to the roof of my mouth: yes, if I prefer not Jerusalem in my mirth. Who takes this daughter of Babylon, wasted and worn with misery, who takes her and says down with her, down with her, who throweth her against the stones without remorse or compunction? What ointment can help these sores and wounds, what words of praise, what kisses on the mouth can help?"

She babbled on. There had been no one else in her life except her mother to whom she could babble as she now did. He saw it rested, soothed her. It related to his own way of spilling his mind and heart. "I sat down under his shadow with great delight," she babbled on, "and his fruits were sweet to my taste. He brought me to the ban- queting house, and his banner over me was love. Stay me with flagons, comfort me with apples: for I am sick of love."

At this last verse Remember sat up and laughed, a short rippling laugh, then she laid her head in his lap again, his hands at her hair and forehead again, as she repeated, "Stay me with flagons, comfort me with apples: for I am sick of love," and babbled on.

Wayfare saw what she was doing, letting go of drolleries, small chaff or follies, bits and bubbles of thought and fancy that came to her mind, resting herself, drinking up thoughts of a freedom she could indulge herself in with him and him only. "Shall I babble on, Master Resolved Wayfare, good master, shall I babble on? Aye was his an- swer, let her babble on. For the days are to pass and we are to drift and dawdle. The beeches may stand bold in the rain and the sea loom brighter yet with its marching dawn, its endless and repeating dawns that we shall not be gazing at together though with every dawn we shall speak the other's name and say, Tomorrow will come beyond any lean shadow of a thin doubt; Tomorrow will come and when it comes we will call it Today and when Today is gone we will dub it Yesterday and say, Farewell, Yesterday, my friend, my love, farewell and be kind to yourself and make for yourself fresh ropes of damask roses if you can, if so can be. And the nights will go on, the nights filled with echoes, an echo here and an echo there, large echoes with the slow sway of tall ships in smooth quiet harbors at anchor, even the echoes of deep hard anchors and the clank of them, the clank of two anchors of iron sworn to hold deep and fast, echoes, little echoes so frail you can reach out your cupped hands and feel them fall into your two cupped hands and when you try to put them away to keep they have melted into the air and when again you wish such a little frail echo you must listen and wait and again let it fall into your cupped hands, echoes of pines, tall commanding pines whereunder lovers stood and spoke of the journey they must not now take together and the journey farther beyond they may be taking, might be taking, could be taking, would wish to be taking, echoes of the zing, the zing of a knife through the air and the sping of it into the wood of a pine and the faint shudder of the haft and handle of it bracing itself after the sudden pause and stop of its wild flight, echoes—Oh God, the echoes we must keep in our hearts!"

Remember turned on her side, raised her hand and pressed it to her shoulder as his answering arms and hands took her. Her arms went round him. The strength of her arms made him glad. They answered to his own strength. On her closed eyes he put kisses. On her hair, then on her mouth, he put kisses and, "We must both be strong for the paths ahead of us."

Her still lips began to move, quivered, then her calm words, "My knees gave way under me and I could no longer stand. The fear in my mind ran down to my knees, the fear of the Evil One working his spell over you and you not knowing. You struck at that fear when you said in your mockery it was not you but the Evil One who has kissed me over and over again. You have been wise so often that now you make me ask myself if it could be that you are free of the Evil One and it is I am victim of his dark ways, that the Dark Conjurer, for his own ends, has planted in my mind that fear. I shall find as the days pass, I truly believe I shall find, that it is you who has kissed me. The tangles and confusions in my heart and mind shall yet come straight and clear."

In the moving of the sun they were now in a clear pool of light that became a tall bowl of silver and blue above them. She opened her eyes to see him in adoration of the play of light making a changing burnish on her braids and coils of chestnut hair.

"I will remember your hair." He paused. "And your eyes will not be forgotten—nor your mouth—nor the strength of your arms nor the strong will that runs in your blood." He paused again. She closed her eyes, and heard him, "I will remember endless things out of your speech and silence—I will keep them, my Remember."

Her eyes still closed, she murmured in a slow singing dreaminess, "Resolved, my Resolved Wayfare."

On a carpet of pines, in a pool of light that rose into a tall bowl of silver and blue, the moments passed and they were lost to each other.

Each knew that the other had made a promise. They were to meet again. How, when, where they were to meet—that would be taken care of since what had now happened between them had the seal of an oath neither had called for the other to speak.

"So long as grass grows and rivers run," he murmured low once as he stroked her face and hair.

"So long as grass grows and rivers run," she pronounced, meeting his own finality.

On the air now came a sound with a threat, a pounding and insistent sound. To the beat and pound of that drum, the doors of Plymouth houses opened to pour their people into the roadways.

Those drumbeats meant Remember Spong must go. She stood up, pulling Wayfare up with her. She threw her arms around him in a fierce embrace. The strength of her—he measured it again in the lean muscles—and the warmth of her blood for him were there in kisses she rained on his face, on his hair. She let go of him, stepped over and picked up his tall hat and put it on his head, then stepped away from him, swept her eyes over him from head to foot, and bowing low, she let out a half-choked cry and a bitter laugh touched with an exquisite bittersweet in her words, "Handsome is as handsome does."

They hid and covered his pack and musket in a clump of under-growth near the Providence trail. They walked to the Plymouth meet-inghouse together and stood by a wide wind-worn cedar forty yards from the front door.

"They are less cruel, your people under that roof, less cruel than Boston, Salem and the others," he was saying. "They are less bigoted and less vainglorious and tyrannical than the others. Yet they have too few seekers. In times to come there will be more seekers, the young now growing. Those who rule and hold the power now are the Past. They brought over that Past from the shores of Europe. I am the Future. I go to seek and find. You have the Future in you. I have seen it. You are tied and fastened without mercy to a piece of the Past. It will not be ever so. We shall meet again. We shall walk together as seekers toward the Future."

She faced him, her shoulders shaken, not moving her hands to the tears that came down her face. "It is as you say."

Soon he would be on the trail for Providence, gone like a bell at the end of its ringing, and you could listen and what you heard would be a memory and not a bell. That was her thought. He saw a temptation wrestling in her for a moment, that she might now reverse her decision and go with him. The code they had evolved forbade that he make any last plea that she go with him. He saw that temptation pass. For a time that neither he nor she could measure in the future, here she must stay. They would be far from each other's faces but they would hold to hope and light.

And Wayfare, brushing her mouth with a light meditative kiss, "So long as grass grows and rivers run." And with her answering kiss in kind, "So long as grass grows and rivers run."

He stood under the wind-worn cedar and saw her walk to the meetinghouse door, nod to the two sentries, and, with her hand on the latch, she turned and her eyes met his. He read her face sad with a heartbreak she had never known before—not lost, but groping and not lacking a thin silver-blue slant of light for her hands and feet.

She opened the door and went through. She walked down the middle aisle neither proud nor humble, mildly dazed, well aware of eyes on her. Her down-looking eyes seemed to know every plank and nail. Nearly every pair of eyes in pew after pew slanted toward her, tried for a glimpse of her face, tried to read why Remember Spong was late and what might have happened to her whose record for early attendance and promptness had been so good these many years.

She seated herself in the high-backed pew where she was expected. Many eyes sought her head and profile. Some of the keener ones, familiar with her face and ways, could read that a change had come to her. Only Remember herself under that roof could tell how deep was the change, that it must grow and go deeper or life would shrivel for her and she would walk in Plymouth as one of the unburied dead. She heard the voice of the preacher droning on. The text didn't come clear to her. She was weaving solemn instructions to herself around a text that kept recurring to her: "We shall walk together as seekers toward the Future."

The sermon ended and outside at the front door there were hints and little queries that Remember warded off with hints and queries of her own. She walked home with her father. They passed the stocks and pillory in front of the fort. And John Spong broke silence with a nod of his head toward the punishment devices and, "He was in good fortune he stood not there in the pillory with his head clamped down."

Remember's eyes blazed. No word came from her. Then her father added as an afterthought that might bring her to her senses, "And you in the stocks alongside him."

Remember's face flashed. She stood still, as did he. They faced each other. Then her words hissed and spewed. "Have I, your daughter, been a slattern, that you should speak to me as though I am filth? Have I, your daughter and the fruit of your wife's womb, been a slut that you should spit on me as unclean? Am I a strumpet of foul and stinking sin who violates the memory of my mother and her archangels?"

They stood with a steady gaze into each other's eyes. The father was the first to turn and take up the walk homeward. The daughter walked alongside, with no further word.

They came to the house that had been home. He unlatched the door and went in. She followed. He threw off his hat, loosened a cord at his wide white linen collar and took himself to his big chair. She changed her brown dress with its wide white linen collar and put on a dark loose dress, lighted a candle, set a table for two, got a fire going to warm a roast of pork, brought corn bread and cider, cuts of the warm meat to the table. They ate little and said nothing. They went straight to their beds afterward without saying good night.

The father knew that a change had come over this child of his loins. He could tell that it was a change not yet finished, that it was a change to go on and on and his wits and his strengths would be helpless against it as it grew and deepened. The nature and working of the change was her personal secret and beyond his fathoming. He would have to break and destroy the Past to understand it and be part of it; she was the Future and he would have to be born again to be of the blood, will and vision of that Future.

Remember in her room was alone and not alone. She lighted a candle and let her eyes linger on and her fingers fondle a small narrow oblong thick parchment filled with a large bold script: the Four Stumbling Blocks to Truth. She blew out the candle. She slid into bed. She was alone and not alone.

Nine miles out, on the trail to Providence that night, with spring water nearby his camp, and a smooth bed of pine twigs under him, looking up at a bowl of moving stars through branches of oak and beech, a man tucked his doublet and cloak around and under him.

"I am the Future." He waved with an open palm of his hand toward the constellations. "And so likewise are you."

The walk with a sixty-pound pack and musket had worn him. "I'll sleep," he laughed, "I'll sleep like a baby." And he did, drifting into sleep with lullaby words, "So long as grass grows and rivers run," and with fingers folded around a tiny bronze plaque graven with the Four Stumbling Blocks to Truth.

BOOK TWO: THE ARCH BEGINS

IS LOVE A NECKLACE?

Robert Winshore stayed overnight with a Whig farmer who knew him as "one of us." He slept poorly and began riding to Boston a little after daybreak. A light snow had fallen. The sun came out. The horse was a small dark bay, four years old, eager to travel. The hills shone, the pines stood grave with affirmations that life could be worse for him.

A tough well-knit body had this rider, six feet tall and the proportions there, his hair dark, wavy and thick hanging over his ears, a straight nose, a ruddy skin, a chin that jutted out somewhat irregular and overly bold, and deep-blue eyes, this morning deep-troubled blue eyes. "It was a mob affair," he broke out to himself. "And I was one of the mob."

He took note vaguely of shy peeps and dim whispers of spring among bushes and branches—April and spring waiting and hidden behind the bluster and snow of March. He thought of the girl he would soon be seeing and how he must keep back from her what was done last night. Nearly a year now he had been shaken by this girl, smitten deep, each wild about the other, each of them snared and swept, each of them beset with secrets they could not tell each other, each of them writhing and groaning under several kinds of pain and desolation.

A white oval of a face she had, framed by chestnut hair in coils that had a dim bronze burnish. She stood six feet but didn't quite seem so. The skin of her cheeks was touched ever so faintly with apple-blush, early apples of late June. The cheekbones and the length of the face gave a hint of the gaunt and perhaps the lonely. Her blue eyes could look at you and you would be meeting her eyes with yours to find that it seemed she was looking through you. And there were moments when a soft dream gaze came crossed with a dark greenish storm-blue, a sea-horizon look that went with her sea-pale skin. The long smooth curves of her eyelashes swept with a perfection not there at all in the tangled and rough shags of her eyebrows.

Months ago it was, away last October and the autumn leaves blowing, she made up a dance for him, naming it: "Love Is a Two-face." She spoke her lines and then stepped and swayed and swirled them, arms, torso and feet in pantomime and moving with the shaded changes of thanks and horror on her face. He could remember lines beginning:

"Is love a necklace I can put on and take off? Is love a shoe I can slip on or kick off, if I please, to the moon?"

Deep was the hold she had on him, deep with a loveliness touched with terror, only less deep than the hold of one other thing, what he most often termed the Cause. He spoke a prayer he might be able to adore and serve both her and the Cause.

Months of elation he had had. It was good to be alive, to be in love with a wild darkhearted girl, to be one joined to others serving the Cause, the great unfathomable Cause. Then he flashed back to the night before. He held up before his face the hand that had slapped the brush of tar back and forth over the face and the gag till the coating was thick with perfect black. And again his conscience gnawed at him. He had done right and he hadn't.

He wrestled with this in many phases as he jogged at a slow trot, walked the horse uphill and galloped an almost level downgrade. And he could come clear on one point. "When I walked into that house I did not know what the deed was to be. I could have refused and made a scene. That would have meant delay and risk besides spoiling their plan. I should have made them understand and agree, before I went with them, that they could not and must not call me to be aught else than a witness."

He rode at a slow trot and mocked bitterly, "And if you had told 'em that, would they or would they not have asked you what kind of a white-livered skunk the Minute Men of Boston had sent out as a representative?"

The mood of gloom was still on him when in Boston he put horse and saddle in the barn of the friend who lent him the nag and walked to the office of the *Massachusetts Spy*, published and edited by Isaiah Thomas.

LIFE IS AN ONION YOU PEEL

They moved to King Street and took places in a crowd about halfway between the British Coffee House and the Bunch of Grapes tavern. From men in the crowd Robert gathered that the victim in the cart was Thomas Ditson of Billerica, a young farmer. Some said Ditson had been caught trying to coax a soldier of the 47th Regiment to desert. Others said he had tried to buy a musket from a soldier of the 47th. Some said he had been tried by British officers and condemned to tar and feathers, and public exhibition as a warning to Boston Rebels.

They watched the parade, the shrilling fifes and the ear-splitting drums, the lines of bayonets, and at the pivot of it all the silent and smutted figure.

Robert and his father stood grim and somber rather than sorrowing. They knew that rather than striking terror to the Sons of Liberty and the Minute Men, it deepened fighting resolves already made and long sworn in solemn oaths.

The parade moved up the street, turned a corner, and the thundering drums were fading.

They turned on the cobblestoned sidewalk. Suddenly Robert Winshore halted, fixed in his tracks. Farther over didn't he see Lieutenant George Frame, whom he knew by sight though Frame didn't know him? And on the arm of Lieutenant Frame, who was it? Yes, wouldn't he know that head, that face? In a swift moment he was facing her, with a cry, "Mim!" and heard her answering cry and they stood with their arms holding each other tight after one kiss.

People stopped to look, asked what this could be. Lieutenant Frame had seen nothing in Marintha Wilming to prepare him for this. Robert's father was less surprised, though he would not have predicted it from what he had seen of Miss Wilming.

After their wild and warm greeting Robert asked if she was going home to Aunt Ellen's and about her traveling bag. "You will pardon us," he said to Lieutenant Frame, Mim adding, after introducing Robert, "I shall hope to see you again, Lieutenant Frame; you have been very kind and thoughtful." To his father Robert explained he was taking Mim home and would be at his room later.

They walked crooked and narrow streets of two-story houses huddled close. They came to wider-spaced lots and the shrubbery

path between two cedars and the home of Aunt Ellen with its first
floor of combined kitchen and dining room at the rear and a small
front parlor and a second floor of three sleeping rooms. Little Aunt
Ellen heard them, came down in a light-blue nightrobe, spoke her
greetings of welcome home, and went back to her sleep.

They had said little in the walk. They said little on the settee
beside the Franklin stove. They had different kinds of silences—
Robert and Mim. This was one of the grateful ones. Their long kisses
on the settee had no tint of reluctance, no misgivings. And they
chatted swiftly an hour or more of things seen and heard since
Robert parted from her in New York. She had been struck with
pleased amazement at Robert presenting to her as his father the man
she had come to like so much on her stage journey. She was warm
and glowing about Ordway Winshore. "You must have further
lights in you I have not seen, to have come from such a father."

The sight of her face, the hold of her hand, the flow of her voice,
went deep in him. His hand was tender, shy and grave on her face
and hair, on her wrists, at her shoulders. And she had her way of
feeding on the look of him, the strengths and the modeling of him
—and beyond that she knew she idolized him for bonds of companion-
ship they had. She had her way now of saying what she had said
before, "You could be homely to look at, homely as a barn made
wrong and twisted by the wind, and my barriers wouldn't stand
against you." Their many hours of singing together, of walks in
the country, of skating and dancing as born partners, his complete
joining with her in grasp of the dances she made up and performed
and her extravagances of speech that some people feared half-mad,
their many quiet hours with few words spoken, the silent comfort
they could be to each other—this past of theirs had grown into
something rare.

Yet little by little there had grown up between them a curious
fabric of fear, a thin woven thing they couldn't touch and handle
and bring out into the open between them because it had its roots
in secrets neither of them could be free to tell. This film of forebod-
ing they kept away from on this night.

Mim brought a small jug of cider she drew from a cask in the
cellar, along with a plate of thin oatmeal cakes sweetened with
maple sugar, after a recipe Aunt Ellen had from a Scotswoman.
They chatted and laughed away their cares and forebodings.

Mim yawned once. Robert said it was the prettiest yawn in the
world and would she yawn again for he liked her yawning face.

They shared a long deep kiss. Robert would be seeing her at the dress shop late next afternoon.

Robert walking the dark twists of one crooked and narrow street tried his memory on slow-spoken words that had come from Mim after a rush of whimsical talk about practical matters. " 'A little and peace with it is the gift of God,' said my grandmother, sitting in the sun at a spinning wheel, speaking it gravely, then smiling, 'Life is an onion—you peel it year by year and sometimes cry.' "

He crept into bed with his father.

"A good night of it, son?"

"Yes, papa."

And their sleepiness was gone.

"Miss Marintha Wilming, a rather wonderful young woman, Robert."

"Perhaps too wonderful for me, I sometimes think."

They actually reveled in their talk about her, each admired her so.

"We see the precious in her, Robert."

"Not many does she let see the precious."

"How many?"

"You and I, her brother Darius, and sometimes Evelyn Trutt, a woman at the dress shop. And perhaps her mother. Mim knows when to guard herself against what others would take to be wild meaningless talk."

"Mim?"

"Short for Marintha—her nickname on the farm ever since she was a baby."

The father told of Stamford and Providence, the bonfires, gallows and tea-burning ceremonies, and Mim saying, "Lost men howling to other lost men where to go" and "Mired men crying to others in the mire how to get foot-loose."

"That sounds like what I hear from her. And I study it and by God it isn't empty and sometimes afterward it gnaws in my heart though I don't know why."

"I've studied about it, Robert. You and I are partisans. We are making history. Only partisans can make the beginnings of history. Through us time and history work. But Mim is timeless. She has elements of the seer and the clairvoyant and she gives a terribly sensitive registration to everything human she meets and sees and hears. She is not afraid of how anything registers in her. With that at times goes an awful loneliness. When she gets too worn with the tragedy of life, as I see her, she shakes herself loose into a quizzical sanity by going folderol and flaunt-a-flaunt."

"That is her, papa, that is my Mim."

And they slept without dreaming and saw no fantasy of a shadow shape standing erect and tar-smutted between two ready and watching bayonet points in the afternoon parade meant to terrorize them.

WALK IN THE MOON

The scud of the moon between clouds, a high wind blowing, silver streaks of mist hanging to the moon and then blown away —this was the night sky over Boston that Robert and Mim saw. They were tired, mentally restless with the packed turmoils of the week. The clean wind, the changing sky, helped as they walked around the Common, up and around Beacon Hill, fields where cows were pastured in summer.

Mim ran ahead and slid along a strip of ice, her foot hitting a rough spot that sent her into the air. Robert rushed toward her, as she made a quick twist of her body, lighting on her feet. He held her close. They laughed together.

Robert was reminded of her dancing for him one time and saying, "My feet were made glad." And Robert also recalled for her her proud words: "When I die my feet will be so glad they will carry me through the Gate of Heaven whoever tries to stop me."

"Too proud. I must have had vanity of the feet when I said that."

This was Wednesday. Next Saturday night he would see her and then leave Boston to be gone for weeks, "God only knows how long." What he would be doing while gone he didn't say. At times a fright came over her that he might love some crazy movement or organization among men more than he loved her. Lights of devotion to her she could see there yet—with an added shadowy abandon she couldn't fathom. Those lights of devotion in his eyes, the touch of adoration in his hands on her, the depths of desire in his kisses, they were there as of old and she counted them her belongings. Could it be they were being overshadowed by this new and growing abandon she couldn't quite place?

Of the fresh reckless flair in him she was jealous. This change in him and whatever brought it she hated. She doubted she would be able to hold her tongue about it. When she twisted it around in her mind and tried to pluck deeper into the motive she had found herself asking, "Have you, Robert, with all these new errands and secrets, become some manner of a sneak?" Then she called herself a poor desperate fool; she must never be that sort of fool before Robert.

They had walked in one of their silences. Mim began talking of how silly and helpless certain women could be. "They scare me with the thought that they are helpless; they don't know in the least how silly and cruel they are. It could happen, I suppose, that I might someday come awake to what I had been doing and see it as silly and cruel—and if I shouldn't come awake that would be more tragic yet."

"I could tell you," said Robert in a burst of candor, "of my being silly and cruel, and it would be terribly involved. One of these days, if we live, I will tell it to you."

"A sweet confession, Robert. Don't soften me when I need hardening.

"What a time it is of hate and hard judgments," said Mim in a spin of feeling. "Why should I hate John Hancock? I did once. I don't now. He is only a two-legged man who will come to an end and be less than dust. Or why should I hate His Majesty King George the Third? I don't. He too is a man on weak legs to get weaker till his end comes. Power crumbles. Riches take flight. The gold men get more often gets them. The finest silk or wool cannot stave off moth and rot. What stands? What lasts? What stays when all these others go? What is proof against death and the rot of dissolution? Could it be love? Could it be a dream softer than fine mist and you could no more take hold of it and say, 'Now I surely have it,' than you could wash your hands in a wind-blown winter moonlight?"

Robert gathered she was saying by indirection that she couldn't go along with him in his zeal for a cause and the kind of hate that must mix with the zeal. She might even hold that their love came first and what he called patriotism second, though of this he wouldn't be sure. Certain he was that she was declaring herself a free human spirit with a sacred heart: she could never be like him a Whig, a Patriot and a Rebel, merely on his wish for her so to be. What she would be in the changes to come she would work out for herself. He knew he was on the danger line when he spoke. "We're young, Mim. We didn't begin this awful trouble that's come on us. It began long before you and I were born. Now we have to take it as it is, as they left it to us. You and I were babies and in our teens when there was high howling, hate piled on hate, over the Writs of Assistance, the Declaratory Act, the Townshend Duties A t. Then seven years ago came the Stamp Act, five years ago the Boston massacre, two years ago the Tea Party. The Continental Congress leaders think we can give the world something never seen before. We can't be sure but we can raise a hope that an American Republic of free men is possible. It could become the light of the world. Liberty of conscience, freedom of worship, we now have, bought with struggle. Further liberties, still other freedoms, we must have. They too will be bought with struggle."

They walked on in silence, came to crooked and narrow streets. The water front opened before them. Under the now clouded moon the sea horizon stood black. "You have spoken tonight," said Mim. "And I could speak. But let it wait. I might say it better Saturday night before you leave."

Robert clenched a fist. He thought of a few nights ago when he asked himself if he had just had the first cold kiss from Mim.

They stood on a wharf. Out along the water level they could see ships riding at anchor with hull lights. The sight of them hit Robert of a sudden. Yes, these were the enemy frigates. They shook him loose from his tangled thoughts of Mim and himself. With pointing finger, and in excited voice, "Yes, there they are, the enemy warships. There they stand keeping the port of Boston closed and dead. There they wait with their guns telling us Americans, On your knees—submit or we shoot you down! They and their guns come three thousand miles to tell us what we can do or can't —ugh!"

In his grunted and loathing "ugh!" Mim heard the new abandon, the fresh reckless flair she hated.

"Yes," and now she pointed a forefinger toward the scene of the Boston Tea Party. "Yes, and over there three hundred and fortytwo chests of good tea flung into salt water to spoil and rot—the criminal rabble—the filthy vile scum."

Out of Robert's mouth came words only she could have pulled: "And I was one of them!"

In silence they walked back to Aunt Ellen's. Robert at the door said she must understand he was sworn never to tell of his own hand or any other man's hand in that wild deed that rocked the Western world and London.

"It is locked in me as a secret till death," said Mim.

He went away with her kiss on his lips. It was no cold kiss. It was a warm desperate kiss.

BRASS CLASPS OF A HEAVY BIBLE

Aunt Ellen said good night; they saw her hand move up the stairway banister to near the top when she turned and with a quiet gravity, "Robert, may the good Lord return thee safe again here."

"Something in the air," said Mim. "Aunt Ellen sniffs it."

"It gets more shaky," said Robert, clenching his hands, unclenching. Then taking one of Mim's hands, they sat close on the oak settee and watched the two heavy stub candles in the sturdy Arabian brass candlesticks. "Action will come soon. We don't know where. I don't know when I will see you again. It may be two weeks or two months."

"We have never had trials, real tests, Robert."

"You've seen changes come over me the last year, Mim, and especially the last three or four months. I've done things hard to tell you about even if I were free to tell you."

"You mean blinding the bound and gagged Hobart Reggs, coating his head and hair and filling his eyes with a brush of warm tar?"

So she knew. Robert loosed his hand from hers, folded his two hands, wove the fingers.

It hurt Mim to go on. But she did. "Sapphira Reggs blabbed it to Mrs. Cavendish and me. She recognized you, said she would swear it was you she saw that night before she fainted."

"I am ashamed of my hand in that. But I wouldn't try to tell you how or why I am ashamed. I was tricked but you wouldn't believe how I was tricked."

Mim's hurt was eased a little. But she went on, "The affair of Silas Ludgate, I am sure, without definite proof, you had a hand in. You meant to throw terror into the Loyalists by nearly blinding a man with smoke in his eyes as he sat cold, naked, bound and gagged."

"That affair, if I had a hand in it, I would defend. An informer is a rat. A rat should be killed. He was mercifully allowed to live."

Here was the new abandon, the reckless flair.

"I see how you Sons of Liberty look on what you do and call it good. In the books and the teachings, in the commandments of God and man, these deeds are crimes. Men sharing in these deeds are criminals."

Robert still folded his hands and wove the fingers. He found his voice and very low-spoken: "Noble words are good. They

serve. But with no actions to illustrate them and enforce their mean-
ing, the words are dead. The Boston Tea Party was better than
ten thousand orations full of bright abstract arguments."

After they sat in silence for a while, Mim said it was just as well
Robert was leaving. She had seen Lieutenant George Frame and
Sapphira Reggs together too much lately; they might be looking
for him.

Robert agreed. Then he asked her what it was the other night
she had held off from telling, hoping to tell it better this night
of his leave-taking.

And the words came: "I must go a certain path alone. After
going it alone I may come to you, if you live, and tell you what I
know then. I don't know it now. I will then." She measured off hard
words: "Now I have slowly come to see you a fool, a bigot, a brute
who sees merit in his crimes and most of all you are what the
preacher meant by a hypocritical party zealot. I think that now.
Yet I do not fully trust what I think. It is you who have that kind
of full trust and that is why you are zealot, bigot, and hypocrite.
Life will teach me while you are gone from me and inexorably life will
teach you while I am gone from you."

"So be it," said Robert. "I know it costs you to say it."

"We are young yet. You said that the other night. It is our hope.
In the worse blood and terror to come we will learn. I can see
they will shake me near to death. I will be swept near the gates of
the lost mind." Mim trembled, her body and voice trembled. Robert
put an arm around her, took one of her hands in his. She went on.
"They will not get me, those dooms that reach for me. My strength
will be a fine thin cord drawn tight and near breaking but it will
hold."

"So I told my father the first time we talked of you," Robert
murmured with dreaminess. Perhaps they should have had this
candor earlier, he thought.

"I loathe your deeds and your excuses and justifications of them.
And I love the companion you have been and the boy you are, my
boy, my only lover, my hope for a home in the hills, for the bright
day," and Mim choked a little at this, "the June day we pictured
for the ceremony and the words 'until death do us part' and Darius
would be an usher and he would drive us to the house and before
going in we would stand under apple blossoms in the moonlight,
under the same trees where last year we had a long deep kiss."

She waited before going on. "My arms will reach for you. My mouth will seek yours. And I will put away the wanting of you. Relentless and whirling events will tell me what I want to know without doubts or reservations. What I see now may be right. If something else is right life will press and burn it into me. Till then I put away from me the want of you, the need of you. And often it will howl and swirl about me and near crush me, the want and need of you."

Robert watched her face pale to a weird white, a faint tremor of blue on her lips. They sat in a long silence, each with a nameless gratitude for the silence they could keep now. And in a fierce interlock of caresses, Mim cried low and Robert felt his eyes go soft. Their mouths were close and they heard the breathing of one another; they were saying by no spoken words that such a farewell should have this kind of bittersweet, this sort of earth tang. The two thick stub candles, the worn calfbound Bible with brass clasps on the center table—they too belonged in this bittersweet of parting.

Robert in his "Liberty Song" at the White Cockade coffeehouse and his words to her under the scudding moon of Wednesday night—he had said the most of it. Little could be added. Mim in her straightaway and poignant talk this night had come to an end of words. So their silence on the oak settee in the low-ceilinged room became them as a garment they had made together.

Into this quiet room of this still house came the sound of footfalls and voices outside, feet coming along the two-plank-wide walk from the gate to the front door, voices that had spoken and then let down. A rough knock at the front door. Mim strode to the door, Robert following a few steps behind. Mim opened the door to the voice and face of Lieutenant George Frame. Might he be permitted to enter? "Certainly," said Mim. At his right elbow was Sapphira Reggs, whose father the Sons of Liberty had tarred and feathered. "My guest, I presume she may enter?"

"Your call is unexpected, but you are welcome," said Mim. "Won't you have chairs?" Miss Reggs seated herself. Lieutenant Frame would come to his errand standing. "Without further ado," said Frame, facing Robert, "my duty here is to put you, Mr. Robert Winshore, under arrest for a criminal assault on the person of Hobart Reggs, who with his daughter here will be the principal witnesses against you. I can also await your conviction of participation in a criminal assault on the person of Silas Ludgate."

While Frame spoke Robert was moving slowly to where the center table stood between him and Frame, whose back was to the front door and his feet on one of the long narrow rag rugs.

"No tricks will help you tonight, Mr. Winshore," said Frame, even-voiced, as he drew a pistol. "You are coming with us. Four of my men outside will take you in custody."

"By what authority is all this?" Robert asked.

"I have the signed warrant for your arrest here in my pocket but you are the extreme and dangerous case where we do not go through the formality of showing the warrant."

"I am to be your prisoner how long?"

"Till your trial when your punishment will be determined."

"A court-martial will try me?"

"Yes, and they will be more just and considerate than you were with Mr. Hobart Reggs."

For a fleeting flash of a moment Robert wondered how Mim's face looked as he played for a few priceless seconds in which to think out the best of five or six chances that ran through his head.

"May I ask—" he began.

"No, there will be no more palaver," came from Lieutenant Frame with a snarl as he lifted the pistol and held it toward Robert's heart.

"My hat and overcoat," said Robert.

"You walk to that front door and step out and we'll bring your hat and overcoat," said Frame.

"A step at a time, one step and then another, that will be obeying your orders?" asked Robert as he moved one small step. Frame was puzzled about what this could mean but seemed inclined to accept it as an admission from Robert that he was ready to go along.

"While I am going along with you one step at a time," said Robert as he moved another small step, "may I ask—"

"You may not ask and you're going to learn to keep your damned Rebel mouth shut," barked Frame.

At the word "shut" the room went dark and the two brass candlesticks clattered to the floor and there was a sound of a body falling, followed by a crackling thump, after which came a bang at the top of the stairway and a rolling rattle down the stairs.

Frame's three grenadiers in front of the house came rushing in, falling tangled and cursing in a chair at the foot of the stairway. After Mim had lighted the candles, they made out what had happened. With a sweep of one hand Robert had sent the two candles and candlesticks to the floor, stooped and with a swift pull at the long narrow rag rug had Frame reeling and toppling to the floor, had hurled the center table over Frame, and then flung one of the loose-legged oak chairs up to the top of the stairway for whatever confusion might follow from its bang and its roll and rattling down the stairs.

A minute, two minutes, a third minute passed. Frame with an effort and a groan sat up and felt of a bump on his forehead where the brass clasp of the heavy calfbound Bible struck him. Frame came out of his daze to cry, "Out the back door, you two, look to the back door!" he ordered and to another grenadier, "Up the stairway and search every corner!"

One whisked up the stairway to find his way blocked by a little one-hundred-and-five-pound woman with a dignified scowl and a righteous voice asking, "Is it murder or robbery come this night to a peaceful house of decent citizens?"

"Did he run this way?" the soldier shouted at her.

"Did who run this way?"

"Robert Winshore, he's under arrest," cried Frame, before dashing to the kitchen and the back door. Through the back door he went to see two of his men trying to revive a third man who lay alongside a sawbuck next the woodshed. This was the grenadier assigned to watch the rear of the house. When he came to his senses the grenadier remembered a man rushed at him and pushed him over the sawbuck and then brained him with a billet of wood.

In the house Mim comforted Aunt Ellen and put her to bed, straightened the room while Sapphira Reggs shook out moans that it was a shame if "that ruffian, that beast" had got away.

Lieutenant Frame stepped back in the house and spoke to Mim with a fine gravity and consideration. "I regret it was necessary to inconvenience you, Miss Wilming. We had allowed Winshore his freedom in the hope of learning more of his associates and accomplices. When we were informed this afternoon that it was certain he planned to leave Boston tomorrow to be absent indefinitely, we made our decision to seek him here."

"He will not trouble you in Boston in the immediate future, you may be sure," said Mim, cool and level-eyed.

"You give me your word of honor, Miss Wilming, that is to your best knowledge and belief?"

"I do, Lieutenant Frame."

"That is sufficient for me. I apologize again for disturbing you and wish you good night."

The house was still again. Mim rested back in the oak settee. Could it be only twenty minutes ago that she and Robert wore a garment of silence together and shared a strange, earthy bittersweet?

I MUST FORGET YOU

Robert learned that Marintha Wilming was under suspicion and they had called several times to press her in questionings of him, of the secret organizations, of his work for them. When Robert came to Aunt Ellen's it was after dark, keeping to the alley and entering by the back door.

Aunt Ellen had come down for a greeting and halfway up the stairs, rather softly, "You'll be safer to make it a short stay, children."

Their arms went around each other and they kissed. Robert didn't want to make anything of it but noticed Mim didn't rub her ear lightly below his collarbone. "She took my kisses without returning kiss for kiss," ran a blur in his head and blood. She slipped out of his arms without being abrupt and yet too soon and too smoothly she did it. That too was a blur in his head and blood.

He seated himself on their old settee, Mim pulled a chair and sat opposite him.

"It broke yesterday," he said.

"Yes, the war has begun."

"I have a message for you—and news."

"I'd as lief you brought me no messages. Enough news there was when we met last."

"What is wrong, Mim?"

"The war is wrong, Robert."

"You know what you're saying, Mim, and you know my answer."

"Agony, dead men, cripples, waste, ruin, women and children waiting for those who never come home."

He looked into her face, a deep and long look.

She went on, her faint smile hard and mocking. "The wedding was to have been in June, the blossom month. In my father's house the wedding and Jake to fill the big Liberty Room with flowers and Darius with his brown hair and brown eyes would usher the invited few to their chairs. Then after the words 'until death do us part' and the rest of it, Darius would drive us to our own little ten-acre place. By then the moon would be up and before going into the house we would stand under an apple tree and look up at the moon

through a latticework of white apple blossoms. And once we joked
that the first baby would be a boy with brown hair and brown eyes
the same as Darius."

The faint smile had faded. Her lips stretched wide over the gaunt
bone structure of her face. It was a mask rather than a face. "Apple
blossoms—pooh—and the moonlight a mishmash with the stink
of stale cheese. What do you and your rabble care? Ashes and blood
now—and good women crying for their lost ones."

"You may yet understand the hearts of your friends and kin-
folk. The sorrow may come less bitter."

Her words sprang. "I know more now than I can understand.
The more I know the deeper twists the bitterness. I trust no one,
not even myself. Tories and Rebels, they both lie and lie how noble
they are, how sacred their causes. On both sides false and cunning
trickeries, crazy hate and defiance. Both sides wanted this war. Now
they have it. Your Sam Adams wanted it. You followed him wanting
it. Now you've both got it."

"A storm has come. It began far back. Sam Adams couldn't bring
it. It began before he was born. A voice, that's all Sam Adams is.
He says what we want said." Robert put out a hand, clutched one
of her wrists. "Before giving you the message and news I came to
deliver, I'm telling you the days to come will bring you lessons. I
have no lesson for you. I leave it to time. I'm not throwing any
persuasions at you. I still value beyond price that fine sincerity of
yours."

"So you say and it may be you know what you say and mean it."

Feet scuffing the plank walk outside sent Robert on tiptoe to the
kitchen. Mim answered the door knock.

"Lieutenant Frame! Would you come in?"

"Thank you."

"I was just going upstairs. Enough of the moon comes in for you
to see this chair. Seat yourself and I will go to the kitchen for candle-
light."

She returned with the two stub candles lighted, set them on the
table. "And now?"

"I have come on two matters. The first is official." And Francis
Frame was grave with a touch of severity though he had the peculiar
moon-round face that puts on severity with effort. His acquaintance
with her was the reason his superiors had sent him to get her
solemn word that she was not playing the role of an informer,
making reports to the Rebels of intelligence picked up among her

Loyalist friends. She gave him as solemn word as he wanted that she was no informer.

"If Mr. Winshore were here, he would testify that I have opposed his views and designs and have tried to prevail on him toward a different course of conduct."

"You may be assured, Miss Wilming, that it will be a pleasure for me to report that you have made these declarations and avowals."

She now asked, "And what was the second matter, Lieutenant Frame?"

His voice shook. "A ball in the leg . . . my brother . . . yesterday . . . above the knee . . . no course but amputation, said the surgeons—" Now she felt sorry for him. This was the grief of a man hit hard.

His lower lip hung loose and his voice was thick, "Death, Miss Wilming, I am not sure but I would rather witness death than a major amputation. You may know the procedure—the ordeal. They bind him down fast with leather straps none of his struggles can break. They proceed with their knives for the flesh and the saw for the bone. In the beginning he moans and screams with the pain. Then he faints away and awakes to go through an agony of healing and then a cripple for life.

"Before the operation"—and now Francis Frame was soft and tender, with no trace of severity—"my brother spoke of you. He said he might not come through. He wished to be remembered to you. He requested me to present to you his compliments and to say to you for him, 'Assure her that I hold her ever in the highest regard.' Those were his words."

"It is sad to hear, deeply sad. You must convey to him my respect and my affection. Give him the message that I speak prayers for his recovery and his future. He will recover?"

"The surgeons believe so. They value his high courage, they say."

"And his future?"

"He leaves shortly for England. The fabrication of a substitute limb when amputation is above the knee has added difficulties. We hope now for his recovery. The plans for his career after that can wait."

Now Lieutenant Francis Frame paused. Mim said nothing. She saw again the official look.

"You have heard, Miss Wilming, that Robert Winshore was in the fighting yesterday? Winshore was the first to find my wounded brother. He dragged him into a barn, then ran out of the barn, shot and killed one of our men and disappeared into the back fields. He was active riding fields and woods between Lexington and Concord with powder and bullets for Rebels whose supplies were exhausted. We consider him a dangerous man."

He paused. "May I have your word, Miss Wilming, that if you hear or know of his return to Boston you will thereupon immediately notify us?"

"What manner of character have I become that you must pay an official call on me at my home in night hours to require a pledge from me that I shall serve you as an informer?"

"It is a matter where we cannot stand on delay, Miss Wilming."

Mim rose and moved toward the door. Lieutenant Frame stood up, moved with her till they stood at the door.

"I am asking you, Lieutenant Frame, I must ask you, to be so good as to come to this house tomorrow night. I shall then give you my decision. Your request is abrupt. I do not refuse it. I ask a day of time. It may be that I shall give you exactly the pledge you ask and give you the fullest possible accommodation. Or it may be that I must follow some other course. It is a matter I must consider."

"I regret I must report to my superiors that I find you hesitant and quibbling. I had higher opinion of you. However I shall call on you at this house and at the same hour tomorrow night."

He bowed himself out the door and his polished high boots scrunched on the plank walk in the moonlight.

On shadow feet Robert joined Mim at the shutters watching the black boots, the scarlet coattails, the blue three-cornered hat, turn off the gravel path and move up the street. Mim after a minute or two stepped out, walked to both corners, went round the house and up the alley in two directions, returned to the front room, to the chair opposite Robert on the settee. "We are safe now, I think, for what little further we have to say."

"Do you remember, Mim," Robert began, as much to himself as to her, and as though what he was saying might help. "Do you remember the night on the green at Lexington in a sweet clean moonlight and we kissed once and kissed again, and later we stood still listening to the slow going down of a wind that an hour before had roared and whined around us as our skates curved on the moon-lit pond? Do you remember?"

Like the thud of a flat stone falling plunk into a quiet pool came Mim's voice, "Is this your message? Time counts. Is this the news you bring?"

He couldn't fathom her. She had seemed far away from him more than once though never before so far away.

"I guess you're right, Mim. I guess I oughtn't be dreamy and maybe instead," here his voice rasped, "I ought be asking you what's got into you?"

She too couldn't fathom him. Now she said he had never been so far away from her. It was too far. It hurt enough for her to say, "You could be cruel to me, Robert. Once I thought nothing could ever happen where you could be cruel to me. That was before the Reggs affair and the Ludgate atrocity."

She could go farther with this and he would sit dumb.

"Of course," and she spoke loud now, she didn't care who heard her or who might come, "of course I remember the kisses on Lexington green and the hush on the snow that was a whisper of music only we two standing still in the moonlight could hear. That's a memory," she went on, "and when both of us think we clean forget it it will come back to haunt us."

She crossed the room and came back with one hand in a clasp, "Now this little folly here I did for the sake of memories. There was an hour in a hazel thicket when we stood tiptoe together and plucked stars from the meadows of the sky and that was a memory. There was another hour we snuggled close in a wagon and tried to bring down a ring of brass chains circling the moon." Now she was crying her words in a low swift murmur and Robert sat awestruck, swept away by her.

"Wear it, keep it in all weathers," she said, as she reached over and thrust a hand inside his coat and into his wool-shirt pocket. "I began making it weeks ago and went through with it and couldn't think of keeping it for myself having you and the memories in mind every moment of stitching it."

Robert reached in his pocket, unfolded and rolled it, clutched and caressed it—a large kerchief of thin blue silk.

"A trifle—keep it—keep it to forget me by," she was saying.

"To live pleasant, to skip the hard places with a light hurt, I might be able to do it, Mim."

"So that's the message you came at danger to yourself to deliver."

"If you care to take it as a message—and I wish I hadn't had to come."

"If there is more, tell it. You can't pile grief too high this night."

His pause was long. He should have made excuses to her mother and not promised. And it was baffling she hadn't rushed questions at him about the reports flying over Boston of the fighting at Lexington and Concord yesterday, why she wasn't asking who, what, when, where, and how did it happen among the neighbors of her youth and childhood. That perhaps was her pride, her clinging to her notion that he shouldn't have gone, he shouldn't have had any part in it. And the press of suspicion and official questioning of her had done something.

She knew there was a light dash of evil in her now mocking, "We have heard of a man risking his life to bring a message to be spoken and then at the final moment forgetting the words," adding as he still sat in his long pause, "There were evenings less dangerous when we said, 'We can't stay here all night.'"

"Marintha." It was both a whisper and a groan. She caught herself sobered and awed, threw it off, and mocked, "Yes, that's the name, you remember the name."

"Marintha," and Robert found himself trying to speak with a disembodied voice, in words detached, monotonous as the regular pendulum of an impersonal clock telling the time to the just and the unjust. "Marintha, yesterday morning the goddam foreign invaders of Middlesex County with a bullet of hate shattered the right arm of your father and with another lead ball of evil aim killed your brother Darius."

In the dim light of the moon through the shutters, she couldn't read his face as she arose. She stood before him, dazed, not certain she heard. He told it again, and again detached, monotonous as the inevitable brass pendulum of time to the just and the unjust:

"They crippled your good father for life and they murdered your sweet and brave brother Darius. I stood at the bedside and saw him die and heard his last words: 'The pain is gone. Tell Mim I will go far down the pleasant valley and meet her with a kiss.'"

She turned and walked five slow steps to the front window. She stood looking through the shutters and half seeing the moonwhite on the grass, on the plank walk, on the cedar branches.

She turned, took two steps as if feeling the way with slow feet, stood silent toward Robert a long moment. Then he saw her sway and crumple to the rag rug on the floor before he could reach her.

He ran to the kitchen for a dipper of water, laid a wet kerchief over her forehead. Her eyelids fluttered and he heard her faintly, "Take me home, Robert Winshore, take me home. You took me too far away. Now take me back." The eyes settled in quiet, little bars of moonlight from the shutters marking her face, her tongue moistening the lower lip, Robert heard her in a pleading, "You wouldn't fool me, Robert, you wouldn't fool me, Robert."

She lifted her head, sank back, closed her eyes and seemed to rest. Then she sat up and pushed at him, wanting him away and not touching her. She straightened herself and shook her head and held it high, gave a ripple of wild laughter as she faced the ceiling.

Then came her words spinning out in laughing ripples, "Now Marintha Wilming is herself again, Robert Winshore. Marintha the bright child with her skates on Lexington green listening to the wind go down, the tall proud howling stallion of a wind become a wee mouse of a vanishing zephyr, we heard it and what of it, sir, I ask, what of it?"

She moved into a heady mockery, a tipsy groping. "What a delightful evening, sir. What a marvelous night we have had, sir, what conversations with the shadows of barn rats and man-killers. A pleasant valley, he said, and he would go far down the pleasant valley and meet his sister with a kiss. And an arm off here and a leg off there and an arm off here and a leg off there—it's like you can drum it on drums of fate—dead in the morning still dead in the afternoon and when the evening stars creep out and look down dead and still dead—an arm off here and a leg off there and when a leg comes off he screams till he forgets his leg is coming off, he can't see, he can't hear his leg is coming off. And if your lover comes it is your duty to tell us your lover has come. He is a dangerous man, a lawless incendiary, and we want our hand on him, tell us when he comes so we may put our hand on him, the rat, the foul and squeaking rat. What smooth and conniving silhouettes of warships on the horizon brought them? And whither goest thou, me lad, and thinkest thee thou knowest whither thou goest?"

In swift ripples of a tipsy abandon it came from her. She paused and now it came slow with a shiver of amazement at her bones. "What sweet angels of fathomless doom have overheard our kind words to each other this night, sir?"

Then again swiftly. "Apples, how many the times Darius and I picked a big red apple, so handsome an apple, and put our teeth into it to find it a mushy wallow of neither taste nor content. And again we met windfalls of scrawny little pippins with no reputation and we filled our mouths with them and glutted ourselves with their scrawny little perfections."

Her hair had come loose on one side and broken ropes of it lay on the wide white linen collar at her left shoulder. Small moon bars through the shutters rested on her head and Robert saw the burnish of her chestnut hair as airy slats of fine bronze.

Now she was far beyond him. He would hesitate at touching her. Time counted. And it didn't. What did they have more of than time for speaking the finalities that hung in the air, for saying what they could not say in the long time, the looming stretch of time ahead of them?

Mim scrambled to her feet, stood at the window, looked out. "Here we can see who might come to listen to our chitchat, our elegant and amusing chitchat."

She bowed, curtsied in mimicry of courtesy and went on smooth and broken, broken and smooth. "Having broken a heart, would you care to pick up the pieces, sir, and put them in a little snuffbox to carry away, to gaze at early or late standing perhaps among yellow pie-eyed daisies, pigweed, ragweed, sow thistle in a cow-pasture fence corner? Or you might give them to an auctioneer and hear him, What can I get to start this? A broken heart—a little mending and it's good as new—what am I bid? Yes, all the pieces of a broken heart in a little oblong of silver and you can take it in your hand and say with sea music, if you can manage it, I remember her, I do, I do, I do, remember remember her and the bits of shadowcreep woven in her thistledown hair, I remember a warm lingering kiss she gave me on Lexington green one night when a brass moonfall came down and a white snowfall drifted on our shoulders."

She made a grotesque mouth. "I'm a clown, always a clown you have found me. How can there be a brass moonfall and a white snowfall at the same time? There must be a mistake somewhere. Yes, there must be a grave error, some figure in the arithmetic of Boston streets and Lexington green got lost and wasn't there when they added, subtracted, multiplied and divided and especially divided." It was wearing her down, losing its weave and timebeat. She was asking, "Or was it a cipher, sir, a naught, a zero, a goose egg, an oval of no promise, no crimson or folly, no bright seduction, deaths instead of weddings, deaths on deaths instead of wedding after wedding?"

She took three quick steps toward the center table, staggered, stood heady and swaying. Robert stepped toward her. She drew back and away, her hands out as though she would push him away. What of fantasy rushed from her now he afterward saw in a dream as a relentless line of white flame destroying itself, eaten, going and gone as it reached an equally relentless black pool of green scum. She would have it so.

"Listen, sir. Let your ears gather my farewell to you, sir. In the sacred name of all the crowning apple blossoms of next June, I promise to forget you. So completely will I put you out of my mind you may know you will not be the least of my thoughts because you will not be among any of my thoughts. I shall kiss my father's crippled arm. I shall stand at the grave of my brother on a Sabbath of gray rain and blowing mist and I shall bless his name and bless his curly brown head of hair and bless his slow brown eyes of faith that never betrayed man, woman, nor beast of burden. But you, sir, I shall forget. Letter by letter I shall forget your name till I cannot remember how to spell it."

Robert saw the very tumult and rioting freedom of her speech had its music of consolation for her, had eased awful and inexplicable thorns piercing her. She now measured slow words. "A dark and tangled wonder has happened that can never be solved. I would have brought you flagons and chasubles, moonmist and rainbows. Instead I brought you the trifle of a kerchief of blue silk, silk for you to remember my heart was made soft as moonmist, and the blue of it blue as a blue moon shining on a blue sea for you to remember me by. And you, what did you bring me, for exchange, by way of barter, by way of a bargain? Why, you brought me the pains of death and the aches of hell."

She swayed. Robert caught her. He held her in his arms on the settee. She sobbed in his arms. He went because there was no mistaking her command. "Don't pity me. I'll do my own pitying. Go now, Robert Winshore. Go and stay gone. I must forget you. The forgetting will come hard but I will forget."

A SHROUD AND A MEETING

Robert was on his back on a bookbinder's table, the window light dim in the corner, a newspaper over his hands, another newspaper having slid away from most of his face, his eyes closed. His stepmother Mary went away, giving a fierce pinch to Mim's arm as though to say, "My prayers go for the two of you."

Mim glided as a frame of shadow on feet of mist to where she stood in reach of the sleeper. She felt herself a sort of ghost and him another ghost, though she asked if a ghost could have a curiosity like hers near to a hunger, and if a ghost could have such thick dark hair as she saw flowing away from his forehead and tousled as though her half-reaching fingers had run through it. High hope she had now. He was alive. She mourned that death had come to his young brother Locke. She exulted, not sure why, over Robert among the living. His eyes were closed. He hadn't heard her. She ran her eyes from his face to his feet where one bare toe stuck out on the left-foot stocking and three on the right. She wanted to reach and touch him. She held back. The first this was she had seen him in uniform. Her right foot touched his three-cornered hat that had fallen off the table. She glanced to the long coat of blue with buff trimmings that hung on a peg above the table. His wool shirt had the same worn look as the stockings, with holes, stains and splotches, two small burnt holes in the shirt sleeve, perhaps from fire sparks while he slept.

Her right hand pressed hard the left-hand fingers as it dawned on her that toil, exposure to raw weather, cares, duties and battle fatigue had worn his rugged body. The pathos of that shirt hanging so loose on his torso, that body her arms had so many times encircled, smote her and a guilt came over her. If he was now better than when he had come home then at that time he must have been scrawny.

He was stirring. He raised his right leg, laid the right ankle onto the left, gave a slow delicious sigh of ease. His eyelids parted and through the slit he looked at his feet, wagged the three bare toes back and forth. Now his eyes came full-open. The pivot of his head brought his eyes around to where they fell on Mim. His eyes dwelt on her face, peered straight into her eyes as his mouth screwed itself into a comic twist and the tip of his tongue came out and Mim half expected he was going to stick out his tongue at her. His face smoothed down and his eyes ranged the length of her from head to toes and then back to her face and eyes.

He shook his head sharply, to make sure he was awake, again ran his eyes over her, blinked and looked again. He then dropped his head to a complete resting position, gazed at the ceiling, closed his eyes tight, held them so a few moments, then opened them wide and flashed them full on Mim. Seeing exactly what he had seen before, he spoke as casually as a man in a dream, "I've seen the ghost of you so many times I'll burn my boots if you're not a ghost now."

Mim stood in her foot tracks. She couldn't move. She couldn't be sure what to do if she moved. She saw in his eyes an unfathomable final something that his father saw and feared. Her shoulders shook. When her eyes closed an instant and opened, two or three large tears slowly dragged down her cheeks.

He raised his shoulders, drew himself to a sitting position, and with a curious soft mockery, "But the ghosts I saw never cried. They were too proud to cry. They wouldn't cry if the sky should come falling down. They wouldn't cry if all the stars in the night sky were crying."

He turned his head toward the ceiling, laughed a hollow ha-ha with a peculiar merry chuckle in it, then turned to her with an appeal not loud but deep-toned, beseeching her with a grotesque mouth, "Jesus, good lady, have a little pity on me. I've had my share of spells with hallucinations. That's the name for 'em—hallucinations. You see 'em. You reach. They're gone. And you're a fool. I've seen you before. I put my hand out for you. And what I got was nothing, a bubble, a bauble, a whiff and a whoof of phantasmagoria and you can look at it and say 'Good evening, my sweet phantasmagoria, how do you fare today and will you walk a piece with me?' and you get no answer and you come out of it with a splitting headache and you poke the fire and pile on wood and roll into your blanket again praying in Sweet Jesus' name for no more phantasmagoria."

His eyes left her. He meditated aloud. "Up on the Kennebec River sleeping in the snow near the Canadian line I had some of the dangdest meals of roast duck with plum pudding and grape-jelly tarts with strong hot coffee, food as fancy as ever a man threw into his belly, and when I came out of it and sat up shiverin in my wet clothes, it was just one more of those tricks, a cheat, a bubble, a bauble."

His head pivoted swiftly to see if she were still there, and, "Stop your crying. Step over here and put your hand in my hand. I'll be danged if I'll reach for you." Their hands met. Their mouths met. His feet swung to the floor and they stood locked and interlocked in moaning and quavers.

Something struck the floor near them. They looked and saw Robert's father and Mary gesturing. They were leaving the printery and had thrown the front door key to Robert and Mim, who plainly wouldn't be leaving.

Suddenly Robert lifted Mim and seated her on the table with her feet dangling. Himself he seated on the table with his back to the wall and his legs crossed under him tailorwise. Then she saw his face cold and he was asking, "How do we know? Can it be we are making a beginning that will have the same end as the last beginning? How do we know?"

A flash of pain crossed her face as he saw it in profile and as it lingered when her face turned toward him. She would have that flash, he thought, if her arm had his rheumatism. He was less cold saying, "I

wouldn't bring you pain, Mim. You're the last person in the world I
would bring pain to."

"Not now, Robert, please don't be ice now. Another time be ice
if you must—not now."

"Who taught me I must teach myself to be ice? It was you."

"I didn't know what I was doing that night. I was out of my head.
I was daft. I was crazy with grief. I was tangled head and foot."

"So I said to myself over and over. You didn't mean it, I said. Up
on the Kennebec River your ghost would keep coming to me and I
would talk with your ghost about it. I was down to skin and bone.
There was one night they cooked a dog for supper. They boiled the
guts of that dog and tried eating it and spit it out. That was about
when I said I must forget you because I began saying to your ghost,
'You did mean it, Mim, and how could you, how could you mean it?'
I had enough bitterness without remembering you told me you would
forget my name and every letter of my name and I could do the same
for you."

His hand went to a pocket and brought out a small fistful. He un-
folded and spread on the table the blue silk kerchief. The tears poured
down Mim's face. " 'I give you this to forget me by.' Those were your
words. 'I give you this to forget me by.' Remembering you began to
hurt so much that I decided it was good advice you gave me and I
should try to make myself forget you. I was forgetting warm clothes,
pleasant firesides, because it hurt to think of them. I was blotting out
memories of good food and clean beds because that hurt. And of all
memories yours hurt the worst, yours gave the hardest pain. And it
got after a while that I could forget you a whole day and sometimes
two or three days not a thought of you."

Mim winced and thrust out her two hands to press his left hand and
drop it.

"I practiced at learning to forget you," he went on. "With practice
I improved at forgetting you. As time went by I said you must have
spoken wisdom and it was important to forget you, never to see you
again, never to let there be a beginning again, for another beginning
could have an end like the last beginning had."

He was tired. His head slumping sidewise said so, his head leaning
at the brick wall, as words came from him in a dreaminess of song
murmur: "Is love a necklace I can put on and take off? Is love a shoe
I can slip on or kick off, if I please, to the moon? In five minutes by
the clock, love can be a thrush pouring flights of song with scarlet

numbers and dancing alphabets—and in that same five minutes be-
fore your eyes that triumphant wild thrush becomes a monkey scratch-
ing a louse at his ribs and a louse at his buttocks while he mocks at you
with his jeering monkey-faces."

He could remember, after all that had passed, the lines she spoke
to her dance named "Love Is a Two-face." He was whispering, "The
jeering monkey-faces, I saw many of them; I hope you saw a few."
He wasn't looking at her and he went on as though she were not
there: "Love is a great gleaming eagle that will sweep you for a ride
to the top of the sky and a spread of green valleys and winding rivers
for your eyes—it happens, it is an event—and love is a buzzard you
can mistake for an eagle to ride, a scavenger who drops you to your
death and takes its time to feed on you and pick your bones white and
polished—this too happens and this too is an event."

He had paused for exact remembering, had hesitated and fumbled
a moment and then gone on, his memorizing of her lines perfect.

"I couldn't say them," said Mim. "I've lost them. I found them when
I found you. I lost them when I lost you, when one of my dreams ran
that you wrote me a long letter of pride and anger and laid it on a fire
and watched it burn. Then in the middle of a sheet of foolscap, having
sharpened a quill to write very fine, you wrote:

> 'My once dearest Mim—Since
> it is thy spoken wish, I
> cross thee quite out of my
> book.   Robert Winshore'

The dream ended there. I like to think if it had gone on you would
have laid this second letter in the fire."

"I could have written it and I could have sent it from the Kennebec
River when there was health and strength in forgetting you. I did
anything that would help forget. I used to make a list in my mind of
all your faults, the faults you yourself admit to and especially the
faults mean gossips give you. That helped, like it helped to repeat an
old saying in one of my father's books: Whosoever hath her hath a
wet eel by the tail."

"That was unclean, Robert."

"And unjust. But it helped me forget."

Were they getting anywhere? What was happening between
them? Mim was asking herself. The answers, for the immediate mo-
ment, came to her.

"Forgive me, Robert, forgive me not for all time nor forever. Only a few days now forgive me. And listen to me for one or two minutes."

"I have talked too much. I could better have slept than talk like I have. Or I could have listened while you told me where in hell you have been since I saw you last." He laughed. It came thin and hollow.

"I was getting to that. We have been prattling here. Since we saw each other you have been to hell and so have I and we haven't begun to tell it. You have done hard duty and met heavy grief today. I didn't know you were in Philadelphia. I came here to work for Cynthia George when she moved her shop from New York. I intended to seek out your father sometime and ask him about you. And I asked Cynthia to let me deliver the shroud I worked on all day so I might learn which son of your father had gone to the Great Valley."

And Robert saw a gray-blue sea-drench in her eyes, ominous resolves beyond his reading now. She slid off the table. She pulled out his feet and straightened him and made a pillow and told him she would bring a chair and sit quietly by him for ten minutes or longer, when she would see him home. "You must do this. Tomorrow, later, we can talk. Another time we can report to each other what we saw, you in your hell and I in mine."

She took his head between her hands and touched his lips with a long foam-light kiss, stood by him with her hands softly alive over his eyes, whispering he must rest and sleep. Then she brought a chair and sat in quiet, watching him ease away into the rest his body and mind sought.

"Two years of storm—and he is ten years older—his face scraped and furrowed ten years older—his knees and elbows older and his right knee joint with its pitiless flashes that still keep coming, the bone joint a hundred and two hundred years older than when I first met him in Boston two years ago."

Mim was talking to herself about Robert as she saw him in the days after Locke's death. "His kisses are less swift and lingering," she said. "Yet I have had slow long kisses from him now that hold the pity of night stars in them. Yes, kisses I have had from him now with a lasting tang of bittersweet I would rather have on my mouth than highly praised honey or candy sweet."

The father saw to it. So did Mary. Robert must have care, attention, rest, sleep, no wearing excitement. They told Mim, no long visits, no long talks, rest, sleep, and whatever might give his mind quiet and his heart consolation. "You are thoughtful," said Mim, letting them know she had earlier considered seeking out Robert but she had kept from going to him afraid of what the shock and tumult of their meeting would do to him. When she did go to him it was not of her planning. When she sewed a shroud on the day of July 4, "I couldn't always see the work I was doing half expecting it was to wrap Robert." They should understand, too, that she had heard Robert tell, and the telling eased him or she wouldn't have let him go on with it, of his hard and humble service at Washington's headquarters and the shaping of an army that after the evacuation of Boston melted half away, of his escape from starvation and death in snow and ice on the Kennebec. When he became too graphic in the mean, the scrawny, the devastating details of what he went through on the Kennebec she would interrupt and lead him away.

"He was out of his mind for some days, I'm sure," said Mim. "And when you try to tell someone else how it happened and how you came out of it, you can make desperate work of it."

Mim saw Winshore and Mary look in each other's eyes with meaning, enough for Mim to know they understood she herself had probably gone out of her mind and if she were to tell Robert about it she would do so gently and delicately, with healing rather than hurt for him.

Winshore's full-throated laugh was gone in these days. At meals or in his chair at a writing table Mary and Mim had noticed him drop his hands and stare at nothing in particular for a while. His talk had less of banter and fantasy. He sought out in her alley cabin the old Negro woman Emmeline one afternoon and mentioned this visit casually at home, "I wanted to talk with her about how it felt to handle Locke and throw him around when he was a baby learning to walk."

In two weeks he would be going, said Robert. The way he said it had finality. He had been where hard decisions are made and men accept those decisions and do the best they can by what of necessity and fate follows.

On a rested horse whose flanks had filled out, saddlebags packed, with a blanket, a pouch of roast pork, smoked fish, wheat bread and apples, Robert rode away. It was a laughing farewell, crackling with jokes and nonsense. They all wanted it that way. He turned a corner waving a blue silk kerchief. In the house Mary Winshore put her arms around Marintha Wilming as the salt tears ran down a face still laughing.

MIM'S FORETOKENING DREAM

Mim moved in with the Winshores; they gave her Robert's room. There came two days when Mim wouldn't eat or talk and the letter to Robert wouldn't get written. Winshore and Mary felt she was sweet, patient and aware in telling them she wished to be left alone and would come out whole and well. On the third day she was saying, "The dream came again and I can't tell it to you as yet."

On that same third day a coughing spell seized her. The doctor joined them in warning her she was letting care and anxiety wear her down. The thick shags of her eyebrows lifted and on her slowly parted lips came a pitiless smile. "You will know when it comes that I have now been through the worst. When the word comes I will be the strongest of you."

In four days came the word and they knew what she meant. It was a note Oates Elwood sent: "Bobby died last night they had to take off both his legs and he didn't have blood enough to carry him through the doctors said. I held his right hand through part of it and never saw a man braver. His last words I could make out he wished he might have seen more of Mim and papa this last year. Before he went on the expedition where his legs froze I heard him say, 'I hope the people to come after will understand what it costs to win a war' and he was sure we were going to win it."

Winshore and Mary sat on Mim's bed and studied her thin and now pinched oval of a white face with a peace on it.

"I crossed a bridge and walked a dark valley before you," Mim said.

"You knew beforehand," said Winshore, "and a peace has come to you."

"A peace with long roots winding around in dreamdust. There was Darius, then my father and mother, and now Robert—and now Robert—all given to a dream thin as the air around and over the elm branches," moving a hand toward the tree outside.

"I tried to write him a letter," Mim went on. "Something kept telling me I couldn't write him a letter to do any good. And the dream kept coming—three nights in a row the dream."

Winshore moved toward her and held her hand. She was dry-eyed and the stronger. He blinked his eyes but couldn't blink away the wet film that came.

"I wept for you too, Ordway Winshore, you who have now given your two sons and have no more sons to give having given all."

His soft brown eyes seemed deeper-set. He asked, "And your dream?"

"Three times it came and no time different. A man walks an open plain toward the sunset. He walks straight into the sunset flare, no pride, no fear, an unbreakable man. He wades into sunset flame. He struggles knee-deep and then waist-high in the moving and changing sundown fire, blood-color fire. He makes a slow turn to face where he has been and he raises his right hand three times to his three-cornered hat as he speaks clear slow words:

"Some go soon and some go late into the sunset. I am one of those chosen to go soon. I have kept my faith in the storm and dream that must ever move in the blood of the American people. Now before going I give my three salutes, one to the American flag, one to my Valley Forge comrades, one to the undaunted and enduring Commander George Washington.

"Then he bowed low again and turned and walked into sheets of blazing maroon cloud. And that was all. The earth dropped away from him and he vanished. That was all."

She paused, then went on. "What could I do with such a dream? I couldn't write it to Robert. I took it as a foretokening. Those days I wouldn't eat or talk with you—those days I wept till I had no more tears. Then it came over me if I was ever to live and laugh again I must keep the wonder of the storm and dream that is on us. We can't see the end. Away off on a mountain forty miles away you can see the white snow glisten and the blue mist change but like Robert and Oat far up in Maine you don't even know the mountain and it's for you to give it a name. Those who never let the wonder die down about what is beyond, they're the ones that'll keep on. Robert died with the wonder still in him, I know. He gave me enough of it for me to keep on.

"And this," Mim went on after a pause in which she reached under a pillow and brought out a closed hand, "this by right belongs to you. I forgot to give it to him when he was here and I couldn't put it in a letter."

She opened her hand. Winshore took from it the bronze plaque and ran his thumb over the Four Stumbling Blocks to Truth. "They don't age, they are timeless," he said as he read:

1. The influence of fragile or unworthy authority.
2. Custom.
3. The imperfection of undisciplined senses.
4. Concealment of ignorance by ostentation of seeming wisdom.

"Aunt Ellen found it near the woodshed door the morning after Robert's furious rush away from Lieutenant Frame and the soldiers who tried to capture him. The silver chain broke."

"It is yours," said Winshore, handing it to her. "I may borrow it from you. It is your keepsake."

She hung it around her neck and put a kiss on it, "One I was saving for Robert."

She read from Robert's last short letter: "Your face and your name they never leave me. When I wrap my blanket around me in a tent or on the bare ground before I sleep I see the hang of your hair around your good face and I hear the ripple of your laugh. The days go by and never a day I don't want you. Keep one kiss I send you now. Keep four more kisses I send you and tie each one in the corner of a handkerchief. The blue silk kerchief you gave me has only one little tear in it. Be lonely for me as I am lonely for you. We must make our loneliness warm with its promises till our spring day. A shining spring with one great day we will have. Keep it tight and keep it sure this one long kiss I send you now."

There was a choke in Mim's throat as she came to the end of the letter. And Mary, as her hand stroked Mim's hair, "You don't weep but you have dry tears."

"Yes, Mary," as the choke in the throat came again.

DAWNS, MANY DAWNS

Again in Philadelphia the Rebels could speak, write, print for the American Cause.

The fourth day of July 1778 came. Over the Winshore house-front doorway hung an American flag that had lain folded and creased under the straw mattress where Mim came through fever and a lung malady and other grief.

"This is your day," Mary had laughed to her husband, smoothing and straightening his yellow linen stock and pinning a tiny rosebud on his coat lapel.

Mary, with Mim and Cynthia George, seemed to be in charge of arrangements that pleased and puzzled him.

At noon Mary answered a door knock and let in Oates Elwood, who said, "They will be here soon." Oat further mystified Winshore with telling him, "It's high time you had this day, sir." Oat and Mary seated Winshore in his large chair at the far corner of the room and Oat went out the front door.

Soon the door opened. A woman walked in, of medium height, full-bosomed, with melting gray eyes, a head of rich glossy black hair, and a smooth neat gown of soft cornflower-blue. Winshore had never seen her before. Mim and Cynthia knew who she was, Oat Elwood's sister Ann. Those who knew couldn't tell whether she ought to laugh or break into tears.

She faced Winshore, bowed her head low and lifted it to look Winshore straight in the eyes and to say, clear-voiced and with no faltering, "Mr. Winshore, I have been queer and I have acted stubborn and I don't know why I have done so. I give you my word now that I am sorry for what I have done that might have been unfair to you. I am sorry about it in a thousand ways." She looked toward Mary standing at the door, then turned again to Winshore. "What more there is to say of any wrongdoings you can hear from your grandson."

Winshore drew in his chin, gripped tighter the armrests of his chair, the wide slash of his mouth in a grimace both tragic and comic.

Mary opened the door and Oat Elwood strode in with an easy solemnity, in his arms a bundle of white batiste, and Winshore made out a pink-white foot at one end of the bundle and at the other end a child face, a child head, a baby boy.

Oat put him slowly and tenderly on Winshore's knees saying calmly, with a touch of austerity, "The name of this child is John Locke Winshore, Jr. Born March 16, 1777, the Year of the Three Gallows."

And at his left Winshore could hear Cynthia George, as though she were ringing merry little chimes, "The child of John Locke Winshore and Ann Elwood, married May 26, 1776, the year of the proclamation of American Independence."

The big hands of Ordway Winshore were roving around the little body he held. Both Mim and Mary flashed to the same guess in their minds. They saw his hands wondering if this was the same feel the hands had when they had roved around the other body, the baby legs and arms, the baby torso and backside of its father.

Now the grandfather peered and was lost at looking into the deep-set and liquid brown eyes, at searching the strands of vivid brick-dust hair, at the wide mouth and the long curve of it. Then Winshore closed his eyes. And Mary and Mim knew he was using the trick he worked to keep back the tears.

No one dared say a word. No one could think of a fitting word. His eyes came open and he gazed from face to face in the room. They saw it was a faraway look that swept out beyond this little room.

"Tomorrow has come to this room and the Future is here," he said, running a hand along the brick-dust hair and searching the soft brown eyes so deep-set, so much like him that they were part of him. "He will see many dawns and one will be the coming true of the dawn his father died for. We shall pray that like his father he will be at home in storm and dream."

He beckoned to Ann, pulled her to a seat on an armrest, put an arm around her and said, "Now tell me more about this wonderful young one."

"He's trying to pull off that rosebud," laughed Ann as she pushed away the mischievous fumbling baby fingers.

"His eyes," Ann went on, "month after month they kept changing a deeper brown till now they're exactly like yours and I couldn't keep him from you."

"How does he walk?"

"You'll see."

Their four hands slid him to the floor. He toddled and wobbled across the room to where Mim crouched and waited and when he did fall it was into her warm arms.

Mim hugged Locke's son, the dying words of Robert flashing to her: "I hope the people to come after will understand what it costs to win a war."

With her arms in a tighter hug around the little one, Mim cried to Ordway Winshore across the room, "He *will* see dawns, *many* dawns."

BOOK THREE: THE ARCH HOLDS

ROD AND DOSS ARRIVE

The two young men put up their horses at the New Era Hotel stable, then signed the hotel register. "Nack J. Doss, New Orleans,

La." wrote the short one. His legs out of proportion to the bodily trunk, he seemed to waddle, at first look, then it could be seen his legs, feet, arms, head and eyes were swift in motion, and his thickset torso had a measured ease. He handed the pen to his six-foot companion with an upward look and a wink into a face with a jutting chin, dark-blue eyes and black hair combed back in waves and crinkles. The man signed, "Rodney Wayman, Atlas, Ill."

After a meal at the hotel, they took a slow stroll around town. They stopped in at the livery stable and talked with Fred Shamp over what was doing in horses. They heard that the best horseman in New Era, Danny Hilton, had gone away for a year, maybe longer, and there would be less excitement in horses with Danny gone.

"Why would a man go away and leave a bunch of horses he'd raised?" asked Wayman.

"Account of a girl wouldn't marry him, they say," said Shamp.

"I've knowed girls would've married him for the horses and taken a chance on him."

"This girl liked the horses, all right. She got boots her own size and put on her father's pants and rode with Danny Hilton around the county. Scandalized the town. Her father's the harness maker here, Presbyterian deacon, laughed at the scandal, thinks the sun rises and sets in the girl's eyes—only child, you know."

In Joel Wimbler's harness shop, Wayman asked, "If I bring you a saddlebag with a broken buckle, do you think you could fix it or put in a new one?"

"I think so. I've got different kinds of buckles."

"I'll be in," and they were out of the shop, Doss saying, "You got no buckle wrong."

"I didn't say so. I asked if there should be a buckle wrong could he fix it or put in a new one."

They had nearly reached the hotel when Doss stopped, pulled Wayman to face him and in gruff mockery in a low tone, "You snake-in-the-grass galoot, you're aimin to be a customer and talk slick to that harness maker and find out about his hoss-ridin daughter. That's why you're goin to bust a buckle."

Joel Wimbler worked swiftly at shaping a new leather clasp for the buckle end and stitching it to the strap end, Wayman saying, "I like to watch a good workman." The door opened silently at a hand familiar with it. The young woman who entered, carrying a banjo case, stood four or five feet from them, glanced around her father's back with a bend of her head to see what he was doing, then rested her eyes on the quarter-profile of the stranger's head, the six-foot length of him, the thick hair black and wavy under the pearl-gray felt hat, the straight nose and slightly jutting chin. He turned now, half aware she was there.

She dropped her eyes and his gaze caught the long curves of her eyelashes cool on a sea-pale skin overlaid with a sun and wind tan. She lifted her eyes to his and saw them caught a moment later at her rough and tangled eyebrows, then back to her own eyes with a steady gaze into them. He may have seen there depths of pool-blue change to the slightest shade of storm-green. They were swift roving glances he took at the straight line of her nose down to her wide mouth, lips neither full nor thin, at the hair under the narrow-brimmed hat, the sunlight heightening the natural burnish of the wave over her ears and the coiled braids of chestnut hair. Then his eyes were back in hers, dropping toward the general sweep of the gaunt and bony frame and lifting again to see a dim blush of winter apples creeping over her face and cheekbones.

His large dark eyes of the deepest sea-blue, a danger-blue, held no threat to her. Her response to them was that she must know more of them. His black hair stood out in tufts of wave and crinkle around the upper half of each ear. The chin stood out, decidedly stubborn, she thought. His straight nose had wide nostrils with black hairs curling in them. The mouth was full-lipped, the lower lip heavy and rounded, a mouth of dreaminess, somewhat sad and it might be cruel, yet there were mockery and song hidden in it and a wealth of laughter.

They agreed afterward they had held a long conversation in silence. They couldn't have told whether it was two minutes or five or ten while their eyes went on in a silent mystic speech new to both of them.

Joel Wimbler with knife, awl, needle, twine and beeswax went through his motions unaware Mibs had come. Wayman dangled a careless left hand with a brushing motion and she heard his velvet-soft baritone, "A banjo," not exactly "bahn" nor yet as flat and nasal as the Northern "ban." Mibs heard herself saying, "Yes" away high and sliding down, giving "a ban" on her highest soprano and the "jo" the nearest she could pitch her voice to a contralto. It came closer to guttural than contralto.

There was a pause. For the life of her she couldn't guess what was coming. It came. His imitation of her was perfection. He too could start away high and arrive at a stop in a comic guttural. He kept his face straight, then she saw one of his eyelids flicker, the corners of his mouth quirking. Her lips parted, her lines of even white teeth shone, and the smile spread to her eyes. Then he smiled open-mouthed and she caught crossplays of light in the dark blue of his eyes.

The father, now aware of Mibs, saw she wanted to ask the fellow to the house that evening and that the fellow wanted to be asked. "You'll take potluck with us," said Joel. Then he took the banjo from Mibs, whittled and chipped, fitted the wooden bridge for holding the strings and told Mibs it was better than the old one.

At supper Wayman did most of the talking. Joel encouraged him. So did Mibs. On Mibs saying, "I'll dry the dishes for Ma and help straighten things," Joel and Wayman sat in the living room while Wayman tuned the banjo and plucked snatches of idle airs. He had decided that the next week he would go out in the country and buy a carload of cattle to ship to Chicago, he said, and plied Joel with questions about the most likely places for him to look over cattle. He rated himself a good cattleman, said he had driven one herd of eight hundred up from Texas for feeding on his father's farm near Atlas, Illinois. And what times he had gone out buying to ship to the Chicago market he had made a profit.

When Mibs and her mother came in all this was explained to them. Mibs blinked her eyes and caught her heart jumping. A fear had smoldered in her that in a day or two he would ride out of town and never be seen again. Now there would be a week or ten days or more he would be in New Era.

On Wayman's urging, Mibs took the banjo for ten or fifteen minutes, played her chords and few tunes, and heard from him, "You have a knack with it." The rest of two hours Rodney Wayman took in stride. From one "instrumental selection" to another on the banjo and from song to song they pressed him for more. Joel had started a fire and threw on a small stick now and then to take from the room the chill of the late October frost.

Wayman was no amateur, the Wimblers saw, some kind of a professional, a teacher maybe and more likely a concert performer or a minstrel man. His skill had come from long practice, from many days of intimate fooling with the instrument; he fondled, coaxed, cajoled, even caressed the banjo.

Wayman played "Sweet Alice Ben Bolt," then began to sing so softly he couldn't have been heard beyond his three listeners. Mibs' long legs shifted and she crossed the right knee over the left. He saw her surprised if not startled, as she searched his face.

Her mother and father said good night, leaving Mibs and Rod for the first time alone.

Mibs went for a pitcher of apple cider and a plate of molasses cookies. She poured a glass and handed it to him, a droop at the corners of her mouth.

"Thank you, Miss Wimbler." He too was utterly grave.

She took her chair, moved it nearer him, their knees almost touching. Their eyes met for a long clean steady gaze. Mibs spoke a nickname, "Pickup Charley." And she smiled at him a tight queer smile.

Wayman straightened, drew in his chin. "Pickup Charley, did you say?"

"Charley Amberson," said Mibs in slow syllables, measuring it as a name.

"Charley Amberson, yes," said Wayman. "And Pickup Charley, that was me and that *is* me."

"I'm pleased to meet you again," said Mibs, her smile less tight.

"I never met you before; I couldn't have forgotten your face if I had ever met it."

"I suppose it *was* a case of where I met you and you didn't meet me." It was some four years back, she told him, the first time she had ever been to a blackface minstrel show, one of the unforgettable nights of her life when she saw and heard Haverstraw's Mammoth Minstrels. And she had gone away with a peculiar lingering wonder about what might be alive with joy and pain, hate and love, back of one of the burnt-cork faces and the voice that went with it. This was the face and voice of Pickup Charley, the Marvel King of the Banjo, also Charley Amberson. It was his instrumental solo, "We Have Lived and Loved Together" that first made her curious about him.

"But the voice that sang of the Mohawk Valley girl, that voice I had snared in my ears to keep and if I ever met it again my ears would tell me, they couldn't go wrong."

She paused. He sipped the last of his cider, ran his eyes to her prim white lace collar, over the black satin bodice sheathing a spare bosom with small and well-rounded breasts, down the loose folds of her satin dress to her small and gleaming button shoes. She was saying, "Did you hear, Mr. Locutor, about the peculiar individual that went into a lager-beer saloon in Chicago and walked out with a gallon of beer in a paper sack?"

And Wayman straight-faced, "No, Mr. Bones, would you be kind enough, Mr. Bones, to inform us what happened to this peculiar individual?"

Then Mibs in a burst of cackling laughter, "Well, Mr. Locutor, I'd be glad to tell you what happened to the gallon of beer in a paper sack —only it ain't leaked out yet!"

"Surely," said Wayman, "you don't remember all those jokes."

"Nearly all. Try me."

"What is the difference between a cat and a legal contract?"

"One has paws and claws and the other has pauses and clauses."

"Perfect—you'll do."

Mibs looked at the tall mahogany clock. "The hour hand says it is ten o'clock."

Gravely he said, "I don't know when I've had so pleasant an evening," adding with a slow dreaminess, "I could stay till the clock says midnight and I could stay on till the light through the windows said daybreak."

Monday evening he would call. Mibs stepped out on the shadowed front porch with him. He took her two hands, pressed them in a tight hold, suddenly pulled her toward him, put a light kiss on her mouth, broke away, and on the steps going down heard from her a hoarse "Goodnight."

THE NEW ERA MELTING POT

Max Mutter was long-shanked, bony, loose-limbed, hatchet-faced and hawk-nosed, halting of speech, his bulging eyes bleary and sometimes bloodshot. Yet his eyes were canny at seeing. He could go on writing an item or an editorial for the paper and carry on a conversation with someone who had come into the office without turning his face and if it was someone he knew he would call the name on hearing the voice. Into a tin box that he kept locked in the bottom drawer of his desk he put sheets of paper week after week, filled with fact, gossip, surmise, that he wouldn't have dared to publish in any of the six columns of the four pages of the weekly *New Era Enterprise*. He wrote:

> *Sunday*. Who are the two men who strode into the Presbyterian church for morning services wearing blue satin shirts? Who was the young woman of a respectable New Era family who kept turning her head and making eyes at one of the men and why did she scandalize that part of the congregation who saw her performance? Would the scandal take on a different color if

it should be generally known that the man at whom she was making eyes was entertained at supper by her parents on Saturday evening and it is known that he left their home at a late hour? Does it add interest to the affair that the young woman has earned a reputation for being a heartbreaker and has twice this year rejected the proposals of two thoroughly reputable men whom she led to her feet with her many wiles?

Max Mutter chuckled. "It is a mess of truths, half-truths. Mibs Wimbler did turn her head for a look at that fellow. I saw her do it over and again. She started it. And he didn't want to keep looking into her eyes but he couldn't help himself. She's a pretty straight girl, Mibs." And again he wrote:

Tuesday. Is the handsome stranger really a cattle-buyer for the Chicago market or is that a stall so he can stay on and make his play with the young New Era woman he has his eye on? What is there to the reports that he is a vagabond of the stage world, formerly a blackface minstrel who turned gambler and then went to the California gold fields and made a failure there? What happened on Monday evening when he went to her home for supper at six o'clock and the sounds of banjo-playing and singing came from the house and it was past midnight he returned to his room at the New Era Hotel?

Thursday. Where did our new-come cattle-buyer in the blue satin shirt stay overnight on Tuesday? Will he prove up as a cattle-buyer or is he a bilk?

Saturday. Was there ever a courtship set New Era by the ears as this one of the handsome cattle-buyer who comes here a total stranger and pays his devotions to a young woman brought here as a babe in arms who saw the town grow up on the empty prairie? Will they marry? Was there some finality about their riding their horses to a branch of Hickory Creek yesterday and in a clump of redhaws amid hazel brush making their campfire and lingering among the embers till past midnight?

Monday. Why, since it is known he was in New Era yesterday, was the abolitionist with sideburns absent from morning church services? And why likewise was the handsome cattle-buyer absent at morning services though the object of his endless attentions was there? And why, at evening services, when one appeared with his wife and the other with his inamorata, should they have discolorations and marks of heavy fist fighting on their faces?

Wednesday. Where and whither and for how long has the handsome cattle-buyer left our midst? How often has it not turned out that the handsome stranger, having had his way with the comely and juicy country girl, has not again been seen? Will he come back to New Era with nice profits from his carload of cattle? If he returns and tries to marry the girl and take her away, where would he be taking her? Was there ever a more sad-faced couple of old folks in New Era than her father and mother?

Friday. What is an editor to do when he has with care and scruples avoided mention in his paper of an affair that has shaken the town with rumors and reports yet finally the affair becomes a matter of public record when the leading man concerned, the handsome stranger, the cattle-buyer, returns from Chicago and proceeds to the county seat at Knoxville and takes out a license to marry the New Era girl he has been courting?

Having thus made a memorandum to go into his tin-box journal, Max Mutter wrote an item to go to press Saturday morning:

> A marriage license was issued at the county clerk's office in Knoxville on Thursday to Millicent Wimbler of New Era and Rodney Wayman of Atlas, Ill.

The editor gazed out at a downpour and said to himself that he must write an item about the heavy rains of the week. Out the window he saw a man pull in his horse, slide off the saddle, tie the horse at a hitching post in front of the *Enterprise* office and come in to say hello.

The man had to stop and tell Mutter the funniest thing to happen in Hickory Grove parts for a long time. After the man had gone Max Mutter wrote the item that ran in the *Enterprise* when it came off the press Saturday:

> Justice of the Peace William Orkney of Hickory Grove came to his office about ten o'clock Friday morning to learn that a couple had been in to see him to get a marriage ceremony performed. On hearing that he was at his home two miles away the couple got on their horses and rode out to his place. They missed meeting him on his way in because he stopped at a farmer's house on business. So the justice of the peace got on his horse to ride out to his home and accommodate the couple by splicing them.
>
> About halfway to his home the justice came to the bridge over Hickory Creek. For two years the bridge has been shaky and an appropriation has been made by the county board of supervisors

for a new bridge but the building of it has been put off from time to time. It interested Judge Orkney to now see that the rising, raging water of Hickory Creek had swept away the bridge.

The justice was sitting his horse in a light drizzle and figuring to himself whether it was two miles or three to the next bridge over the Hickory Creek. As he studied his predicament, he saw two horses coming down the long slope of the road, the riders walking their horses easy on account of the slippery mud and slush. As they came near he made out a man and woman, the woman in man's pants and wearing a rubber coat and a slouch hat.

They called hello to the justice and stopped their horses at the creek edge, laughing as though they were having a good time. The justice hollered back his hello. The woman hollered, "We're trying to find Mr. Orkney, the justice of the peace."

"I'm Mr. Orkney," he hollered.

"We want you to marry us," the woman hollered.

"Have you got the license?" the justice called.

"Sure we got the license," the woman laughed and hollered.

And the man fussed at his inside pocket and pulled out a paper and held his one hand over it to protect it from the drizzle.

"Read it," hollered the justice of the peace.

The man read the paper and the justice of the peace sat his horse studying. The light drizzle of rain began coming into a heavy downpour and the woman had a big smile on her face as she hollered, "Come on, Mr. Orkney, marry us right here and now and you'll never be sorry for it."

"Give me the names again," Mr. Orkney called.

The man smiled as he took out the license again and hollered the names clear and clean over the yellow roaring onrush of Hickory Creek.

The justice repeated the names twice to make sure he had them correct. Then came the voice of the justice, clear as you could ask, over the tumultuous babbling waters: "Do you, Rodney Wayman, take this woman Millicent Wimbler to be your lawful wedded wife?"

"I do," said the man as he stretched out his right hand and took hold of the woman's hand.

"And," called the justice, "do you, Millicent Wimbler, take this man Rodney Wayman to be your lawful wedded husband?"

"I do," came her sober reply.

"Then," cried the justice of the peace in a high-keyed tone, "I pronounce you man and wife and may God bless the both of you as long as you live."

Mr. Orkney was about to turn his horse and ride away when he saw the bridegroom out of the saddle, handing the reins to the woman, pick up a stone, wrap something around it and then throw it across the creek. Mr. Orkney off his horse picked it up to find a ten-dollar bill wrapped around the stone.

Mr. Orkney got on his horse, threw two kisses to the bride, and rode to Hickory Grove saying such a thing as had happened would never happen again, "Not in my lifetime."

Wet to the skin, singing in the rain, reckless and gay, the newly married couple rode their horses, with detours because of washed-out bridges, to New Era.

WAGON HONEYMOON—AND HOME TO ATLAS

In the dark before daybreak the wagon moved out of New Era on the Tuesday following the Friday that Mibs and Rod were married. There had been hours of silent picking, packing, sorting of her things to go in trunks and boxes for this sudden honeymoon trip to the home of her husband.

They had loaded the wagon the night before. Her father and mother had both held her tight in their arms and wept and she had wept with them; then Rod had held their hands and spoken words that had small crumbs of comfort. "I promise you before God I'll try to be a good and faithful husband to your precious child."

In this November before the fixed day of December 9 John Brown was to tread the gallows and meet his Maker. Omri Winwold rode home from the Atlas post office and read in four different semiweekly newspapers about the excitement South and North over John Brown.

A walk of an hour and he would sleep better. Omri walked toward Atlas, saw a fire alongside the highway. He walked toward it as slowly the fire winked away into darkness.

Omri came to where the fire had been. Nearby were two horses. Then his eyes lighted on a wagon and saw the iron rim of the left hind wheel loose, half off. Omri stooped a little and saw a man and a woman in blankets, the woman sleeping, the man open-eyed, awake and wary, low-voiced, "What do you want?" At Omri's beckoning, the man slid from between the blankets without waking the woman, a Colt six-shooter in his right hand. Omri walked to the middle of the road, the man following. Again he asked, as his right hand swung the six-shooter, "What do you want?"

"Wheel rim nearly off?" "Yes." "I live the next house, my farm, less'n a mile. We got room and could put you up tonight, if you want. Or you stay here and come morning we got breakfast for you and maybe help on the wheel."

The man put the six-shooter in his left hand, put out his right to shake with Omri, while his face broke into a big smile and in the starlight Omri could make out a line of white even teeth. "You're good for sore eyes," said the man. "I belong hereabouts. My name's Rodney Wayman. You might know my folks the other side of Atlas."

"My name is Omri Winwold. I've met your folks and I've heard of you."

"We're on a honeymoon. My wife under the wagon. Married up in Knox County ten days ago. Drove to Oquawka and took steamer and got off the landing over here this morning. If you'd come an hour sooner we'd have gone to your house for the night. I wouldn't think now of waking her."

"You're shivering, young fellow. Back to bed with your wife and come early for breakfast."

After helping Rodney Wayman and his wife to a new wagon wheel, Omri had visited them several times. Rod's father, Randolph Rutledge Wayman, was tall, cadaverous, pleasant-spoken, with an endless sense of humor, and a pride in the State of Virginia; he often seemed a Virginian rather than an Illinoisian.

Omri's keen eyes had roved over Rod and Mibs as a couple, as young persons with their wagon honeymoon over. In their house and his own, on a sleigh ride to Pittsfield and back, at a lecture in the Presbyterian church by a missionary returned from India, Omri had watched their open conversation and jokes, their covert and almost invisible signals, the curious and quietly accepted understandings between them. Though they completely disagreed in viewpoint on whether slavery was a monstrous wrong, on whether a war was coming, outside of such areas the two of them ran spiritually, mentally and temperamentally in an extraordinary harmony. And as physical mates they gave one surprise after another to Omri's searching and pondering eyes. "I'd guess it's near to the same thing Bee and I had in what few weeks she didn't have one of her spells," said Omri to himself. "Whether they walk across a room together, or she passes him the butter at table, or he helps her into her cloak, it's always got a touch of style and grace."

His fourteen months as a banjo king and soft-shoe dancer with Haverstraw's Mammoth Minstrels, with gay garrulity Rod told much of it to Mibs. Of the six months with a wagon show in California and nearly two years of prospecting and mining with Nack J. Doss, he had talked little. The memories were bitter, what with rotten food, endless hard work, ten months straight not getting a sight of one woman. Then a fight with two robbers they killed and Doss laid up and suffering six weeks with a head wound, drinking and gambling days in San Francisco when Doss won nearly as much as Rod lost; then the six-week stage trip across the plains to Illinois with something over twelve thousand dollars in gold apiece. Last year Rod with other cowmen had driven eight hundred Texas longhorns up from the Southwest, fed them for market on the Wayman farm, and said he was sure his profit ran somewhere over two thousand dollars and he needed a bookkeeper.

Of nothing else in California, it seemed, would Rod talk as freely and repeatedly as of a hard-drinking Scotch-blooded young architect whose white face had strength and valor along with his fair and girlish quality, his tall forehead with a fall of hair the color of oat straw.

"And what kind of a young woman was it that fooled him?" Rod asked. "Probably a pretty thing, very practical and cold, him on his deathbed mocking at her, 'She was chaste as the snow and when the time came she was all snow, all ice, her head, feet and bosom all snow and ice.' She thought him queer in his worship of the Arch, his never-ending quotation from away back, 'The arch never sleeps.' He oughtn't to have died. It was too soon. It'll stick with me long as I live, that boy, he wasn't much more than a boy, on a lumber bedstead with wooden slats and a straw mattress, and him saying, 'Love stands and hangs by an arch. Hate breaks the arch. The rainbow is an arch. Where you find truth, love, harmony and lasting strength, there an arch bends and curves over it as a blessing and an oath. Unity, union, you get it only with an arch. Hate and pride break the arch. Love and understanding build an unbreakable arch.' "

Omri had seen tears come to Mibs' eyes on this. "Rod loved that boy. He couldn't any more pity or blame that boy than he could himself. That boy is part of Rod now. Those moody spells of his, when he won't talk to me nor anyone, I think it's these other people alive in him and he's too near them."

A day in mid-January it was, Mibs standing at an ironing board and talking with Barbara Wayman, who was tearing a variety of cast-off clothes into strips for weaving a rag carpet, and Mibs asked what a woman generally does when she is going to have a baby. "I think it will be in August or September," said Mibs. As a phrase of sacred music to Mibs came Barbara's low voice, "That baby, my first grandchild. If it's a boy, I want him like Rod, if it's a girl, I want her like you."

EVENTS, SEASONS, A BOY BABY

The months marched on across the year of 1860. Punctuations came, days when what happened seemed like nothing before. The Winwolds and the Waymans read of national and world affairs in a Republican weekly at Pittsfield, with further details from dailies and semiweeklies out of Springfield and St. Louis.

Rod, with two other men, arrived at Atlas in mid-July with a herd of cattle from Texas, Arkansas and Missouri. He was sunburned, his wavy black hair grown long and tumbled, a little under his regular weight of a hundred and eighty pounds, hard and lean. He kept watch over the locations and feeding of the cattle for market, riding to the house two or three times daily to see Mibs, to be near her, to laugh with her, when she was in a light mood, about what was to come in August. They had their own big room at the end of the house and of evenings they brought out the two guitars they now preferred to the banjos, though there were times when a certain impetuous hammering gaiety called for the banjos.

Omri told them the first week in August, halfjoking but more in truth, "You two wind yourselves around each other singing like you do when you waltz."

"That's good for a woman to hear when she's not in waltzing trim," laughed Mibs.

Rod was helping the men put in a fence of Osage-orange hedge when he was called one afternoon in late August. At the house, though, there was nothing he could do. In the room with Mibs were a doctor and nurse, and Rod's mother. For a time Rod sat in the big living room and shut his eyes and clenched his hands as the screams came from his wife. There was a lift and an abandon to her screams. Or again they were long wavering high-pitched moans. Rod went out on the front porch and sank in a chair. Then came a series of low sobs, hushed moans scarcely reaching his ears, they were such soft quavers. He first thought she had grown weaker. Then his hands loosened a clench they were in. A grim smile came to his mouth. His lips parted to half groan in joy, "I can't be wrong. My Mibs has made a fight and she's won."

Ten minutes later his mother took him in to see Mibs, her face whiter than the pillowcase. Her eyes slowly opened to look straight into his as though on opening they couldn't have met any other eyes. Her right arm turned over with the palm up for him to say nothing for now except in the touch and hold of their two hands. He couldn't think of words, no more could she. Then they let him peep into the cradle at a bundle and his eyes got only the red raw impudent mouth and nose of the newcomer.

"A boy," came the clear whisper of his mother. And he went out and got his fourteen-foot blacksnake whip and whirled it and whanged it at anything and at nothing.

A week later, when Mibs had finished nursing the baby and laid it in the cradle and wiped the milk off its chin, she stood erect to her full height, bent her head and looked down at the little one closing its eyes in sleep. Rod came in, said nothing and joined Mibs in gazing down at the raw pink body, on this sweltering August day wearing only a diaper. "Know what it is?" said Mibs. "He's God's kiss," said Rod.

In September the marriage of Rod's brother Brock and Cedora Winwold drew the two families closer. Omri deeded a hundred-acre piece of land to the couple. For the time, for another year at least, they would live with Brock's folks because Brock now knew the run of the Wayman farm better than anyone else.

The march of the seasons went on. The leaves turned yellow and rusty, turned brown and gold, fell and scattered before wind, rain, frost. The same as any other year the leaves did this. And not the same as any other year, and not at all like any autumn before, the drama of politics was played out act by act with players and audience wondering and troubled over what next. For the first time the South had, in effect, one solid monolithic party and any rival of it unthinkable. In the North the race was between Douglas and Lincoln.

One of the two would be the next President. For the first time the Republican party marched in immense torchlight processions of citizens and voters with a new organization, the Wide-Awakes, young men uniformed and drilled, supposed to be ready for possible danger not mentioned.

The standing corn had mostly been husked, the last of the leaves blown away from ash and maple, oak and sycamore, when in November the American voter spoke. Lincoln was elected. His vote in round numbers gave him nearly a half-million more than Douglas. Ten Southern states reported no vote, not a single ballot cast, for Lincoln. The other candidates combined had nearly a million more votes than Lincoln. "We'll hear," said Omri, "that Lincoln got only a plurality and not a majority of votes. We'll hear that he's a sectional man elected by sectional votes. Which he is."

The snowfalls came that winter about like any other. Out of the same sky fell the snow and over the same land lay hushed in quiet or went whirling and wind-driven about the same as any other winter. Yet to Omri Winwold and to Mibs Wayman it wasn't the same snow and the winter had no likeness to any other they had known. The news came week by week. State by state seceded. State by state in the South called up troops, laid out money for guns and supplies, took over forts, ships, mints and other properties of the Federal Government.

"The war has begun," Omri said to himself. "The war is here. The shooting will begin soon after the new President is sworn in."

Early in March of 1861, near fourteen months ago, Rod had kissed good-by to Mibs, had thrown high in the air the baby Clayborn Joel Wayman. He was going to New Orleans for a visit, long put off, with Nack, then to Texas, where he would buy a mustang and a herd of cattle to drive North for feeding for market on their farm.

April had come, the South and North armed and marching. Nack J. Doss and Rodney Wayman took commissions as captains in the Confederate Army, little doubting, with many others, the war would be over in sixty or ninety days. A guilt lay in Rodney's mind that in those exciting weeks of drill and preparation he sent no letter to Mibs. And when one day in May he had a letter written to her, mail service North and South no longer operated.

Now in Tennessee he handed a letter to a man with family and wagon heading for Cincinnati and paid the man to see the letter

mailed in that Ohio city. He had written the news of himself, his
hope the war would end soon, then home again to see the little one
born last August.

After the terrific Shiloh battle had come his first shivers of mistrust
that the South could win the war. Dark the hour for him and Nack
when late in April came news of the forts guarding New Orleans sur-
rendered to the Union fleet and land forces. There was left the
Cause. For the Cause, for "honor," he would go on. If his name
was on some bullet of destiny marked for him he would meet it, with
only the single and bitter regret that he couldn't have had more
bright days and songs with his children and the one woman who never
faded from his visions and hopes.

The patch of white moonlight had moved off Nack's face. Rod
stepped over and knelt for a long look at the face. He wiped away a
splatter at the left temple, brushed the hair back from the forehead,
stroked the beard once. He took from the pockets a silk handkerchief
and a large bandanna. He bundled in the bandanna a wallet, a jack-
knife, a box of matches, a pipe and pouch of tobacco, a few coins, a
small round chunk of pure-gold bullion out of California days carried
as a luck piece. The watch, still ticking, he put into a vest pocket. The
associations of these familiar and sacred pocket articles somehow
threw him back to a hospital visit when Nack said, "Death is a
funny customer anyway you look at him, Charley." And now
suddenly he ran back to a sunny afternoon in California when he and
Nack had washed their only shirts and hung them to dry. He had
asked Nack, "How would you prefer to die?" And Nack had
drawled, "Since you ask me, Charley, I'll tell you. What I'd like
would be this, I'd like on my ninety-eighth birthday to be hanged
for rape."

Rod located a little depression of ground, dug out leaves and sticks
from it and heaped them at the side. He went back to the body, and
remembering a man in his company whose shoes had given out so he
fought barefoot in the big battle, Rod took off the boots and socks.
The gray uniform, others could use it, but reverence commanded
burial in it. He laid the body in the prepared place, hunted out the
silk handkerchief to cover the face, then heaped leaves, sticks, a few
handfuls of earth for ritual, then piled heavy branches over and
around. Alongside this shallow grave he slept, awoke soon and was
long in falling to sleep again. Then came a short flash of a dream
that repeated and came always the same, of a man riding a horse in

the sky straight at the sun and singing. Into the blinding inconceivable light of the sun the man rode singing and was gone.

In his added cares and duties now Omri had less time for visits and social affairs. He would have gone more often to see Mibs could his wits have devised any thoughts to comfort her. He saw her pressed and torn from many directions. She wanted the Union to win through and perhaps more yet she wanted Rod to live. Omri no longer dared to ask ever so gently, "Any news at all of Rod?" Two years now and no letter from Rod and no word from anyone who had heard of him. Omri saw one grinding twist at her heart, the fear of Rod one of the thousands shoveled into pits and graves marked Unidentified.

In former days he had seen Mrs. Wayman a light and a comfort to Mibs. Now barriers had risen between them. Could Mibs have spoken her Union feeling to her husband's mother? No—Omri was sure. Yet that feeling had somehow betrayed itself or Mrs. Wayman's intuition had read it. This was Barbara's best-beloved son gone South and no word from him in two years, along with the quixotic grief that Brock, her other son, had given his life for the Union.

Omri saw that to Mibs Rod was becoming a phantom, unreal for the present, and Mibs ready to put him in the past as one cherished and adored. He saw Mibs having only one vital consolation—the two children. The second one, born five months after Rod left in March of '61, and named Rodney Wayman Jr., had his father's black hair and jutting chin, and his mother's blue eyes. Omri saw the gay Mibs of yesterday only when the children were awake. Then she could laugh, sing, speak follies and make faces. "They'll keep her," he said. "She'll come through for all the black bats I've seen flying far back in her eyes."

BATTLE WOUNDS AND PRISON HUNGER

The soldier Rodney Wayman opened his eyes and turned them in different directions. With little moving of his stiff and sore neck and his head with a ringing pain in it, he kept looking. Now he remembered the place. This triangle of land, covered with gravel, small stones and several boulders, had seen hard fighting the day before. His company with two others had driven the enemy out of it in the morning of that day, had lost it about noon, had with reinforcements retaken it only to lose it again late in the afternoon.

Dropping his eyes he saw that his captain's coat of gray wool and the gray wool shirt underneath were gone. He let his aching head drop back on the gravel and closed his eyes. He wondered about how completely senseless he had been during the night when a coat and shirt could be pulled off him. The burning pain above the elbow of his left arm, as that arm was jerked around to get sleeves of coat and shirt loose from it, should have brought him awake. Then he remembered he had not eaten since yesterday morning. In the close fighting through midday and afternoon there hadn't been time to eat, and near sundown he fell. He could have kept his feet with his bad left arm. It was the sudden scraping grind over the left temple and alongside of the head that brought him down. He had known nothing since then from late afternoon and through the night till this gray light of daybreak. His free right hand went into a trouser pocket and found it empty. He waited for a little strength and moved his hand up over the left side of his head. He could feel the hair wet with blood. His fingers lightly traced the path of the bullet. Had the lead ball struck a quarter- or a half-inch lower he would be lying as still as those nearest him. He had come awake to shiver with cold and each shiver brought fresh pain to the left arm. He was numb, hungry, thirsty. Now that he thought of it he was thirsty more than anything else—and his canteen gone.

In a Union field hospital three days later his wounds were dressed and he heard a surgeon's judgment that he might be up and around in three or four weeks. In a Union Army hospital in Nashville he got better; riding in a railroad boxcar to Louisville two days he got worse. Three weeks in Camp Morton Hospital near Indianapolis with nourishing food and the care of an able and friendly surgeon; then Rod was taken by a guard who led him away and dropped him into the swarming slithering human mass of prisoners.

In Camp Morton prison Rod saw men slowly go to pieces in mind and behavior, little by little and day by day losing sense and feeling about what was filth. He had seen once brave men in battle feed like hogs and dip their hands over and again and eat what they picked from the swill tubs back of the hospital kitchen. Rod had joined with others to shame, cuff and beat these swill-eaters, making an example of one offender by throwing him headfirst into a barrel of swill.

The physical corruption of Camp Morton spread its odor. Enforced bodily neglect, degradation and filth gave its stench night and day. Worse yet an incessant rot played in the mind and worked at the invisible fibers of men. Prisoners of tried valor in battle combat slowly became shadows. Some turned mute, refused to talk or listen, in quiet and baffling ways went daft and somehow died, which was their goal.

Somewhere in the upper realms of the authority holding them, believed Rod and some of his intelligent companions, fraud and collusion operated by which food rations meant for them never reached them. Their hate grew ever deeper for the prison guards, men never in front-line service, lacking a sportsmanship rather common among soldiers in the field, guards known to be shirkers with political pull to keep them safe from campaign marches and firing lines.

The time was evening, just as the bugle sounded for the men to get to their bunks and before the night patrol reached the prison yard. A ditch had been dug next to the Camp Morton twenty-foot wall to keep prisoners from reaching that wall. Here men rushed to overturn a privy shed into that ditch. This made a bridge for the men who swarmed over it with ladders they raised to the top of the wall. Those ladders had been slung together in fast time that very day, from bunk planks spliced with blanket and clothing strips. While the ladders were being set up two guards fired and hit no one. The desperate prisoners below hurled stones, bottles filled with water, hunks of hardwood, that sent the guards running. By their speed, timing and wild abandon, by their cool keen preparations and their seasoned quality as soldiers, every man in the Plan got over the ditch, up the ladders and over the wall. A few were caught the next day. A few made for Canada and reached it. Most of them headed south. They had the names of towns and neighborhoods where over half the people favored any kind of an immediate peace to end the war, these people being known as Peace Democrats or Copperheads, many thousands of them members of one secret society, the Knights of the Golden Circle, or another named the Sons of Liberty. This element in Indiana had sent to the state legislature a controlling majority to block measures and proposals of the Unionist Governor of the state. Part of this element was co-operating with Confederate Army officers in Canada organizing attacks to be launched over the Canadian border on Great Lakes shipping and cities.

Into southern Indiana, sprinkled thick with Southern-blooded Confederate sympathizers, the ragged and desperate prisoners made their way, found clothes, food, hiding places for rest and going on with new strength.

Nearly half of the escaped men, in their butternut rags, with their telltale skinny bodies and staring haunted eyeballs, were brought back, sullen and worn, to the chills and vermin of Camp Morton where famished human creatures still ransacked daily the swimming particles of the hospital swill barrels.

Among the permanently missing at Camp Morton, no longer answering roll call, was Rodney Wayman. He had followed the ladder men over the privy-shed bridge. Three stones, each about the size of his fist, he had thrown at a sentry up on the wall. Two of the stones missed. The third he spit on and let go and saw it hit the left elbow of the sentry; he hoped it broke the bone. It gave him a fierce new strength to see the sentry turn and run. Up the flimsy shaking ladder he went and over the wall without time to take a farewell look at the most evil house of shame his sight and smell had ever met.

The week after the Camp Morton escape, a woman and two small children came to the officer in charge of the prison. She had a note from the Governor of Indiana attesting she was loyal to the Union cause, should be extended every courtesy and an opportunity to interview her husband, who was a prisoner.

"Mrs. Rodney Wayman," read the officer, looked up at her, and curtly, "I think I have heard the name." Then bringing a paper from a desk pigeonhole and scanning it, "Yes, the name is here, Rodney Wayman." Then he told her, brightly he believed, "Your bird has flown, madam. He departed from our hospitality a week ago, without notice or authority. As he is no longer resident here an interview with your Rebel husband is not possible."

She was dismissed. She would have liked to see the prison, perhaps talk with men who had known her husband, who could tell her how he looked and behaved. One fierce satisfaction with shivers of ecstasy ran through her—only bold unbroken men of live wit and unspent strength could have carried through such a dash for freedom.

When she arrived at the Wayman farm late the next evening a letter was handed Mibs. She opened it, read it in less than a minute, read it over and again during the evening. She slept with it in a pocket of her nightgown. It was from Rod, postmarked Cincinnati. "God leaned down and gave me a lift," he wrote. He was alive and well, would rejoin his regiment, would write her when he could, would see her when the war ended, God willing, his prayers always including her and the two little ones and his father and mother.

Mibs laughed over his being alive and well, caught his song-voice and a personal quirk of his eyes and lips in "God leaned down and gave me a lift." And she cried over how long it might be before his homecoming.

She blew out the lamp, crept between the sheets and pillowed her head with a whispered moan, "Oh God, this bed feels empty!"

NEW ERA HOMECOMING

A bloody month, May of 1864—the statistics from Virginia and Georgia battlefields a steady drip, a red drip—the open and hidden agony beyond computation or narrative. Europe looked on, wondering what the end would be. The controlling opinion of men and journals in Britain and on the Continent, as the news reached them from across the Atlantic, held to one viewpoint: if the Union armies won, America would in a long future stand as a world power, incalculable and beyond reckoning or prediction.

Omri Winwold out of his reading and thought tried to interest Mibs in the immensity of the political and military drama of the hour. She had ridden over to his farm one May afternoon for their first visit in many weeks. He could only half interest her in the national and international issues. She told him of her trip to Indianapolis and her face had a brightness, her eyes brilliant and her lips swift as he had not seen her in two years or more.

Mibs' old-time voice rippled thrushlike the simple informative sentence, "Rod is alive and well, hard as nails, a regular tiger and a fighting devil," rushing on with details of the escape from Camp Morton. The news gushed from her that a short sweet letter had come, postmarked Cincinnati. Rod was alive and heading south to join his regiment, praying for the end of the war so he could join her and the little ones—she had to share this news with Omri.

They had been standing on the front porch, overlooking an orchard and a planted cornfield, trees leafing out, the smell of fresh green earth in the air, and forty feet away four cherry trees clad in hosannahs of white blossoms. Mibs pointed to the four trees: "A year ago I was saying what do I care about them blossoms, and today they are a sacred hushed white song telling me believe believe believe." She brought her face close to Omri's in saying this. He read her as wanting a fighting chance, ground to stand on in a little daylight.

"Don't be too gay," said Omri.

Now, before going, Mibs' face and mood changed. She was traveling the next day up to New Era. Her father, restless through the first year of the war, at fifty-five years of age was commissioned in the commissary service. After Chattanooga and a long siege of malaria and typhoid, he had been furloughed home, taken to bed with a relapse, as Mibs' mother wrote.

With her two children Mibs was to have her first visit in New Era in more than four years. "Our letters got shorter and fewer these four years," said Mibs to Omri. "You know how mixed and tangled things are under the Wayman roof, some things I couldn't even tell you. How could I write them about Rod, gone for years and not a word from him? How could I write them about Rod's mother, her fine friendship with me, a beautiful and lovable woman and her mind slowly failing under the agony and inanity of the war? I couldn't have written them long-enough letters, even if there had been time, to make clear to them the miseries that aren't clear to me."

Omri walked with her, saw her mounted and riding away.

Joel Wimbler was far gone, a white shrunken face, a wasted body, when one of his pale bony hands lay in the hand of his daughter. Most of his hair had fallen away. She had to search his face for what she had known there. The high moment for all in the house was the wan queer smile at his lips and eyes as his right hand held first one and then the other of the hands of his two grandsons. He died with his mind hazy, too weak for words.

It smote Mibs, and her conscience wrangled with her as she saw the white thin war face of her mother. The old-time still look, inner peace with herself while the world went by, now had the pinch of pain. Not even the grandchildren could give her ease or comfort, it seemed. "I heard they were born and they were boys and that was all," she said once to Mibs. She saw her mother at times a sort of ghost, bones clothed with a weary and withered flesh. Once when tears came and she had lain down alongside her mother and tried to put an arm under her mother's head, she felt her arm gently pushed away and no words why. From day to day for a week after her father died, Mibs was going to say good-by and leave with the two children. Something told her from day to day not to go.

On the sixth day the mother's only words were, "I don't want to live. I think I began dying when you left us. I did die when Joel died, only you haven't buried me yet." The next day a doctor was there with Mibs and they saw Brooksany Wimbler give her last breath. And there had been one brief moment of wakefulness when her eyes opened in quiet, when Mibs saw again the old still look on the mouth and the words came that pierced Mibs, melted and shook her, the words along with a soft hand taking Mibs' hand, "I don't blame you, darling, you had to, and I love you all."

She was leaving New Era because it would hurt to stay, though she knew very well that in Atlas too it would be hard going. She visited with only a few.

Abolitionist Hornsby Meadows stood out as the New Era hero. Dispatches mentioned the bold attacks, hard riding and endurance under fire, of his cavalry regiment. He seemed to have a high record in the army for the number of enemy troops he had personally sabered to death. "I don't know what to think when I hear of the chances he takes," said his wife Fidelia to Mibs. "Sometimes I wish he wasn't so much of a hero. By his letters I can tell he enjoys the war and he is glad he lived to see the war come."

The two women talked long. They had mutual travail, griefs, doubts. Each went to bed at night and got up in the morning wondering how and where was the husband. As Mibs was leaving, their arms went about each other and their cheeks pressed in low moan and dry sob.

Mibs' hand was on the doorknob. Again she was about to go. Fidelia was saying, "What's that you're wearing there, around your neck?"

"In a leather trunk my father made, I found it at the bottom, under letters, papers, keepsakes. Years ago I saw it and it didn't mean anything to me and I clean forgot it." They stepped to a window in the sitting room, Mibs loosened a silver cord at her neck and held in the clear daylight a bronze plaque. Together they read the words:

The Four Stumbling Blocks to Truth

1. The influence of fragile or unworthy authority.
2. Custom.
3. The imperfection of undisciplined senses.
4. Concealment of ignorance by ostentation of seeming wisdom.

THE DEEPER SORROW THAT HAS FORGOTTEN HOW TO WEEP

The annual return, the airy and mystic float of dogwood and shad-blow in blossom, had come to Virginia in 1864 in the old merry month of May—and two armies set for a clutch at each other seeking a stranglehold.

The battles of the Wilderness and Spotsylvania Courthouse rolled up the most terrible cost in dead, wounded, missing, that any modern war in Europe or America had seen. In smoke, fog and rain sagged the battle lines. No one could tell the entire dripping and crimson tale of the thousands of individual combats, struggles, sacrifices, acts of devotion or fear, that composed the battle drama as a whole.

To Rod this Virginia battle was like Chickamauga, his men driven back, firing from behind trees, from behind logs and stumps, out of thickets where they hugged the ground. Reinforcements came and orders to charge. They swept over the clearing and into its bordering woods. It was here that Rod lay with six men behind a protective log. He asked for volunteers to run for a thicket forty yards toward the enemy line. One man made it. A second one made it. The third one fell halfway. The other three hesitated. Rod said, "I'll make it, and then you come."

He had made nearly thirty yards when he stopped with a jolt. He spun round, slowly and dizzily, and sank into a mass of dwarf juniper. Vaguely, dimly, he knew of a burn and a gash running along the jaw and the right side of his face.

Hours later, before opening his eyes, he caught the smell of hay, of cattle and horses. And sounds came to his ears, voices somewhat hushed, curious confusions of feet, wheels, horses. He opened his eyes on a large barn. He lay with straw between him and bare ground, in a wide aisle between stalls on both sides, haymows above the stall rows. On both sides of the aisle lay lines of men with their feet toward each other, enough space between the feet for litter-bearers. He gave a slow sidewise turn of his head toward the right. He forgot the surges of pain in bone, flesh and nerves as his eyes roved the officer in blue next to him. The broad round shoulders and thick arms were familiar. So was the profile of the head. And the sideburns triangular and pointed, the wide positive mouth and the strong nose— there could be no mistake. Out of New Era days—abolitionist Hornsby Meadows it was. So long ago now seemed their fight over politics, with the gossips wondering if Mibs' rejection of Hornsby might not have been a factor. The moans of the man were a kind of breathing for the relief of pain; they were no call for pity.

Rod wasn't sure but the man was in mild delirium. He stared over the haymow opposite and with half-choked sounds tried to sing the lines, "In the beauty of the lilies Christ was born across the sea. . . ."

The words came blurred. He turned his head and looked at Rod. "Shot in the lungs, sir, shot in the stomach," and as his eyes gathered the gray uniform coat of Rod he added, "Compliments of the Southern Confederacy, sir." His eyes opened wider, the brown eyebrows lifting ever so slightly, and now he was saying a little above a whisper and the words clear, "Where have I seen you?"

"Long ago, before the war."

"I remember, I tried to kill you with my bare hands."

"Man, don't think about that now."

"You married Mibs Wimbler?"

"Yes."

"Will you tell her I forgive her?" Rod saw the man's eyes go glassy and his two hands come folded near the hole in his lungs, and then in a dim sigh the words, "Tell her I forgive all."

Rod spoke slowly and thickly the words "I'll tell her, I'll tell her." And he knew the man didn't hear his words and the man lay beyond whispers or thunder.

Captain Rodney Wayman of the new arrivals at Johnson's Island prison off Sandusky, Ohio, was a prison veteran. The other prison was for the Confederate rank and file. This one was for commissioned officers of the Confederate Army. Excellent care they had given him in a northern Virginia hospital where the bullet wound on the jaw and the right side of the face had slowly healed and left a five-inch scar, a red line that curved over the jaw in a fishhook shape. His ragged uniform with six bullet holes in it, a few pocket articles, a blanket—these were his slim possessions.

It lay in his calculations that Mibs, with others, should they learn where he was, would try to get him out. On this point he had fear. And the fear had an added hold on him because of his weakened body. Sometimes his hands trembled, chills came, then a sweat.

He wrote Mibs one six-line letter, then tore it up, in fear of he knew not what, for he had ended, "I have known the sorrow of endless tears and the deeper sorrow that has forgotten how to weep."

He was spending more time in his bunk, half awake, half alive in meaningless reverie. His leg scurvy got no better, his mouth sores grew worse. One week a dream came two nights straight. He lay in a four-poster mahogany bed between sheets of fresh white linen. He saw a white shape enter the room through the door without opening it. This white shape began moving toward him gliding rather than walking. At the door, before gliding through, she turned and spoke to him in quavers of low wailing: "Four years thy feet have wandered, Charley Amberson, four pitiless years, Charley Amberson, consider there is such a garment they call love, Charley Amberson, beware of a burnt garment and the bitter ashes of love, Charley Amberson." He woke from the dream and could sleep no more.

He was startled one day passing a nearly finished barracks house where two carpenters were hanging a door. The face of one of them was familiar. He couldn't place it. He came back, went up close to the man, then walked away. Now he was sure; the face was that of a brother of Ed Houseworth, the Atlas storekeeper. Alfred Houseworth—everybody called him Al—was a good carpenter when he worked but he was known as easygoing and would lay off work for spells of hard drinking.

The next day Rod's feet strayed again for another look at Al Houseworth. He saw Al lay down a scantling and look up to say, "Was you ever in Atlas, Illinois?" It was a pleasant question. It warmed Rod. He answered, "That's supposed to be my home."

"Ever hear of a fellow named Houseworth there, Ed Houseworth?"

"You're his brother Al; we met in his store a couple of times."

"I heard about your goin South to fight. You've had hard times."

"I'm hoping you don't tell them you saw me here."

"Why not?"

"Because I'd just as soon not have 'em know I'm here."

"If they knowed you was here they'd help you, wouldn't they? Maybe they'd get you out of here."

"I wouldn't want 'em to get me out of here till the war's over."

"Sounds queer, but there's a lot of queer things in a war. Tell you what—"

"Yes."

"If I write any letters back there I won't tell 'em about you."

"I'll thank you to say nothing, I'll appreciate it."

"All right, Mr. Wayman, Captain Wayman. I'll keep mum but it looks foolish to me."

A week later when another carpenter told Rod that Al Houseworth had been furloughed home with disability, Rod could only speculate and guess. He couldn't know that in the decrees of circumstance, so often whimsical and sometimes terrific, Al Houseworth held a long session and spent a pleasant afternoon in the Wayman farmhouse with three persons. They were fascinated with what came from his testifying lips. They poured for him from a bottle of old

Monongahela whisky. Mr. Wayman poured. So did Omri and Mibs. They kept at him and had him repeat more than once every scrap of a word that had come from Rod. There were days Rod couldn't walk, yet there could be thanks he was still alive. The high point of truth and fact stood forth that after the four long years of hazard he was not dead. And Omri saw the pallor of Mibs turn whiter when Al said, "He's thin, what they call *gant*. I couldn't help sayin after a second long look at him, 'Why, it'd take two of you to throw a shadow.' "

Two civilians from Sandusky, one of them a United States Marshal, came to him and said they had orders and he would go with them. Rod was a little sullen and somewhat suspicious when they put a round black sealskin cap on his head, had him step into overshoes, had him slide into a cowhide overcoat heavy with a hairy warmth. They led him to a small rowboat mounted on runners, had him climb in, and they walked alongside as two soldiers pulled the vehicle over the ice to the Sandusky shore. They walked him the few blocks to a wooden frame building, the New York Central Railroad station. There, in the waiting room, they handed him over to a woman, the Marshal saying to her, "Here's your man and now you take good care of him."

She was in a cloak of blue wool and a blue wool cap. He was encased in the wide loose-hanging stiff cowhide overcoat. Their arms went around each other but it wasn't a real hug. The two long kisses on the mouth had more reality. Yet they were weird kisses. Both knew that in the former days they kissed as equals, as partners strong and matched for kissing. Now it was she alone who had strength and blood.

In his eyes she saw deep in the sockets a dim lurking flame. That was as good to her eyes as any kiss he could now give her. He was still a fighter. Though far spent he was no beaten man. He would mock at himself. She knew that. She would expect it. Mockery at himself would be his resource and weapon.

She had seen, in a flashing instant, the five-inch fishhook scar of red on his right jaw. She wouldn't ask about that now. His hands that trembled so as he held hers and that went on trembling after she let them go, she wouldn't mention either for a long time.

"Mibs, my Mibs" were the only words that came from him after her cry of "Rod!" He sank to a bench under the weight of his overcoat and a kind of thunder pulsing in his wrists and forehead temples.

A little strength came and she heard his hoarse whisper, "The children—tell me."

"The one you've never seen is named Rodney Wayman Jr., and has your black wavy hair. And Clayborn Joel, he's strong, lusty, all you could ask."

"That's enough. Let me dream about it." And he leaned his head back on the bench and folded his hands that Mibs noticed had become quiet. As her eyes now really caught his hands of skin-and-bone fingers—telling her the whole frame of him was little more than skin and bone—the tears came and she wiped them away and clenched her own hands and set her teeth in a resolve she mustn't cry again.

The cast-iron coal stove nearby glowed a rusty red. "Never so warm since last summer," said Rod as he rose. She helped him out of the heavy cowhide overcoat and he sank on the bench again, laying aside his sealskin cap. Several bystanders, also waiting for the westbound train, began eying him as Mibs herself for the first time gathered the gray uniform, ragged, patched, stained, grease-spotted, creased from head to toe, a bullet hole at one shoulder, a bullet hole in one sleeve—his only suit of clothes reporting by its surface signs that he had for months worn it every day and slept in it every night.

The black dank beard of him covered a face too fine to hide; Mibs didn't want those ugly hairs over his mouth, the subtle corners of it. The hair of his head she noticed as limp and matted, the old waviness gone, and when she saw on the right side of the upper forehead the beginning of a scar and a line, an indentation of the hair over that line, a shudder ran through her. Heavy trouble, deep sorrow, had been her portion. What he had shared was Agony, firsthand, raw, wild, fleeting, credible only to those who were part of the events. In this last he would be to her, in degree, a Stranger, for all time. And it gave her no care. For his wounds, for the limp she had seen as he came into the station, for his tremulous hands, for his shattered skin-and-bone body, she had a sacred regard and a depth of reverence she believed would carry them through.

The smooth clean skin of her face—he had not been close to anything quite like it in a long time. She was pale and there were plain furrows of care at chin and nostril and her black dress he sensed as very sober and proper. A half-inch strip of lace at the top of her collar caught his eyes that moved to her white neck. He had forgotten that any neck anywhere could be so clean. His eyes moved over her face again wondering how skin could be so clean and smooth. Hairy faces, chapped and pitted faces, here and there scurvy faces with running sores—he had been so near them as company night and day that now it was a revelation and a luxury to look at these unspoiled unspotted smooth-flowing cheeks and chin.

She held his right hand, saw his eyes open and heard his husky and throaty "You're good for sore eyes, Mibs, my Mibs." She waited and heard him, "One thing—tell me—how did you get me out?—I hope it was clean."

"You're an exchanged prisoner. You walked out today because down South somewhere another man as far gone as you walked out to go home to his people."

"But they stopped exchanging prisoners a year ago." And she could see he paused to summon strength to say what was for him hard to say. "Don't you know I wanted no special favor?"

"I knew it well." She pressed his hand. "I sorrowed over it and I revered you for it." Then she too had to pause and summon strength for what was not easy to say to him at this moment. "Do you wish now to go back to Johnson's Island so that a man let out of Andersonville Prison in Georgia today must go back to Andersonville?" She felt his bony fingers press hers. And she was saying, "We reach Chicago tonight. Tomorrow night you're home with Clayborn Joel, and Rodney Jr. you've never seen; you'll have every comfort and put meat on your bones in no time." She saw a slight shrug at his spare-boned shoulders. "How do you feel about it?"

His hands trembled again and he stared at the coal stove. "Mibs, I'm just one of God's mistakes. I feel like a rat, since you ask, like a privy rat." She searched his face. He didn't look at her and went on. "They were killing them over on the Island—killing them to eat— not a rat left on the Island." He turned to find her anxious eyes searching his. "Mibs," he went on, "do you know I'm so dirty I'll wash and wash and I'll never be clean again, it won't come off?"

She had expected this mockery. And she exulted, for no one else on earth could have caught as she did a thin edge of trifling in his tone, a vagrant humor that told her he was no hopeless case.

"I'll do the washing, my lord and master. I'll see to the washing myself. I'll get you out of your clothes and put you into that big tin bathtub full of hot water. I'll do the scrubbing and when I'm through you'll laugh and say you're clean all over."

For the first time he now smiled and she saw two teeth gone near one mouth corner. She helped him to the door of the men's closet, heard his patient, "I'm what they call a chronic case."

In the further waiting before the train came in, Mibs noticed Rod

indifferent to the curiosity-gazers. A dozen or so of people seemed
spellbound in their interest. Here was a piece of the war. Here was a
wreck out of the well-known war. Men and women peered at this
specimen, this fish out of the brine of war. And the specimen went
along as though he had learned much about what is called privacy
and among the least of his personal needs was the right to seclusion.

The train came in. The seats up near the stove at the end of the car
were filled. Rod kept his overcoat on. Mibs had him lay his head on
her shoulder a good part of the time and she saw him sleep an hour.

They stayed overnight in Chicago at the Briggs House. They ar-
rived after dark the next night at the Wayman farmhouse near Atlas.

Rod made slow gains. A sickish yellow tint in his skin took on
more of white and pink, at times. On some days his mildewed look
was gone. Mibs had burned his clothes with their filth. She had per-
sonally scrubbed his body in hot baths and he had admitted, "Yes,
I'm clean now," though later she heard from him, "It may be I won't
feel clean till the memory is gone."

Slowly by weeks the dysentery had left Rod. But the hand tremors
kept coming back. He would knock over the pepper reaching for the
salt. The red five-inch fishhook scar on his right jaw Mibs studied
many a time with infinite thanks the bullet had not plowed into
mouth, nose or an eye.

One fact stood out. Mibs flung it gaily and daily at Rod. Every
week he gained weight. From a hundred and fifteen pounds in Feb-
ruary he went to a hundred and thirty-two in the first week of April.
"The scales tell it," she warbled at him. "We'll be singing and waltz-
ing again this summer."

Then from Rod a flow of speech came in a slow measured drawl,
as though out of long thoughts and as though the two of them were
one and had ahead of them all the time there is: "Sometime I'll tell
you about the Union people of East Tennessee, about women who
learned how to kill in cold blood, about an ambrotype of a girl in
my coat pocket and why I couldn't give it to her, Shiloh and the
night march in mud and the wounded in wagons with rain and hail
on them, how Doss died and what a man he was—Chickamauga,
Camp Morton and the escape, fighting at the Wilderness, Spotsyl-
vania and Hornsby Meadows dying next to me in an old barn with a
message he forgives you all—malaria and then the ride to Johnson's
Island—how God leaned down and brought you to me—how many

times I lost everything but you and one thin sliver of shimmering light and that was my pride in the Lost Cause. My faith in that cause has been hammered on brutal and awful anvils, shot and burnt in the smoke and steel of a thousand battlefields from the Potomac to the Rio Grande. But that pride lives, a bond between men who can never forget what they went through together. I have them and I have you and the two of God's kisses."

She had him lie down, with her alongside, a blanket over them. He closed his eyes and one hand sought hers. She looked from his face out the window to the hemlock tree and its evergreen and five stars fixed over it and beyond that a baby moon, a silver slipper of a moon.

THE ARCH NEVER SLEEPS

Mibs read the news to Rod in April of the surrender at Appomattox, a few days later of the assassination of the President in Washington. Omri read for them a paragraph from the dead President's Second Inaugural:

" 'Neither party expected for the war the magnitude or the duration which it has already attained. Neither anticipated that the cause of the conflict might cease with, or even before, the conflict itself should cease. Each looked for an easier triumph, and a result less fundamental and astounding. Both read the same Bible, and pray to the same God; and each invokes his aid against the other. It may seem strange that any men should dare to ask a just God's assistance in wringing their bread from the sweat of other men's faces; but let us judge not, that we be not judged. The prayers of both could not be answered—that of neither has been answered fully. The Almighty has his own purposes.' "

Rod was shut-mouthed for two days. Then Mibs heard him for the first time singing clear-voiced, full-voiced. They took up two guitars and sang together "In the Bright Mohawk Valley."

A great grief had hung over the land since April 14, the night it was said there was blood on the moon. The tolling of bells, the muffled boom of cannon and minute guns, had marked moments of ceremonial. There had been lashing rains and the red gold of rolling prairie sunsets and great bonfires lighting the sky while crowds stood with uncovered heads to see a coffin pass in the night.

Mibs had slept lightly. She saw the moon go down and the sky left in the keep of quiet stars.

She woke Rod. They hitched a span of horses, put a valise and a basket of food in the buggy and took to the roads. Along the roads two and three hours before sunrise they passed or they followed other rigs. There were buggies, wagons, gigs, horsemen—by the hundreds moving in the night toward one point, one center—by the thousands they saw them as they neared Springfield an hour or so after sunrise.

They stood in line at the state capitol building, ahead of them thousands of city and country folk. It had been so all night long and all of the morning and afternoon of the day before—thousands waiting in line and moving on for a look at the face in the coffin. That final look itself, the moment or two of gazing at an embalmed body amid heaped fragrance of blossoms, what the eye caught and kept was less in itself than the ritual act of being present and paying silent salutation.

They followed the cortege and procession to a burial vault and stood on a green hillside and heard prayers, hymns, the reading by a Methodist bishop of the Second Inaugural.

Rod and Mibs took turns driving home, sleeping and driving by turns, saying little, saying almost nothing, brushing shoulders, snuggling close at times.

The moon rode white in a silver haze. Past midnight they neared Atlas and home. Rod came out of a short sleep and a long silence to say, "Mibs, do you know—"

"Yes, Rod?"

"I love the old Union, I believe I do truly love the old Union."

"Yes."

"But we won't talk about it. And, Mibs, old girl—"

"Yes, young feller?"

"Been thinking about one letter you never got. You know how it ended?"

"About time you were telling me."

" 'I went out and counted the stars. Every star I counted had your name on it. Does that make sense?' "

"Are you talking or was that the letter?"

"That was the letter."

She had him say it again. She pulled to the side of the road, made him throw back his head and count stars. She dropped the reins. She took his head between her hands and gave him long soft kisses on mouth and eyes.

The horses began moving on a slow walk. They knew it was time to go home. Mibs snatched the reins and put them on a slow trot.

One summer day when apple blossoms were flagrant and luminous in whitening the air the news came. The commander of the Army of Northern Virginia, an idolized figure and a man of few words, had as a paroled soldier applied for a pardon that gave him full restoration of his rights as a citizen of the United States.

Rod learned of the advice of his old commander: "Our returned soldiers must all set to work, and if they cannot do what they prefer, do what they can. They must put themselves in a position to take part in government and not to be deterred by obstacles in their way. There is much to be done which they only can do."

Rod and Mibs drove to the courthouse in Pittsfield, had his signed application for pardon made correctly, and sent on to Washington. Driving home they went out of their way to stop at the Winwold house. Omri ran fingers through his snow-white muffler beard, slanted an eye at Mibs, said he had heard her tell it but now for once he would like to hear from Rod about the San Francisco boy, the young architect.

"He was pure Scotch, as I understand," said Omri. "A woman had fooled him and failed him and he drank hard. He quoted that ancient line, 'The arch never sleeps.' Then he went farther. That's what I'd like to hear from you, Rod."

Rod stood up. It made him restless to remember it. He leaned against a porch post. "The arch never sleeps. When the arch holds, all else holds. Love stands and hangs by an arch. Hate breaks the arch. The rainbow is an arch. Where you find truth, love, harmony and lasting strength, an arch bends and curves over it as a blessing and an oath. Unity, union, you get it only with an arch. Hate and pride break arches. Love and understanding build unbreakable arches."

They drove away, Mibs at the reins. Rod said, "They're a beautiful couple, Omri and his wife."

"Yes, but their waltzing days are over."

"And who wants to waltz life away?"

"I do. I want a thousand waltzes with you I've missed."

"You can have 'em—since we're good waltzers."

"Good? We're the best in the United States."

"The whole world, you could have said." And he pulled a tassel of hair down over her ear. "The whole world—why not?"

Mibs turned her head with her eyes slanted at Rod. "Yes, darling, always and ever when you and I see the whole world through the same arch."

EPILOGUE

PETE AND ANN: EVENING OF MIST

The woman in the taxicab watched the raindrops splashing on the skylight glass roof, a September rain, the year 1943. She saw the blowing sheets slow down to a gray drizzle. Her eyes turned toward a man dashing from the front entrance of the Veterans' Hospital. She swung the cab door open and when he had leaped in and closed the door, their arms went around each other.

Of the fourteen million American men and boys who had gone into the Second World War, the one in captain's uniform alongside her was the one she preferred to see this day in her Army Nurse uniform. Now they sat holding hands, once in a while fingers gently pressing, looking at each other with sidelong glances, occasionally turning a head for a full open-eyed gaze, one at the other. He had telephoned to his sister the message for her, "Of course I'd like to see Ann but I couldn't talk. There's little to say." He saw her underweight yet stocky of build, her black hair falling in locks and strands of movement around her ears, a face of natural pallor, eyes that on second look were a deep brown almost black, a mouth of mournful lips slow in breaking into a smile.

She saw him perhaps twenty or thirty pounds under his normal two hundred, and six feet two, bony shoulders, his uniform coat loose on him. His chest was still hairy, came one sudden random thought to her, as in days when they had gone swimming together. Her eyes fell on the back of his hairy left hand and one finger with a thickened knuckle joint—she had seen him make the flying tackle which broke that finger.

Now after three years of not seeing him she believed he could be, as before, sudden and casual—like herself. He had been stringing along that last college year with two other girls besides herself when one night he suddenly told her, "You're the one and only for me."

Then her soft laugh, "I won't have to think it over."

They made no plans, no pledges. He handed her a thin silver ring saying, "It don't mean a thing but sometime if the cards come up right maybe we'll go in for wedding bells." As she slipped the ring on her finger she gave him her gayest laugh, "You mean nobody's plighting no troths today." That was all. He had been sudden and casual about going into the Army without telling her beforehand. And as she looked back now she was hazy about how and why she had drifted into training and become an Army Nurse—and the letters between them had been few and rather factual, more informative than romantic.

She had deep curiosity, a few slight misgivings, and nothing at all like fear about the present and temporary arrangement of the large blue goggles he wore, with wide flesh-tinted temple pieces running back to the ears, and the well-made mask rather marvelously simulating his nose and fitted so smoothly on the upper lip and the face contours that your eyes couldn't detect the edges of it. She rambled swiftly in memories of him, of how changeable she had seen him, of how there was no telling when next you met him whether he would be high and proud or low and humble.

The taxi rolled along Henry Hudson Parkway and their eyes caught a long bridge in thin evening mist. There was a level horizontal line picked off in parallels of light. There were dangling loops of light, quiet yellow dots on faint blue fog, saying, "A bridge, if you wish to cross a river this night."

"Nice, hey, Pete?" with a sweep of her hand toward the bridge.

"I like it, purty."

He had, in the old days, usually said "purty" for "pretty." Now it was more like "kurty," somewhat like an amateur ventriloquist speaking for the dummy on his knees. He couldn't make his lower lip muscles do what he wanted them to do.

Walking out of the Blue Dipper after the show Ann clung to Pete's arm and liked it. On the street a drizzle of rain came cool and pleasant on her face. They waited a minute or two for a taxi. "You smell that rain?" she asked.

"It's good, I like it." And she knew the feel of that film-drifting drizzle pleased him more than the floor show, more than the drinks and the float of faces and the gabble and the crowd starting to dance and the jangle of the swing orchestra.

In the taxi on the way to her apartment, Pete said nothing. To the sudden and vehement outburst that came from her he answered with pressure from his large-knuckled right hand in hers. It poured from her in a hoarse fury with some of her syllables in cool black velvet.

"Yes," she began. "Yes, I guess so. Those faces, those dancers pro-
tecting themselves from the war—a chill kept creeping over me and
I was saying to myself, 'Oh, God, this isn't new, it goes with every
war.' It's old, so old you wonder how old it can be and whether it
goes back to Cain and Abel. These people with satisfied faces taking
the war as a thing far away somewhere, never real to them till it
shatters their own doorways and blows them into the street with
ashes in their hair and mouths, blood streaking their white faces and
oozing bellies."

His hand tightened on hers. For a moment it shot pain to her
knuckle joints. He knew she was near tears. They rode in silence,
each aware of only dry tears, his hand saying, as she believed, "You
haven't told the half of it; it can't be told." Then her voice sharply,
gutturally, "Nice people, their names get in the papers as nice people.
They keep the war far away. They know the war is not nice. The
nearer you get to the real thing it stinks with the stink of death and
the boys in the dark crying, Medic! Medic! They don't want to smell
it or hear it and they guard their minds and imaginations against it.
They have worked out a technique of mentally holding their noses
and stopping their ears so the war will always be far away."

His hand in hers again brought pain to the knuckles. After another
silence she mumbled, "I won't go on, Pete. I had to get that load off
my mind." They rode to the apartment building where Ann was stay-
ing. They could see through the revolving door the night elevator
man with his eyes on them. Pete pressed her hands in his, leaned close
to her face. "Good night, Ann, it was worth the time." He made no
move to kiss her, though she believed he at least half wanted to. And
she came near reaching her lips toward him.

She held back believing he would rather she didn't. She went
through the revolving door with a "Sweet good night and sweet
dreams, Pete." She stood inside and watched him, saw him turn and
look toward her in his trench coat, his cap visor gleaming over the big
blue goggles. She saw him wave to her; she waved back, saw him
enter the taxi. As it pulled away he threw her a kiss. She threw him
one and blew with her lips out on the opened palm of her right hand
toward him.

The elevator man in a dark-blue uniform coat spoke easy as he
pulled a lever and the car started, "He was in the war?"

They reached the sixth floor. She was getting out when she
answered, casual as he had been, "Yes, he was in the war."

*

At Bryn Mawr, Ann and her roommate Maria Enders, Pete's sister, had written for the college paper, played with short-story writing and poems. With two years in the Army she had forgotten about writing, many weeks too rushed in duties for letter-writing. Now her mind played with an unwritten dispatch about herself which might have run:

London—Ann Flaherty, 24, daughter of a Chicago paving contractor, a Bryn Mawr graduate, will be on a plane for the United States this week on indefinite leave from her duties as a nurse. "It will be sort of homelike on the plane," she said. "I served as a nurse on six flights ferrying wounded to England and carrying medical supplies on return flights. Now I am under orders to keep to my berth and rest and get healed." She was in a plane loaded with hospital supplies that crashed. They lifted her out of a burning plane and after giving her first aid put her on another plane. "I didn't know what happened," she said, "and the first split second when I came to I thought I was still on the plane that crashed. Then several bright and curious pains began reminding me something had happened and I didn't know what it was till they told me."

Her own little story ran smoother as reading than that of Captain Peter Enders, thought Ann. It might run in part like this, as Ann spoke it in low tones in a voice just above a whisper:

"Captain Peter Enders of the —th Army, —th Regiment, in an operation in Sicily took a hand with men of his company in several vivid exploits. Interviewed in an English hospital he told of his Lieutenant Jacob Zinski leading a platoon up a mountain slope in search for land mines and booby traps. Two explosions lighted the night darkness, followed by enemy fire from machine-gun nests.

"Half the platoon came crawling back on their hands and knees. One reported to Captain Enders, 'Jake is out there!' and the two crept out, zigzagged on their bellies, 'chancing we might help him,' said the Captain. They crawled over slippery bodies of men still warm and the life breath gone. They came to three men in a pile, two of them fallen across Jake's body.

"They bent and crouched low carrying back to their lines Jake's body, a torso with one arm and a head still attached to it.

" 'The same day, in a house that had served as enemy head-quarters, we saw an officer sit down in a chair and in two seconds every stitch of clothing blown off him and burns all over him with only a fair chance he would live,' " said Captain Enders.

" 'Two days later it was I opened the door of a village house, as I had opened the doors of four other houses that day to talk with people living there. In this house the people had gone away. We believed it some kind of a hideout. Two of us jammed our shoulders against the door and broke the lock. The blast that came killed the other man. He was between me and the main force of the explosion. The next I knew I was in the hospital with a face full of shell fragments. Beyond that I don't care to speak.' "

Ann turned off the light, spoke softly to herself. "Yes, beyond that you don't care to speak. You haven't told me a word of it and I still have the ring you gave me and I don't wear it because you say you'd rather I didn't. But you told your story to your sister, and she told me."

JUSTICE WINDOM'S SEALED ENVELOPE

At Hopecrest, where the shadow and voice of the old Justice still lingered in hallways and rooms, the days went by with a strange quality of fury and quiet intermingled for Raymond, the grandson of Justice Orville Brand Windom, and his wife Maria Enders Windom, known to her familiars as Mimah. The wide-fronted, two-story stone house, the large wooded yard with its spread of old oaks and elms and its clump of Scotch pines, the rugged boulder tall as the old Justice himself and wider than it was high, which he had named Remembrance Rock—these led toward quiet. The overhead drone of transport planes and bomber formations, the solemn and implicative newspaper headlines, the broadcasts and announcements pouring from radio sets in relation to mankind's first truly global war—these made the brutal music of the fury of the world storm.

In this mingled quiet and fury Ray and Mimah had read aloud to each other from day to day the long manuscript of Justice Windom, written to them and for them, Books One, Two, Three—the earliest colonists three hundred years ago grappling with a vast naked un-tamed continent; Lexington, the Declaration of Independence, Valley Forge and the works and self-denials of great men with an utter and complete faith in the American Republic they were founding; the windings of doom, strife and prayer out of which came the amalgamated American Union of States fated to become a world power.

Before and after their daily readings, sometimes as an interruption, came the terrific bulletins, from the colossal and almost incredible Normandy beachheads through the fights and marches across France and the Low Countries into Germany itself, umbrellas of thousands of planes, airborne troops in co-ordination with pronged tank attacks and the ever-advancing masses of infantry, this in the west of Europe while on the eastern front day by day and mile by mile the Red Army pressed the invaders of Russia back toward their Faderland.

At the bottom of the box they found a sealed envelope with instructions they should open it after reading Books One, Two, Three. Breaking the envelope they read:

My dear children: You have now made with me the long journey of the time of America in the making. You have glimpsed at what America has cost.

Live with these faces out of the past of America and you find lessons. America as a great world power must confront colossal and staggering problems. Reckoning on ever-fresh visions, as in the past, she will come through, she cannot fail. If she forgets where she came from, if the people lose sight of what brought them along, if she listens to the deniers and mockers, then will begin the rot and dissolution.

The hard beginnings, the chaotic obstacles of days when the Republic seemed lost, these must be remembered. To lose them is to lose the Republic.

The day has come for you to know more about Remembrance Rock. It is, as I often told you, a place to come and remember. I am not sure why I was sensitive about it and held back from telling you what has been placed under the Rock for remembrance's sake.

First to go under the Rock was a handful of dust from Plymouth, Massachusetts. Alongside it was placed a Colonial silver snuffbox filled with earth from Valley Forge. Next came a little box of soil from Cemetery Ridge at Gettysburg where my father fought, and side by side with that a handful of dust from the Argonne in France near where my son fell in a La Fayette Escadrille plane.

Now I would request of you that you add to these little sacred deposits some of the rainbow-tinted sand that Ray sent to Mimah from a South Pacific island, adding to it a little black volcanic ash from another island taken at high cost. Perhaps to this last you could add a handful of earth from ground in Italy or France where Mimah's brother Pete shared with his comrades in struggle or sacrifice. I would suggest that this humble and private ceremonial, as between ourselves, be performed on some day shortly after the end of the war. You may use as you please a tiny object, a sacred relic, which I have enclosed in a flat metal-and-leather case at the bottom of the box which I request you do not open till the day of the ceremonial.

And now please know this is not my final word to you. One further memorandum for you I have given to an old and valued friend. What he brings you at the war's end is my last testament and I pray God keep you.

Ray's face changed. He rose, not a word to her, walked out of the room. From a window later Mimah saw him walking around Remembrance Rock, bareheaded, then standing before it a long while, hands in his two back trouser pockets, his elbows triangled back. Not long after, he lay flat on the grass, face down, a late September sunlight falling through yellow afternoon haze. She smiled to herself, shook her head and smiled. Ray was gaining on himself. He was loosening his thongs. Bowbong had reached into him. So had Remembrance Rock and its dream dust.

WHEREIN THE LONELY SPEAK

Pete had come to Hopecrest for the week end. He sat in the library with Ray and Mimah in the early afternoon listening to a news broadcast. Then he walked with a fine easy deliberation to a window that looked out toward Remembrance Rock. Mimah had read to him Bowbong's memorandum about the memorial dust under the boulder. Pete at the window stood motionless, composed, his hands folded in front of him. Mimah's love of her brother was made of both adoration and reverence and she saw him now as a still image that could be struck into bronze. Years there had been when her love for him included considerable intimate understanding. Now she acknowledged that since his return from the war he was beyond her fathoming. She could see certain dark new strengths and she was afraid they might be too stark and ruthless. She was sure he had no slightest vestige of pity for himself. She had seen his composure and peculiar poise, usually having a definite element of warmth rather than cold, act as a tonic and serving health to the mind and will of Ray, who once said, "There are times Pete is good for me like Bowbong was."

As her eyes ranged him there at the window she flashed to old days when he had kicked, passed, or run with a pigskin ball down a field and stadium crowds had yelled themselves wild and his helmeted face with a handsome grin had been spread two columns wide in newspapers the country over. That seemed to her now hundreds of years ago. Not until this morning had he shown her his face before his adjustment of the mask and goggles. He had put her fingers to his chin where a shell fragment had torn flesh and bone loose, a new chin of metal and plastics replacing the old one. He would be returning to the Valley Forge surgeons for months to come in the slow rebuilding of the lower part of the nose and small sections of cartilage in the upper part.

The sister smiled and laughed when her brother did and she was certain he didn't guess that she went straight to her room and stood at a window looking toward Remembrance Rock and burst into tears, shook with sobs, then clenched her hands, dried her tears, said to herself aloud, "What kind of a fool am I to be weeping? Why should the sister of that kind of a man be crying?" Then she went down to breakfast and neither Pete nor Ray had ever seen her at once so beautifully gay and solemn.

Later that morning alone with Pete she had said to him, "Ann phoned me today. She'll be out late this afternoon." "Yes?" drawled Pete. And Mimah softly, "When I think about you and her I can't help feeling she's got what you need."

And Mimah was amazed at what shook loose from him in a low-toned outburst roused by her few innocent words. "Yes, a dogface like me ought to be living next to her to offer his mouth to her sweet lips. Yes, I should make her life a mess. She can do better than hook up with me. She's got everything. I'm plain nothing wrapped carefully in nothing and the loose ends tucked in. She's keen with a wild streak in her I love down to my toes. I can't do it. She'll get a man that's all there, his face in one piece. I'd rather she hate me for all time than drag her into a mess. Tell her I said so."

Ann came into the room with Ray. She and Mimah put their arms around each other, Mimah laughing a merry greeting, Ann murmur-

ing something in low contralto, a little somber, the words not clear.
She wore a light gray-blue wool suit, the jacket widely parted show-
ing a white sharkskin blouse, its row of white buttons running high
to the throat, the curves of her full bosom and strong shoulders set
off with grace.

Pete stood looking out the window. Ray and Mimah fussed around
in small talk for several minutes before Pete turned and walked with
slow ease to Ann, took her hand and said, "Good to see you, Ann."
She held his hand, "Lovely to be with you, Pete," peering at the blue
goggles, trying to fathom what could be lurking in the small light-
hazel eyes behind those goggles.

They took chairs and listened to a broadcast from London. Pete
had met the news commentator, a North Dakota- and Minnesota-
raised boy, of Norwegian parents, a man troubled about humanity
and the present global war and the possible next global war. Ever
probing, questioning, unblinking, he was relentless:

> The soldier knows the real story of the war; he feels it sharply,
> but he couldn't tell it to you himself. . . . The war treats no
> two exactly alike; and so even two soldiers from the same front
> sometimes don't understand each what the other is talking
> about. . . .
>
> This war must be seen to be believed, but it must be lived to
> be understood. We can tell you only of events, of what men do.
> We cannot really tell you how or why they do it. We can see,
> and tell you, that this war is brutalizing some among your sons
> and yet ennobling others. We can tell you very little more.
>
> War happens inside a man. It happens to one man alone. It can
> never be communicated. That is the tragedy—and perhaps the
> blessing.

There was more and the broadcast ended. The words had sunk
deep. There was silence, faces seeking faces.

Ann at last moved slowly, her face serene as she walked with an
easy slouch toward Pete and pulled a chair alongside his. Having
seated herself she glanced sidewise toward him. He half stooped for-
ward, scrunched his shoulders, bent his head and gave her a long up-
ward gaze through the goggles. She turned her head away as though
she didn't care to meet this twist of his or perhaps as though pre-
ferring to act as if he were not there. Then she couldn't help herself.
She gave her eyes to him. She gave him beseeching black eyes. He

began speaking low-voiced, slow. "Did you hear what that fellow was saying from London? Did I get him right, did you?"

"He was saying you know what you went through, but we don't."

"No, he said it different and he said it better. You didn't listen. Tell me more he said." There was almost a touch of impudence in his tone. Ann covered her face with her hands. "Let me think."

"You don't have to think, I'll tell you."

Ray looked with curiosity at Pete, Mimah with anxiety. They watched the very deliberate Pete put a faraway gaze toward the window; he gave the impression that what he was to say had its origins beyond this room. He pursed his lips and the words dropped slow with an exceptional clarity for him. " 'War happens inside a man. It happens to one man alone.' " He turned toward Ann, again with scrunched shoulders, the head bent and looking upward into her face. " 'It can never be communicated.' "

After a long searching look into Ann's face Pete straightened, turned the line of his goggles toward the window and the far outside world again and very slowly, " 'That is the tragedy—and perhaps the blessing.' " Pete rose casually from his chair, stood before Ann, took her head between his two hands, bent toward her, his palms at her temples, his fingers moving in her hair, saying with tension and in a half-whisper, " 'War happens inside a man. It happens to him alone. It can never be communicated.' "

She was white-faced, with swift blinking eyes. He held her so a moment. Then he let go and sauntered to the door; he stood in the doorway perhaps a half-minute while his goggles moved as though his eyes behind them swept the room. Then he stepped away into the hall. The moment his shoulders faded at the doorway Ann turned to Mimah in a sharp moan, "Did he know me? Do you think he knows me?"

They turned to hear him as he stood in the doorway and there was pain in his cry, "Does he know you? Of course he knows you. He knows you're Ann Flaherty and you've got the face God gave you. He knows Ann Flaherty one time was going to marry him. And he knows and she knows it's off, it's all off, it's gone and clean-gone."

Then days went by and weeks moved into months and the great clock of the war ticked off deaths and dooms by the millions and it was far into the next year before Pete and Ann met again.

BRIGHT WONDER AND A DARK PRIDE

The four walked to Hopecrest, Pete alongside of Ray, Mimah up ahead with Ann. It was the evening of V-E Day, the war in Europe ended.

Ann told Mimah, "I'm not sure I would have come if I had heard Pete was coming."

"You're taking it hard, Ann."

"Does he say anything about me?"

"He's the same. Models himself on the Chesapeake Bay clam. Not a word from him, not since long months ago when he said he adores you so completely he can't think of living with you because you're so wonderful."

"I'll wait a little longer. If it doesn't clear up I'll clear out. He's got some disease of conscience, I guess. That's what I say anyhow. And maybe mine is sick too and I ought to tell you and him more than I do."

At Hopecrest Pete stood alongside Ann at a tall window and looked toward the fresh floodlights blacked out more than three years till this night. "I could wish I was back on one of those planes," said Ann to Pete, "bringing water to one basket case, fixing the pus drain of another, getting morphine for a boy crying to his mother he was lonely. If you were on that plane, you'd let me do something for you."

"When we used to talk about getting married I could look you in the face and tell you to look me in the face."

"Why not try and see? Trying won't hurt. You'll never hear a whimper out of me. Can't you see that?"

Pete sipped the last of his Scotch and soda, toyed with the glass in his two hands, looked into her face and eyes, and she would have liked desperately to pierce through the blue goggles and see what could be moving in his eyes. "It's too complicated. Sometimes I think I'm coming out of it. If and when I do I'll tell you."

Her mind wasn't on her drink. She had sipped about a fourth of her glass. She was saying, "So that's the way we stand?"

Later, after the final movement of a symphony on the radio, they sat in unbroken silence. Then Pete rose, stood before Ann, took her head between his two hands, gave a gentle slap to one side of her face and then to the other. "Stick around, little girl. We might be chums yet. God only knows. I'm putting it up to God. You better do the same." He walked to the doorway, turned and stood facing them. They all rose. Pete was saying, "It's bedtime for me. Good night."

Ann fell on Mimah's shoulder, laid her head there. "Help me to stick around like he says." She was sobbing. "Help me. You heard him, didn't you? We might be chums yet. He said it like that. We might be chums yet, God only knows." Later they called a taxi for her.

She would breakfast with her father, a Chicago politician and man of affairs whose fortune of a half million or so had come in part from street-paving contracts along with selling coal to the city. His heart rich and warm toward his daughter, she barely hinted to him of her main grief and he read her, "It's trouble of the heart y've got, Ann." If it was money she needed for any wish of her heart she could draw on him for any amount, he let her know.

Out at Hopecrest Mimah didn't sleep so good, her mind on Ann having said, "Maybe I ought to tell you and Pete more than I do," her mind on the bright wonder and dark pride of Ann's voice.

DREAM NIGHT AT HOPECREST

August 6, 1945, and four hundred planes swept over southern Kyushu of Japan, their bombs shattering the munition plants of Tarumizu. On the same day, a lone Superfortress over the coast of Honshu turned in its course to cross its target, a city of three hundred and forty-three thousand people—and let go one bomb. Down the skyway the bomb started while the Superfortress crew followed instructions, "Scram! Get the hell out of here!" The seconds passed, fifty-two seconds exactly—then the bomb went off. In a quiet flash more dazzling than sunlight it broke over the city of three hundred and forty-three thousand people. A column, a cloud, an umbrella of dust, smoke and chaos, rose, mushroomed and spread. Two-thirds of the city of Hiroshima laid level and wiped out in wreck and ruin, the human corpses seventy thousand, the sick, wounded and disabled twice as many as the dead—this foreshadowed what?

The Japanese surrendered. The people's V-J Day came August 14. Nils Rolstadt, the Danish physicist, telephoned Ray and Mimah he was coming over to see them. He arrived and handed Ray the memorandum entrusted to him by Bowbong. Ray glanced at the paper and put it in Mimah's hands. She read aloud:

"Dearest Ray and Mimah—You have heard. The news has come. You and Ray share it. You watch its awful impact. Now you see the human family moves out into a fresh adventure. Will it end in a smoking day of doom or a bright dawn of promise?

"In the changed world you now enter, my children, armies and navies as we have known them will vanish. The science of mass manslaughter will be statistical and in split seconds, now you see a city and now you don't.

"And in this possible next war, incalculable in speed and finality, the brave man vanishes, the action ending before he has a chance to be brave—valiant and coward, women and babies, sick or idiot, strong heart and faint, go down in one wide kinship of annihilation.

"My friend Rolstadt told me of this event while it was preparing. He can tell you of round-the-earth rockets, of cosmic-ray experiments, of biological warfare, each as ghastly in its potentials as the Atomic Bomb.

"Indeed a changed world you enter, my young dear ones. Now a war can begin before it is declared. When the blights and epidemics commence and the crops fail and the deaths run into millions it will be understood the next war has begun with no certainty who has begun it. To this have we come."

Rolstadt was hearing this for the first time. "I brought this paper to you sealed as he gave it to me. I hear Bowbong's voice in it."
Mimah read on:

"Man goes on, my loved ones. Man does not stop. Often I heard Rolstadt, 'Man is a changer. God made him a changer.' It is within possibility that you, my dear ones—you may become the witnesses of the finest and brightest era known to mankind. You shall have music, the nations over the globe shall have music, music instead of murder. It is possible. That is my hope and prayer—for you and for the nations. Now I bid you farewell and say Amen."

Then came his bold sweeping signature in full, Orville Brand Windom.

Pete came in. His usual slouch had an added easier roll to it. Mimah said, "You're not jingled, but you *are* feeling pretty good. I asked

Ann; she'll be in soon. She's staying overnight. Says she might be heading for a job in Chicago or on the West Coast next week."

"Maybe for the best." And Pete was casual as before.

Mimah heard the doorbell, met Ann in the hall, and told her of Pete's face. "Twenty-eight operations in two years, Ann. And now nearly as good as new. He showed me today. A few weeks, he says, and the mask and goggles come off."

"God, that's lovely to hear," came Ann's throaty whisper. "We can see his eyes again."

Ann entered the room, nodded to Ray and Rolstadt, took a chair next to Pete, whose goggles seemed to move in slow ranges over Ann from head to hips to knees to toes. Pete mumbled a vague something. Ann was going to ask him to repeat but let it pass. She looked translucent as a blue cloud, her face smooth as a white pebble under clear running water, wearing a light-blue gown that held the snug and even flow of her curves from shoulders to knees.

Rolstadt rose to go. To Ray he said, "Bowbong talked about you the last time I saw him. I think you know what he said." In the momentary smile on Ray's face Mimah could see a clean bright boyish streak out of earlier days.

Through the evening it wasn't easy for the two couples. Pete seemed the least troubled of the four. Ray had begun to join Mimah in her feeling that Pete was making his break with Ann too hard for her. They were afraid they caught a touch of the wanton and cruel in his casual manner toward her.

With a grumbled and half-defiant good night, Pete at the door of his room said to Mimah, "If I ever marry, and no matter who, I will live alone and so will she. I think I'm learning to live alone and like it."

Mimah knocked softly on the door of Ann's room at seven-thirty in the morning. Hearing Ann's voice, "Come in," she opened the door. She kissed Ann, sat on the bed and heard Ann tell a dream of herself lying on the grass with Pete in a warm sun before Remembrance Rock. Then it seemed the Rock gave birth to a big basket of birds it had held locked and waiting, juncos, wrens, redwings, scarlet tanagers, cardinals, the robin, the grosbeak, the catbird, garrulous bluejays, yellow canaries, unknown uncanny scavenger birds, two large lugubrious crows, kingfishers, teal, herons and cranes, white gulls, homing pigeons, a pair of mocking birds gushing and trilling, and two lovebirds blue-white-and-red that sat a moment one on Pete's shoulder and one on Ann's before their wings fluttered and took off and away into the thin silver-white flimmer of the cloud shawl.

They sat staring at the Rock. They had seen it tremble as it opened and shook loose one of its many secrets; now again it stood locked, silent, inscrutable. Ann turned to Pete, a shudder running through her, "Is the show over?" And Pete's voice came casual, offhand, baffling again, even cold, "The show's over."

Ann said to Mimah, "I woke up crying. For weeks I haven't cried, thought I had hold of myself. I head for Chicago tomorrow. Back home with father for a while, then maybe a job on the West Coast, far from here."

Mimah sat on the bed, hunting for words to console, to heal. The words wouldn't come. A film of tears blurred her eyes. She lay down and threw her arm around Ann and they held each other. Ann broke away with a little laugh, pushed away sheet and blanket, jumped to the floor, and scampered to the bathroom.

Mimah waited, plucked at vague figures on a spread. Then she saw Ann come out of the bathroom carrying her pajamas, hanging them in a clothes closet and walking to throw on the bed her underthings, stockings, blouse, and skirt for the day. Mimah leaped off the bed, stood before Ann, startled and wide-eyed, her eyes dropping from Ann's face and then shifting, scared and blinking, over Ann's scrawled body, shoulders to knees. "Ann, you should have told me." The words seemed to choke and gag in her throat. "Good God, my sweet old friend, you should have told me."

"A hell of a thing to tell," said Ann with a cool smile. "A woman's a woman." And Ann was less cool and her full lips trembled as she took note of a flash of storm-green in the blue eyes of her old chum. By that flash of sea-tint she knew that a whirlwind of mixed anger, love and pity raged in Mimah.

Ann dressed. They went to breakfast. They saw Pete off for a consultation with his favorite Valley Forge surgeon, who was in Washington for the day. "Ann leaves with her father for Chicago tomorrow," Mimah had said to Pete, who was nearly gay in his answer, "We'll make it a farewell party this afternoon."

Morning passed into afternoon. Pete and Ann sat on a davenport at a window corner overlooking the big rear yard. Ray and Mimah drove away for an hour, returned to see bottles of bourbon, fizz water and ginger ale on the table before Pete and Ann. They put on records; Mimah hovered and flitted about, trying not to seem nosy, yet under her poised exterior anxious and shaken over whether a final farewell afternoon was on between Pete and Ann. She noticed Ann pouring smaller and fewer than Pete with the bourbon and Pete mildly jingled taking his liquor straight. She couldn't make out what Ann was hearing from Pete's mildly lush tongue, "Love is where two people smash into each other with the idea two bare legs and toes to toes makes a marriage, which it don't." With a pathetic boozy animation Pete was saying, "Love is where two people are hungry for something they don't know what it is but they're going to find out and when they do it's something else again." Pete thought this was keen and gave it the approval of such a smile as his not yet fully recovered face muscles would permit. Ann replied with a sad mouth, "Love is where two people lie and lie to each other about how much they mean to each other and when they run out of lies they put their love in a little coffin and bury it." Ann knew that it was Pete's un-fathomable bitterness rather than the straight bourbon that brought her reply.

What-all passed between them Mimah would like to know. Each guess Mimah made had a hurt in it. Five o'clock had come with lingering sun slants through the window when she coaxed Pete to go upstairs. She put him to bed to sleep it off. At seven she went to call him for dinner. She shook him awake, came in later when he had washed, dressed and adjusted his mask and goggles. Then she spoke to him, low-toned yet command in her tone: "Pete, if you believe I ever loved you so much as a little finger, listen to me. It's Ann. I saw her this morning in her room. For the first time since the Bryn Mawr days, I saw her naked, but not as God made her. All over that curved beautiful body of hers to her knees, she's scars. Neck to knees long sweeping crisscross scars, crazy red and white spots, splotches of scars. Shoulders to hips, breasts to knees—scars and red splotches, I swear. The plane she was on in Africa crashed. We heard that. We didn't get it clear. It caught fire. She was lifted out of that plane on fire. For weeks she had hell. Not enough whole skin left on her for grafting. You know the new skin grafted on has to come from the person burned."

"You're telling me, where I been!"

"Forgive me, Pete, I'm telling it the best I can. You know, of course, they could have taken the skin off her face, but that wouldn't have been enough to do any good."

"Besides making a difference with her face."

"She's haunted about you. You lost what she didn't. You both lost, but it's about even—she's a woman. Can you think at all, Pete, about what I'm telling you?"

"What I think comes easier than it did."

"You know one thing you and Ann have together?"

"Like what?"

"No gripes, both of you game, marvelous what you take in your stride. I've never seen anything like it. Ray says the two of you do him good, away inside help him."

She could feel her heart slump. Then her heart came back. She mustn't try to read him. She doubted whether at high moments he could read himself. It could be too that he had learned certain controls. And she must hold to the idea that what was going on far inside of him was a secret to which he had a right. She rebuked herself for what there was of unfair prying in her attempt to get what was hidden under the icy echoes in his "Thanks, Mimah. Thanks a million."

Dinner saw Pete sober, inscrutable, near wordless, his goggles often pointed toward Ann and held long. Pete sat mute except once when Ann quoted some surgeon, "How tight to tie sutures is a matter of experience, I try to err on the loose side," and Pete kept mumbling, "Err on the loose side, is that so?"

Soon after dinner came Ann's taxi. "I'll put her in," said Pete. When after a few minutes, he returned to the living room, Mimah asked, "What was the last you said when you put her in the cab?"

"Good night, Ann, it was worth the time—like that."

"Will you write to her?"

"Could be. I might."

DREAMDUST AND LOVE

At Remembrance Rock at high noon they laid in metal-bottomed crevices the little prepared copper boxes—gravel from Sicily, sand from Utah Beach on the Normandy coast, rainbow-tinted sand from a coral atoll in the South Pacific, harsh black volcanic ash from Okinawa. They packed in soil at the base of the boulder, leaving no sign of the sacred receptacle underneath.

They stood by, hands folded in front of them, keeping a silence during one minute of sacramental time. They were Captain Raymond Windom and his wife Maria Enders Windom, Captain Peter Enders and five friends. What the group had done was their private affair, in an intimacy of fellowship that belonged to them alone.

They walked to the house in a quiet sunfall of early autumn, faint streaks of brown and gold, sudden spots of yellow and crimson, in the air the unseen feet of the yearly return of falltime.

Ray, Mimah and Rolstadt in the living room heard Pete in the hallway calling, "Hey, you!" five or six times.

They heard feet on the stairs. They saw entering the room, arm in arm, Pete and Ann Flaherty.

The pair stood before the surprised others. From Pete came the serious words, "How do we look? Would you say we look like a couple, fair enough?" Mimah's heart missed a beat, her eyes falling on Ann's left hand wearing a long-absent and nigh-forgotten silver ring.

"Captain Enders," broke in Ray, "with all due respect, what the hell's been going on here?"

"You request a report, Captain Windom. Then Captain Enders begs to submit the information that early yesterday morning his conscience lay heavy on him and his memory twisted inside of him with a blue and lonesome pain he couldn't stand. He put in a telephone call to Chicago for Miss Ann Flaherty. She caught a plane for Philadelphia. She went off the deep end and got married, hitched and spliced forever to Captain Enders, each of them duly showing their dogtags to the justice of the peace. They began their honeymoon in the Ben Franklin Hotel registered as Captain and Mrs. Pete Enders. From the window of her room here Mrs. Enders saw the ceremony at Remembrance Rock. Now soon the bride and groom are going out to the Rock and watch birds come flying out of it, a thousand birds fluttering and circling in a spiral up to the blue yonder."

"Before you go," said Ray, "join with us in the last thing Bowbong asked us to share with him."

Ray opened the small flat metal-and-leather packet from the bottom of the box. It held a bronze plaque with a silver neck chain. They read the plaque—the words of Roger Bacon seven centuries ago:

The Four Stumbling Blocks to Truth

1. The influence of fragile or unworthy authority.
2. Custom.
3. The imperfection of undisciplined senses.
4. Concealment of ignorance by ostentation of seeming wisdom.

It passed from hand to hand. Ray read it aloud, then handed it to Mimah. Mimah fixed the clasps of it around Ann's neck, saying gravely, "You wear it one year and I'll wear it the next." Ann couldn't hold back the tears.

Pete said low-toned to Mimah, "I can't tell her what the chemist said to his wife: 'Go ahead and cry! What are your tears? A moderate percentage of phosphate salts, a touch of sodium chloride and the rest is all water, just plain water.' "

On seating themselves for lunch and raising their glasses of Burgundy, Ray spoke toasts. And when Ray later said to Mimah, as between them, "You seem to be glad from your shining hair clean down to your fast and wicked feet," Mimah said, "I am," and again went back to Mary Windling in 1608: "My feet may go to hell though my soul will not follow my feet. The good Lord should not have made my feet so glad."

Ann Flaherty Enders at the other side of Ray had heard. She smiled to Mimah. "Say it again, for me, to Pete," which Mimah did.

Then Mimah gave the toast of Mary Windling in 1608: "To the storms to come and the stars coming after the storm."

Autobiographer

Carl Sandburg

Photograph by Edward Steichen   *Courtesy of* U.S. Camera

Montage late September 1939 on completion of writing the four-volume
Abraham Lincoln: The War Years

Born in Illinois of Swedish Immigrant Parents

Photograph by Paula Steichen Sandburg

With his mother in 1926

Married to Lilian Paula Steichen in Milwaukee, Wisconsin, 1908

Photograph by Edward Steichen

Mr. and Mrs.—the Sandburgs in 1920

Recognized as a Poet
Chicago Poems, 1916

Photograph by Edward Steichen

"Meanly Done" by Ivan Opffer

Vanity Fair, 1920. Courtesy of Ivan Opffer

THE "CHICAGO" POET.

CARL SANDBURG.

A BRAVE FIREMAN THIS IS HOW HE EARNED HIS TUITION AT COLLEGE

THE PRIMITIVE URGE IN SUMMER HE WANTS TO WIND A RED HANDKER-CHIEF AROUND HIS NECK AND JUMP A RATTLER

CARL SANDBURG HE ENTERTAINS A GROUP OF ADMIR-ING FRIENDS

Courtesy of the Chicago Daily News

Storyteller for Children

The Rootabaga stories were written for daughters Margaret, Janet, and Helga

With Helga (left) and Janet (right), 1921   *Photograph by Edward Steichen*

Wide World Photos, 1945

The two new stories herein were first told to grandchildren Karlen Paula and John Carl

Established as a Biographer
Abraham Lincoln: The Prairie Years, 1926

At time of publication

Photograph by Dana Steichen

With Lloyd Lewis, the one man with whom he most enjoyed singing duo

Singer and Song-Seeker
Songs gathered in roving over America were presented in *The American Songbag,* 1927

Welcoming help from guitarist Andrés Segovia, whom he reveres

Photographs by Robert Buchbinder, 1938

Pulitzer Prize Winner for History, 1940
Abraham Lincoln: The War Years

Lincoln life mask by Volk and Carl Sandburg's hand

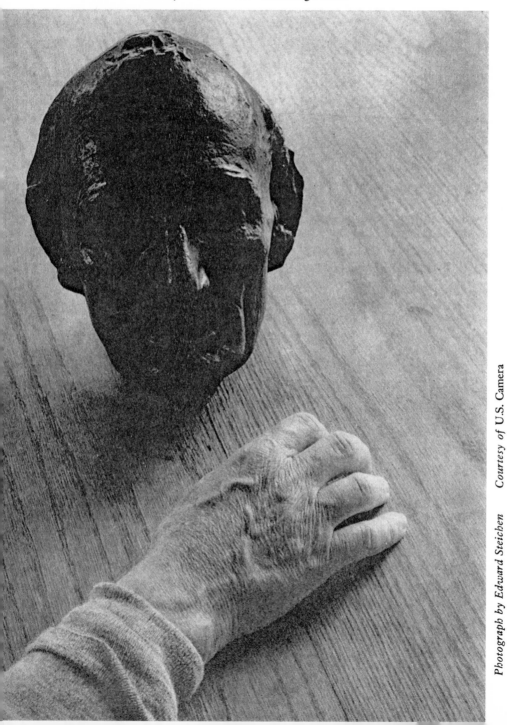

Certain cartoonists paid salutations   *C. D. Batchelor in the New York* Sunday News

Fitzpatrick in the St. Louis Post-Dispatch

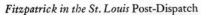

CARL SANDBURG LOOKS HOMEWARD.

Photograph by D. J. Russell

With Governor Henry Horner of Illinois (left) and ex-Governor John Winant of New Hampshire (right) at Knox College Centennial, Galesburg, Illinois, 1937

Photograph by Dr. I. W. Schmidt

As narrator of Aaron Copland's "A Lincoln Portrait," he rehearses with André Kostelanetz, who conducted the performance of the work by the New York Philharmonic

Sculpture by Jo Davidson, 1939   *Photograph by Alexander Alland*

The Sandburgs in 1942

Outside the barn that housed their Chikaming herd of goats at Harbert, Michigan

On the Lake Michigan dunes
holding a Nubian kid

Photograph by Edward Steichen

Recent Years

With (left to right) Edward Steichen, Allan Nevins, Fanny Butcher, Ralph Newman (partially hidden) at 75th birthday celebration in Chicago, 1953

Douglas Southall Freeman made the presentation of the Gold Medal for History and Biography awarded by The American Academy of Arts and Letters, 1952

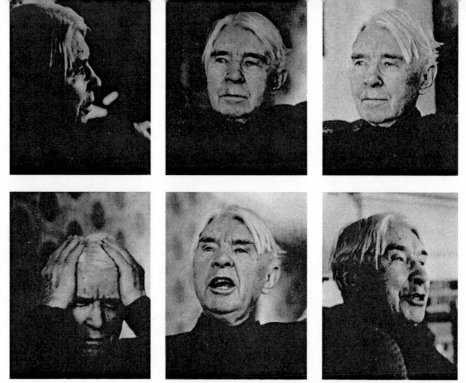

Wisconsin State Journal *photographs by Ed Stein*

Meeting reporters three hours in the home of William T. Evjue, Madison, 1956

In Chicago, 1957 *Photograph by Harry Callahan*

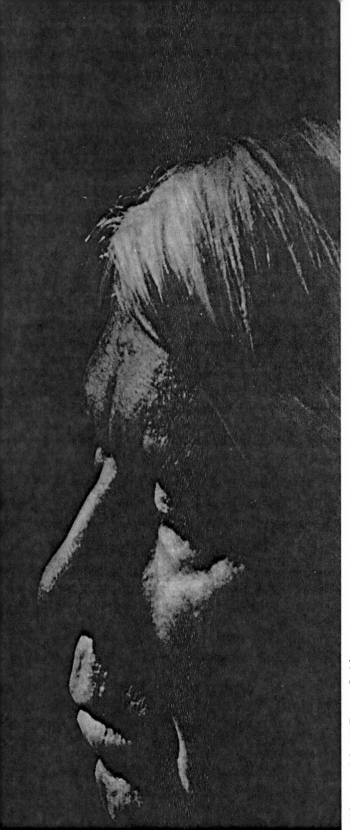

Creative Solitude

"There is such a thing as creative solitude—a certain kind of loneliness out of which have risen the works of the creative spirits of the past. They were not afraid of being alone; they had learned how to use their loneliness."

Photograph by W. Eugene Smith

Publication of Always the Young Strangers *on January 6, 1953, marked Carl Sandburg's seventy-fifth birthday. This is his own story of the first twenty-one years of his life, a volume that John K. Hutchens in the New York* Herald Tribune Book Review *called "a memorable American autobiography that superbly recaptures the boyhood of the artist Carl Sandburg became, that fondly but truly paints the portrait of a prairie town in a time long gone." Robert E. Sherwood, in the New York* Times Book Review *felt "compelled to put my neck in the noose with the statement that* Always the Young Strangers *is, to me, the best autobiography ever written by an American. . . . By striving to tell no more than an intensely personal story, Sandburg has achieved the universality of a Pilgrim's Progress."*

Approximately ten per cent of the book is represented in this sketch of the young Carl Sandburg growing up in Galesburg, Illinois.

Always the Young Strangers

MAN-CHILD

A big unseen bell goes "Bong!" Knots come loose, long-woven bonds break from their folds and clutches. "It is my time now," says the mother while tugs and struggles in her womb say, "My time too has come." There is a tearing asunder of every last hold and bond, the violence of leaving the nine-month home to enter a second and vastly larger home. In the mother and the child the crashes and explosions go on, a series leading to the final expulsion. Not till then can there be a birth certificate, a name and a christening, a savage small mouth tugging at pink nipples.

In my case the announcement came, "*Det är en pojke*," the Swedish for "It is a boy." The first baby, some three years earlier, was my sister Mary. They wanted a boy. I was a welcome man-child.

My father was a "black Swede," his hair straight and black, his eyes black with a hint of brown, eyes rather deep-set in the bone, and the skin crinkled with his smile or laugh. He was somewhat below medium height, weighing about a hundred and forty-eight, well muscled, the skin of his chest showing a pale white against the grime when his collar was turned down. No sports interested him, though he did make a genuine sport of work that needed to be done. He was at the C.B.&Q. blacksmith shop, rated as "a helper," the year round, with no vacations, leaving home at six forty-five in the morning, walking to arrive at the Q. shop at seven, never late, mauling away at engine and car parts till twelve noon. He walked home, ate the noon "dinner," walked back to the shop to begin work at one and go on till the six o'clock whistle. Then he stood sledge alongside anvil and walked home.

His hands thick with calluses, he was strictly "a horny-handed son of toil." It would take him ten or fifteen minutes to get the soot and grime off hands, face, and neck. He poured the cistern rain water from a tin pail into a tin basin on a washstand, twice throwing the used water into a tin pail on the floor before the final delicious rinsing at a third basin of the water that had run off the roof into the cistern. The calluses inside his hands were intricate with hollows and fissures. To dig out the black grit from the deep cracks took longer than any part of the washing. Even then there were black lines of smudge that failed to come out. Then came supper and often his favorite meat, pork chops fried well done. In late spring, summer, and early fall, he would often work in the garden till after dark, more than one night in October picking tomatoes and digging potatoes by the light of a moon. In the colder months he always found something to fix or improve in walls, floors, chairs, tables, the stove, the coal shed, the cistern, the pump. He liked to sew patches on his jeans pants or his work coat, having his own strong thread and large needle for replacing lost buttons. In those early years he read a weekly paper from Chicago, *Hemlandet*, the Swedish for Homeland. Regularly he or the mother read aloud, to each other and the children, from the Swedish Bible.

And the mother, young Clara Mathilda Anderson who had married my father, what was she like? She had fair hair, between blond and brown—the color of oat straw just before the sun tans it—eyes light-blue, the skin white as fresh linen by candlelight, the mouth for smiling. She had ten smiles for us to one from our father. Her nose was recessive, retroussé, not snub. Her full and rich white breasts— how can I forget them, having seen the babies one by one, year on year, nursing at them, having seen her leave the washtub to take up a crying child and feed it and go back to the washtub? She was five feet five inches in height, weighing perhaps one hundred and forty, tireless muscles on her bones, tireless about her housework. She did the cooking, washing, sewing, bedmaking, and house cleaning for the family of nine persons. At six o'clock in the morning she was up to get breakfast for her man, later breakfast for the children, and meals for all again at noon and at evening. Always there were clothes to be patched, the boys sometimes wearing out a third seat of trousers and having the other kids hollering, when the shirttail stuck out, "There's a letter in the post office for you!" As we got into long pants, the knees always needed patching. Playing marbles in the spring, wrestling, and scuffling, we wore holes at the knees of pants, going bare at the knees till "Mama" patched them. That was always our name for her when we spoke to her or of her in the family circle. The father always called her "Clara," spoken in Swedish as "Klawrah."

*

Of the house where I was born I remember nothing. This was a three-room frame house on Third Street, the second house east of the Chicago, Burlington & Quincy Railroad tracks, in Galesburg, Illinois. The date was January 6, 1878. A few years later we moved to another three-room one-story house, on the north side of South Street, three doors west of Pearl.

Two memories of the little South Street house stand clear. On a Sunday John Krans and his wife drove into town from their thirty-acre farm seven miles out of Galesburg. They went to Lutheran church services with my father and mother and drove back to our house for a dinner of fried chicken, mashed potatoes, and gravy. I, still wearing dresses and about three years old, stood at the back door and watched John Krans snap a halter to the bit of one of the horses and tie the halter to the pump. Then Mr. Krans came into the house, gave me a pat on the head, and began talking with the folks. I stood watching that team of farm work horses, well-matched iron-grays hitched to a farmer's light market wagon. Then it happened. On a sudden impulse, I ran out to the pump, got my hands on the halter and pulled it loose. I climbed up a wheel and got myself onto the seat. I had the reins in my hands—oh glory! I was going to call "Giddap" to the horses. Then my father and Mr. Krans came rushing out of the house. They had me hauled down from that wagon in a flash. Then came a scolding and reproaches. I was ashamed because I couldn't explain. I felt guilty of doing something terribly foolish. The horses were facing the garden, which was no place to take a pleasant Sunday drive.

The second memory is of late summer. South Street was dusty. The black dirt had been ground fine by wheels and horseshoes over many days of dry weather. I was standing in the middle of the street. Along the wooden sidewalk across the street from our house came a Negro woman known as Mammy Lewis. She was the first woman of black skin I had ever seen and a few days before I had heard neighbor boys older than I hooting at her. Now she was walking along with long slow steps, looking straight ahead. Standing there with bare feet in street dust, I poked my head toward Mammy Lewis and called in my loudest jeering child voice "Nigger! Nigger! Nigger!" Mammy Lewis, a servant woman of good reputation, as I later came to know well, stopped and turned slowly to see who could be so mean and low as to cry like that at her on a sunny summer morning. We were about twenty feet apart. I could see her eyes glisten. I heard her voice, a marvelously deep harsh contralto. And she was saying words that came slow and clear and made me know her dignity and her righteous anger. She was saying, "I'll get a pair of scissors and cut your ears off!" I heard her. I believed her. I picked up my feet and scampered breathless into our house and clutched my mother's skirts. That morning I didn't dare tell my mother what had happened, though later I managed to get it told. She gave me a talk in Swedish. What I had done was bad manners, was not Christian, and I should look out about following the ways of the older neighbor boys. Sweet and soft she could say, *"Var en snäll pojke"* (Be a good boy).

When I was about four we moved two blocks over to Berrien Street and a ten-room house with a long roomy third-story garret running the length of the house, a four-room cellar having floors in the two front rooms. A two-compartment privy had a henhouse back of it. The lot was three times the size of the South Street place, had a big garden with several gooseberry bushes, a front yard with five tall soft-maple trees, a picket fence, a brick sidewalk, and a ditch in front. It was really two houses and lots. Over the front door a small tin sign read "Aetna Fire Insurance Company" to show that the house was insured, and two sign numbers said that we lived at 622 and 624 East Berrien Street. Here the emigrant Swede August Sandburg set himself up, with due humility and constant anxiety, as a landlord. The two east rooms of the first floor, along with the two cellar rooms under them, were rented to different families across the years, never vacant for more than a day or two, while the large upstairs east rooms always had a renter.

THE HOUSE ON BERRIEN STREET

The house on Berrien Street was a challenge to my father. He couldn't see himself paying—or wasting—money for repairs. He became a carpenter, a bricklayer, a house painter, a paperhanger, a cabinetmaker, a truck gardener, a handyman restless and dissatisfied unless there was something to fix or improve on the property he owned or was paying for. What he made or fixed with his hands wasn't always finished perfectly smooth and correct—but it would do. I was his helper, his chore boy, my brother Mart later throwing in. When the roof needed shingling I went up the ladder bringing him shingles. When a pump was ailing he let me down on a rope to put on a new leather sucker. When a cistern had its yearly cleaning I was let down barelegged to shovel mud and silt into the bucket he drew up with a rope. A chair or table getting wobbly, my father brought it down to his cellar workbench and had me holding a kerosene lamp to light him while he chiseled, fitted, mortised, and hammered. I might after supper have taken my place at the kitchen table to read J. T. Headley's *Napoleon and His Marshals*, from the Seventh Ward school library. And I might be saying to my father, "It's a good book and I want to know about Napoleon," but he would say, "Sholly [Charlie], you let Napoleon go for tonight and hold de lamp for me."

Monday was Washday. When I was strong enough to carry a pail of water I went out the kitchen door, down eight steps of the back stairway, eight more steps to the cistern, where I lifted the cover and let down a bucket and filled the pail. After enough trips to the cistern there would be water for two washtubs, one tub with warm water and a washboard for soaping and rubbing, the other with cold water for rinsing the clothes and running them through the attached wringer. On summer and vacation Mondays I often turned the wringer while my mother fed the clothes into it. On many winter Mondays I carried the basket of clothes out to the back-yard clothesline. In a blowing wind I pressed wooden clothespins to fasten bed sheets, shirts, drawers, handkerchiefs, stockings, and diapers on the rope clothesline. Often I found the clothes left in the basket had frozen stiff. Coaxing those frozen pieces of cloth to go around the rope for a wooden pin to be fastened over them was a winter sport with a challenge to your wit and numb fingers in Illinois zero weather, with sometimes a wild northwest wind knocking a shirt stiff as a board against your head. I remember more than once taking a basket into the kitchen for the clothes to thaw out while my fingers thawed out.

The pump in the back yard was wooden and had a wooden handle. I became part of the pump and the pump became part of me. The pump stood about fifteen steps from the foot of the stairs going down from the back door of the house. I took an empty galvanized iron pail from the side of the kitchen sink, opened the door to the back hall, opened the back door, and went down the stairs and then to the pump. I set the pail under the pump spout, put my two hands on the pump handle, pushed the handle down, pulled the handle up, and went on pumping till water poured out of the spout and filled the pail. Then I carried the pail to the back stairs, up the stairs to the back door, the hall, the kitchen door, and the kitchen sink. I did this a thousand times, at least, or it could have been two or three thousand times. Others did this same chore but I was counted the oldest boy, the handy strong boy who was called on. What we brought into the house was "fresh water," or in Swedish *friskt vatten*. In the warm months water standing in a pail an hour or two didn't taste good and the call was for fresh water, the father saying, "*Friskt vatten, Sholly.*"

In a summer dry spell when the pump handle came up light and loose, pulling up no water, I knew the water was low at the bottom of the well and the pump needed "priming." I would go back to the kitchen and get a pail of cistern rain water, pouring it down to the leather sucker and the tubing. Then I would push and pull at the pump handle till at last the pump spout was running glad and free and saying, "Here is your water!" And on hot sweltering summer days when butter melted and stayed melted in the kitchen, mother would put it in a small tin pail, tie a doubled grocery string to the handle, and I would lift the cover of the well platform and let the butter down to become cool and hard again.

There were winter mornings when my hands in mittens went around the pump handle and I pushed and pulled and couldn't budge it. They would be watching from the kitchen window. They saw me skipping back to the kitchen. They were ready with a pail of hot water. I poured this down the pump, sometimes ran back to the kitchen for a second pail of hot water. After the pump was thawed out I pumped and carried in two pails of water to last the family till the next morning, when again we thawed out the pump. And this, of course, meant carrying in extra pails of water from the cistern, where there was no pump and you let down your galvanized iron pail and broke the thin ice and pulled the pail up with a rope. I got acquainted with the difference between a fresh-water well and a rain-water cistern.

Three or four times it happened I would push and pull at the pump handle and no water came. Papa looked it over and said it needed a new sucker. He cut leather and shaped a new sucker. He let me down into the well on a rope, told me what to do, and stood looking down telling me more what to do. I was glad when he pulled me up and we could say the pump was fixed and the new sucker worked. It was a good pump, and whenever it didn't work it had a good excuse and you couldn't blame it.

Coxey's Army in the news for months, men out of work marching on Washington to ask Congress to get them work. And the Panic, the Hard Times, definitely reached Galesburg. Except for watchmen, the railroad shopmen went from a ten-hour day to a four-hour day, the checks on payday less than half what they were used to.

We learned to eat bread spread with lard sprinkled with salt, and we liked it. When lard was short we put molasses or sorghum on the bread, which was not so good. We were lucky in our garden giving a bumper crop of potatoes. The land laughed with spuds. As Mart and I helped the Old Man dig potatoes and carry the bushel baskets into the cellar, we saw him do the only writing of his we had ever witnessed. For each bushel brought in he would chalk on a ceiling rafter a straight vertical line. When there were four verticals he would cross with a diagonal line, meaning we had five more bushels, by golly.

A little co-operative of neighbors sprang up. They borrowed a horse and wagon and hauled to town a hog from John Krans, a hog bought below the market price then, "the price near nothing," laughed Krans, whose wife was a cousin of our mother. Two lots away from us, outdoors in front of a small barn, I first saw a hog killing. I carried home a bucket of blood from which Mama made a tasty "blood pudding." Mart and I hustled home with a ham and hog sections from which we had across the weeks that winter pork chops, pork loins, side meat, spareribs, cracklings, sowbelly, pig's knuckles, lard for frying and for bread spread.

There was a note of doom and fate about the big railroad whistle in those Hard Times months. For years we had heard it at seven in the morning, at twelve noon, and at one and six o'clock in the afternoon. Now it blew at eight in the morning and twelve noon only. It was the Hard Times Clock saying, "Be careful, watch your pennies, wait and hope!"

FATHER AND MOTHER

My father liked company and his face was rich with smiles at meeting our nearest kin, the Holmeses and Kranses, and others. He had instincts about workmanship, about being a craftsman. The

Berrien Street house had his handprints over hundreds of places, in foundation bricks and mortar, in roof shingles and chimney bricks, in floor boards he had set and nailed, in paper he had hung on walls. Many a night I held rolls of wallpaper for him and he on a stepladder would hand me down a brush to be dipped in a paste pot. He could stand off from the house and look at it and say, "It is mine because my hands are part of it."

Why did my father, with his exceptional manual cleverness and variety of skills, never learn to write? Had he cared to will to write he could have learned to write the letters of all the words he knew. The desire wasn't there. He never cared for books. Life seemed to have enough stories for him without storybooks. In our early childhood years he read to us from the Swedish Bible but seldom till later years did we see him spend hours or half-hours reading it for companionship or the learning of wisdom from it or any music its verses might have for him. And seldom did he quote from it. He read the weekly *Hemlandet* a half-hour and let it go at that.

When I became a carrier with a "route," delivering the daily *Republican-Register*, and brought home an "extra" copy, my father spent little or no time on it. When there was big news the others gave it to him. The reading habit never got him. Several times when I had my boy head in a book he said with no touch of fun in it, "Sholly, you read too much in de books—what good iss it?"

If he had had even a surface desire to write, he could have learned from his wife or from any of his children with only a few nights of fooling around with the shaping of letters. He never hungered to write, never felt the need for it.

The mother had ways and habits quite different from the father. Though she seldom kissed the children, she often gave a pat on the cheek or on the head along with a beaming smile, which the father almost never did.

We knew he was taking life in hard ways. As the years passed there came by slow growth layers of muscle making a hump on his right shoulder. He was day on day swinging sledges and hammers on hot iron on an anvil. We knew him for a strong man who could hold up his end on a piece of work, but we saw him many an evening come home after the ten-hour day, his shirt soaked with sweat, and he had no word nor murmur though he looked fagged and worn. After washing he would slump into a chair as though now every bone and muscle in his body could be glad and easy.

*

Mama's wedding ring was never lost—was always on that finger as placed there with pledges years ago. It was a sign and seal of something that ran deep and held fast between the two of them. They had chosen each other as partners. How they happened to meet I heard only from my mother. I had asked her how they came to marry and she said, "I was working in a hotel in Bushnell [Illinois], making the beds and helping in the kitchen. He came to Bushnell with the railroad gang. He came to the hotel and saw me and we talked and he said he wanted to marry me. I saw it was my chance and soon went to Galesburg and the Reverend Lindahl married us and we started housekeeping." A smile spread over her face half-bashful and a bright light came to her blue eyes as she said, "I saw it was my chance." She was saying this at least twenty years after the wedding and there had been hard work always, tough luck at times, seven children of whom two had died on the same day—and she had not one regret that she had jumped at her "chance" when she saw it. One sheet of paper kept as sacred over the years was a certificate signed by S. P. A. Lindahl that on the 7th day of August, A.D. 1874, in Galesburg they "were united in marriage by me."

We heard her among other women at times speaking of "my man." She had pride in him for the way he struggled barehanded for his wages, for his anxiety in his homemaking, for the religion they had together and "the All-seeing God" they spoke of and worshiped together.

On two occasions she argued with him and defended herself against his charge of wasting money. It happened one morning when he was away at his job, a bright summer day and mother doing a wash in the cellar. I came in to see a well-dressed man talking to her. She had quit washing and was listening to him. He was showing her a sample of a book. Here were the covers and here were sample pages—the real book was five times bigger. Mama's face and blue eyes were shining. She was interested. He was saying that education is important. And how do you get education? Through books, the right kind of books. Now this book was no trash affair. It was a *Cyclopaedia of Important Facts of the World*. You have this book around and the children can't help reading it. They will find here the facts about the great battles of the world, how many people live in Illinois or California or Sweden, the national debt, the Washington Monument and how many feet high it is, the names of all the Presidents of the United States. Knowledge—that is what counts when your children go out in the world—knowledge! "The more they learn the more they earn!"

Mother was a little dazed by now. He was speaking her own mind as to education and knowledge. The Old Man would have been scowling and shaking his head. The mother was more than interested. She took the sample and turned pages. She looked down into my face. Would I like the book? I said yes in several ways. She signed her name for the book. She had the required seventy-five cents ten days later when the man came with the book. I hugged it. I sank myself in its many facts and felt proud here was a book of our own that I didn't have to take back to the school library or the Public Library. I read a thousand facts and remembered perhaps a hundred, though I still can't say how many feet high is the Washington Monument. But I was proud of my mother. She had eagerness about books. She would have read many shelves of books if she could have found the time.

About this *Cyclopaedia* the father grumbled—a waste of money, let the children get "eddication" in the schools. It was later he made a real fuss. This time I was there again when the book agent came, not the same man, but well dressed and polite, handy with his tongue, like the first one. His book was three times bigger than the *Cyclopaedia*, bigger pages, two columns to the page, many pictures, *A History of the World and Its Great Events*—nothing less—with special attention to the famous battles of all time. I liked the feel of the sample and the look of the pictures. Mother again looked down into my face. She was not quite so bright, not so sure, as the last time. But I was surer I would like this book. It had all kinds of fighting in it. I said we ought to have it. Mother signed again. This time it was a dollar and a half. That was more than a day's pay of my father. But mother signed and had the money when the book came two weeks later.

I won't go into the scene the Old Man made when he saw the book and heard the price paid. He stormed and hurled reproaches and cried aloud we were heading for the Knoxville poorhouse. "*I bela min tid*"—in all my time. "*Gud bevara*"—God help us. It was a sorrow and a shame. If it ever happened again he didn't know what he would do. It was a real grief with him. It ended mother's listening to book agents.

The mother had visions and hopes. She could say with a lighted face, "We will hope for the best," as I bent my head over *A History of the World and Its Great Events*. The Old Man would stand over me saying, "Wat good iss dat book, Sholly?" And I had no answer. I didn't like his saying such a thing. But I had some dim realization

too that he had in mind mortgages on which payments must be made.
In his way he was as good as any of the Greeks at Thermopylae or
any of the Swedes fighting with Gustavus Adolphus in the Thirty
Years' War—but at the time I didn't know that, and I was a long
time learning it.

SCHOOL DAYS

A case in Chicago had us kids and all Galesburg stirred up. We
heard about it, read about it, and talked about it, from May 5 on
through every day of that year of 1886. On the night of May 4, a
police captain marched one hundred and eighty of his men to a
meeting on the Haymarket, where the captain lifted his club toward a
speaker on a wagon and said, "In the name of the people of the State
of Illinois I command you to disperse." Then came a crash like a bolt
of wild thunder. Someone had thrown a dynamite bomb straight
where the policemen stood thickest. When it was all over seven
policemen were dead.

Then came the murder trial of eight men and we saw in the
Chicago papers black-and-white drawings of their faces and they
looked exactly like what we expected, hard, mean, slimy faces. We
saw pictures of the twelve men on the jury and they looked like
what we expected, nice, honest, decent faces. We learned the word
for the men on trial, anarchists, and they hated the rich and called
policemen "bloodhounds." They were not regular people and they
didn't belong to the human race, for they seemed more like slimy
animals who prowl, sneak, and kill in the dark. This I believed along
with millions of other people reading and talking about the trial. I
didn't meet or hear of anyone in our town who didn't so believe then.

The trial dragged on and the case went to higher courts and the
governor of Illinois, and two of the eight men were sentenced for
life, one for fifteen years, and five to be hanged on November 11,
1887. I was nine years old, nearly ten, when we were let out of the
Seventh Ward school at three-thirty on the afternoon of November
11, 1887. Us kids had been asking and were still asking what would
happen. In a world where there could be anarchists doing the things
that anarchists do, who could tell what would happen next? We had
heard about the crowds and mobs who swarmed around the court-
room when the trial was on. We knew that the jurymen leaving the
courtroom were guarded by policemen with hands on their revolvers

and sharp eyes for any bomb thrower. And the wild news had come to us on the day before that one of the anarchists, a bomb maker, had somehow got, probably from a woman fascinated by him who visited his cell, what he told her he wanted. It was a "fulminating cap" that exploded dynamite. He had put it in his mouth, bit his teeth into it, and blown part of his head off. There was one, we said, that wouldn't have to be hanged.

We walked from school that afternoon of November 11 a block and a half south on Seminary Street. On the other side of the street we saw walking fast toward us a railroad man we knew. We heard him call out, as he went on walking fast, to another railroad man about ten feet ahead of us. I can never forget the four words that came from that man across the street. He had the big news of the day and was glad to spread it. The four words were "Well, they hanged 'em!" That was all. The man went on walking fast, more than happy. You could tell that by his voice, by the way he sang it out with a glad howl. No need to say more. Everybody knew what had gone before. The end of the story was "Well, they hanged 'em!"

Something tight in me came loose and it was the same with the other kids. We looked into each other's faces and said, "I'm glad it's over, ain't you?" and, "They had it comin to them and I'm glad they're dead," and, "A lot of people will be glad today, won't they?"

My mother said, "I don't like to tink of all dose men dead wit ropes around deir necks. But dose arnashists are bad people. Satan had his hand in it." My father came home from the shop, had one arm out of a coat sleeve, was shaking his head and saying, "Dose arnashists, dose arnashists." And getting the other arm out of its sleeve, he went on, looking at mother, "Dey killed and so dey ought to be killed." Then turning to Mary, Mart, and me, "Dey killed and so dey ought to be killed."

Five years later I sat in a gallery and heard John Peter Altgeld in a campaign speech in the Opera House. Not a word came from him about the Haymarket bomb and the anarchists. But a few months after he was elected governor he pardoned the three "anarchists" at Joliet and gave out a sixteen-thousand-word message on why he did it. It took me over two hours to give a slow reading to that message in a Chicago newspaper. "The jury which tried the case was a packed jury selected to convict," wrote Altgeld. He named the jurymen who had said in court that they had read about the case and they believed the men on trial were guilty. With the kind of a jury that was picked it was sure beforehand that the men on trial would be found guilty.

The governor wrote that the judge threw in questions and remarks before and during the trial showing he believed them guilty before the evidence was in, and instead of a fair trial it was a farce and a mockery of justice. The man who threw the bomb had escaped and there was no evidence to show that he was connected in any way with the men on trial. The police of Chicago had shot and killed strikers, wrote the governor, and they had broken up labor meetings and had beaten many heads bloody—and the man who threw the bomb probably did it on his own for "personal revenge."

I knew as I moved through that sixteen-thousand-word message, crammed with what I now took to be sober facts and truth, that I wasn't the same boy as five years before when I was glad about four men hanged. The feeling grew on me that I had been "off my nut," along with millions of people like myself gone somewhat crazy.

Newspapers howled that Altgeld himself was an anarchist. Police officers and politicians joined in the howling. In their hate they couldn't find names nasty enough to call him. I had seen him and heard him. I leaned toward him, feeling he was no cheap politician. I heard Republicans and Democrats saying, after the pardons, "Altgeld has killed himself in politics. He can never again be elected to a big office." He ran for governor of Illinois and was beaten, ran for mayor of Chicago and was beaten. He had been a millionaire, owned a tall office building in the Loop, and what he owned was swept away, some of it by trickery.

Years later I heard Edgar Lee Masters, who had known Altgeld, saying, "He had violet eyes, strange and quiet violet eyes. They stripped him to the bone, drove him into a terrible loneliness, but I don't believe those who say he died of a broken heart. He had hidden strengths. In his fifty-four years he lived a thousand years. It could be that five hundred years from now his name will stand out like that of Cromwell or William of Orange." It was a far cry back to that afternoon when I heard those four words in a glad howl, "Well, they hanged 'em!"

I finished the Seventh Ward school. I could feel I was growing up, halfway toward being a man. It was quite a change to walk twice a day to the Grammar School downtown and walk a mile home again. They came from all ends of the town to the Grammar School, many new faces to see and new names to hear, many more boys and girls from the well-off families with better clothes.

The Grammar School stood a short block from the Public Square.

Between stood the Old First Church, built more than forty years before by the First Settlers. The long oak beams holding it together had been hauled by horses from miles away and hewn by the axes of old-timers. The benches inside were black walnut. The old building could say, "When I was built this town had only a few hundred people in it and you could walk across the town in three or four minutes to the cornfields and pastures." In a few years they tore down the Old First Church and sold the great oak beams and black-walnut benches as used lumber. They could have moved that fine quaint antique of a building to some vacant lot to stand as a loving memorial to the pioneer founders of the city, but there didn't seem to be enough care, sentiment, or imagination for such action.

Straight across the street from the Grammar School stood the two-story house where Henry R. Sanderson lived. He had been mayor of Galesburg and had a son George, who would later be mayor, and another son "Bay" we liked to watch playing shortstop on the Galesburg team. We used to see Henry R. Sanderson with his long white beard and quiet face. We heard how when he was mayor he had taken Abraham Lincoln into his house as a guest in the year 1858 when Lincoln came to debate with Douglas, how he had helped with towels and warm water for Lincoln to take a bath. Sanderson could tell of Lincoln meeting a man named John T. Barnett in Galesburg and remembering that years back he and Barnett were spear-fishing in the Sangamon River, with Lincoln holding a torch high up so as to keep the light out of his own eyes. And Barnett had called out, "Abe, bring down that torch. You're holding it clear out of Sangamon County." Lincoln pointed at Barnett and said to Mayor Sanderson, "This is the man."

ALONG BERRIEN STREET

If we saw a man of slight, wiry build, a light-brown silken beard over his face, his head held high and bent forward peering through spectacles, a small tan valise in one hand, walking east as though his mind was occupied with ideas a million miles from Berrien Street and Galesburg, we knew it was near eight o'clock, when Professor Philip Green Wright would take up a class at Lombard University some six blocks away. We didn't know then his grandfather was Elizur Wright, a radical and an agitator who had a stormy career as secretary of the American Anti-Slavery Society and who later worked out and compiled the first dependable actuarial tables used by the large life insurance companies. We didn't know that this funny-looking fellow would become a truly Great Man and forty years later I would write the sketch of him for the *Dictionary of American Biography*. As a boy I didn't have the faintest dim gleam of a dream that this professor would in less than ten years become for me a fine and dear friend, a deeply beloved teacher. He walked with queer long steps, stretching his neck to peer away past the next corner. We would imitate his walk and we didn't know in the least that he had streaks of laughter in him and in time to come would write one of the funniest musical comedies ever seen on the local Auditorium stage even though he was a mathematician, an astronomer, a historian, an economist, a poet, a printer and a bookbinder, a genius and a marvel. All we knew then was that his figure and walk were funny and we liked to watch him and it was near eight in the morning.

There was a row of buildings running west from Chambers Street on the north side of Berrien. Every one of those buildings has its curious memories that stick in the mind. What I remember so often seems trifling and meaningless yet it sticks, faces and places that will be there so long as I keep what might be called "my right mind." On the corner stood the wooden grocery building with its sign "Swan H. Olson & Bro." Swan had a red chin beard, always neatly trimmed, waited on customers quietly and politely. He had arrived from Sweden in 1854, twenty years old, worked on Knox County farms, and in 1862 enlisted as a private in Company A of the 102d Illinois Volunteer Infantry, fought in the Atlanta campaign, marched with Sherman to the sea, across the Carolinas and on up to Washington for the Grand Review. Not until later years when I studied the marches and campaigns in which Swan Olson served did I come to a full respect for him. He was a foot soldier whose feet had taken him more than two thousand miles. He had been in wild and bloody battles, had waded creeks and rivers and marched in heavy rains day after day carrying rifle and blanket roll—but you couldn't tell it by seeing him measuring a quart of cranberries for Mrs. Nelson or hanging out a stockfish in front of the store on a winter morning to let the Swedes know their favorite holiday sea food had arrived.

Of the days of play and sport in the street in front of our house one tender and curious memory stands out. The house next east to ours straight across the street was an average two-story frame affair, with a porch perhaps fifteen feet long. In the street in front of this house was our home base when playing ball. Often we saw on that porch in a rocking chair a little woman, her hair snow-white with the years. She had a past, a rather bright though not dazzling past, you might say. She could lay claim to fame, if she chose. Millions of children reading the McGuffey and other school readers had met her name and memorized lines she had written. For there was in the course of her years no short poem in the English language more widely published, known, and recited than her lines about "Little Things":

Little drops of water,	Little deeds of kindness,
Little grains of sand,	Little words of love,
Make the mighty ocean	Help to make earth happy
And the pleasant land. . . .	Like the heaven above.

She was Julia Carney, her sons Fletcher and James being Universalists and Lombard graduates, Fletcher serving three or four terms as mayor of Galesburg. There she sat in the quiet of her backward-gazing thoughts, sometimes gently rocking, while we hooted and yelled over hits, runs, putouts. There she sat, an image of silence and rest, while the air rang with boy screams, "Hit it bang on the nose now!" "Aw, he couldn't hit a balloon!" To us at that time she was just one more nice old woman who wouldn't bother boys at play. We didn't know that her writings were in books and newspaper reprints that reached millions of readers. The Carneys were good neighbors and she was one of them—that was all we knew.

I have played baseball on a summer day starting at eight o'clock in the morning, running home at noon for a quick meal, playing again till six o'clock in the evening, and then a run home for a quick meal and again with fielding and batting till it was too dark to see the leather spheroid. On many a Saturday I had sold the *Sporting News* at five cents a copy, and I had read about the "leather spheroid."

Four lots to the east of our house was a vacant double lot where we laid out a small diamond. At the time a good-natured Jersey cow was pastured there for a few weeks. We never knocked a ball that hit the cow but when the ball landed near her and the fielder ran toward her it disturbed her. Also it disturbed the owner of the cow, who said he would have the police on us. So we played in the street till the day the cow was gone and we heard it had been sold. Then we went back to our pasture.

Our early games among the Berrien Street kids were played in the street, barefooted, keeping an eye out for broken glass or rusty cans with sharp edges sticking up. The bat was a broom handle, the ball was handmade—a five-cent rubber ball wrapped round with grocery string. The home plate was a brick, first base a brick, second base a tin can, third another tin can. We played barehanded till we learned how to get a large man-sized glove and stuff it with cotton, wool, or hair to take the sting out of a fast ball.

The days came when we played in the cow pasture with a Spalding big-league regulation ball. We gathered round the boy who first brought it to us and said we could play with it. "Well, what do you know!" we said. "A dollar and a half." And we told it around as a kind of wonder, "We been playin today with a dollar and a half." We would hear "Fatty" Beckman ask, "Is Skinny Seeley comin today with that dollar and a half?" Sure he was. He was bringing the same ball that Amos Rusie was throwing in the big league, the same ball Big Bill Lange was hitting so hard with the Chicago team.

Across a few years I could from day to day name the leading teams and the tailenders in the National League and the American Association. I could name the players who led in batting and fielding and the pitchers who had won the most games. I filled my head with this knowledge and carried it around. There were times my head seemed empty of everything but baseball names and figures.

An idea began growing in me that if I played and practiced a lot I might become good enough to get on a team where my talent was appreciated. Once on a minor-league team I would have my chance to show what I could do and I might end up in the majors—who knows about a thing like that? I didn't mention it. It was a secret ambition. I nursed it along and in what spare time I could find I played where the boys were playing, did fairly well in left field on a scrub team.

Then came an afternoon in early October. I was sixteen. Skinny Seeley and I went to a pasture in the second block north of the Lombard campus. Skinny and I knocked up flies. He was hitting some long and high ones to me. I had managed to buy secondhand a fielder's glove, a regular big-league affair I was proud of. I was running for a high one. I believed I would make a brilliant catch of it, the kind of catch I would make when maybe one of the minor-league clubs had taken me on. I was running at top speed. Suddenly my right foot stashed into a hole and I fell on my knees and face. When I looked at what had happened to my right foot I saw a gash in the shoe leather and blood oozing from the tangled yarn of the sock. I saw too that in the eight-inch hole there was a beer bottle, broken in half, standing on its bottom end, and into the top of this my foot had crashed.

I limped across the pasture, about a block, to the house of Dr. Taggart. He was at home. Out on his front porch he had me take off the shoe, then slowly the sock. He cleaned out the bleeding cut, picked out yarn and glass, applied antiseptic. Then he brought out a curved needle and sewed four stitches at about the middle of the foot just below the instep. He bandaged my foot and I limped home. My mother spoke sorrow and pity. My father asked when would I ever learn any sense and quit wasting my time with baseball.

From that day on I was completely through with any and all hopes and dreams of becoming a big-time ballplayer. I went on playing occasional games and have never lost a certain odd tingle of the hands at holding a bat or catching a baseball. Those four stitches in the right foot marked the end of my first real secret ambition. I began a hunt for new secret ambitions, but they were slow in coming.

FIRST PAYDAYS

About 1890 I carried a newspaper route. At one house set well back a man would often be at home and expecting me and more yet, expecting the latest telegraphed news over America and the wide world. This man expecting me would step out of the door to take the paper from my hand. He was the most roly-poly fat man in town. There were other fat men who stood bigger and weighed more, but no others so roly-poly. He was round everywhere you looked at him, no straight lines, even his back curved. He was a waddly barrel of a man, with a double chin, a round face, a gray silver mustache and goatee. This was the Honorable Clark E. Carr, mentioned often as the Republican Party boss of Knox County and having a hand in national politics. He had been appointed postmaster by Republican Presidents. He was to serve as United States minister to Denmark.

He liked to be called "Colonel" Carr, encouraged people to call him "Colonel" and editors to print "Colonel" in front of his name. I believed "Colonel" Carr had sometime and somewhere marched his men on dusty roads in sweltering sun and had seen men fall wounded and dying. But later I learned that the Civil War governor, Richard Yates, had appointed him a staff colonel, so he was a commander without a regiment, an officer who never reached the marching and fighting fronts.

At a later time I heard Colonel Carr in a campaign speech poke fun at himself for being so fat and roly-poly. At Copenhagen he had worked out some schedule that let American pork into Denmark at a lower tariff. He mentioned this and the collops of fat and flesh on him shook with his laughter as he added, "When I was the minister to Denmark the American hog obtained recognition!"

As a young man he was the Illinois member of the Board of Commissioners who made up the program for the exercises dedicating the cemetery on the Gettysburg Battlefield. He rode in the parade to the battlefield and had written that he noticed President Lincoln on a horse just ahead of him and how Lincoln sat straight in the saddle at first and later leaned forward with arms limp and head bent far down. This roly-poly man taking the *Republican-Register* from my hand had met Lincoln in party powwows, had heard Lincoln tell stories, and Clark E. Carr said of Lincoln, "He could make a cat laugh." In 1864 he made speeches up and down Illinois for Lincoln and at Quincy had spoken before a wild crowd of ten thousand people from the same platform as Bob Ingersoll, the Peoria lawyer.

Of course the twelve-year-old boy handing him his evening paper didn't know what made Clark E. Carr so important. I knew that he had for more than thirty years met and shaken hands with all the big men of the Republican Party. I knew he could make speeches and statements that got printed. I didn't know that even though he swung a lot of power in the Republican Party he couldn't get it to give him what he wanted most of all. I learned later that he wanted to be elected to Congress and go to Washington and be a statesman. Several times he came near getting what he wanted most of all and those against him stopped him.

At the Carlin store, where I would stop on my route to dry and warm my feet, I saw a young man carrying boxes and bags out of the store to a delivery wagon. He was a six-footer with big shoulders, a round head and face, a strong jaw and chin, a pleasant smile. How could I know, since he didn't know it himself, that he would go on and on and up and up? When later he began driving a handy wagon with a shanty on it out among the farmers and small towns he did well at getting new subscribers to the *Republican-Register*, yet also about the same time making friends with many key men of the Republican Party workers. He quietly smashed an old party machine, was elected county treasurer, took over two or three banks and joined them into one bank where he was at the head, took over the *Republican-Register* and joined it with the *Evening Mail* so he was the publisher of the new Galesburg *Register-Mail*. In politics it became a saying, "We won't know what the ticket will be till we, see Omer Custer."

When I sat by the Carlin grocery stove, looking up from reading the Chicago papers, to see Omer Custer with a sack of flour on one shoulder and a sack of sugar on the other, he couldn't figure for sure that the day would come when he would be the top man in Knox County banking, politics, newspapers, owning the first modern hotel in Galesburg, carrying the name of Hotel Custer. Nor as Omer clucked to the horse and said "Giddap" did he have the faintest glimmering that some thirty years later he would be managing the campaign of Governor Frank O. Lowden of Illinois, a rather able and honest governor, for the nomination for president of the United States by the Republican National Convention. And when Lowden's chances looked bright and rosy, with the nomination almost in reach, and people were saying Omer Custer would be the next postmaster general, there came out of St. Louis a scandal that wrecked the Lowden band wagon and the country got Harding instead of Lowden for President. Neither Omer on his delivery wagon nor Charlie with his newspapers at the stove drying his mittens, neither had a crystal ball for reading the moist, mystical future that lay ahead.

I was fourteen and coming near fifteen in October of 1892. My mother would wake me at half-past five in the morning. She had ready for me when I came down from the garret a breakfast of buckwheat cakes, fried side pork, maybe applesauce or prunes, and coffee. I walked to the house and barn of George Burton, who had two milk wagons. It was a walk of about two miles to get to where I was ready for work.

In this October were days I had a sore throat. I went to bed two days and sent word to Burton that I wasn't able to work. Reporting for work, I explained to Burton and he looked at me with suspicion and not a word. I still had throat pains and was weak, for two days eating little on account of it hurt the throat to swallow. I didn't explain this to Mr. Burton—he already looked suspicious enough.

That same week Mart went down with a sore throat and it was four days before he was up and around. Then the two youngest boys of the family stayed in bed with throats so sore they couldn't eat. Freddy was a baby two years old and Emil was seven years old this October. Emil had a broad freckled face, blue eyes, a quick beaming smile from a large mouth. He was strong for his age. He and I wrestled, scuffled, knocked off hats, played tricks on each other, and I read to him my favorites from the Grimm stories. We liked the same stories and he called often for "The Knapsack, the Hat, and the Horn."

We moved a narrow bed from upstairs down into the kitchen, our one room with a stove in it. Next to the west window, with afternoon sun sometimes pouring in, we put Emil and Freddie side by side in the one bed, each with a throat looking queer, what had been pink and red having turned to a grayish white. They seemed to be getting weaker. And though we knew it would be a dollar and a half for a call from Doctor Wilson, I walked to his Main Street office and told him the folks wanted him to come as soon as he could.

Doctor Wilson came in about an hour, stepping into our kitchen in his elegant long black coat, white shirt and collar, a silk necktie, thin reddish hair, and gold-rimmed eyeglasses. He had a good name as a doctor. He took a flat steel blade from his case. He put this on the tongue of Emil and pressed it down and looked keen and long at Emil's throat. He did the same for Freddie. Then Doctor Wilson stood up, turned to the faces of my father and mother and said three words. His face was sober and sorry as he spoke those three words: "It is diphtheria."

Late that afternoon the city health commissioner nailed a big red card on the front door of our house: DIPHTHERIA, warning people not to come to our house because it had a catching disease.

On the third day when Doctor Wilson made his third call, he took the pulse and the temperature of the two boys, looked long and careful into their throats, and said they were not making any improvement. He shook his head and said something like, "All we can do now is to hope. They might get better. They might get worse. I can't tell." Late that afternoon we were all there, with a west sun shining in on Emil and Freddie where they lay with their eyes closed and still breathing. It was Freddie who first stopped breathing. Mother, touching his forehead and hands, her voice shaking and tears coming down her face, said, "He is cold. Our Freddie is gone." We watched Emil. He had had a rugged body and we hoped he might pull through. But his breathing came slower and in less than a half-hour he seemed to have stopped breathing. Mother put her hands on him and said with her body shaking. "Oh God, Emil is gone too."

The grief hit us all hard. In the Front Room the marble-topped center table with the big Family Bible was moved to a corner. In its place in the center of the room were two small white caskets. Neighbors and friends came, some with flowers. The Kranses and the Holmeses came to look at the faces of their two little relations. The Reverend Carl A. Nyblad spoke the Swedish Lutheran service. A quartet sang "Jesus, Lover of My Soul." The undertaker moved here and there as though it was like what he did any day, and you couldn't read anything in his face. Mother cried, but it was a quiet crying and she didn't shake her shoulders like when she said "Oh God, Emil is gone too." Mart and I didn't cry. We kept our eyes dry and our faces hard. For two nights we had cried before going to sleep, and waking in the night we had cried more and it was our secret why we weren't crying at a public funeral.

We saw the two little white caskets out the front door and put in the black hearse with glass windows at the sides and the end, four black tassels on the top corners. We followed in a closed carriage. At the grave we heard the words, "Ashes to ashes, dust to dust," saw the two little coffins lowered and a handful of earth dropped on them, the sober faces of the Kranses and the Holmeses having grains of comfort.

We were driven home in the closed carriage, the father and mother, the sisters Mary and Esther, the brothers Mart and I. We went into the house. It was all over. The clock had struck for two lives and would never strike again for them. Freddie hadn't lived long enough to get any tangles in my heart. But Emil I missed then, and for years I missed him and had my wonderings about what a chum and younger brother he would have made.

I didn't know when I heard Philip Sidney Post making a speech at a Republican rally or when I saw him walking on Main Street that I was looking at a great fighting man, one of the best soldiers that answered Lincoln's call for troops in '61. He was a young lawyer out in Wyandotte, Kansas, when the call came. He went east to Galesburg, enlisted, and became second lieutenant of Company A, 59th Illinois Volunteer Infantry, fought in some of the bloodiest battles of the war, taking wounds, getting honorable mentions, moving up to major, colonel, and brigadier general. Pea Ridge, Perryville, Murfreesboro, Chickamauga were bloody grounds, and Post was there.

After the war his corps commander, General George H. Thomas,

asked the secretary of war to make him a colonel in the regular
army, writing that after the Pea Ridge battle Post "even before his
wound was recovered . . . rejoined his regiment."

The War Department, after his wounds healed, sent him to San
Antonio, Texas, in command of sixteen infantry regiments. It was
nearly thirty years later that General Post with two other men came
into the Union Hotel barbershop, where I was a porter. All three had
shaves. Two had shines. One of the two whose shoes I shined was
Philip Sidney Post. If I had known where those feet had been in their
time I would have tried to turn out the best and brightest shine I
ever put on shoe leather.

I haven't looked up General Post's record in Congress. He lived a
plain life, didn't come into big money and didn't seem to need it.
In his day and time I took him for just one more politician, his
right hand not sure what his left hand might be doing. And now I
have a sneaking fool pride in my heart that one time I shined his
shoes without knowing where the feet in those shoes had been.

THEME IN SHADOW AND GOLD

Farnham Street where it meets Fifth was a country road when I
walked barefoot in its dust, the land pasture or cornfield. On a piece
of ground a house went up there and in that house Galesburg had the
bloodiest crime of passion in its history. The man had been drink-
ing but he couldn't have been clumsy drunk, for the fast and horrible
work he did on the night he came home to find a man in bed with
his wife. He sent a bullet into the man's body and a bullet into his
wife's right arm. He put two razor cuts in the palm of his wife's
right hand and slashed a deep cut in the left side of her neck from
below the ear to the mid-line of her throat. Across the man's throat
his razor swept from the left ear nearly to the right ear, severing the
jugular vein. The bed was blood-soaked and the pools not yet settled
when police officers arrived in the morning.

"The fight lasted two or three minutes," the killer testified when
on trial. His movements around the unlighted upstairs room must
have been fast, his feet quick and his hands working in a wild fury.
He was found guilty of manslaughter and sentenced to fourteen years
in the state penitentiary. Mart joined eighteen character witnesses—
among them a college professor, a physician, and men the killer had

worked for—who testified that "before his recent trouble his general reputation as a peaceable and law-abiding citizen was good." He served his time in Joliet, came back to Galesburg, lived a quiet life, and died, having had occasional news from his two married daughters and grandchildren in Chicago. Mart said to me, "He was that gentle and easygoing that he was about the last man in town I would have expected to hear was a killer and a double one. He told me that once before the last awful night he had caught the same man in bed with his wife. He warned them but they stayed in bed and jeered at him and said he didn't have the nerve to kill a flea." After he had served five years, Mart and others tried for a pardon or a parole but couldn't swing it. The affair was involved, complicated in motives, and not lacking in light on why hard liquor in excess is termed "tanglefoot."

I had my "puppy love." Day and night her face would be floating in my mind. I liked to practice at calling up her face as I had last seen it. Her folks lived in the Sixth Ward on Academy Street next to the Burlington tracks of the Q. They usually left a crock on the porch with a quart ticket in it. I took the ticket out of the crock, tilted my can and poured milk into my quart measure, and then poured it into the crock, well aware she was sometimes at the kitchen window watching my performance, ducking away if I looked toward the window. Two or three times a week, however, the crock wasn't there and I would call "Milk!" in my best boy-baritone and she would come out with the crock in her hands and a smile on her face. At first she would merely say "Quart" and I would pour the quart, take my can, and walk away. But I learned that if I spoke as smooth and pleasant a "Good morning" as I could, then she would speak me a "Good morning" that was like a blessing to be remembered. I learned too that if I could stumble out the words, "It's a nice day" or "It's a cold wind blowing" she would say a pert "Yes, it is" and I would go away wondering how I would ever get around to a one- or two-minute conversation with her.

I was more bashful than she. If she had been in the slightest as smitten as I was, she would have "talked an arm off me." But she didn't. It was a lost love from the start. I was smitten and she wasn't. And her face went on haunting me. Today I can call up her girl face and say it's as fine as any you'd like to rest your eyes on, classic as Mona Lisa and a better-rounded rosy mouth. I had no regrets she had smitten me and haunted me. I asked for nothing and she promised the same. I could say I had known my first love. It was a lost love but I had had it. It began to glimmer away after my first and only walk with her.

I dropped in with another boy one summer night to revival services at the Knox Street Congregational Church. There I saw her with another girl. After the services a chum of mine took the other girl and I found myself walking with the girl of my dreams. I had said, "See you home?" and she had said, "Certainly." And there we were walking in a moonlight summer night and it was fourteen blocks to her home. I knew it was my first or last chance with her. I said it was a mighty fine moonlight night. She said "Yes" and we walked a block saying nothing. I said it was quite a spell of hot weather we had been having. She said "Yes" and we walked another block. I said one of the solo singers at the church did pretty good. And again she agreed and we walked on without a word. I spoke of loose boards in the wooden sidewalk of the next block and how we would watch our step, which we did.

I had my right hand holding her left arm just above the elbow, which I had heard and seen was the proper way to take a girl home. And my arm got bashful. For blocks I believed maybe she didn't like my arm there and the way I was holding it. After a few blocks it was like I had a sore wooden arm that I ought to take off and have some peace about it. Yet I held on. If I let go I would have to explain and I couldn't think of an explanation. Not for a flickering split second did it dawn on me to say, "You know I'm crazy about you and crazy is the right word." I could have broken one of the two blocks we walked without a word by saying, "Would you believe it, your face keeps coming back to me when I'm away from you—all the time it keeps coming back as the most wonderful face my eyes ever met." Instead I asked her how her father, who was a freight-train conductor on the Q., liked being a conductor and did he find it nice work.

We made the grade at last. The fourteen blocks came to an end. I could no more have kissed her at the gate of her house than a man could spit against Niagara Falls and stop the water coming down. Instead of trying to kiss her I let go her arm and said "Good night" and walked away fast as if I had an errand somewhere. I didn't even stand still to see if she made it to the front door. I had made the decision I wasn't for her nor she for me. We were not good company for each other. If we were, at least one of us would have said something about what good company we were. I still adored her face and its genuine loveliness, but it had come clear to me that we were not "cut out for each other." I had one satisfaction as I walked home. My bashful right arm gradually became less wooden. The blood began circulating in it and my fingers were loose instead of tight and I could wiggle them.

HOBO

I was nineteen years old, weighed one hundred and forty-two pounds, nearly a grown man. And I was restless. The jobs I had worked at all seemed dead-end with no future that called to me. I decided in June of 1897 to head west and work in the Kansas wheat harvest. I would beat my way on the railroads and see what happened. I would be a hobo and a "gaycat." I had talked with hobos enough to know there is the professional tramp who never works and the gaycat who hunts work and hopes to go on and get a job that suits him.

I would take to The Road, see rivers and mountains, every day meeting strangers to whom I was one more young stranger. The family didn't like the idea. Papa scowled. Mama kissed me and her eyes had tears after dinner one noon when I walked out of the house with my hands free, no bag or bundle, wearing a black-sateen shirt, coat, vest, and pants, a slouch hat, good shoes and socks, no underwear, in my pockets a small bar of soap, a razor, a comb, a pocket mirror, two handkerchiefs, a piece of string, needles and thread, a Waterbury watch, a knife, a pipe and a sack of tobacco, three dollars and twenty-five cents in cash.

It was the last week in June, an afternoon bright and cool. A little west of the Santa Fe station stood a freight train waiting for orders. The conductor came out of the station and waved a yellow flimsy in his hand. As the train started I ran along and jumped into a boxcar. From then on I stood at the open side door, watched the running miles of young corn, reading such station names as Cameron and Stronghurst, names of villages and towns I had heard a thousand times and had never had sight of. Crossing the long bridge over the Mississippi my eyes swept over it with a sharp hunger that the grand old river satisfied. Except for my father, when riding to Kansas to buy land, no one of our family had seen the Father of Waters. As the train slowed down in Fort Madison, I jumped out and walked along saying, "Now I am in Iowa, the Hawkeye State, my first time off the soil of Illinois, the Sucker State."

I bought a nickel's worth of cheese and crackers and sat eating and looking across the Father of Waters. The captain of a small steamboat said I could work passage to Keokuk unloading kegs of nails. I slept on the boat, had breakfast, sailed down the river watching fields and towns go by, at Burlington, Quincy, and Keokuk shouldering kegs of nails to the wharves. At Keokuk I spread newspapers on green grass near a canal, and with coat over shoulders, slept in the open with my left arm for a pillow. I washed face and hands at the canal, using soap from my pocket and drying with a handkerchief. Then I met a fellow who said, "On the road?" I said "Yes." He led me to where he had been eating bread and meat unwrapped from a newspaper. "I got three lumps last night," he said, and handed me a lump for myself. A lump was what they handed you if they wanted to give you something to eat at a house where you asked for it. My new friend said, "I got a sitdown before I got the lumps." At one house he had been asked to sit at the kitchen table and eat. That was a sitdown.

He named Cincinnati Slim and Chicago Red and other professional tramps he had traveled with, mentioning them as though they were big names known to all tramps and I must have heard of them. He named towns where the jail food was good and how in the winter he would get a two or three months' sentence for vagrancy in those jails. "Or I might go South for the cold weather," he said, "keepin away from the towns where they're horstyle." So now I had learned that where they are hostile they are "horstyle" in tramp talk and it has nothing to do with horses.

On the Fourth of July, with crowds pouring into Keokuk, I saw a sign "Waiter Wanted" in a small lunch counter near the end of Main Street. The owner was running the place by himself. He said I could make myself useful at fifty cents a day and meals. He showed me the eggs, lard, and frying pan, the buns and ham for sandwiches, the doughnuts and the coffee pot. Soon he went out, telling me I was in charge of the place and to be polite serving customers. This was ten o'clock in the morning. Three or four people drifted in before eleven-thirty, when he came back, feeling good, he said, and he would help through the noon rush. Five or six customers came in the next two hours and he sat in a quiet corner taking a sleep while I handled the trade. There were not more than two customers at any one time and I flourished around, got them what they called for on our plain and simple bill of fare. I felt important. Maybe after a while

I might work up to be a partner in the business. I ate a ham sandwich with two fried eggs and coffee.

The owner woke up and went out saying he would be back soon. Three o'clock and he came in feeling better than the last time he came in. He had forgotten to eat at noon and there being no customers around, I offered to fix him two fried eggs, which I served him with a bun and coffee. He went out saying he would be back soon. I served two customers while he was gone. Five o'clock and he came back "stewed to the gills," slumped himself in a corner on the floor, and went to sleep. I fried myself three eggs and ate them with two buns and coffee. I fixed two sandwiches with thick cuts of ham, put them in my coat pockets along with two doughnuts, opened the money drawer and took out a half-dollar. With my coat on one arm, I closed the front door softly, and that night slept in a boxcar that took me halfway across the State of Missouri. For a poor boy seeking his fortune I hadn't done so bad for one day.

In Kansas City Mrs. Mullin had a sign in the window of her restaurant on Armour Avenue, "Dishwasher Wanted." She took the sign out when the Swede boy from Illinois made himself at home in the kitchen with the mulatto chef and the one waiter, also a mulatto. I had good times in that kitchen. The chef was fat, jolly, always cheerful. The waiter was handsome, brown-faced, gay, and he could sing. Noontime was the rush hour of the workers from the meat-packing plants nearby. It was a fight in that dish trough to get enough dirty dishes cleaned for serving the customers. I swept the eating room morning and afternoon and mopped it on Saturday.

My sleeping place was the end of a hallway with my cot curtained off, and I washed and shaved, using my pocket mirror, at a sink and faucet in the hall. I was tired one morning when I said to the chef, "I don't care whether school keeps or not." I remember the laugh of the chef as he told the waiter, "Gus says he don't care whether school keeps or not." I was going by the name of Gus Sandburg. Why I changed from Charlie to Gus I don't know. George could sing either old-time songs or late hits. One afternoon he sang a sad song that had me melting. I said, "That's pretty fine, George. It sure gets me." He said, "I'll sing that for a sweet girl tonight and she'll give me anything I ask her for." I believed him. Only a woman with a heart of stone wouldn't soften to the way George sang, I believed. He took a liking to me and would sing again special songs I called for.

I was up at six in the morning and had the eating room swept for customers who began coming in at six-thirty when we opened. I worked every weekday till eight o'clock at night except for an hour or two in the afternoon. I had three good meals a day. The chef would ask me what I wanted and fix it for me as though he was an uncle of mine and nothing was too good for me. I had Sunday off and walked miles around Kansas City comparing it to Galesburg, Peoria, Keokuk, and Chicago.

In a week or so the wheat harvest in western Kansas would be ready. Mrs. Mullin paid me my second week's pay of one dollar and fifty cents. I thanked her and said good-by and saw the sign "Dishwasher Wanted" whisked back into the street window. Shaking hands with George and the chef and saying good-by wasn't so easy. They were goodhearted men who had made everything easier and brighter for me.

In a windy rain I jumped out of a boxcar and found a sleeping place under a loading platform for stock cars. About seven o'clock in the morning I read the station sign and learned I was in Hutchinson, Kansas. I had heard it was better not to hit the houses near the railroad. They had been hit too often by 'bos. I walked eight or ten blocks and hit two houses. "Have you got any work I can do for breakfast?" They took one look at me and shut the door. At the third house a woman sent her daughter to get me a saw, showed me a woodpile and a sawbuck. For an hour I kept the saw going, piled the wood, and went to the house. The smiling mother and daughter led me to the family table, set fried ham and potatoes, applesauce, bread and coffee, before me. After I had eaten they handed me a large lump. I thanked them forty ways, walked Main Street to see what Hutchinson was like, and went on to my loading platform. Unwrapping the lump, I found fried chicken and bread that would make dinner and supper, along with two pocketfuls of apples that had come down in the wind and rain the night before.

Newspapers said the country was pulling out of the Hard Times. Yet there were still many men out of work, many men who had left their homes hoping for jobs somewhere. You could see these men riding the boxcars and sitting around the jungle hangouts. Some had learned hobo slang. Some didn't care for it. There was always a small fraternity who knew each other at once by their slang. They were professional tramps, who divided into panhandlers and petty thieves.

In one jungle a panhandler, for no reason I could think of, got confidential with me and two other gaycats. He pointed to a spindly fellow somewhat well dressed who seemed shy about mixing with other fellows around. "See that squirt over there?" he said. "He's a pimp. They beat him up and threw him out of a Kansas City whorehouse last week." It could have been, and then maybe not. He was speaking his mind and made it clear that as a panhandler he had little respect for a pimp and there was a social chasm between them. I remembered him at a later time when a panhandler told me, "I always get a good feed at a whorehouse unless there's a pimp around. The pimps are too goddam jealous of us."

I was meeting fellow travelers and fellow Americans. What they were doing to my heart and mind, my personality, I couldn't say then nor later and be certain. I was getting a deeper self-respect than I had had in Galesburg, so much I knew. I was getting to be a better storyteller. You can be loose and easy when from day to day you meet strangers you will know only an hour or a day or two.

In one jungle was a little fellow in his middle forties who said that every summer he would break away from Chicago and take to the road, working now and then. "What I like," he said, "is to sleep under the stars. Do yuh know the stars is a great study? I never read a book about the stars but I never get tired of lookin at 'em and watchin how they move and change. The stars make me feel that whatever is wrong with the world or with me sometime is goin to be made right. The stars is the only book I read." He had a question he said kept bothering his brain: "Why does God make it rain on the ocean where there is plenty of water and not on the desert where the rain is needed?" He wanted more light on that. "I like to watch the workins of my own mind," he said. "The longer I live my mind gets to be more of a mystery to me."

At Lakin, Kansas, I noticed on a timetable that I was six hundred and eighty-four miles from Galesburg on the Santa Fe. I figured what with detours I had traveled a thousand miles since I left home. I worked with a threshing crew some three weeks around Lakin. The job finished on one farm, we moved to another farm with a different farmer and family. The work came easier with getting used to it. The dust in your nose and eyes, the chaff sliding down your sweating back, you got used to. I moved on by fast freight to Rocky Ford.

Thousands poured into Rocky Ford for the Melon Day celebration. Watermelon and cantaloupe were handed out free to everybody. I rode a crowded passenger train that evening—sitting on a small board over the rods of a truck between the wheels of the train. I changed for a freight train where I had a boxcar sleep and got off in the morning not knowing where I was. I didn't bother to go back and read the station sign. I ate a sandwich as I walked west on the railroad track. The day was sunny and cool. My eyes caught high rises of tumbling land I had never met before. "Jesus," I said, "those are the Rocky Mountains." I hadn't planned it but there they were, rolling formations of rock and pine lifted away high. "There's the Hand of God," I said. I couldn't think of anything before in my life that had me using that phrase, "the Hand of God."

I walked on to Canyon City, took a look at the outside of the state penitentiary and felt good that I wasn't inside. I picked pears, earned meals and a few half-dollars, went on to Salida, where I spent two days. Then I took a Colorado Midland train heading back east aiming for Denver. It was night. There wasn't an empty boxcar on the train, and for the first time I was riding the bumpers late at night. I didn't know what a stupid reckless fool I was. My feet were on the bumpers. My hands were on the brake rod so in case my feet should slip I could hold on and not go under the wheels. Suddenly I was saying to myself, "You damn fool, you've been asleep." My numb brain was saying that when you go to sleep on the bumpers you're in luck if your hands don't loosen and topple you down under the moving train. I would watch myself and not go to sleep again. We had been running along maybe an hour when again I caught myself coming out of a sleep. From then on I wouldn't trust myself to be still for even a second. I kept changing my position. I kept moving my feet and hands. I beat the sides of my head with my fists. I kicked one leg against the other. An hour of that and the train stopped and I got off and thanked God and the everlasting stars over the Rockies. Many a time later I said that the Angel of Death hovered over that train that night and saw me standing and sleeping and brushed past me with soft wing tips saying, "Not yet for this boy. He's young yet. Let him live."

I saw Pikes Peak so I could say I saw it. At the Windsor, a first-class hotel in Denver, I washed dishes two weeks, for a dollar and fifty cents a week, a cubbyhole for a room and meals as good as were served to the silk-hat guests. Then came the question whether I should head for the West Coast or east to Galesburg. I admitted I was a little homesick for the faces and streets of Galesburg. Where a passenger train was on slow speed out of the yards I hopped on the steps of a Pullman vestibule. A conductor and porter ordered me off. I got off and saw the train slow to a stop. I climbed on top of a Pullman car, lay with my head toward the engine, swore a solemn oath I wouldn't go to sleep. The car rocked and shook going around curves and my hands held tight so I wouldn't slide off the roof of the car. It was a cool September night and the train speed made it cold. I still had no underwear. I buttoned my coat, turned the collar up and tied a handkerchief around my neck. I went to sleep twice and coming out of it kept hitting and kicking myself to stay awake.

Daybreak came. An early farmer waved to me and laughed. I saw we were pulling in to a division point, McCook, Nebraska. I climbed down and started to walk out of the yards. A one-eyed man in plain clothes with a club and a star stood in my way. "Where did you come from?" His tone was horstyle. "I just got off that train," I said. He gave me my orders in a more horstyle tone: "We don't want the likes of you in this town. You get back on that train." There were no trainmen in sight as I climbed back to where I had been riding. I had a daylight view of the Nebraska landscape from McCook for thirty miles to the next stop at Oxford. No one was waiting for me at Oxford. I went to a lunch counter, where they let me into the kitchen to wash the cinders and soot out of my head, hair, ears, and neck. Then I ordered a monster breakfast of ham and eggs, fried potatoes, bread, coffee, and two pieces of pie, paying thirty-five cents in cash.

I caught a freight for Omaha. The Hotel Mercer took me on as dishwasher at a dollar and fifty cents a week. The pastry cook was a sweet Creole girl from New Orleans. The vegetable man, a fast potato-peeler, was John Whitney, and I hope he did well after what came to happen. The hotel was leased and run by a fancy-dressed tall man who slid and slunk rather than walked around the place. He was known as Wink Taylor. I didn't notice him wink at any time but he probably had the name because he was quick as a wink. At the end of the first week I didn't get my standard pay of a dollar and fifty cents nor at the end of the second week. Then came the word that the Hotel Mercer was foreclosed, and Wink Taylor vanished. He owed me three dollars that never got paid.

I had one last sleep in the Mercer, crossed over to Council Bluffs and had a breakfast of one pork chop, fried potatoes, and bread and coffee for five cents. Then I caught one freight train after another till I came in sight of Galesburg the afternoon of October fifteenth. I had timed it so that I wouldn't feel on my head the crashing club of the night policeman Richardson, known far and wide as "that god-dam nigger bull in Galesburg."

I walked along Berrien Street till I came to the only house in the United States where I could open a door without knocking and walk in for a kiss from the woman of the house. They gave me a sitdown and as they had had only two or three letters from me, they asked me where I had been and I told them the half of it. When I showed my father fifteen dollars and a few nickels, he said the money would come in handy and I should watch it. The clean bed sheets that night were not so bad. Mart said that along in August he had read in a newspaper 'bout a hobo riding the bumpers in western Kansas who fell off the bumpers and was mangled to death. The folks hadn't read it and he didn't tell them. "But I was afraid, Cully, that maybe it was you." Then I told him about how in Colorado it could have been me and I was a fool.

What had the trip done to me? I couldn't say. It had changed me. I was easier about looking people in the eye. When questions came I was quicker at answering them or turning them off. I had been a young stranger meeting many odd strangers and I had practiced at having answers. At home and among my old chums they knew I had changed but they could no more tell how than I. Away deep in my heart now I had hope as never before. Struggles lay ahead, I was sure, but whatever they were I would not be afraid of them.

SOLDIER

President McKinley declared war and I was sworn into Company C, Sixth Infantry Regiment of Illinois Volunteers, on April 26, 1898, for two years of service. The regiment had been part of the State Militia. Company C was a living part of Galesburg, had its drill hall, marched in uniform with rifles and bayonets on public occasions, went to Springfield once a year for regimental maneuvers. The company needed a dozen recruits to fill its quota and I was among the earliest. I knew most of the privates, had worked for Corporal Cully Rose at the Auditorium and had gone to school with Con Byloff, who was first lieutenant. About three-fourths of the members were from Galesburg and the rest from farms and country towns around Galesburg. They elected their own officers and you could hear fellows, "No West Pointers in *this* regiment."

When I quit my job and told the family I was going for to be a soldier they were a little sad and somewhat puzzled. They knew they couldn't stop me from going, as I was set on it. Mart spoke for the family, "We'd like the honor of having a United States soldier in the family but we don't want you to be killed." I said it might not be a real war and if it was I might not get shot because some soldiers always come back home. And besides, having seen the West I would now see the East and maybe the Atlantic Ocean and Cuba.

Our family and hundreds of others were all there when the train carrying Company C pulled out from the Q. depot. I saw my mother crying and waved to her with a laugh and she laughed back through her tears. The *Republican-Register* said, "The scene growing out of their departure was one such as is witnessed but few times in the life of a generation."

On the fairgrounds at Springfield we were quartered in an immense brick building used for livestock exhibits. While still in civilian clothes I was handed a Springfield rifle and put through the manual of arms and company drill. I was certified as enlisting at "twenty-one years of age, five feet ten inches high, ruddy complexion, grey eyes, brown hair and by occupation a painter." It was the first I had heard that my complexion was ruddy. And as I was ten months short of being twenty-one years of age I think I may have told them I was twenty-one and therefore old enough to be a soldier and full citizen.

In about ten days I slid into a uniform, a heavy blue-wool shirt, a coat of dark blue with brass buttons that went to the throat, pants of a light-blue wool cloth double as thick as the coat cloth. This was the same uniform that the privates under Grant and Sherman had worn thirty-five years before, intended for wear in those border states of the South where snow fell and zero weather might come as at Fort Donelson the night Grant attacked. The little cap was a cute trick. It wouldn't shed rain from your ears and above the stiff black visor it ran flat as though your head should be flat there. I felt honored to wear the uniform of famous Union armies and yet I had mistrust of it.

In a big room of the state capitol building a hundred of us stood naked and one by one passed before an examining surgeon. He was a German with a pronounced accent and a high falsetto voice. He listened to our heartbeats. He had us open our mouths and hold them open so we felt like horses to be auctioned. He called off his findings to a recording clerk. He was no stickler for regulations, this surgeon. When our little friend Joe Dunn came along he was found to be an inch or two short of the required height. The tears began running down Joe's face. The surgeon looked toward officers nearby, who gave him a nod. And he wrapped the measuring tape around a finger, measured again and found that Joe would pass.

We roamed around the capital, walked past the governor's house, out past the home of Abraham Lincoln. We gawked at statues of dead statesmen sitting and standing, dead generals riding horses, and I think we found one statue of a private soldier in a cape overcoat, standing with his musket at ease and ready for the order "Atten-SHUN!"

On the train to Washington rumors ran thick and fast about how soon we would be shooting Spaniards. On the day coaches we had each a wicker-covered seat to sit in and to take our night's sleep in. At some stations crowds met the train with cheers and smiles. The train arrived in Washington and the night was dark when it was shunted to Falls Church, Virginia. We marched two miles to level ground with underbrush and woods around it. We dipped our tin cups into a shallow creek, filled our canteens, and drank the murky water because we were thirsty. We put up tents and slept on the ground, two soldiers to a tent. The next morning we went to the woods, cut saplings with crotched sticks and branches and made bunks to lay our blankets on.

We drilled. Across late May and all of June we drilled. We learned the bugle notes from reveille, mess call, sick call, assembly, to tattoo and taps. We filled our canteens from a piped water supply and washed our shirts, socks, undershirts, and full-length drawers at the murky creek in the woods. Most of the time we ate field rations as though we were in a campaign, bean soup and pork and beans more often than any other items. Our company cook was a prize—Arthur Metcalf, with his moon face and wide mouth having a smile that forgave you all your sins except murder. He did the best with what the War Department, through its quartermasters, let him have. I saw him one morning patiently cut away from a flitch of pork about a quarter of it that was alive with maggots. This was seven miles from the City of Washington where the Department of War had its office.

My tent mate was Andrew Tanning, as clean, scrupulous, and orderly a corporal as ever served Uncle Sam. What I didn't know or couldn't guess about army regulations he was there to tell me. He took for himself the number of his rifle and would enter the tent saying, "Here comes Old Thirty-eight."

Our captain was Thomas Leslie McGirr, a second-rank Galesburg lawyer, a tall heavy man with a distinct paunch, heavy jaws, and a large mustache slightly graying. He kept by him a large yellow-haired St. Bernard dog named Smuggler, who in sight of the men was occasionally fed juicy sirloin steaks. Our first lieutenant, Conrad Byloff, seemed to be a born commander. He had the voice, the posture, the eye; the men had depths of affection for him. Our second lieutenant was Daniel K. Smyth, a scholar and a gentleman ever considerate of his men.

Ten of our company were Knox students and two were from Lombard. Some twenty or more were farm boys. At least twenty had had fathers, uncles, or near kinsmen in the Civil War. All had mixed motives in enlisting. Love of adventure, or a curiosity about facing dangers and standing hardships, was one and, I would judge, the outstanding one. A mystic love of country and the flag was there in degree among most of the men. Breaking away from a monotonous home environment to go where there was excitement could be read in the talk of some fellows. At least two of the older men had troublesome wives at home. The hope of pensions after service was sometimes definitely mentioned. Over all of us in 1898 was the shadow of the Civil War and the men who fought it to the end that had come only thirty-three years before our enlistment. Our motives were as mixed as theirs. I think many of Company C went along with my old chum Bohunk Calkins saying, "I want to find out whether I'll run when the shootin begins." The tall, thoughtful Charlie Winders hoped he wouldn't get shot, expected to come home and be a lawyer, though he couldn't have guessed at Camp Alger that he would end up in Seattle as general counsel of the Northern Pacific Railway.

How can you possibly forget a first sergeant who trains his voice every day by six and eight times calling off a hundred names? After a few weeks some of the men without looking in a book could call the roll from Benjamin Anderson to Henry Clay Woodward as smoothly as F. Elmer Johnson, first sergeant, who kept records, read orders, and was the hardest-worked man in the company.

Of the nine sergeants and eleven corporals I couldn't think of one that I hated and with the most of them I kept a lifelong friendship. Oscar S. Wilson, a Knox student, managed to be a true and devout Christian and an efficient corporal. Corporal Ed Peckenpaugh was up and down the company street and only the hard of hearing failed to get his baritone giving out "I Guess I'll Have to Telegraph My Baby." It was no surprise that later he led a choir and sang baritone anthems in a large church in Brooklyn, New York. Corporal James

Switzer was the company bugler, a handsome boy of seventeen, nick-named "Mim." Years later I would walk into his office at the LaSalle Street station in Chicago where he was the passenger traffic manager of the New York Central Railway system. And on my saying, "How are you, Mim?" he would say, "Hello, Cully."

On leave for a day we walked two miles to Falls Church, took a trolley to Washington, saw the Capitol and wondered what Congress was doing, walked past the White House and tried to guess how President McKinley was feeling. I had my first look at the Ford Theatre outside and inside and the outside of the Peterson House across the street.

For our State Militia caps we got felt hats with wide brims, and to replace our Springfield rifles we were issued Krag-Jörgensens. July sixth saw hustling and gabble. We began riding an Atlantic Coast Line train across Virginia and North Carolina to Charleston, South Carolina. We had our first look at tobacco and cotton growing, at the mansions, cabins, and hovels of the South, and at stations here and there men selling bottles of "cawn lickah" that had the color of rain water. We slept overnight in our coach seats and the next day quartered in big cotton warehouses on the wharf. We went swim-ming next to the wharf, and you could see the Illinois prairie boys taking mouthfuls of Atlantic Ocean water to taste it and calling to each other, "It *is* salt, isn't it?"

We saw lying at anchor the *Rita*, a lumber-hauling freighter, the first ship our navy had captured from the Spanish. Six companies of the Sixth Illinois boarded her on July eleventh, each man given a bunk made of new rough lumber. Running your bare arm or leg over it you met splinters. The air below was heavy, warm, and humid. On clear nights several hundred men brought their blankets up and covered the upper deck as they slept.

The *Rita* arrived in Guantánamo Bay, Cuba, on the evening of July seventeenth, our band playing and cheers coming to us from the decks of famous battleships, the *Oregon*, the *Indiana*, the *Iowa*, and more cheers from cruisers and torpedo boats. In the morning Colonel Jack Foster and staff officers went ashore to come back soon with word of Santiago taken and we wouldn't be put ashore to fight in Cuba. Some men were disappointed. Others were satisfied. Also, it was reported, there were ashore some four hundred troop cases of yellow fever and Colonel Jack had been ordered to get back to the *Rita* at once.

We sailed out of Guantánamo Bay, three thousand troops on the transports. Rumors ran that we were going to Porto Rico. If we had been reading United States newspapers, we would have believed we were going to land at Cape Fajardo near San Juan, the capital of Porto Rico. The War Department so believed and expected and therefore was sending transport fleets from Charleston and Tampa to be of help when we landed at Cape Fajardo and moved to attack San Juan. Of this we, the men and officers of the Sixth Illinois, knew no more than the nakedest Zulu in the African jungles. Even the commander of the three thousand men on this expedition to Porto Rico, General Nelson A. Miles, who had commanded a brigade in Grant's army in 1864, didn't know where we were going. When we sailed out of Guantánamo Bay he believed like those who read the United States newspapers and like the secretary of war that we would land on the north coast of Porto Rico at Cape Fajardo.

Then about halfway, about mid-passage of our cruise to Porto Rico, General Miles changed his mind. After he changed his mind he was sure of where we were going. Instead of landing at Cape Fajardo on the north coast we would land on the south coast of Porto Rico and he had picked the spot. It seemed that as his ship sailed the idea came to him that since the War Department had told the newspapers and the newspapers had told the world where his expedition was going to land and march and fight it might be safer and easier to land somewhere else where he wasn't expected.

Soon after daylight on July twenty-fifth we sighted a harbor and moved into it. Ahead we saw gunfire from a ship and landing boats filled with bluejackets moving toward shore. We were ordered to put on our cartridge belts and with rifles get into full marching outfits. We heard shooting, glanced toward shore once in a while and saw white puffs of smoke while we stood waiting our turns to climb down rope ladders into long boats called lighters. We were rowed to a shallow beach where we dropped into water above our hips. Holding rifles over our heads, we waded ashore. We were in Guánica, a one-street town with palm and coconut trees new to us. We expected to be ordered into action against Spanish troops somewhere in the town or nearby hills. We were marched to a field near the town where we waited over noon and afternoon. We ate our supper of cold canned beans and hardtack and soon after were ordered to march.

When we came to a halt we waited in the dark and heard shots that seemed not far away. This was the one time on that island when most of us expected to go into battle. And it didn't happen. We waited and marched back to our fields near Guánica. A story arose that Sixth Illinois troops that night did some wild firing, some of their bullets hitting the transport on which General Miles was sleeping, others of their bullets hitting a ship carrying Red Cross nurses. I can merely testify that neither Company C nor the companies on our flanks did any firing that night. It could have been that the shots we heard sounding to us like enemy fire were from the Krag-Jörgensens of Sixth Illinois boys aiming at random at an unseen enemy. Some of us had been "shaking in our boots" and it would have been a relief to shoot at anything in any direction. We heard in the morning that bluejackets from the ship *Gloucester* and regulars with artillery had killed four Spanish soldiers, driven a troop of cavalry to the hills, and there was no enemy in sight or hearing. We heard later too that the secretary of war and many others in the United States were stupefied to learn that General Miles had changed his mind and begun operations on the south coast.

We marched to Yauco and on to Ponce, finding those towns surrendered. We had camped in a wooded ravine two nights. After the first two or three hours of mosquito bites, sleeping in our underwear and barefoot, we put on our pants, wool shirts, and socks, for all of the moist heat. The mosquitoes were large, ravenous, pitiless. "They came with bugles sounding mess call," said one man with a swollen face. On the second night I followed others in wrapping my rubber poncho around my head. After an hour I would wake with an aching head from foul air breathed over too many times. I would throw the poncho off, beat away the mosquitoes, wrap the poncho around my head again, then sleep till awaking with a headache—and repeat.

On roads and streets as we marched were barefooted men and women smiling and calling to us "*Puerto Rico Americano.*" For four hundred years this island had been run by a Spanish government at Madrid. Now it was to be American and it was plain that the island common people liked the idea and had more hope of it. More than once we saw on the roadside a barefoot man wearing only pants, shirt, and hat, eating away at an ear of parched corn. We saw knee-high children wearing only a ragged shirt and their little swollen bellies told of something wrong with their food, not enough food and not the right kind.

We camped at Ponce a few days and then began a march up mountain roads. The August tropic heat was on. We carried cartridge belt, rifle, bayonet, blanket roll, half a canvas pup tent, haversack with rations, a coat. We still wore the heavy blue-wool pants of the Army of the Potomac in '65 and thick canvas leggings laced from ankles to knees. On one halt after another there were men tearing their blankets in two so as to lessen weight to carry. I tore a third of mine away. Some let the whole blanket go. Men fell out, worn-out, and there were sunstroke cases. We passed more than one on the ground raving about the heat. It was an eight-mile march upgrade. We halted for the night on a slope above the road. We were sleeping and all was quiet about midnight. Suddenly came a shriek. Then a series of yells and shrieks and several companies of men rushing headlong down the slope to the road. Men sleeping or just awakened were trampled and bruised. It was found that one of the bullocks hauling carts loaded with supplies and ammunition had got loose and hunting for grass had tramped on a sleeper who gave the first piercing shriek that was taken up by others. We went up the slope and back to our sleep calling it the "First Battle of Bull Run."

We camped on a slope on the edge of Adjuntas, where we saw the American flag run up. Cook Metcalf over a long afternoon had boiled a tinned beef we named "Red Horse." For all the boiling it was stringy and tasteless, "like boiled shoestrings flavored with wallpaper." We had set up our pup tents, laid our ponchos and blankets on the ground, and gone to sleep in a slow drizzle of rain. About three o'clock in the morning a heavy downpour of rain kept coming. We were on a slope and the downhill water soaked our blankets. We got out of our tents, wrung our blankets as dry as we could and threw them with ponchos over our shoulders. Then a thousand men stood around waiting for daylight and hoping the rain would let down. Daylight did come. Metcalf did manage some hot pork and beans with coffee. Midmorning the sun did come out and we dried and marched on to Utuado.

There at Utuado came news, "The protocol has been signed and peace is declared and we are ordered back to Ponce." Marching down the mountain roads we had climbed came easy along with rumors that we would take transports home from Ponce and replacements were on the way. Rains beat down and we were lighthearted and cried, "Hurrah for the protocol!" It was a new funny word we liked. Instead of "Good morning," we said, "How's your old protocol?" We slept a night in a building used for drying coffee. Each man fitted nicely into a dry bin enclosure rich with a coffee smell.

At Ponce many of us weighed to see what we had sweated and groaned out. All but a half-dozen men had lost weight. My one hundred and fifty-two pounds in April had gone down to one hundred and thirty pounds in August. Many were gaunt and thin, with a slightly yellow tint on the skin of hands and faces. Uniforms were fading, here and there ragged and torn. Hats had holes in them. On some hats the fellows had written in purple with indelible pencils the names of places we'd been.

Our transport with the whole Sixth Illinois sailed for New York. We were divided into messes of eight men for rations. A tin of "Red Horse" would be handed to one man who opened it. He put it to his nose, smelled of it, wrinkled up his face, and took a spit. The next man did the same and the next till the eight men of the mess had smelled, grimaced, and spit. Then that tin of "Red Horse" was thrown overboard for any of the fishes of the Atlantic Ocean who might like it. Somehow we got along on cold canned beans, occasional salmon, and the reliable hardtack. What we called "Red Horse" soon had all of our country scandalized with its new name of "Embalmed Beef." It *was* embalmed. We buried it at sea because it was so duly embalmed and every suck of nourishment gone from it.

On the transport we went through a ceremonial we had gone through many times before. A circle of men might be sitting on deck talking and jollying when one would call out "Shirts off! Time for inspection!" Then each man ran his eyes over all parts of the shirt, especially the seams, picking the graybacks and crushing them. Underwear and pants were more of a problem. In camp we boiled them occasionally when there was time and a big kettle of water. But only a bath all over with sizzling hot water would get those in armpits and other hideouts where they were dug in. This I had learned the year before in hobo jungles.

We sailed into the port of New York at night, docked at Weehawken, and in the morning saw a small crowd looking up at us and waving hands and hats. On the dock I bought a loaf of white bread for a nickel and a quart of milk for another nickel. As I ate that bread and milk I felt that I had been an animal and was now a human being—it was so clean, tasty, delicious. We roamed around New York City; men and women stopped us to ask where we had been, some to ask if we had news of regiments their boys were in, others to ask what we might want in the way of food or drink. There was hospitality that made us feel good about the country. They acted like we were heroes. We had our doubts about that but we did know we could use more fresh victuals and boiling hot water with strong soap.

As for history, Theodore Roosevelt summed it up in a speech at the Stockyards Pavilion in Chicago which I covered for a newspaper.

He happened to mention the Spanish-American War and added with a chuckle and a flash of his teeth, "It wasn't much of a war but it was all the war there was."

The war, though a small one, was the first in which the United States sent troops on ocean transports to fight on foreign soil and acquire island possessions. It was a small war edging toward immense consequences.

Again on a train of coaches with wicker seats we rode and slept, reached Springfield, Illinois, and camped there while our muster-out papers were arranged. When our train pulled into the Burlington station at Galesburg on September twenty-first we had been gone only five months but we looked like we had been somewhere. The station platform swarmed with a crowd that overran Seminary Street for a block to the north, and from there on to Main Street the sidewalks were lined thick with people. I caught my mother's face and others of the family laughing and waving their hands high.

I went that evening with Mary to a farmhouse near Dahinda where she was teaching a country school. They put me in a room with a four-poster feather bed. I climbed up on the mattress, laid my head on a pillow, and sank into the feathers for a sleep. I tossed around a half-hour, then got out of the bed and in thirty seconds went to sleep on the rag carpet on the floor.

The next day I went to home and mother. Mart said, "Well, you didn't get killed, did you?" "No, they didn't give me a chance." "Well, what did you learn?" Mart went on. "I learnt more than I can use." "Well," said Mart, "last year you was a hobo and this year a soldier. What's next with you?" "Maybe I'll go to college." "College! Jesus, that'll be something!" came from Mart.

My father gave me a rich smile that spread out and around his mouth and went up into his twinkling eyes. He gave me a handshake that wilted me. He said he stayed on the job the day before and when shopmen asked him why he didn't take the day off and go join the big cheering crowds, he said, "I will see my boy at home and he will tell me everything." Mother said it had been a big summer for him, with the shopmen and neighbors often asking him, "How's the boy, Gus?" or "Company C is getting a long ways from home, Gus. We hope your boy comes through all right." Mart told me such talk hit our Old Man deep and it seemed that now he was sure he was an Americanized citizen. He liked it where it said in my muster-out papers, "A good soldier, service honest and faithful," and said we should frame it to hang on the Front Room wall. I gave him fifty dollars of my muster-out money, which amounted to one hundred and three dollars and seventy-three cents. He was walking slower, moving around slower, his shoulders more bony so that the hump of muscle on the right shoulder stood out more.

We were in the newspapers that week. The Army and Navy League gave us a banquet at the Universalist Church and the Ladies' Society of the First Presbyterian Church another big dinner. The biggest affair was an oyster supper in the basement of the First Methodist Church where President John Huston Finley of Knox read a poem about our exploits. It was a free-going poem with nice touches of humor and a printed copy of it in a little book with red covers was presented to each member of Company C.

In nearly every life come sudden little events not expected that change its course. Private George R. Longbrake of Company C, whose back yard on Brooks Street touched our back yard on Berrien, had spoken to me on the transport about my going to Lombard, now a university, where he had been a student for a year. He asked whether I would enter as a student if, as he believed, they would give me free tuition for a year. I said yes. So after all the cheering and the church banquets were over, he came to me saying the arrangement had been cheerfully made at Lombard. Private Lewis W. Kay, one of the two Lombard students in Company C, had died of fever about the time of our muster-out.

Then came Wiz Brown, who was the keenest wit in Company C, saying there was a fire-department job vacant. The department had two "call men." They slept at the department at night and in the daytime when the fire whistle blew and was heard over the town, they went to a telephone; if it was a big fire they bicycled to it as fast as their pedals would take them. A call man was paid ten dollars a month. "That's nice money, Cully, and I'm sure if I speak to Mayor Carney he'll appoint you," said Wiz. He appointed me. I bought a bicycle and a blue shirt with a big collar that buttoned far down the chest and two rows of pearl buttons of silver-dollar size. I began sleeping on the second floor of the Prairie Street station house. We were sixteen men sleeping in one room. Alongside each iron frame bed was a pair of rubber boots with pants and when the alarm bell rang we stepped out of bed, pulled up the pants, ran to slide down a brass pole and hop on the chemical wagon or the hose cart. Chief Jim O'Brien gave me a glad hand and said, "Considering where you been, Charlie, I think you'll make a good fireman."

I enrolled at Lombard for classes in Latin, English, inorganic chemistry, and elocution, drama, and public speaking. That was what I elected. They had an "elective system." I had to leave class when the fire whistle blew but that wasn't often enough to bother either the class or the professor. I was going to get an education. So I hoped.

Often in the 1890's I would get to thinking about what a young prairie town Galesburg was—nearly twenty thousand people, and they had all come in fifty years. Before that it was empty rolling prairie. And I would ask: Why did they come? Why couldn't they get along where they had started from? Was Galesburg any different from the many other towns, some bigger and some smaller? Did I know America, the United States, because of what I knew about Galesburg? In Sweden all the people in a town were Swedes, in England they were all English, and in Ireland all Irish. But here in Galesburg we had a few from everywhere and there had even been cases of Swedish Lutherans marrying Irish Catholic girls—and what was to come of it all? It didn't bother me nor keep me awake nights but I couldn't help thinking about it and asking: What is this America I am a part of, where I will soon be a full citizen and a voter? All of us are living under the American flag, the Stars and Stripes—what does it mean? Men have died for it—why? When they say it is a free country, they mean free for what and free for whom, and what is freedom?

I said I would listen and read and ask and maybe I would learn. By guessing and hoping and reaching out I might get a hold on some of the answers. Those questions in those words may not have run through my mind yet they ran in my blood. Dark and tangled they were to run in my blood for many years. To some of the questions I would across the years get only half-answers, mystery answers.

Biographer
and
Historian

Steichen the Photographer

Published in 1929 in an edition limited to 925 copies, the book contained forty-nine photographs by Steichen, reproduced by the then new Knudsen process. No attempt was made to write a formal biography, as the author explains in his foreword:

Biographies of contemporaries are difficult. Years of the mellowing tests of time are an advantage in doing a full-length book portrait of any individual. There are opinions, judgments, facts, surmises, secrets, that look better in print fifty years after the subject has gone where the woodbine twineth and the lizards sleep on the idle slabs in the lazy sunlight. Yet there are men whose contemporaries can't keep still. Out of love and fun, sometimes hate and ill will, they must write—and out of such writings is laid the basis for later biographies worthwhile. I told friends of Steichen, "He throws a long shadow and ranks close to Ben Franklin and Leonardo da Vinci when it comes to versatility." And they said, "We would like to get out a little book now." So here is the little book, wherein the author may be allowed prejudices in writing about his wife's brother. It is not at all a statement of the life, career and works of Edward Steichen. It is a little record and memoir of data, opinion and whim, as between friends.

Roughly sixty per cent of Carl Sandburg's loving memoir of the fifty-year-old Steichen follows.

I

A painter was making a portrait of J. Pierpont Morgan, Sr. And wanting a photograph to help toward a speaking likeness, he told Mr. Morgan there was a young camera genius who should be called in. Mr. Morgan was willing. He stipulated merely that the young camera genius should work fast. He would sit two minutes.

The famous financier reached the painter's studio on time to the dot. Edward Steichen was there with his camera. In fact, a half-hour earlier Steichen had been posing the janitor of the building in different parts of the studio, assuming that God's good sunlight would work the same way on a great financier's face as on that of a jocular janitor.

Steichen pointed to a chair and requested Mr. Morgan to sit. Mr. Morgan laid his big cigar to one side and did so, though he was not at ease and his posture was lacking in accustomed poise. The camera clicked for one exposure.

"Now," said Steichen, making it snappy though not too snappy, "would you please sit a little differently? Just swing your head around and we'll have it. Just swing your head around!" And Mr. Morgan swung his head around, exercised the muscles of his neck, and brought his massive head back to the same place and position it had started from.

"That's good! That's excellent!" was Steichen's outburst—though Steichen knew that Mr. Morgan was faced and postured precisely as in the first exposure. What had happened was that now Mr. Morgan's head rested where he himself had put it of his own choice and volition—which was what Steichen wanted—the subject was at ease, comfortable, which makes a difference in the look of the eyes and the pantomimic speech of the shoulders.

Again the camera clicked. "Thank you, sir," said Steichen. "Is that all?" inquired Mr. Morgan. "Yes, sir."

The great Wall Street umpire had been in the studio exactly two minutes. He clapped his big hat on his head, reached for his big cigar that in a moment jutted from the face in the relation of headlight to locomotive, and shot from the corner of his mouth the remark, "I like you, young man. I think we'll get along first-rate together."

The portrait painter took charge of the financier, escorting him to the elevator, where Mr. Morgan took out a roll of bills, picked out five hundred-dollar notes, and said, "Give this to that young man."

Two prints were brought to Mr. Morgan by Steichen. He looked on the first one, called it good, and ordered a dozen prints. The second one Mr. Morgan didn't like. He tore it in two and once again. The action was a quick insult to young Steichen, whose heart was strong or it would have broken.

One may be a wizard in banking, railroad and industrial reorganizations, and fail at knowing a photograph that wins. Steichen toiled for months till he got an enlarged print, perfect for his purposes, of the rejected photograph. On exhibition the next year it made an impression on all who saw it. Miss Belle da Costa Greene, librarian to Mr. Morgan, declared it in her opinion the greatest portrait ever made of the redoubtable, picaresque subject who had sat for it. She took the print to Mr. Morgan, who claimed he had never seen it till then. He authorized Miss Greene to buy it. However, that particular print belonged to Alfred Stieglitz, editor of the magazine *Camera Work*, in which it was to be reproduced. A bid of $5,000 was made by Mr. Morgan for the print. And the bid was refused. Then an order was placed with Steichen for the now recognized masterpiece of portraiture. And Steichen held off for three years before delivery of the wanted picture. He once said, "That was my childish way of getting even for the tearing up of the first picture."

On the same day that Steichen made the famous Morgan photograph he had another adventure. It was a day of contrast. After that sitting he hopped into a cab and a half-hour later was at the Savoy Hotel with his camera aimed at Eleanora Duse, the Italian actress who took her roles without facial make-up.

"She was completely unconscious of the camera," says Steichen. "Never before nor since have I photographed any person so completely unconscious of the camera." She would forget all about Steichen and the hooded black instrument. "Hold that!" was the word. And for a fraction of a second she would hold it—and then move. She was told to keep in her hand a bunch of roses. She did—then bowed her head, smelled of the flowers, and lifted her head. "I was so spellbound I didn't care," says Steichen.

Five plates were no good because she moved. But the sixth! That was a picture! Mystical, exalted, delicate, tragic. When shown the bad plates she smiled and offered to sit again at the Steichen studio. She arrived at the hour appointed a few days later, and said, "I don't feel a bit like having my picture taken—let's chat." And she perched on a packing case and she and Steichen talked like two school chums about people and faces and art—while a secretary looked at a watch, impatient over appointments being broken.

II

Well—that day in which Steichen photographed within two hours the most massive realist of the American financial world and the most delicately shaded genius of dramatic art then on American shores—

that day was only a few years after he had said good-by to Midwest America—he was only twenty-seven years old.

By turning pages backward we come to the time when he was a toddler in Hancock, Michigan, kicking his toes at a ceiling, blissfully unaware of time exposures and perfectly obedient to his chromosomes. His father worked in the copper mines. His mother had a good head and fingers; she made hats and ran a hat store for women. At seven and eight the boy was in the green grocery business—in a footloose way—with low rent and overhead—carrying a basket from door to door and selling lettuce, string beans, cabbage and carrots from his father's garden. He sold newspapers and magazines—and after a while had the money for a camera. He had not yet decided to be an artist. The camera interested him as a piece of machinery, delicate and of strange moods. The little black box would tell truth wonderfully—and again was a monstrous and comical liar.

A very loving and much loved mother wanted her boy to have advantages. Nothing could be too good for him. The copper country was too far from the centers of true learning. She was a mother— with hopes tall as the angel wings of a Raphael or a Correggio. A tag was fastened to his coat lapel one day in the railroad station at Hancock. He was nine years old. They were billing him through to Milwaukee and the Pio Nono (Pius the Ninth) College preparatory school, where he matriculated and began studying his lessons.

In a drawing class at the Pio Nono school Destiny connected him up with art. He brought in sketches he had made through using transparent paper (which was cheating) and on which he had received help from older persons (which also was cheating). He roughed up some of the firm clear lines made through transparent paper (which was not merely cheating, but was cheating "with felonious intent"). Now the priest gave high praise to his sketches. So did others of the elders. His mother declared, "He must be an artist, he shall be a g-r-e-a-t artist!" From then on he was in for it. And the family moved to Milwaukee, then as now the art capital of Wisconsin.

One day when business was better than ever at the hat store for ladies which his mother was conducting, she gave him money for a bicycle. He rode to the Western Union office, got a job as messenger at fifteen dollars a month (regular pay was ten dollars), and went whizzing around as the first rubber-tire telegram-delivery service seen in that city. The Western Union superintendent heard about him, called him into the head office, and said, "I wanted a look at a boy who has new ideas."

The boy had an eye for the latest devices of applied science, asking eagerly, "How does it work? What makes it go? Why is this? And why is that?" He took the bicycle to pieces and put it together again with all pieces fitted. He took apart an old Waterbury watch and assembled it, having two parts left over! Yet the watch ran—and how and why bothered the boy's head. He showed it to a family friend, a watch repair expert, who said, "I have never had any luck making watches go with two pieces left out."

Extra money was coming in, tips from people thankful to the boy who made quick telegram deliveries on a bicycle. He threw these dimes and quarters into a small cigar box stuck between loose plaster in the wall of his bedroom. With this cash in hand one sunny fall day he started for Chicago and gave himself a week at the World's Columbian Exposition. He looked, read, listened and rambled among all the marvels of modern mechanics and art, lived on chocolate most of that week and kept enough of his money to buy an electric motor. At home in Milwaukee he mastered by himself the leading principles of the science of electrodynamics. He built an electric railway and cars. He tried to hitch the motor to a little red wagon so he would have a horseless vehicle—but it was no go. He decided he would wait before making an automobile.

III

Then Edward at fifteen years of age was signed up as a four-year apprentice with the American Lithographing Company of Milwaukee. He was given a broom and told to sweep out the works every morning; he washed windows, cleaned cuspidors, delivered goods, ran errands. For the first year his wages were nix, nothing at all; the pleasure was all his. The second year he got two dollars a week, the third year three dollars and the fourth year four dollars.

Extra money was coming in. He got twenty-five dollars in real coin for a program cover design used for the Deutscher Club annual banquet. He painted water colors of Indian heads, busts and heads of women; these were sold in department stores; Gimbel's had a window exhibition of them. When the brewery workers, the allied printing trades or the turner societies held a picnic he was on hand with his camera. Snapshots were so much per. Then throughout the year he was doing a photo portrait business, cabinets and specials at so much a dozen. And every spare dollar he laid by; he had a Purpose.

He organized the Milwaukee Art Students League and was elected president. They hired a hall, employed instructors, engaged models, put on exhibits. It was the era of Eugene Field's declaration in a nearby city, "When Chicago gets going she'll make culture hum."

He was now able to say to the lithographing company that he could better himself elsewhere unless they could better him. The boss saw him painting one noon hour; a pretty birdie in a pretty nest. The boss liked it. He was promoted to the drafting room at twenty-five dollars a week, which soon jumped to fifty. He was designing posters now. One day it was beer, another day patent medicine, that he was ordered to exploit and sing and make attractive through color and line.

One fall morning the boss said, "We want pigs and corn shocks to show lifelike in your next poster." And Steichen rode his bicycle out among the farmers and made photographs of pigs and corn shocks to look at as he drew them for the poster. In that shop this had not been done before.

Next he designed ladies' hats, which his mother made according to design. As she put them in the show window she said, "I'll never sell these hats," the son replying, "Well, people will see them in the window and then come in the store to see what else there is!"

He fashioned one poster that gained renown—on the long lower flourish of a capital letter C he presented a luxuriant, luring, voluptuous feminine figure representing health, contentment and heart's desire—and roundabout her the legend:

CASCARETS

work while you sleep.

This was emblazoned on billboards from coast to coast. As an artist he was speaking to the nation.

There was looming before him now a career as a poster designer and a commercial art illustrator. Those chances, however, he was throwing away. For years he had been playing with the camera—and how! Noontimes, evenings, holidays and Sundays, he was taking negatives and developing and printing. It interested him that sometimes painters looking at a print would say, "What a swell painting that would make!" as though if well made it might not be far superior to a painting, as though for a record and by way of a document it might not surpass what any master painter might put on canvas.

Once he joggled the camera while making an exposure and the Elders said of the resulting photographic print, "That's art!" They were the Elders. They probably knew what was what. So young Edward went on joggling his camera as he made exposures of plates. He learned too how to spit on the lens so the resulting prints came out blurry, vague, "arty."

What is art? And by what sign, badge and token shall we know an artist when we meet one? He was asking these questions of others and himself. The lithograph company was getting from him what they wanted and according to their ideas of art. The dollar-a-dozen photo portrait customers were having their express wishes served.

The young fellow Edward J. Steichen, however, was getting what he wanted and was having his wishes served only after toil, trials, tribulations; he sought out birches by moonlight along the road to Sheboygan; he rode at dawn out of the city into fields and woods near Whitefish Bay, sketching and using the camera, and wondering what essential creative life there was to the pictures and paintings and the photographs he made for himself regardless of the Elders and those who murmured of a photograph, "My, what a painting that would make!" In himself he had the toughest customer of all to satisfy. He felt something desperately experimental and far from finished about every painting or print he completed.

Other men—far off—were toiling—lighted with hope—about the fascinations of this theme, this lure—called Art. It was an abstraction as vague and baffling, as spiritual and beckoning as those others called Religion or Democracy. In a few books and magazines, in stray reproductions of paintings the young Steichen felt human movements at work; they were a breakaway from traditions that had ruled art for centuries. The Impressionists, followed by the Post-Impressionists, the secession societies in Europe—what kind of strugglers were these men?

He was reading eagerly every issue of *Camera Notes*, edited by a pioneer spirit and a genius of photography, Alfred Stieglitz. He had seen photographs of the sculptures of Rodin and read plays and essays of Bernard Shaw and Maurice Maeterlinck. He would go to New York, to London, Paris, Brussels; he would see these men; he must get closer to the living human movements of art. He went to more picnics with his snapshot camera; he stirred up more trade in the dollar-a-dozen photo portraits; he saw his savings grow; he had a Purpose.

Of course, for three years he had sent paintings to the Chicago Art Institute and the jury had rejected them. Of course that might mean something—or nothing. He was young. And who were they?

In 1898 all of his photographs were accepted in the Philadelphia Photographic Salon. The next year all of his offerings were taken in a similar exhibition in the Chicago Art Institute. Did we say "all"? We must correct that. A painter was a member of the jury and refused to admit all of them, over the protest of the other jurors, two accomplished photographers, Alfred Stieglitz and Clarence H. White. The few prints admitted, however, were given a place of honor on the walls. One was "The Pool," a mood of water and woodland, a little piece of Wisconsin breathing ever so softly at twilight.

Letters came: "Go on with your camera work." They were from such men as Stieglitz and White. He reckoned up his savings, packed his bags for New York and Europe, kissed the family a big laughing farewell; they said, "Good-by, Gaesjack"—and the Midwest chapter was ended.

IV

In New York, again he asked himself "What is art?" as he saw on an immense downtown billboard the lengthy, luxuriant, recumbent Lady of the Cascarets daily gazed at by tens of thousands of people who didn't know but what maybe the Metropolitan Museum of Art is a field for the tombs and mausoleums of dead artists.

He walked into the New York Camera Club and found Alfred Stieglitz, great man and prophetic spirit. Stieglitz was organizing an exhibition. "What have you got under your arm?" he asked Steichen, who opened a portfolio of platinum prints, sketches in oil, lithographs, pen-and-ink, pencil and charcoal drawings.

"You have been working," said Stieglitz. "I am amazed at the variety of your efforts and the amount of ground you cover. . . . Are they for sale?" "Huh . . . why, nobody wants to buy them." "I'll buy some. What price?" "Huh . . . I don't know." "Well, you don't look any too rich. I'll give you five dollars apiece and rob you at that."

It being Stieglitz, the friend, the counselor, apostle of bigger and better camera work, Steichen was jubilant about selling several photographs at five apiece. That same week, however, when the *Century* magazine editors asked Steichen what his charge would be to go to Philadelphia and make a photograph he told them twenty-five dollars and expenses. They were surprised; the customary price was five dollars. Steichen didn't get the commission. They were nice about it—and would be nicer yet.

When he put on his exhibition of photographs that year of 1901 in London, there were reviews and critiques; the young American's work was odd, peculiar, *outré*, bizarre, impertinent but not quite important. The writers generally hailed Steichen "with hospitable hands to a bloody grave." Stunts, tricks, whimsies, trifles—so they said—in the manner and lingo that John Ruskin employed as regarded James McNeil Whistler.

Yet there was a five per cent of the commentators who saw something. Bernard Shaw was lighted with enthusiasm; where others viewed the camera as merely mechanical, he saw it as emphatically *un*mechanical. There was a thrill in posing Shaw. "He was easy as a big dog to photograph."

Steichen found corroboration of some of his wilder dreams in the companionship of the tall ascetic Irishman who could drop his clown mask and write, "True, the camera will not build up the human figure into a monumental fiction as Michael Angelo did, or coil it cunningly into a decorative one, as Burne-Jones did. But it will draw it as it is, in the clearest purity or the softest mystery, as no draughtsman can or ever could. . . ."

The next year, 1902, saw Steichen in the big annual exhibition of the Paris Salon—with two paintings accepted. The next year he sent to the Salon a group of photographic prints labeled "Drawings," accompanied by a letter to the jury informing them of what he had done. They were free to interpret "drawing" as that of the sunlight on the negative plate. "I wanted to get 'em past the doorman," Steichen explained of this incident.

Thus far it was a great piece of news. The New York *Herald* published a cabled article that the Paris Salon had received and was to show photographs. The story went over the world. The Paris edition of the *Herald* published it. Vienna, Moscow, Rome had their art worlds stirred by this fresh information. Then came the kickback. The photographs were withdrawn when the Salon opened. There was a committee announcement that the regulations provided for no such entry. What had happened was that the newspaper publicity given the affair smacked of too far a departure from established practice and tradition in conducting the Salon. One jury member told Steichen later they feared in future years they would be flooded with photographic prints.

This play of Steichen's was like him. He does such stunts, is always on the brink of shattering an established practice and tradition. He could get away with what he did in this instance because he was the only respected photographer in the world who had standing as a painter with a record of pictures accepted at the Salon.

One day Steichen was dining at the home of Fritz Thaulow, Norwegian, painter of running water, member of the jury of the Paris Salon. Steichen had made a photograph of Thaulow, who had sent a generous check in payment—as though photographers should be paid no less than distinguished painters for their work and time. "I'd like to meet that grand master, Rodin," said Steichen. "You would, would you?" said Thaulow. "I can fix that. We go this afternoon." And with Mrs. Thaulow—three of them on bicycles—they were soon at Meudon, the country studio of Rodin, ten miles from Paris.

Rose meets them; she is the leading lady of the place; shy of people; sometimes spoken of as a primitive woman, a peasant; she knows the Thaulows and gives them her quiet smile. "Soon the Master will be here."

Over the rim of a hill at twilight comes first a broad black hat, then a silhouetted head with a majestic beard, nose and eyebrows, then the short stocky torso. "God! What a photograph that would make!" Steichen was crying. And when he told Rodin in a stammered French, "*Cher maître*, it is the greatest ambition of my life to make a great photograph of you," the Old Man laughed to Thaulow, "Fritz, you see enthusiasm is not dead yet."

Auguste Rodin, then the most original and talked-of sculptor, had been commissioned to produce a statue of Balzac. He did; the deep-chested writer of a shelf of books trying to gather the whole human procession; the midnight coffee drinker; in a dressing gown; a massive struggling torso. There was hubbub and furor. "He has put the sublime Balzac in a flour sack." The society that had commissioned Rodin to do this work refused to accept it.

Rose cooks dinner. Rose brings wine. Rodin is rested and mellowed after a day's work. Fritz says, "Now, Steichen, bring on your pictures." And the sculptor looks at photographs, gets revelations of a new phase of art. At the evening's end he says to Steichen, "Consider my studio yours. Come whenever you like."

Twice a week, off and on, for six months, Steichen rides his bicycle out to Meudon. Then one day—when he is good and ready—he takes his camera along. He spends ten minutes posing the Old Man. Then he goes away with a plate that after its development has him shouting hallelujah. A superb head, born to be a clear-lined silhouette, is shaped in a sublime black mass against the luminous white of his Victor Hugo statue, gazed at from the right side and higher up by the somber, contemplative figure of "The Thinker." As a photograph it is a masterpiece of portraiture, an allegory, a document, virile, tender, a marching song without words.

One night at Meudon the Balzac is moved into the open air on a slope overlooking Paris. Moonlight shines down. All night long Steichen works with his camera and "that charlatan, Light." Exposures range from one minute to an hour and a half. At breakfast an envelope is under Steichen's plate. He opens it to find 1,000 francs. "I did not know it would be so much work," says the Old Man.

Three nocturn prints come. Life, death, light, night and "Balzac in his dressing gown changed into a stone image enveloped in vapor." Rodin receives the photographs and sends Steichen a bronze of "The Walking Man." He calls Steichen "my son" (*mon fils*). Thereafter Steichen photographs each new work at the Meudon studio.

Steichen roams the studio one afternoon. His paintings are failures; the world doesn't care about photographs; he is no good, no use; why can't he have the strength, courage, wide human faith, that has produced these bronzed shapes in stone? Rodin finds him in tears. "What is wrong?" "Oh, I've never done anything in my life and I never will. Everything is wrong and I'm the wrongest of all." Rodin puts his arms around the young man and says, "Now I know you are a great artist and have the right stuff in you. If I didn't still have such moments I would know I was through—finished."

Once Rodin told of days in poverty; he couldn't hire a model; and there was a man hard to look at, with a broken nose, who came twice a week to clean the workshop, the atelier. "I had to have somebody to model and I made this fellow sit for me. At first I could hardly stand it. Then as I worked I found his head really had a wonderful shape. In his own way he was beautiful. That was how I came to model '*L'Homme au Nez Cassé*' [The Man with the Broken Nose]. That man taught me many things."

Steichen heard a woman, an American tourist from Xenia, Ohio, ask Rodin, "What do you think of the Impressionist school of painters?" The Old Man studied a moment and gave a reply that was aplenty. "There . . . are . . . only . . . good . . . painters . . . and . . . bad . . . painters."

All things young Steichen had ever heard or surmised about toil and craftsmanship, technical preparations and endless strivings for special results, were learned again, were confirmed in a thousand ways as he went here and there in Europe making photographs of Great Ones who interested him. Maeterlinck, Anatole France, George Frederick Watts, Bartholomé, Lenbach, Bebel, Jaurès, Matisse, Gordon Craig, Isadora Duncan—this is but part of the list. Seeing these persons, talking with them, photographing them, was a season of learning. He was a poet, had moods, impulses, reveries, a soft heart. He was impressionable. He was beginning to learn that back of this equipment for the artist must be controls, method, workmanship, technique.

He was painting a portrait of Georgette Le Blanc, the wife of Maeterlinck. During the first sitting, a door at the end of the room opened a few seconds and was softly closed. Maeterlinck had entered the room without entering—as if in one of his plays. The next day Steichen was to meet Maeterlinck, the delicate mystic, the sage of words so often compact of violet shadows and little foam feathers of speech. He first saw "the Belgian Shakespeare" in overalls—stretched under an automobile, crawling out and standing a six-footer, oil and grease on hands, face and clothes. A husky garage mechanic from Altoona, Pa., rather than a mystic poet of the regions of the invisible and the inaudible.

Maeterlinck looks over a portfolio of Steichen photographs. "Why! Why! Why! I am amazed!" he says, if we translate his French correctly. Then he writes a gracious little article for the Steichen number of the Stieglitz magazine *Camera Work*, a precise and concrete utterance, appropriate from a poet who makes his own motorcar repairs.

V

Steichen was back in New York in 1902—a stripling of twenty-three years—alive with unrest, seething with plans for work—established in a little room at 291 Fifth Avenue, which later became the headquarters of the Photo-Secession movement. Growing to include painters and sculptors of the modernist trend, the movement was designated as 291. You could get a man's number in the art realm by finding whether he was for or against 291—or just a neutral, a noncombatant and a bystander. Alternating with exhibits of photographs were one-man shows of Rodin drawings, Gordon Craig etchings and stage designs, productions from Matisse, Picasso, Brancusi, Negro sculpture, Max Weber, Arthur Carles, John Marin, Marsden Hartley and Georgia O'Keefe.

The voice and mind at the focus of 291 was Alfred Stieglitz, a tireless war horse, pioneer and apostle. During difficult years for Steichen, Stieglitz bought photographic prints, many of which were reproduced in *Camera Work*. He paid Steichen from fifty to a hundred dollars for these prints; they are not only the best photographic prints Steichen made then but are the only representative record that exists of that period. The original negatives are lost or went under in the World War that came.

Two exhibitions in 1903 brought money to Steichen. Soon he would be a going concern. He had been hard pushed at times in Europe. Once he sent a hunger cry to the greathearted mother in Milwaukee and she had mailed him all the money with which she was going to pay the hat-store rent the next week. God seemed to be listening, for business picked up; a heavy rain on a Sunday afternoon in summer sends the picnickers to the milliner for new hats on Monday.

The *Century*, a magazine of importance then, published in its February 1908 number a leading article titled "Progress in Photography—with Special Reference to the Work of Edward Steichen." Charles H. Caffin sketched Steichen as a master photographer and a painter of exceptional genius. Fifty dollars apiece was paid by the *Century* editors for the reproduction rights to the six Steichen photographs used to illustrate the article. Three months previous, in a leading article, "The New Color Photography" by J. Nilsen Laurvik, the *Century* used two Steichen color photographs, paying three hundred dollars for reproduction rights.

Henry R. Poore, landscape painter and author of a book, *Pictorial Composition*, was writing in the *Camera* of "the daring and surety" of the Steichen photographs on exhibition at 291. "In Memoriam" impressed him as "a heroic nude which could well adorn the sepulchre of a de Medici side by side with the marbles of Michael Angelo." This critic went further, declaring of Steichen's portrait of Rodin, "One should not say he recalls Rembrandt, but rather at this rate Rembrandt will, in time, remind us of Steichen. Not that this particular print has the subtleties of Rembrandt's luminous shadows, but it has all and more of the great gamut of chiaroscuro upon which the master played."

And so our hero was battling along in the dual role of painter and photographer—one of the steady uncompromising young strugglers in the movement that brought what is known in America as modernist art. The 291 Fifth Avenue attic was a rallying point. They toiled, made mistakes, had their fling of follies and vanities. And yet they created. They evolved theories and originated viewpoints that were to become operative twenty years later when "modernist art," the touch of the Cubist, the Post-Impressionist, the Abstractionist, were to be seen in multiple forms in millions of homes, in so common and wide-flung a medium as the newspaper advertisements. . . . In 1908 the editors of *Everybody's Magazine* paid Steichen five hundred dollars apiece for reproduction rights of photographs of Theodore Roosevelt and William Howard Taft.

VI

Steichen locates on a three-acre place, a studio, garden and farm, at the village of Voulangis, thirty miles from Paris. The camera is a neglected instrument; on tripods in a garret the long-legged spiders climb. The seeker is painting—landscapes, portraits, flowers, panels, mural decorations. He is still "finding himself." He is thinking things over. He will not force his growth. He can wait. His moods are up and down. Days wear different faces. On one he might be saying as he cried out to Rodin, "I've never done anything and I never will." Or again, "I am as determined as the tides of the sea and as patient as the Roman Catholic church."

A few years pass and there are people arriving in Voulangis asking for Steichen, the gardener, the plant breeder. They get from him new varieties of Oriental poppies; he has developed new colors and types of a pure blue petunia, an extraordinary perennial delphinium or larkspur. On a smaller scale he has made interesting developments in begonias, rambler roses, iris. The National Horticultural Society of France awards him a gold medal. His original three-acre field has spread to seven acres. He is versed in the books of Mendel, Darwin, DeVries, Bateson and Burbank and is especially interested in finding a method of having acquired characteristics transmitted. He cannot bring himself to accept the Wisemann theory of the time, that acquired characteristics are not transmissible.

Several experiments look like progress on his theory. Certain conditions have an effect on the germ cell of plants under observation;

they take on new ways; they pass these ways or traits on in their seeds to their descendants. So it seems. Not yet, however, have all the evidences been gathered.

He takes a row of 500 or 1,000 poppy plants when they are young, and walking alongside mutilates them; they grow up deformed, some of them throwing up aborted flowers in all kinds of curious shapes and twisted stems till there is nothing normal about that row of plants; they don't seem to be poppies any more.

Now the seeds of these aborted flowers are gathered and sown in large quantities and given intensive cultivation. And some of the plants throw up aborted flowers, whereas seeds gathered from a normal, untouched row of poppies (the "witness group," as plant breeders say) all produce perfect flowers.

It is the year of 1914, the month of August, and about 1,000 seedlings of the third generation of plants under observation are coming up and getting ready to bloom the following year. But the drums in the village are calling the first reserves to the colors. German cavalry scouts ride over the poppies and ride back. In later weeks French and British soldiers pitch tents over the blue petunias and the iris, over seedlings of the mutilated and of the witness groups.

Steichen takes his family out of the war zone, goes to New York, paints and photographs in a halfhearted way during the years till the United States enters the war, goes into the air service and is sent to France with the first group of the American air corps as a technical adviser in the organization of the entire aerial photographic service.

During the second battle of the Marne he is made chief of the photographic section, placed in command of all the photographic operations in the American sector of the front. General William Mitchell recognizes Steichen's ability and is responsible for his rapid advancement.

Three-fourths of the information that the army operated on was obtained or verified by aerial photography. The photographic section under Capain Steichen's command comprised fifty-five officers and 1,000 troops. Five biplanes made reconnaissances daily, going twenty to twenty-five miles in enemy territory opposite the American sector. A series of photographs was made each day and assembled so as to give a complete picture, from the air, of the enemy terrain occupied or perhaps to be traversed, to troops.

Naturally, in this work, no soft nor blurry photographs were required. An absolutely meticulous definition of line was wanted, information of unmistakable finality. General Mitchell and Captain

Steichen laughingly agreed that anyone caught making "art photo-
graphs" would be shot at sunrise without court-martial, witnesses or
benefit of clergy.

On landing in France in 1917 the first French newspaper Steichen
had read announced the death of Rodin. In Paris he interviewed Gen-
eral Pershing and was appointed the commander's representative to at-
tend the funeral. The French premier, Clemenceau, had been a lifelong
friend and supporter of Rodin, and Steichen witnessed a historic burial
ceremony, for an artist, during wartime. Clemenceau had called
from the front a platoon of shock troops to fire the last salute;
squadrons of army planes circled overhead as the final tributes were
spoken. French officials, academicians who damned Rodin in under-
tones, delivered eulogies; a woman arose to say that Rodin was the
first artist who had an understanding of woman. All this was at
Meudon and the beloved Old Man was laid in a grave in front of his
studio, next to the grave of Rose, his wife, who had died a few
months before her man.

As the war rumbled on, Steichen went zooming in airplanes and
roaring in motorcars in assorted weather, all hours of day and night;
studied over the best lenses for use in the cameras that clicked off
exposures from underneath biplanes traveling a hundred miles an
hour, 15,000 to 20,000 feet above enemy territory they were photo-
graphing; sympathized with the sturdy lads who almost suffocated in
the little pup-tent darkrooms, cellars and dugouts used in field service;
developed the art of reading lines, shadows, blurs, camouflage in the
finished prints of the day's duty.

The war over, Steichen had a Legion of Honor ribbon and the
rank of colonel. But he was a perplexed artist.

VII

Steichen painted two portraits for which the sitters paid $5,000
each and then at forty years of age gave himself a postgraduate
course in photography. He did a thing of "daring and surety."
Though he was a photographer of established reputation on two
continents, he toiled alone for a year—as though he might be learning
for the first time and rehearsing all that he ever knew for sure about
the camera and "that charlatan, Light." He locked himself up and
did nothing but experiment for a year. It was like the tale of Paganini

spending a year in a mountain cave perfecting his technique with finger exercises.

He is back at Voulangis—alone—a year. He photographs a white cup and saucer ten hundred times. He sets that white cup and saucer against a black background and makes one thousand photographic plates of them. He studies, compares, notes—on how to get the maximum amount of realism.

The cup and saucer were placed on a light wedge, with painted strips of all shades from the whitest white possible to the nearest possible absolute black. He was seeking the photographer's controls as between the blackest black velvet and the whitest white paint in the sun.

So goes Steichen always—a seeker. He is profoundly mystical, richly and warmly sentimental, affected by faces, voices, flowers. And he seeks the most precise mathematical controls of his medium so that his results will have what he wants them to have.

He drifts. On a gondola on the Grand Canal of Venice, he drifts. A gondola passes with Isadora Duncan and five of her pupils. "We are going to Greece, Steichen. Come along and make pictures of us in the Parthenon," says Isadora. They talk further. Their friendship goes back fifteen years; one of his earliest well-wrought photographs is of her; he has seen her dance in public and for friends; he has talked hours and days with her and absorbed her theory of art as an emotional expression guided by strength and discipline won from great forces of nature.

Next morning they start; they go to Athens, to the Parthenon. It is "overwhelming" to them; that is the word they agree on—overwhelming. It is an hour before Isadora can lift her arms and even dare begin to try to pose. Three masterpieces of photography result from that day's work. One feels great portals, immense walls, far blue sky, and prayers and song in this trio of prints. They are pictures to live with, silently and solemnly alive and breathing almost silently. Steichen posed Isadora Duncan with two of her pupils beneath the Caryatids. That photograph is a superb document. A California-born woman, child of pioneers of the covered-wagon days, stands as a specimen of grace and dignity equaling, some say surpassing, the women of the high time of Grecian art.

Steichen is now about ready to quit painting, to swear off brushing oils and pigments on canvas. One morning his gardener places before him on the breakfast table a painting, a copy of a Steichen picture.

"Where did that come from?" Steichen asks François, a Breton peasant in wooden shoes, an ox of a man raised on potatoes and cabbage. "I did it," replies François. "You painted that picture?" "Yes." "Why," shouts Steichen, "it is better than mine!"

He buys the painting from François. He keeps it. Years pass and many throwouts go to the trash cans. But the François painting is kept as a treasure, a mascot, a signpost, a guidon, a talisman. "It was the one thing needed to finally convince me that so far as I was concerned painting was the bunk," says Steichen.

There had been many previous incidents also persuasive of the fact that there are no standards in pictures; all goes back to personal taste; it is anybody's guess what is a work of art. One high light for Steichen was the time a group of artists held a canvas in the rear of a mule whose tail was frequently dipped in paints of various colors. Back and forth switched the tail of the mule, fixing a design in paint on the canvas. The resulting picture was hung in an exhibition, its origin unbeknownst to the world outside of the jokers involved.

The picture was not outlawed. It got by. It amused, mystified and pleased enough beholders to convince Steichen that all is not well, that there are cankers and superstitions, in a world of aesthetics that rejects abstractions on the one hand—and on the other hand with ignorant pride and pathetic scorn rejects such documents of light and love as the Steichen portraits of J. Pierpont Morgan, Auguste Rodin and Eleanora Duse.

So Steichen said, "I'm through with painting." But he wasn't. He was through only with the world of painters and critics who devote their days to Blah. He was flinging himself head foremost into an adventure in measurements and deductions, trying to find a series of equations and ratios that hold throughout the living forms of the natural world, hoping to formulate a set of figures that would balance and guide him in drawing. He went to plants, trees, flowers, seed pods—and came with such frequency on certain proportions and ratios of growth that he worked out a system of equations and adopted it. And having it fast and safe what should he do with it?

He decided his audience must be among children. He created The Oochuns. They are very triangular. And as triangles they are absolutes. Their government has things done decently and in order. They are as lovely as living things with long acquired rhythms. They are dignified and beautifully old, yet fresh as a red autumn dawn with green ducks across the sky. Let it be said no man can tell what The Oochuns are. The Oochuns alone can reveal themselves. We may say, however, that they are as tender as Hans Christian Andersen and as precise and thoroughly reasoned as Albert Einstein.

However, there was a living to make, an income to be earned, in New York, whither Steichen had returned and was doing camera portraits. The Oochuns would require color process printing; there wasn't time to work out the method of presentation. The Oochuns now sleep in abstract little beds, living sweet abstract lives, knowing that someday they will be hauled forth to the gaze of a pleased world. Yes . . . there may be Oochuns on the walls of schoolrooms one of these days.

VIII

About now Condé Nast and Frank Crowninshield were publishing in *Vanity Fair* a photograph of Steichen himself in the midst of a page of camera workers, with Steichen designated as "The Greatest Living Portrait Photographer." Shortly after, he became photographic editor of *Vanity Fair* and *Vogue*—at a salary regarded as dizzy—and soon justified.

On a trip to Paris for *Vogue*, Steichen went out to the Voulangis studio and he and the gardener had a heyday, so to speak. All they did was to take about $50,000 worth of paintings, representing a large part of twenty years of Steichen's work, out into the garden and make a bonfire of them. It was a sacrament of fire at high noon. At first Steichen came near crying as the flames licked up the oils and canvas. Then he sang the song he and Billy Mitchell gave in duo during the war:

"Where will we all be one hundred years from now?
Pushing up the daisies, pushing up the daisies,
That's where we'll all be, one hundred years from now!"

Back in New York again in his studio in the Beaux Arts Building he cut into shreds a remaining twenty odd paintings in oil and called for the janitor to remove them as rubbish. The frames went to the Whitney Studio Club for distribution among hopeful students.

So now he could be surer of himself when saying, "I'm through with painting"—though he knew The Oochuns might be laughing at him. If they did he would fix them with the taunt "Oh, you're not paintings at all; you're just mathematical equations and rhythms of life streaked with paint, that's all you are."

Now he was producing that remarkable album of days and people, puppets and miracle children, which has been the outstanding feature of *Vanity Fair*. They march across its pages, a fascinating parade of actors, singers, playwrights, authors, dancers, vaudevillians, prize fighters, performers of stunts and creative artists. We would give much for a like record out of a civilization of a hundred or a thousand years ago. Yet Steichen's art here is limited; he deals with a world separate from steel mills, aviation, mass production; engineers don't count. It is a world alien to the immense grotesques of the primary industries, tools, daily bread and the Pittsburgh sky line at night.

Each month now he was hanging an exhibit of photographs for tens of thousands of people, for many discriminating observers. His studio on the seventh floor of the Beaux Arts Building, overlooking Bryant Park, in New York, was a workshop and laboratory. Steadily —across definite periods of time—there came slight changes in technique—sharper and higher lighted outlines where that was wanted, along with a surer manipulation of all dusks, shadows and silhouette apparitions.

He gave special study to making photographs intended for the printed page; his work was to point up and join with that of the caption writer, layout man, engraver, printer, pressman. When a photograph is planned for halftone reproduction, to be located in the midst of type letters and impressions of black ink, the making of the photograph is then a special piece of work. The feeling that governs the craftsman in such work is different from that in making a print to be hung on a wall, kept in a portfolio or otherwise have its life alone and away from printer's ink. The handling of light and shadow in a photograph for a magazine page, reading section or advertising required a new technique.

The competency and relevancy of Steichen photographs in eye-witness quality and in workmanship having wide human appeal had long interested the J. Walter Thompson Company, an advertising organization in the Graybar Building in New York. They signed a contract for his services exclusively in advertising photographs. Steichen was being paid as much as $1,000 for a single advertising photograph, and during the second year of his contract he was approached by all of the leading agencies and turned down more than $50,000 of work in that year.

Steichen found enjoyment in this new work. In helping sell tooth paste, through photographs, he has made lovely and rippling pictures; they argue, these pictures do, that teeth are an accessory or essential in human loveliness, that love may work better if both parties have teeth worth gazing on. In helping sell a skin lotion, he has made masterly photographs of human hands; one of the prints in this series shows the hands of a woman kneading dough; as a picture it has a Rembrandt homeliness and essence.

And so Steichen has reached a paradoxical position as an artist. On the one hand, through the Condé Nast magazines known as "the quality group," he reaches a maximum of the select and aristocratic audiences of America. On the other hand, through the J. Walter Thompson advertising photographs in the big-circulation magazines, a single photograph running in several magazines the same week or month, he reaches almost the total literate population of the country.

In a week of work now he might have Mrs. Irving Berlin, Rudolph Valentino, George Gershwin, Sherwood Anderson and Mrs. Reginald Vanderbilt as callers in the Beaux Arts Building studio for portrait sittings. Lady Diana Manners and Elinor Patterson would be photographed for an advertisement of Pond's Cold Cream. A long afternoon might be spent on staging a container of Pond's Skin Freshener and Tonic amid mirrors and white jonquils. And a morning might go into a prolonged camera study of the white oblong flakes of Lux.

After photographing a granddaughter of J. Pierpont Morgan, Mrs. Arthur Woods, he would make negatives that week of Gene Tunney, Norma Talmadge, Jack Dempsey and Eugene O'Neill. These sittings would be interspersed by long sessions with Welch's Grape Juice and Simmons Mattresses.

A model arrives at ten o'clock one morning; she has a handsome face, a winning smile, translucent eyes; her ankles are symmetrical and she has grace of person. She spends three hours posing with her hands and forearms for Steichen; she is an office girl; this is her day as a model; she takes care of her own hands. For the purpose lissome, languorous hands are not sought; they should be hands that can wait on themselves; the picture is of hands only; this is to be a photograph for Jergens' Lotion with millions of people reading the claim and legend underneath it, "Almost instantly softens and whitens the skin." The electrician, Mac, understands his boss is working under high pressure when a sharp cry comes, "Great Scott, Mac, where's your light? Shove another floodlight on the left. Throw a spot over the right hand. Step up the arcs."

The majestic Clare Eames, drawn to a commanding length of frame, and the twinkling Bessie Love doing a Charleston might be on a day's schedule which ends with experiments in the photographing for *Vogue* of a pair of mauve pearl kid evening slippers with diamond-shaped inserts of silver mesh.

Two colored boys deliver to the studio a large packing case from *Vogue*. "Put it here," says Steichen. They wrestle it to where Steichen says. On nearing the hall elevator, one is heard to say, "Who was dat?" And the other, "Don't you know who dat is? Why, dat's Mistah Ol' Man Vogue hisself."

Jack Dempsey would have remarked to Steichen, "I can see you're a great artist." Gene Tunney would have commented, "It's evident you're a real craftsman." These are the identical words.

"George Arliss came in to be photographed," said Steichen once when asked about co-operation between portrait photographer and sitter. "He is a very good actor, but he carries his profession with him. He was thoroughly bored. We sat around and I tried to be polite with him, but I realized finally that I was wasting his time and mine, and the magazine's money. Finally, I said: 'Mr. Arliss, you are acting like a spoiled child.' Then he came to life, 'Well—well—!!' But he instantly realized what I was after, that I was merely trying to get his goat. He smiled and we worked hard and successfully. That's one way of breaking through a sitter's inertia."

Between whiles in such a week Steichen might be working on prints of large leaves of mullein proliferant and brooding, of succulent and maternal apples, of foxglove pouring downward in a white waterfall of leaves, of a fiercely energized grasshopper captured in many attitudes ("I followed that grasshopper around all last Sunday"), of a meeting of a big and a little sunflower ("Like a big nun wrapping herself around a little orphan"), of a sunflower having innumerable florets, each with pistil and stamen of its own, and an independent flower by itself ("It looked like a *grande* rosette, an imperial decoration of the Emperor of Scoogemagootch awarded to one of the Knights of Squallymagog for distinguished service—those receiving it are members of the Order of the Children of the Golden Sun"). Asked about a certain print he might say, "That is an experiment related to the satiny texture of the petals of a Japanese tree peony."

If a man understands how to make a photograph of a grasshopper or a cup and saucer he understands basic things about what a magazine needs or what an advertising client wants. Steichen draws a parallel. "If Clara Bow gets a serious scar on her face she's through. If Charlie Chaplin gets a scar on his face he can go on. Clara Bow couldn't lose a leg and go on; Charlie Chaplin could."

It seems to be Steichen's theory that the technique and the creative imagination of a man can work as surely in commercial art as in "art for art's sake." He believes his *Vanity Fair* portraits of Charlie Chaplin, of H. L. Mencken and of Evelyn Brent, as offhand instances, are as good as his best portraits in the noncommercial field. He sees as many aesthetic values in certain shoe photographs for *Vogue* as in photographs of roses and foxglove to which he gave the limit of his toil and creative pressure.

"If my technique, imagination and vision are any good I ought to be able to put the best values of my noncommercial and experimental photographs into a pair of shoes, a tube of tooth paste, a jar of face cream, a mattress or any object that I want to light up and make humanly interesting in an advertising photograph."

IX

Steichen is a naturalist and a man of science in the sense that Leonardo da Vinci was. One could draw parallels between Steichen and Ben Franklin; he has performed experiments as original as Franklin's kite-flying or the weighing of mid-ocean water. Only chance prevented his development in a field of plant breeding that might have led to accomplishments akin to those of Burbank; we do not yet know what he may do if he lives and has the years to work out his plans on his recently acquired 240-acre farm at Umpawaug, Connecticut. He goes back of the evolutionary theory, as did Jacques Loeb, and believes that if we can know more about life in its most elemental forms such as a colloid or a plant, we will know more about how it came to be, how it evolved.

In the personal development of the human individual he finds a brusque change in characteristics is similar to mutations in plant species. Back of the last stroke bringing mutation, which stroke may seem violent and cataclysmic sometimes, is a long internal silent preparation. "I find I can trace the process in myself," Steichen says. "Going along a railroad one day I see a thing I have seen many times. But this day I suddenly *see*. 'Tisn't that you *see* new but things have prepared you for *a new vision*."

He hunts ideas, old and new, gives long study to Chinese painters and the civilizations back of their art—and learns all to be learned about the telepex, a machine that uses front and profile photographs to sculp figures with an accuracy of definition impossible to sculptors chiseling from life. He, whom Rodin called "*mon fils*," telepexes himself and gets put on a page of *Vanity Fair* with other Machine Age sculptures. Radio arrives, he masters the essentials and with two years of experiment develops a new radio receiving and amplifying apparatus in his studio, adopts it for use with phonograph records; vocal performers hearing themselves say, "That singing is better than we can sing!" He goes to a marathon dance and looks on from eleven o'clock at night till six in the morning, watching couples who have been on their feet continuously for four hundred hours, excepting a fifteen-minute rest period after each hour of dancing; eating, drinking, shaving or arranging make-up while dancing; they Charleston, Black Bottom or turn cartwheels for a ten-dollar bill. Steichen goes away thinking and talking for weeks about the chances of reversing and reorganizing old biological processes, ancient habits of eating and sleeping, in the life of man; he would like to see scientists take a lot of the dancers to experiment on as he did with red poppies and blue petunias in his Voulangis garden. The chromatic harmonica, the musical saw, the Movietone, the swift elevators in the new Graybar Building, all must be gone into as keenly as his first electric motor or camera when he was a boy.

To ramble through fifty or a hundred of his photographs is to come in touch with something of the world of art and the world of science and then something else beyond those worlds, for which we do not have words. Grasshoppers, frogs, stalks and stems of plants are so rendered that we range between emotions of art and speculations of science. A tenement back yard in New York is delivered, through a photograph, alive with a hundred pages of O. Henry.

Imagine the days and months of toil and enthusiasm necessary to photograph "The Life of the Sunflower," from the germinating seed to the seed pod of potential successive generations. He was registering the facts of natural phenomena and carrying on a quest for art forms and working standards. This is the joining of artist and naturalist.

"What is this?" he is asked about a print. "That is a delphinium and iris *aurea* contrasting the sneak of light up the iris with the soft wooly delphinium; it is just a pictorial contrast of texture, height and shape." "And this?" "Foliage of Hemerocallis or day lily." "And this?" "Common flag and iris *aurea*—the light runs up the stems like lightning."

He will die telling God that if he could live a few years longer he might be the photographer he wanted to be.

His mother once said at the yearly Christmas dinner, "I suppose you want a camera in the coffin with you when you are buried." He answered, "Yes—and over the grave put my radio set." He will die a seeker and a listener.

We look at a tropical begonia, a sumptuous plant, telling of sudden heavy frost, of strife and collapse, death. "Completely licked," says Steichen. As a picture it captures the essence of a living form that had rich, triumphant life, suddenly took awful punishment and then passed out leaving its agony registered in the twist and droop of its last sprawl. It could be titled "Completely Licked" and is more impressive than the "Dying Gladiator."

He speaks to moths, sunflowers, poppies as if they are kindred humans, half chuckling as though they might answer questions, or as if they are opponents trying to outwit each other. "Let's look at you," and down comes a tall sunflower to have its face scrutinized. "I'll get you yet, little fellow," to a moth.

A day's work with one butterfly resulted in many prints—and one masterpiece, "The Diagram of Doom." The tall living figure of dark wings crossing an intensely white lighted space of sun is doing the best he can. Just around the corner waits Luck—with club or caress.

Explaining in brief what another print is about he gives it a title in the manner of Chinese painters. "Early Hoar Frost on Rambler Rose Vines Climbing a Plum Tree in My Voulangis Garden." Or of another—"Pale Blue Spirals of Delphinium Early in the Morning with Dew on the Bloom."

"The Wheelbarrow," a print Steichen favors, records a wheelbarrow loaded with earthenware flowerpots, suggesting an infinity of terra-cotta tubes in mute, inglorious transit. One looking at it might cry, "Billions! Billions! And billions!" As a piece of workmanship, or art (which may be a better or worse word than workmanship), it measures up to Steichen's requirement that creative art give an object or experience a new existence and essence of its own. In "The Wheelbarrow" one feels Steichen's long thought and brooding over the fixity of species of life forms.

X

A passionate and grave sincerity governs Steichen's work and is told on his face; he might be taken for a piano or violin virtuoso; we

say virtuoso because physical dexterity, capacity with hands and
arms, goes with his equipment. He has large hands; they are an out-
standing feature; he has needed well-sized, gifted hands.

He eats rapidly, finishing his victuals before others at the table.
He is six feet high, has never been sick except two or three times in his
life when overwork and overeagerness about work brought him down;
his father and mother are marvels of strength and endurance. Sum-
mer and winter he sleeps with his feet sticking out from the bed-
covers; he sleeps as a child of Adam, wearing neither pajama shirt nor
trousers. He works in a blue or gray negligee shirt, coat off, through
a camera portrait sitting. He circles camera and sitter, darts swiftly
from under the camera hood and back, on his own errands. His coat
invariably has in it the little crimson quarter-inch silk ribbon, the
Legion of Honor award. He used to work all day and most of the
night till in the winter of 1926 he found he had lost the habit of
sleeping at all; old Mother Nature was handing him revenge and
pay; he was sent to Asheville, North Carolina, to stay in bed a month
and sleep. Since then he has reorganized his habits and learned to
forget his work more, get outdoors more and sleep more.

Once in his middle thirties when responsibilities and work loomed
heavy ahead of him, he said to his father, mother and sister on leaving
the Midwest for New York, "Well, if the worst happens we'll die
with our back to the wall." He gives all he has to the work in hand,
bets big on the future, has play and song hours with two daughters
and idolizes two baby granddaughters.

He recognizes limitations and once laughed out, "A fellow can't
stay on Broadway a long time and give the customers what they want
without being something like the north end of a horse going south."

He has had defeats and bitter disappointments; enough to kill off
any army mule; and is a classical instance of a man stubbornly con-
trolling the design of his life to a far degree. . . . Asked why an
artist of much promise a few years earlier was turning out no work
worthwhile, he said, "It's simple—he won't work—that's all."

Once when a certain loud-mouthed busybody and faker of the art
world was mentioned with the query "What can we do about him?
Isn't there anything?" Steichen replied, "The only way to stop him
is to kill him—and we haven't got time for that—it's all we can do
to find time for our own work."

Every year of his life that he has been in North America during
Christmas week he has journeyed to have dinner with his mother and
folks. The day after New Year's the mother cries, he puts his arms

around her, tells her, "It's all right, Old Girl," and goes away for another year. The mother plans a Christmas cake beforehand, tells what is going into it, shows it in the baking pan before it goes into the oven, talks about it and shows it again as she puts on the trimmings and fixings. After it is eaten, the son says, "Now a cake like that has an existence of its own; a personal essence is created around it. I call such a cake a Work of Art."

Two of his nieces were shown a certain photograph of Abraham Lincoln and were asked, "Who is it?" They answered, "Uncle Ed." Though essentially melancholy and brooding, he has a comedian's heart for difficulties, for hours with friends, children, good fools.

He recites Longfellow's "The Wreck of the Hesperus" with gusto, once carrying it so far that a seven-year-old girl burst into tears over the angry sea, the lost ship and "drownded" passengers. He knows dogs, has a repertoire of dog barks, crouches and attacks with dog-fight growls—and would be a popular hit at running a vaudeville dog act.

He can imitate after-dinner speakers, and in his talk about any scene or people his voice and face accompany with mimicry, rhythm and intonation. He takes off Charlie Chaplin's imitation of Raquel Meller's impersonation of an old Spanish woman peasant with a shawl —or tells of a sky ride with General Billy Mitchell trying to beat a storm that almost overtook them and if it had would have finished them—or the entrance of Geraldine Farrar into his studio to be photographed before a concert tour. "Such a grand sweet old lady that has a girl heart yet and knows just how to play her role for her age." He can tell of persons who say "photo" or "photygraft" or a nice old codger who for years has been saying "phortorgraph" with a screwed-up face.

Once when a woman snob frozen with dignity, sickly superior, obeyed all suggestions with patronizing contempt, refused to sit in and have a nice photograph made, Steichen said afterward, when it was all over, "It was too bad—I saw she was trying to meat-ax me— I couldn't help it—but when the photographs were finished—I had meat-axed her." After a big sitting sometimes the studio looks like a cyclone had blown through. A very neat lady arrived by appointment. "Oh, you are moving?" "No, madame, it's always like this."

He can be a child with children, loose, easy, make-believe. He can eat an apple with big bites, loud smacks and a ravenous face. He knows, with children, when to clump and guffaw and when to walk tiptoe, beckon, whisper and mystify.

There was a poet in Steichen's time who issued a book of verses in the year 1920 with this dedication:

To

COL. EDWARD J. STEICHEN
Painter of nocturnes and faces, camera engraver
of glints and moments, listener to blue
evening winds and new yellow roses,
dreamer and finder, rider of great
mornings in gardens, valleys,
battles.

Lincoln Collector:
The Story of the
Oliver R. Barrett Collection

In every one of his Lincoln books, Carl Sandburg has paid special tribute to Oliver R. Barrett, as a friend, "a collaborator and commentator." And in 1949 he paid the greatest tribute of all by writing a book about the man and his collection.
David C. Mearns, in the New York Herald Tribune, *said:*

Lincoln Collector is a kind of consummation for three inseparable Illinoisans; Lincoln brings to it the majesty of his incomparable experience and expression, Sandburg his poet's magic, and Barrett the mastery of material which is for him fulfilment. This is more than a source book, though it is that and in fine, sound measure. It is more than a picture album, though few books have been, as publishers used to say, so "profusely illustrated." It is a rippling, billowing, flapping, visible standard of America. . . .

With such magnificent material, it is obvious that between them, Lincoln, Sandburg and Barrett have produced a magnificent book, a treasury of Americana, a memorable representation of a people and a time.

Oliver Barrett died seven months after Lincoln Collector *was published, and his notable collection was later auctioned. The passages selected aim at a sketch of Barrett himself and are only a minor part of the book.*

About the year 1886, some twenty years after the death of Abraham Lincoln, the thirteen-year-old boy Oliver R. Barrett began what was to become a massive and diversified collection of Lincoln letters, documents, relics, and related source materials. In his home town of Pittsfield, Illinois, there was the memory of Colonel D. H. Gilmer, who had volunteered for the war, received his commission from President Lincoln, fought in several battles, and met his death in combat at Chickamauga. In line with an announced appointment policy of preference for a veteran or his dependents, President Lincoln appointed Colonel Gilmer's widow to be postmaster at Pittsfield. The daughter, Lizzie Gilmer, could remember that as a girl swinging on the front gate she saw the visiting lawyer and politician Abraham Lincoln come out of the Gilmer house. And Lincoln took hold of Lizzie, swung her high in the air, kissed her, and put her back on the gate to go on swinging. So that became a tradition; likewise the story of another Pittsfield woman, Susan Scanland, who freely gave her opinion of Lincoln—"The laziest man there ever was, good for nothing except to tell stories." Susan had fixed a turkey dinner for Lincoln and other menfolk, and six o'clock came and half-past six, and the dinner went cold, because Lincoln was spinning yarns for a crowd of men at a drugstore.

As a boy in Pittsfield, Barrett's interest in Lincoln was first deeply awakened in a grade classroom. The one Negro pupil sat alone in a front seat, a double seat. And when a boy or girl whispered, the teacher thought it proper to make such guilty boy or girl, as a punishment, sit beside the Negro girl, who was always smiling, had big gleaming eyes, didn't mind at all. One day the teacher called out, "Ollie Barrett, you sit down beside this girl." He took the seat as ordered and heard the snickering of boys who sent spitballs and pieces of chalk against his neck and head. Going to the back of the room for a drink of water, as the rules permitted, the Barrett boy suddenly was out the room, slammed the door, and ran home to tell his mother and get sympathy. His mother gave him a hug, talked long with an arm around him, told him about Lincoln, about slavery and emancipation and the terrible war. Then the mother told the boy she would fix it with the teacher—and if Ollie was a good boy she would take him to Springfield—he was going to have his first ride on a railroad train. Spring came and the mother did take her boy to see the capital, the tomb, and the old Lincoln home.

The custodian of the tomb then was John Carroll Power. Here the boy saw for the first time the dress of the actress Laura Keene and heard that the dark stain was the blood of Lincoln. From this somber moment Power turned to telling of the robbers or ghouls who had tried to steal the body of Lincoln and who escaped from the clutches of Power and of waiting detectives.

"My boyish mind wandered away," Barrett once reminisced, "and I looked around and saw a pair of old Congress gaiter shoes on a glass shelf, and I got to thinking and wondering, imagining Lincoln treading around the White House wearing those shoes." Later he heard Mr. Power say, "Now there are the shoes belonging to one of the robbers that night," adding that once a smart schoolteacher had asked him, "Well, if you could get the shoes off the robber, why didn't you get the robber?" Mr. Power told her, "We will come to that later." And later Mr. Power did explain to young Barrett and his mother that the tomb robbers took off their shoes and hid them in bushes so as to sneak in quietly, detectives finding the shoes after the robbers vanished.

In reverence and quiet the boy and his mother sat on the hillside sloping up from the tomb, the mother leading the boy on in a deepening interest in the man whose moldering bones lay enclosed at the foot of the hill. They then went to the plain two-story corner house where Abraham Lincoln and his family had lived. In charge there they met Osborn H. Oldroyd, who was later to go to Washington and establish a museum in "the house where Lincoln died." They found Oldroyd widely informed, kindly, and he took them upstairs and down, pointing to beds, chairs, tables, cabinets, relics, giving young Oliver a few souvenirs.

Then back to Pittsfield, sixty-odd miles from Springfield, and having its own Lincoln associations. Here were men and women who could remember the little redheaded "printer's devil" who later became editor of the weekly Pike County *Free Press*, young John G. Nicolay. In his mother's autograph album young Barrett found a poem written by Nicolay. Later Nicolay was to be private secretary to President Lincoln and coauthor of an immense biography of Lincoln. Here the other coauthor, then a boy, John Hay, came from nearby Warsaw to attend Thompson Academy, a small seminary school in Pittsfield and to strike up an acquaintance with Nicolay that was to last far beyond their association as secretaries to Lincoln. Here too Milton Hay, an uncle of John, had practiced law, and later sold his home to young Barrett's grandfather and moved to Springfield, his law office near that of the Lincoln & Herndon firm.

Sensing Oliver's newly whetted interest, the mother took the boy up to the attic of their house. Here he saw bullet molds, candle molds, a hoop skirt that boys had used for a tent, grants of land to the boy's grandfather, documents signed by presidents of the United States. His hands came on an envelope marked "verry Precious," and his mother showed him the letter in the handwriting of Robert Burns a niece of Burns had given to Oliver's father.

Then they opened a trunk made of deerskin, the hair turned outside. The boy saw something like one million used postage stamps. The boy's father during years of duty with the Freedman's Aid Society had laid by all used stamps that had come his way, having heard that when he got a million, they would bring a small fortune. Then, when he learned that used stamps would bring him little or nothing in the open market, he put his million of them up in the attic. The boy Oliver found that many of the stamps were rare and brought good prices; he managed to sell them, and with this income bought autographs and letters. In Pittsfield and elsewhere the boy sought and gathered Lincoln letters, tokens, handbills, newspapers, and miscellany bearing on Lincoln and his times.

He set out on a canvass and got enough subscriptions to the *Youth's Companion* to win a small printing press. He set type and ran off a circular: "WANTED, Letters of Famous Men." He sent this circular to postmasters over a wide area, requesting them to put it where post-office patrons would see it.

One book the boy often took from a shelf was titled *Europe through American Spectacles*, and he always turned to the place where it told of his father. The Reverend George J. Barrett was in Italy, and a crowd, beggars, lazzaroni, began following the stranger from America. After a time Mr. Barrett grew tired of the way they near-jostled him, pointed at him, and jabbered at him in words he couldn't understand. Mr. Barrett stopped in his tracks. He put the fingers of one hand in his mouth. Before their eyes he snatched out his teeth. They gaped. They turned and ran—as though next he would snatch off his head—probably possessed of the Devil. And soon as they were gone Mr. Barrett opened his mouth and put his teeth in again.

The young collector, a high-school graduate at seventeen, had been advertising in country weekly newspapers for old letters and autographs. He had worked out a form letter, paying boys at school a penny a letter to copy it, sending this to notables everywhere asking for autographs and old letters.

The Pittsfield youngling struck up a correspondence with the Boston poet and essayist Oliver Wendell Holmes. The elder enjoyed the points and queries put to him, took time to answer the boy and wish him well, took time to write for the boy two verses of "The Last Leaf," a poem that Lincoln knew "by heart" and recited aloud.

Two determinations had been moving the young fellow: first, to be a collector, second, to be a lawyer. In 1896 Barrett graduated in the law class of the University of Michigan and entered on a lifelong practice of law. There was an interlude. In April 1898 he enlisted in the Fifth Illinois Volunteers. Next November, having advanced from private to corporal, his muster-out papers read: "Battles and engagements—None; Skirmishes—None; Wounds—None."

Once, in early practice in the lower courts of Peoria County, Illinois, Barrett's client was Jack Armstrong, a farmer whose uncle, Duff Armstrong, years ago had been freed of a murder charge. In that famous case Lincoln produced an almanac as evidence there was no moon nor bright moonlight by which witnesses could see what they said they saw. In the case of Duff's nephew, the landlord, following a procedure called "distress for rent," had gone to Jack Armstrong's farm, loaded on wagons and hauled away crops, a piano, and other chattels for rent payment. The time, as established by witnesses, was 4:38 P.M. and thereafter. Barrett rose and pointed to the old English law which says that such a seizure of property, for rent payment, must take place between sunrise and sunset. Next Barrett produced an almanac showing that sunset on that day occurred at 4:35 P.M.— wherefore the landlord was three minutes later than the law allows! Barrett's almanac saved Jack Armstrong's crops and piano as Lincoln's almanac saved Jack's uncle's neck. All of which the old Chicago *Inter-Ocean* considered a fine Midwestern folk tale, and one Sunday gave it a whole page.

Across years the correspondence of Barrett ranged far and wide. When he heard of a Lincoln letter or a paper or a relic having Lincoln associations, he would write his inquiries about it. Whether it was a farmer who had found a letter that his father, a Union soldier, had received from Lincoln, or whether it was a well-known item in the hands of an experienced and sophisticated collector, Barrett would gather his information about it, what condition it was in, whether it might be sold, whether sometime it was going to be put up at auction. In the course of time it became widely known that the attorney Barrett welcomed at his office anyone who had material bearing on Lincoln or on actions, events, characters that interwove with the life of Lincoln. It would make a considerable story by itself, the variety of Lincoln folk and kin who came on one errand and another to Barrett's office.

One of these, a man of national reputation, twice happened to come to the Barrett office, without a previous appointment, on days when Barrett was engaged in a trial and couldn't possibly see his caller. What the caller wanted particularly was President Lincoln's gold watch chain. The caller was chairman of the board of the Pullman Company, Robert Todd Lincoln, eldest son of President Lincoln. He made offers to Barrett of Lincoln documents to be given in exchange for the gold watch chain of his father. From Charles Moore, chief of the Manuscripts Division of the Library of Congress, came a letter to Barrett advising an exchange "if you want to make the heart of an old man very happy." An exchange was agreed on, but before its conclusion Robert T. Lincoln died.

The watch chain had been part of the estate inherited by Mrs. Lincoln. The chain is a curious specimen of goldsmith's craft, many strands of fine-spun gold being intricately woven, the mesh so fine that the fingers of one hand can roll the chain into a ball. The English playwright John Drinkwater, struck with admiration of the keepsake, told Barrett he would try to find a goldsmith who would make him a replica of the chain, Drinkwater later reporting that the goldsmiths he interviewed were baffled, saying: "There used to be men doing that kind of work but we don't know of any nowadays. A machine to reproduce it would be of prohibitive cost." A California delegation that called at the White House gave this token to Lincoln as a specimen of what fine metal and workmanship they had in their state. The chain shows plainly in several Lincoln photographs, looped through the second buttonhole from the top of the vest. The new watch chain replaced one of silver links that Lincoln gave to Dennis Hanks, who many years later sold it to a man who sold it to Barrett.

The collector's wife often comes in for discussion among collectors. To be happy, her hobby must be a husband who has a hobby. This sentiment has been heard where collectors forgather. For some years after his marriage Barrett had a system when bringing home an armload of books or manuscripts. He laid them gently and quietly outside the front basement window. Later at night he would go to the basement and, as casually as you please, bring his new acquisitions upstairs as if from his old basement stock. This smuggling system came to an end when a law partner, in retaliation for a practical joke, repaid in kind and told how the system worked. The collector was forced to devise new methods.

In the story of how this Lincoln Collection came to be gathered, it would not be permissible to omit mention of the foremost candy man of the Midwest, Charles Frederick Gunther, born March 6, 1837, in Wildberg, Württemberg, Germany. He was five years old when his family sailed for America and settled in Somerset County, Pennsylvania. At eleven he was riding a daily mail route through mountains, twenty-five miles each way, his pay twenty-five cents a day. He went to schools, public and private, and when the family moved to Peru, Illinois, in 1850, he began at fourteen to earn his own living. He worked in a country store, then a drugstore, later became a bank cashier with his name on the window. Out of Peru associations he saw chances for the ice business in the South. On starting for Memphis in 1860 he told friends, "The South needs ice." He was working on plans for more and better ice in the South when the war broke. The Confederates pressed him into service and appointed him purchasing agent of the Confederate ship *Rose Douglas*. Union forces took him prisoner; late in the war he was exchanged, and headed back to Peru, Illinois.

Over the South and the Midwest he traveled for a large candy firm of Chicago. Then in 1868 he began on his own the manufacture and sale of candies made from German recipes known to his family. The name of Gunther come to stand supreme with a host of candy buyers and eaters. Then the Chicago fire wiped out Gunther's shop and store. Word came that Marshall Field, the merchant and financier, wanted to see him. Field told him the city of Chicago must go on, and offered him a loan for a fresh start in business.

Gunther opened his new shop and store and was on a road leading to fortune. He was short and stocky, with a round face wearing mustache and chin beard, later a goatee. People liked his cheerful face and twinkling eyes. He was lighted with enthusiasms, not merely well known for his candies but with a reputation as a collector. With reference to the Civil War and its documents, letters, relics, people far and wide had heard of his interest and his readiness to buy in the field. This, however, was but one phase of Gunther's collecting. On one of his many journeys abroad with Mrs. Gunther, it was told, he acquired an assortment of mummies in Egypt, and wishing no delay in transport, he reserved sleeping-car berths for his cargo of ancient dehydrated Pharaohs.

Time came when Gunther had an eight-story building, one floor filled with miscellany, crammed with humpty-dumpty boxes and chests. He proposed to his collector friend Oliver R. Barrett, "Buy the whole kit and caboodle." Barrett said that all he would like would be letters, documents, papers of interest to him and of pertinence to the rest of his collection. Across years, from then on, Barrett carried on his labors amid the immense accumulations of Gunther, searching and sifting in the loot of battlefields and the dusty findings from garrets and closets.

One Saturday Gunther telephoned Barrett and Barrett went over to hear Gunther: "I know you like Lincoln, but I like Washington better because he treated the Germans better than Lincoln. Washington treated Von Steuben and others better. I would rather let the Lincoln go first. I have picked out twenty letters, all long. I have my taxes to meet today." Barrett was waiting. Gunther went on, "Take those twenty Lincoln letters." And Barrett went away with a great windfall for one day.

In another session when Barrett saw a manuscript in the handwriting of Robert Burns—the verses of "Auld Lang Syne"—he said, "I want this." Gunther replied, "I know how you feel. I went over to England and I got it and I had to pay a lot of money."

Barrett: "I want it now. You know how it *feels* to have it, and I *don't* know how it feels."

Gunther: "I will sell you this 'Auld Lang Syne' and you write out the receipt and put in the receipt that any time I want it, I can buy it back at the same price."

Barrett took it home. A week later Gunther was on the phone: "Bring back the 'Auld Lang Syne.' You know, I haven't been able to sleep. I hear the waves of Lake Michigan pounding at night and I think about it. I walk down Michigan Avenue thinking about it, and now it is gone and I am not going to last many years. Let me have it back."

Barrett brought back the manuscript. Years passed. Then one day Barrett stood before Gunther and said, "I can't sleep, and I want that 'Auld Lang Syne.'" Gunther smiled. They were brothers. Gunther said, "You just double the price and I will let you have it, and you can take it along." And in the passing of time Barrett would not have been surprised on any day to hear Gunther say, "I want that 'Auld Lang Syne.' I can't sleep."

A death in a family brought into Barrett's collection a document he had long sought. It had occurred to Barrett that many more letters had been written by Lincoln to Horace Greeley than had come to light in publication. Greeley had been one of the most incessant of letter writers to Lincoln and many of his long epistles had brought immediate and pointed replies from Lincoln. "Where are these replies of Lincoln?" asked Barrett. He went to Chappaqua, New York, the old home of Greeley, and interviewed Greeley's daughter, Mrs. Clendennin, the wife of an Episcopal rector. From her he learned there had been a fire in the house that had burned all of her Lincoln letters except one. The First World War was then going, her daughter's husband with the U. S. Armed Forces, and Mrs. Clendennin couldn't think of selling the letter. She led Barrett to a corner of the room, pointing to the Lincoln letter in a frame on the wall, and with a pleasant smile: "I could never sell that. It's got to go to my daughter." It was an abrupt, peremptory Lincoln letter. Greeley had written to Lincoln of "confidential" information he had of two Confederate ambassadors in Canada waiting and ready to cross over from Canada and talk peace terms and end the war; Greeley believed the "ambassadors" had full power from their government to negotiate. The affair was involved. After various outcries from Greeley, Lincoln sent John Hay to New York with a letter to Greeley. In a hotel parlor Hay delivered the letter to Greeley, who read in part:

> I am disappointed that you have not already reached here with those commissioners, if they would consent to come, on being shown my letter to you of the 9th Inst. Show that and this to them; and if they will come on the terms stated in the former, bring them. I not only intend a sincere effort for peace, but I intend that you shall be a personal witness that it is made.

The peace negotiations of Greeley proved much of a farce. Mrs. Clendennin mentioned that another Lincoln collector, Judd Stewart, had made offers for the letter. Barrett said, "If you ever want to sell it just send it C.O.D. for double his offer." Barrett thanked her, she had been kindly; she would let him know of any development in regard to the letter.

Thus the matter stood as the years passed till the day Barrett received a letter from the Reverend Clendennin saying: "Now that our dear daughter has gone over to the better country we have decided to part with Lincoln's letter." Now they could meet Mr. Barrett's wish and let him have the letter.

Barrett had a deep feeling about the manuscript of the autobiography that Lincoln, after his nomination for the presidency, wrote on request of Jesse Fell of Bloomington, Illinois, and sent to Fell with a letter. That letter had come into Barrett's hands in a purchase from the heirs of Osborn H. Oldroyd. Barrett wanted the autobiography and exchanged letters with the Fell sisters, who owned it. Their nephew, editor of the Bloomington *Pantagraph*, came to Barrett's office one Saturday afternoon. They readily agreed on the value of the manuscript. The banks were closed. Moreover, the editor said there was another to be consulted and that he would leave the autobiography with Barrett and come back on Monday. Barrett said, "No, you bring it back on Monday." Soon Barrett read in the paper of his sudden death. Afterward Barrett learned that the death of the nephew had seemed almost a warning and that the Fell sisters were not going to part with the manuscript.

As against the occasions when death interposed there were times when life interfered, once in the form of a young woman. At the home of Jesse W. Weik in Greencastle, Indiana, amid boxes, trunks, chests and bundles, the coauthor with William H. Herndon of a famous biography of Lincoln showed Barrett his collection. Suddenly in the processional of items came a paper that had Barrett groggy. "It was a letter of my father to Herndon," says Barrett, "and of his meeting Lincoln on the way to the duel with Shields. No offer of mine for this letter of my father seemed to interest Weik. He would sell it only in case I bought the whole collection. Finally I showed him a bank draft I had brought with me. I told him I would give him for my father's letter a blank check signed by me and that he might fill in the amount and I would not even take a peek at it until he had cashed it at the bank. That letter of my father to Herndon stayed in the Weik collection until his death."

It was earlier that they had practically agreed on a sale of the whole collection. Then Weik began to have moments of pause. His talk ran about his granddaughter, a slim, swift-moving girl, gliding quietly in and out of the rooms. Weik's eyes followed her as one to be cherished. She was making herself useful getting the dinner, and that her sweet bloom and frailty needed his care and protection was plainly in the thought of Jesse Weik.

"His eyes kept on following her," says Barrett. "It seemed that almost in a moment his desire to sell dried up. He ended the hope I had when he said that she meant so much to him, that he hadn't a great deal more to leave her than the collection, that if he sold it now he couldn't know what might become of the money, but he could feel that he had done his duty by her if she could have it when he was gone."

There was a schoolteacher in Chicago having an interest in an inheritance case. The suit was lost, but in the course of the action she heard about the opposing counsel, Oliver R. Barrett, being more interested in Lincoln letters than he was in law practice. After the trial she telephoned Barrett, inviting him to come to her home and see some letters Lincoln had given her father. In company with his fellow collector, Alexander Hannah, Barrett called on her.

Her story was simple. Her father was a cabinetmaker whose shop was directly under Mr. Lincoln's law office. Into her father's shop one morning of February 1861 had come Mr. Lincoln with a sheaf of papers in one hand, saying he was going to put them in the stove. Her father had said to Mr. Lincoln, "Why not let me have them?" And into the cabinetmaker's hands went letters of friendly and anxious men giving counsel or sending good wishes and prayers, letters warning of assassination by gunshot or poison, letters of ridicule and belittlement and wild curses—inquiries from a gun inventor and a desperate beggar, and the long letter of a horse thief who wished to turn informer and share a reward with Lincoln. This series might be termed the Hot Stove Letters.

The findings set Barrett on a quest. He was asking whether it could be that Lincoln's old house desk was still around. If so, how could it be located? If found, would there be anything in it? He began in Springfield among the houses roundabout the old Lincoln home. "I canvassed that whole neighborhood just like you would looking for witnesses in a lawsuit. I went from house to house knocking and asking if they knew anything about Lincoln or an old desk he had. I came finally to a house where the woman in the doorway was saying, 'Why, yes, sure enough' she had in the house the old desk of Mr. Lincoln himself. I can see her face now but I didn't tax my memory with her name."

She asked him into the house, led him to the desk. There in each of two pigeonholes was a bundle of letters addressed to Lincoln, postmarked late 1860 or early 1861. She had never read the letters, had never untied the threads and strings that bound them. At an auction sale of the Lincoln household effects she had bought the desk, had regarded the letters with something of reverence and a feeling they should be kept. She was willing to let Barrett have the letters, but refused to part with a diary that had been kept by her daughter reporting early days in Springfield, including parties where she saw and talked with the Lincolns. And whereas the Hot Stove Letters mostly wanted to kill Lincoln, the Old Desk Letters wanted to help him or show their faith in him.

One winter morning in early 1861 there was a little bonfire going on in the alley back of the Lincoln house in Springfield. A woman stood by watching the fire. She was Mrs. Abraham Lincoln. From a house opposite came a woman, on a fast walk, saying as she came into the alley, "Good morning, Mrs. Lincoln. What are you doing here?" "Just burning some old letters we don't want to take to Washington." "Why can't you let me have some of them?" "Well, I guess you're welcome to them."

Out of the black ashes the woman's fingers managed to scrape five letters the flames hadn't touched. She spoke her thanks to Mrs. Lincoln and took the five letters home.

Somewhat like this the story was often told, here and there in Springfield. More than seventy-five years after, there were men who wondered what might be in the letters and whether the letters still existed. In the course of time they learned that it was a man and not a woman who had plucked the letters from the alley bonfire. They located the man's granddaughter in Jacksonville, Illinois—Mrs. Laura Jane Hopper. Alexander Hannah, boon companion and fellow collector of Barrett, asked if it could be true that some letters had been saved out of an alley bonfire started by Mrs. Lincoln. This was so, Mrs. Hopper assured Hannah. And she still had the letters, had kept them through a long term of years. In the end they passed to Barrett and Hannah, who divided them.

Two of the letters that Mary Todd Lincoln in house-cleaning hurry and worry came so near destroying carry intimate domestic exchanges between Lincoln and his wife. The letters give somewhat the tones and voices of the Lincoln marriage at its best, periods of connubial serenity. They give support to the impression that whatever there might have been of bliss or strife in the Lincoln household, there were, at times, amicable discourse and even plain domestic happiness.

There were manuscripts Lincoln didn't care to burn or give away on leaving Springfield. These he put into a carpetbag that he turned over to Elizabeth Todd Grimsley. She remembered how distinctly he said to her, in effect, that this "literary bureau" was put in her custody and if he should not return to Springfield for it, then she might dispose of the manuscripts as she thought best. This was in early 1861 and "Cousin Lizzie," as Lincoln called her, thought he spoke a little absent-mindedly, as though he had plenty else on his mind. The carpetbag held what of his writings he wished to preserve and he did not care to be encumbered with in Washington.

After the death of President Lincoln, Mrs. Grimsley would occasionally mention to friends the carpetbag of manuscripts. She would hear a request or a hint from one who would prize a paper that held handwriting of Lincoln. At least five times Mrs. Grimsley handed over a Lincoln manuscript to another person. Then came the day when she still had the carpetbag but it was empty of Lincoln writings. There was no puzzle or mystery as to what had happened to the precious contents of the carpetbag. In good conscience and doing her best to "clean up and get things straightened," the naïve housemaid had taken the scrambled papers in this old carpet sack as rubbish that ought to be burned—so she burned them.

Years later Barrett in a series of interviews managed to track down five of these carpetbag manuscripts. These include two fragments of memorandums on slavery, one on the Constitution, the nine sheets on which Lincoln wrote his lecture on "Discoveries and Inventions" delivered in 1859 in various places and on February 22, 1860, before the Springfield Library Association.

On Barrett's first visit to the farm of Lincoln's father near Charleston, Illinois, and to the homes of Lincoln kinfolk in that neighborhood, he was told of the previous visits of William H. Herndon and others and learned that Herndon had secured all of the letters that had been written by Lincoln to the home folks. There was, however, an old trunk that previous visitors had paid slight attention to or not seen at all. In this trunk the family papers had been kept and there were carefully preserved documents and letters dated from December 1813, legal papers signed by Thomas Lincoln and Sarah Bush Lincoln, in every instance Thomas signing his name in full and Sarah signing with her mark X. Included were papers of the Hall family who had moved with the Lincolns from Indiana to Goose Nest Prairie.

Here too were many letters of all the kinfolk, including Dennis Hanks and his children, some members of Sarah Bush's family, and an account book of John D. Johnston mostly concerning whisky sales. And the family had still retained the letters received from Herndon, the earliest being one of September 1865.

When Abraham Lincoln's father died in a Goose Nest prairie log cabin on January 17, 1851, the son was not at the bedside. Shortly after, however, he visited his stepmother, Sarah Bush Lincoln, joining in a reunion of kith and kin. And they gave the best of their information and belief to a record of the marriages, births, and deaths of the Lincoln family.

In Abraham Lincoln's handwriting this record went into the family Bible. Time passed, and a few years after the death of President Lincoln his cousin Dennis Hanks, leaving Charleston for a visit with his daughter, removed from the family Bible the record leaf written by Abraham Lincoln. In 1888 this documentary page came into the hands of Jesse Weik, Weik noting, "Dennis tore out and wore out the Bible record." Though creased and worn, it still serves students and biographers.

Barrett finished a research that tells us what it was that Abraham Lincoln wrote in the five lines of the upper right-hand corner of this Bible leaf, a creased corner that got worn or torn off and lost. On those five lines Lincoln wrote the birth dates of his father, Thomas Lincoln, and his mother, Nancy Hanks, and the date of their marriage. Having this data, we are able now to correct the mistaken dates chiseled on gravestone and memorial tablets and to fill in the blanks where many chronicles are vague or incomplete. The missing five lines of the Bible leaf record as restored through the Barrett research read:

"Thos. Lincoln was born Jan. the 6th A.D. 1778 and was married June 12th 1806 to Nancy Hanks who was born Feb. 5th 1784.

Sarah Lincoln Daughter of Thos. and"

And how can we be sure these are the five lines that Lincoln wrote? By four separate and different pieces of evidence:

1. John D. Johnston, a son of Sarah Bush Lincoln by her first marriage, copied from the family Bible the entire record made in Lincoln's handwriting in an account book, where it may be seen today, the outstanding item alongside a record of numerous sales of whisky at 50 cents a gallon.

2. John J. Hall, a grandson of Sarah Bush Lincoln living with her at the time Lincoln wrote the family-Bible record, also made a copy of that record before Dennis Hanks removed it. Hall's copy was kept in the Lincoln cabin until 1891. Visitors to the cabin often saw this

copy. On at least three occasions Hall's copy was given publication. *The History of Coles County*, published in Chicago in 1879, has this entry: "While in the old cabin where he [Thomas Lincoln] lived and died, we were shown the family record copied by Mr. Hall from a leaf of the family Bible. . . ."

3. In a large scrapbook where plain handwriting tells us it was "made by Nancy A. Hall, great-granddaughter of Sarah Bush Lincoln, Goose Nest Prairie, near Charleston, Ill.," is a clipping of one of a series of newspaper articles titled "Half Century in Coles County," by John Cunningham, Chapter 11, "Pleasant Grove, The Lincoln Family." The writer tells of relic hunters carrying off family records, though "Mr. John Hall has a copy . . . of a leaf from the Lincoln family Bible, which I give entire." Then follows the text with the birth dates identical with the record in the county history and the John D. Johnston account book.

4. There is still another newspaper clipping, this from the St. Louis *Globe-Democrat*, saying: "Mr. Hall retained nothing [of family relics] but a copy of the family record, the only genealogy kept by the Lincoln family, incomplete though it was, which is given in full below."

Newspaper clippings pasted in this Nancy Hall scrapbook report stories and sayings among the Lincolns. Short-spoken, humble, and reverent was the blessing young Abraham often heard at table, if this account in one newspaper is correct:

"John Hall, a near relative of Abraham Lincoln's stepmother, says that Thomas Lincoln returned thanks at every meal, always using the same words, 'Fit and prepare us for humble service, we beg for Christ's sake. Amen.' "

A yarn not yet included in any Lincoln biography is reported in this same scrapbook. The evidence seems to be that Thomas Lincoln was a worthy husband of Nancy Hanks, the mother of Abraham Lincoln, who died when he was a child, and of Sally Bush, the beloved stepmother. But the only account we have from Thomas Lincoln in this regard is in this scrapbook newspaper clipping:

"One day when alone with her husband, Mrs. Lincoln said, 'Thomas, we have lived together a long time and you have never yet told me whom you like best, your first wife or me.' Thomas replied, 'Oh, now, Sarah, that reminds me of old John Hardin down in Kentucky who had a fine-looking pair of horses, and a neighbor coming in one day and looking at them said, John, which horse do you like best? John said, I can't tell; one of them kicks and the other bites and I don't know which is wust.' It is plain to see where Abraham Lincoln got his talent for wit and apt illustrations."

When on a March day in 1837 the twenty-eight-year-old Abraham Lincoln rode a borrowed horse from New Salem to Springfield to begin practice as a newly licensed lawyer, he didn't know where he would stay in Springfield. At the general store of Joshua Fry Speed, he asked what he would have to pay for bedclothes for a single bed. That would come to $17, Speed figured. Cheap enough, said Lincoln, but he didn't have the money and would have to ask credit. Speed offered to share with Lincoln his large room and double bed upstairs over the store. A friendship of these bedfellows began that ripened and deepened and lasted across Lincoln's lifetime. Lincoln had many friendships, with various and limited degrees of intimacy, but to no other man did he write so extended a series of long letters, the larger part having to do with love and marriage complications of the two men.

Fourteen of these letters written by Lincoln to Speed came into the Barrett Collection. J. S. Speed III, a kinsman and heir, wrote to Barrett saying he had had correspondence with New York dealers, but would prefer to have the group of letters go into a private collection, and if Barrett wanted them he would sell them. Barrett wrote Speed to send along the letters and put a C.O.D. draft on them. A few days later a banker phoned Barrett to come see him. The banker was anxious, even somewhat alarmed. When Barrett arrived the banker said it seemed someone had stolen what was in the box and left nothing but some old Lincoln letters. "Just what I want," said Barrett. The banker explained, "Those are all handwritten, and a book is much easier to read. I just don't understand it." Barrett later reminisced, "I don't know whether he ever understood it, but I got the letters."

Death struck, a fame arose. A tradition, running in labyrinths, grew in fact and fable. One of Barrett's few modest ventures in verse-writing compresses his feeling about Lincoln in a four-line meditation:

Slow, oft with faltering step that seemed to stray,
A homely man, but plain in truth and right, pursued his troubled way.
Unsought, unknown, the fame that waited close beyond those years of
    woe and blood,
He only knew, he wished and sought, mankind and country's good.

ABRAHAM LINCOLN

"For thirty years and more I have planned to make a certain portrait of Abraham Lincoln," Carl Sandburg *wrote in his preface to* Abraham Lincoln: The Prairie Years, *published in 1926. "It would sketch the country lawyer and prairie politician who was intimate with the settlers of the Knox County neighborhood where I grew up as a boy, and where I heard the talk of men and women who had eaten with Lincoln, given him a bed overnight, heard his jokes and lingo, remembered his silences and his mobile face."*

This portrait was as far as the author intended to go; he wrote a piece for inclusion in the foreword in which, he said some thirty years later, "I made an attempt at covering all the rest of [Lincoln's] life by the device of an introduction. This introduction would begin at the death of Lincoln and work back to the day he left Illinois. The reader could then turn to the book and begin with the birth of Lincoln." The piece was discarded when Carl Sandburg decided to continue his Life of Lincoln, but fortunately it was preserved, and the author was persuaded to allow it to be privately printed in a limited edition in 1953 for circulation among his friends. A Lincoln Preface was later syndicated in newspapers throughout the country, and as the opening of the Lincoln sketch herein, it is presented to the general reader for the first time.

Of The Prairie Years, *William Allen White wrote in the New York* World *on its publication:*

Carl Sandburg, the poet, has put a poet's patience and a poet's vision into a beautiful monumental prose story of Abraham Lincoln. Here are more than a thousand pages in two large books. Detail is piled upon detail. Little details, seemingly irrelevant, apparently incompetent when they are added to other details, become tremendously material. That is the Sandburg method; the method of the naturalist artist. . . .

In these two volumes telling of Lincoln in his prairie years are
pages and pages of background accurately worked in, most in-
telligently placed. And as one reads chapter following chapter,
one finds the child, the young man, the lover, the lawyer, the
patriot growing, filling out in stature, growing in grace, growing
in some mysterious way as a man grows out of his environment
into life through aspiration until he becomes the follower of
visions, the homely self-deprecating seeker of the Holy Grail.

No one but a poet with a poet's patience and a poet's under-
standing heart could have written this book. It will stand as one
of the great portraits of Lincoln before he went to the White
House. . . . Here stands no plaster saint, but a clumsy, shrewd,
ambitious, affectionate man. . . . Here on the prairie, Sandburg,
the poet, is at home, and here this Lincoln, made with the poet's
hands, takes on reality, strong, rank, pungent, gorgeous reality.

*In the midst of his extended research for the later Lincoln vol-
umes, Carl Sandburg took time out to write a study of* Mary
Lincoln: Wife and Widow, *with documents edited by Paul M.
Angle and published in 1932. Fanny Butcher in the* Chicago
Tribune *said it "is written with infinite understanding. . . . Jus-
tice is in every page, judicial impartiality. . . . In such a fashion
thus judicially can the story of Mary Todd Lincoln best be told,
and Mr. Sandburg tells it memorably."*

It was not until 1939 that the four-volume Abraham Lincoln:
The War Years *was ready for publication. Charles A. Beard
wrote of it in* The Virginia Quarterly Review:

Never yet has a history or biography like Carl Sandburg's
Abraham Lincoln: The War Years appeared on land or sea. . . .

Few if any historians have ever labored harder in preparation
for composition. [Mr. Sandburg] has traveled widely and
searched widely. Great collections of Lincolniana he has scru-
tinized and used critically. He has examined mountains of news-
papers, letters, diaries, pamphlets, stray papers, documents, rec-
ords, Congressional debates, posters, proclamations, handbills,
clippings, pictures, cartoons, and memorabilia, great and small.
Work with the paper sources he has supplemented by journeys
all over the country, interviews with survivors of the war years
and their descendants, and walks over fields and plantations. And
indefatigable thoroughness characterizes his preparations and his
pages. . . .

An air of grave thoughtfulness hangs over the lightest words. The searching, brooding spirit of the laborious historian pervades the treatment of every large problem. With this, that, and many things, specialists will doubtless quarrel more or less gently. . . . But when specialists have finished dissecting, scraping, refining, dissenting, and adding, I suspect that Mr. Sandburg's work will remain for long years to come a noble monument of American literature. . . .

Yet Lincoln is not portrayed in these pages as the mighty hero, the great wise man who foresaw things perfectly and moved with unerring wisdom to the great end. He is shown as a poor limited mortal, of many moods, tempers, and distempers, stumbling, blundering along, trying this and trying that, telling jokes, bewildered, disappointed, grieved by his fractious wife, weeping now, laughing then, ordering this, cancelling that, trying to smooth ruffled personalities, looking upon mankind, like Marcus Aurelius, as composed of little creatures playing and loving, quarrelling and fighting, and making up again, all without much rhyme or reason—Lincoln steadfast in his purpose of saving the Union, and, if possible, reducing the area of slavery or getting rid of it entirely. . . .

A week's reading, which nearly finished my dim eyes, carried me along as in a tumultuous flood, amused, entertained, delighted, toward a conclusion which I had long been maturing. Why is it that the formally educated and polished are so often futile in the presence of vast movements of history? Why is it that so many makers of history on a large scale spring from somewhere near the earth of Antaeus and manage to do things on a colossal scale, displaying profound wisdom in the operation? The answer which I had been darkly maturing, Mr. Sandburg has clinched for me. It is that the great philosophies and systems of thought which adepts pile up, teach, and parade, so far as they are valid for life, derive from a few common-sense aphorisms, fables, and maxims evolved by ordinary humanity in its varied efforts to grapple with the stuff of life. Out of the mouths of babes cometh wisdom. Lincoln was the fablist, the aphorist of the age, strong of will yet supple, facing the storm as farmer wrestles with the toughness of the soil and the tempests of the seasons, and speaking a language, even in crude jokes, which struck the chords of the primordial that endures at or near the bottom of every civilization and carries on when the top has rotted away.

The six-volume Life totals one and a half million words. After many years Carl Sandburg yielded to popular demand and distilled a 430,000-word one-volume edition of Abraham Lincoln: The Prairie Years and The War Years, *published in 1954. To give the reader a sustained portrait, the excerpts selected deal with Lincoln the Man, and interwoven is a chapter on his romance and marriage from* Mary Lincoln: Wife and Widow.

A Lincoln Preface

In the time of the April lilacs in the year 1865, a man in the City of Washington, D. C., trusted a guard to watch at a door, and the guard was careless, left the door, and the man was shot, lingered a night, passed away, was laid in a box, and carried north and west a thousand miles; bells sobbed; cities wore crepe; people stood with hats off as the railroad burial car came past at midnight, dawn or noon.

During the four years of time before he gave up the ghost, this man was clothed with despotic power, commanding the most powerful armies till then assembled in modern warfare, enforcing drafts of soldiers, abolishing the right of habeas corpus, directing politically and spiritually the wild, massive forces loosed in civil war.

Four billion dollars' worth of property was taken from those who had been legal owners of it, confiscated, wiped out as by fire, at his instigation and executive direction; a class of chattel property recognized as lawful for two hundred years went to the scrap pile.

When the woman who wrote *Uncle Tom's Cabin* came to see him in the White House, he greeted her, "So you're the little woman who wrote the book that made this great war," and as they seated themselves at a fireplace, "I do love an open fire; I always had one to home." As they were finishing their talk of the days of blood, he said, "I shan't last long after it's over."

An Illinois Congressman looked in on him as he had his face lathered for a shave in the White House, and remarked, "If anybody had told me that in a great crisis like this the people were going out to a little one-horse town and pick out a one-horse lawyer for president, I wouldn't have believed it." The answer was, "Neither would I. But it was a time when a man with a policy would have been fatal to the country. I never had a policy. I have simply tried to do what seemed best each day, as each day came."

"I don't intend precisely to throw the Constitution overboard, but I will stick it in a hole if I can," he told a Cabinet officer. The enemy was violating the Constitution to destroy the Union, he argued, and

351

therefore, "I will violate the Constitution, if necessary, to save the Union." He instructed a messenger to the Secretary of the Treasury, "Tell him not to bother himself about the Constitution. Say that I have that sacred instrument here at the White House, and I am guarding it with great care."

When he was renominated, it was by the device of seating delegates from Tennessee, which gave enough added votes to seat favorable delegates from Kentucky, Missouri, Louisiana, Arkansas, and from one county in Florida. Until late in that campaign of 1864, he expected to lose the November election; military victories brought the tide his way; the vote was 2,200,000 for him and 1,800,000 against him. Among those who bitterly fought him politically, and accused him of blunders or crimes, were Franklin Pierce, a former president of the United States; Horatio Seymour, the Governor of New York; Samuel F. B. Morse, inventor of the telegraph; Cyrus H. McCormick, inventor of the farm reaper; General George B. McClellan, a Democrat who had commanded the Army of the Potomac; and the Chicago *Times*, a daily newspaper. In all its essential propositions the Southern Confederacy had the moral support of powerful, respectable elements throughout the North, probably more than a million voters believing in the justice of the cause of the South as compared with the North.

While propagandas raged, and the war winds howled, he sat in the White House, the Stubborn Man of History, writing that the Mississippi was one river and could not belong to two countries, that the plans for railroad connection from coast to coast must be pushed through and the Union Pacific realized.

His life, mind and heart ran in contrasts. When his white kid gloves broke into tatters while shaking hands at a White House reception, he remarked, "This looks like a general bustification." When he talked with an Ohio friend one day during the 1864 campaign, he mentioned one public man, and murmured, "He's a thistle! I don't see why God lets him live." Of a devious Senator, he said, "He's too crooked to lie still!" And of a New York editor, "In early life in the West, we used to make our shoes last a great while with much mending, and sometimes, when far gone, we found the leather so rotten the stitches would not hold. Greeley is so rotten that nothing can be done with him. He is not truthful; the stitches all tear out." As he sat in the telegraph office of the War Department, reading cipher dispatches, and came to the words, Hosanna and Husband, he would chuckle, "Jeffy D.," and at the words, Hunter and Happy, "Bobby Lee."

While the luck of war wavered and broke and came again, as generals failed and campaigns were lost, he held enough forces of the Union together to raise new armies and supply them, until generals were found who made war as victorious war has always been made, with terror, frightfulness, destruction, and valor and sacrifice past words of man to tell.

A slouching, gray-headed poet, haunting the hospitals at Washington, characterized him as "the grandest figure on the crowded canvas of the drama of the nineteenth century—a Hoosier Michael Angelo."

His own speeches, letters, telegrams and official messages during that war form the most significant and enduring document from any one man on why the war began, why it went on, and the dangers beyond its end. He mentioned "the politicians," over and again "the politicians," with scorn and blame. As the platoons filed before him at a review of an army corps, he asked, "What is to become of these boys when the war is over?"

He was a chosen spokesman; yet there were times he was silent; nothing but silence could at those times have fitted a chosen spokesman; in the mixed shame and blame of the immense wrongs of two crashing civilizations, with nothing to say, he said nothing, slept not at all, and wept at those times in a way that made weeping appropriate, decent, majestic.

His hat was shot off as he rode alone one night in Washington; a son he loved died as he watched at the bed; his wife was accused of betraying information to the enemy, until denials from him were necessary; his best companion was a fine-hearted and brilliant son with a deformed palate and an impediment of speech; when a Pennsylvania Congressman told him the enemy had declared they would break into the city and hang him to a lamppost, he said he had considered "the violent preliminaries" to such a scene; on his left thumb was a scar where an ax had nearly chopped the thumb off when he was a boy; over one eye was a scar where he had been hit with a club in the hands of a Negro trying to steal the cargo off a Mississippi River flatboat; he threw a cashiered officer out of his room in the White House, crying, "I can bear censure, but not insult. I never wish to see your face again."

As he shook hands with the correspondent of the London *Times*, he drawled, "Well, I guess the London *Times* is about the greatest

power on earth—unless perhaps it is the Mississippi River." He re-
buked with anger a woman who got on her knees to thank him for
a pardon that saved her son from being shot at sunrise; and when an
Iowa woman said she had journeyed out of her way to Washington
just for a look at him, he grinned, "Well, in the matter of looking at
one another, I have altogether the advantage."

He asked his Cabinet to vote on the high military command, and
after the vote, told them the appointment had already been made; one
Cabinet officer, who had been governor of Ohio, came away person-
ally baffled and frustrated from an interview, to exclaim, to a private
secretary, "That man is the most cunning person I ever saw in my
life"; an Illinois lawyer who had been sent on errands carrying his
political secrets, said, "He is a trimmer and such a trimmer as the
world has never seen."

He manipulated the admission of Nevada as a state in the Union,
when her votes were needed for the Emancipation Proclamation, say-
ing, "It is easier to admit Nevada than to raise another million of
soldiers." At the same time he went to the office of a former New
York editor, who had become Assistant Secretary of War, and said
the votes of three congressmen were wanted for the required three-
quarters of votes in the House of Representatives, advising, "There
are three that you can deal with better than anybody else. . . .
Whatever promise you make to those men, I will perform it." And
in the same week, he said to a Massachusetts politician that two votes
were lacking, and, "Those two votes must be procured. I leave it to
you to determine how it shall be done; but remember that I am
President of the United States and clothed with immense power, and
I expect you to procure those votes." And while he was thus em-
ploying every last resource and device of practical politics to consti-
tutionally abolish slavery, the abolitionist Henry Ward Beecher at-
tacked him with javelins of scorn and detestation in a series of
editorials that brought from him the single comment, "Is thy servant
a dog?"

When the King of Siam sent him a costly sword of exquisite em-
bellishment, and two elephant tusks, along with letters and a photo-
graph of the King, he acknowledged the gifts in a manner as lavish
as the Orientals. Addressing the King of Siam as "Great and Good
Friend," he wrote thanks for each of the gifts, including "also two
elephant's tusks of length and magnitude, such as indicate they could
have belonged only to an animal which was a native of Siam." After

further thanks for the tokens received, he closed the letter to the King of Siam with strange grace and humor, saying, "I appreciate most highly your Majesty's tender of good offices in forwarding to this Government a stock from which a supply of elephants might be raised on our soil. . . . Our political jurisdiction, however, does not reach a latitude so low as to favor the multiplication of the elephant, and steam on land as well as water has been our best agent of transportation. . . . Meantime, wishing for your Majesty a long and happy life, and, for the generous and emulous people of Siam, the highest possible prosperity, I commend both to the blessing of Almighty God."

He sent hundreds of telegrams, "Suspend death sentence" or "Suspend execution" of So-and-So, who was to be shot at sunrise. The telegrams varied oddly at times, as in one, "If Thomas Samplogh, of the First Delaware Regiment, has been sentenced to death, and is not yet executed, suspend and report the case to me." And another, "Is it Lieut. Samuel B. Davis whose death sentence is commuted? If not done, let it be done."

While the war drums beat, he liked best of all the stories told of him, one of two Quakeresses heard talking in a railway car. "I think that Jefferson will succeed." "Why does thee think so?" "Because Jefferson is a praying man." "And so is Abraham a praying man." "Yes, but the Lord will think Abraham is joking."

An Indiana man at the White House heard him say, "Voorhees, don't it seem strange to you that I, who could never so much as cut off the head of a chicken, should be elected, or selected, into the midst of all this blood?"

A party of American citizens, standing in the ruins of the Forum in Rome, Italy, heard there the news of the first assassination of the first American dictator, and took it as a sign of the growing up and the aging of the civilization on the North American continent. Far out in Coles County, Illinois, a beautiful, gaunt old woman in a log cabin said, "I knowed he'd never come back."

Of men taking too fat profits out of the war, he said, "Where the carcass is there will the eagles be gathered together."

An enemy general, Longstreet, after the war, declared him to have been "the one matchless man in forty millions of people," while one of his private secretaries, Hay, declared his life to have been the most perfect in its relationships and adjustments since that of Christ.

Between the days in which he crawled as a baby on the dirt floor of a Kentucky cabin, and the time when he gave his final breath in Washington, he packed a rich life with work, thought, laughter, tears, hate, love.

With vast reservoirs of the comic and the droll, and notwithstanding a mastery of mirth and nonsense, he delivered a volume of addresses and letters of terrible and serious appeal, with import beyond his own day, shot through here and there with far, thin ironics, with paragraphs having raillery of the quality of the Book of Job, and echoes as subtle as the whispers of wind in prairie grass.

Perhaps no human clay pot has held more laughter and tears.

The facts and myths of his life are to be an American possession, shared widely over the world, for thousands of years, as the tradition of Knute or Alfred, Lao-tse or Diogenes, Pericles or Caesar, are kept. This because he was not only a genius in the science of neighborly human relationships and an artist in the personal handling of life from day to day, but a strange friend and a friendly stranger to all forms of life that he met.

He lived fifty-six years of which fifty-two were lived in the West —the prairie years.

Abraham Lincoln:
The Prairie Years

WILDERNESS BEGINNINGS

In May and the blossom-time of 1808, Tom and Nancy Lincoln with the baby Sarah moved from Elizabethtown in Kentucky to the farm of George Brownfield, where Tom did carpenter and farm work. Near their cabin wild crab-apple trees stood thick and flourishing with riots of bloom and odor. And the smell of wild crab-apple blossoms, and the low crying of all wild things, came keen that summer to Nancy Hanks. The summer stars that year shook out pain and warning, strange and bittersweet laughters, for Nancy Hanks.

The same year saw Tom Lincoln's family moved to his land on the South Fork of Nolin Creek, about two and a half miles from Hodgenville. He was trying to farm stubborn ground and make a home in a cabin of logs he cut from timber nearby. The floor was packed-down dirt. One door, swung on leather hinges, let them in and out. One small window gave a lookout on the weather, the rain or snow, sun and trees, and the play of the rolling prairie and low hills. A stick-clay chimney carried the fire smoke up and away.

One morning in February 1809, Tom Lincoln came out of his cabin to the road, stopped a neighbor and asked him to tell "the granny woman," Aunt Peggy Walters, that Nancy would need help soon. On the morning of February 12, a Sunday, the granny woman was at the cabin. And she and Tom Lincoln and the moaning Nancy Hanks welcomed into a world of battle and blood, of whispering dreams and wistful dust, a new child, a boy.

A little later that morning Tom Lincoln threw extra wood on the fire, an extra bearskin over the mother, and walked two miles up the road to where the Sparrows, Tom and Betsy, lived. Dennis Hanks, the nine-year-old boy adopted by the Sparrows, met Tom at the

357

door. In his slow way of talking Tom Lincoln told them, "Nancy's got a boy baby." A half-sheepish look was in his eyes, as though maybe more babies were not wanted in Kentucky just then.

Dennis Hanks took to his feet down the road to the Lincoln cabin. There he saw Nancy Hanks on a bed of poles cleated to a corner of the cabin, under warm bearskins. She turned to look at Dennis and threw him a tired, white smile. He stood watching the even, quiet breaths of this fresh, soft red baby. "What you goin' to name him, Nancy?" the boy asked. "Abraham," was the answer, "after his grandfather."

In the spring of 1811 Tom Lincoln moved his family ten miles northeast to a 230-acre farm he had bought on Knob Creek, where the soil was a little richer and there were more neighbors. The famous Cumberland Trail, the main pike from Louisville to Nashville, ran nearby the new log cabin Tom built, and they could see covered wagons with settlers heading south, west, north, peddlers with tinware and notions, gangs of slaves or "kaffles" moving on foot ahead of an overseer or slave trader on horseback, and sometimes in dandy carriages congressmen or legislative members going to sessions at Louisville.

Here little Abe grew out of one shirt into another, learned to walk and talk and as he grew bigger how to be a chore boy, to run errands, carry water, fill the woodbox, clean ashes from the fireplace. He learned the feel of blisters on his hands from using a hoe handle on rows of beans, onions, corn, potatoes. He ducked out of the way of the heels of the stallion and two brood mares his father kept and paid taxes on. That Knob Creek farm in their valley set round by high hills and deep gorges was the first home Abe Lincoln remembered.

Four miles a day Sarah and Abe walked to school. In a log schoolhouse with a dirt floor and one door, seated on benches with no backs, they learned the alphabet A to Z and numbers one to ten. It was called a "blab school"; the pupils before reciting read their lessons out loud. Their first teacher was Zachariah Riney, a Catholic, and the second one, Caleb Hazel, a former tavern keeper. Under them young Abe learned to write and to like forming letters and shaping words. He said later that "anywhere and everywhere that lines could be drawn, there he improved his capacity for writing." He scrawled words with charcoal, he shaped them in the dust, in sand, in snow. Writing had a fascination for him.

*

In December 1816, Tom Lincoln with Nancy, Sarah, Abe, four horses and their most needed household goods, made their break-away from Kentucky, moving north and crossing the Ohio River into land then Perry County, later Spencer County, Indiana. They traveled a wild raw country, rolling land with trees everywhere, tall oaks and elms, maples, birches, dogwood, underbrush tied down by ever-winding grapevines, thin mist and winter damp rising from the ground as Tom, with Abe perhaps helping, sometimes went ahead with an ax and hacked out a trail. "It was a wild region, with many bears and other wild animals still in the woods," Abe wrote later, where "the panther's scream, filled night with fear" and "bears preyed on the swine." A lonesome country, settlers few, families two and three miles apart.

About sixteen miles from the Ohio River they came to a rise of ground somewhat open near Little Pigeon Creek. Here the whole family pitched in and threw together a pole shed or "half-faced camp," at the open side a log fire kept burning night and day. In the next weeks of that winter Tom Lincoln, with help from neighbors and young Abe, now nearly eight, erected a cabin eighteen by twenty feet, with a loft. Abe later wrote that he "though very young, was large of his age, and had an axe put into his hands at once; and was almost constantly handling that most useful instrument." Abe or Sarah had to walk nearly a mile to fetch spring water. Tom dug several wells but they all went dry.

A wagon one day late in 1817 brought into the Lincoln clearing their good Kentucky neighbors Tom and Betsy Sparrow and the odd quizzical seventeen-year-old Dennis Friend Hanks. For some years Dennis would be a chum of Abe's. The Sparrows were to live in the Lincoln pole shed till they could locate land and settle. Hardly a year had passed, however, when Tom and Betsy Sparrow were taken down with the "milk sick," beginning with a whitish coat on the tongue, resulting, it was supposed, from cows eating white snakeroot or other growths that poisoned their milk. Tom and Betsy Sparrow died and were buried in September on a little hill in a clearing in the timbers nearby.

Soon after, there came to Nancy Hanks Lincoln that white coating of the tongue; her vitals burned; the tongue turned brownish; her feet and hands grew cold and colder, her pulse slow and slower. She knew she was dying, called for her children, and spoke to them her last dim choking words. Death came October 5, 1818, the banners of autumn flaming their crimsons over tall oaks and quiet maples. The body of Nancy Hanks Lincoln lay in peace and silence, the eyelids closed down in unbroken rest. The children tiptoed in, stood still, cried their tears of want and longing, whispered and heard only their own whispers answering.

Tom Lincoln took a log and he and Dennis Hanks whipsawed it into planks, planed the planks smooth, and made them of a measure for a box to bury the dead wife and mother in. Little Abe, with a jackknife, whittled pine-wood pegs. And while Dennis and Abe held the planks, Tom bored holes and stuck the whittled pegs through the holes. This was the coffin they carried next day to the little timber clearing nearby.

So Nancy Hanks Lincoln died, thirty-four years old, a pioneer sacrifice, with memories of blue wistful hills and a summer when the crab-apple blossoms flamed white and she carried a boy child into the world.

Lonesome days came for Abe and Sarah in November the next year when their father went away, promising to come back. He headed for Elizabethtown, Kentucky, through woods and across the Ohio River, to the house of the widow Sarah Bush Johnston. They said he argued straight-out: "I have no wife and you no husband. I came a-purpose to marry you. I knowed you from a gal and you knowed me from a boy. I've no time to lose; and if you're willin' let it be done straight off." She answered, "I got a few little debts," gave him a list and he paid them; and they were married December 2, 1819.

He could write his name; she "made her mark." Why the two of them took up with each other so quickly Dennis Hanks later said, "Tom had a kind o' way with women, an' maybe it was somethin' she took comfort in to have a man that didn't drink an' cuss none."

Abe and Sarah had a nice surprise one morning when four horses and a wagon came into their clearing, and their father jumped off, then Sarah Bush Lincoln, the new wife and mother, then her three children by her first husband, Sarah Elizabeth (thirteen), Matilda (ten), and John D. Johnston (nine years old). Next off the wagon came a feather mattress and pillows, a black walnut bureau, a large clothes chest, a table, chairs, pots and skillets, knives, forks, spoons.

"Here's your new mammy," his father told Abe as the boy looked up at a strong, large-boned, rosy woman, with a kindly face and eyes, a steady voice, steady ways. From the first she was warm and friendly for Abe's hands to touch. And his hands roved with curiosity over a feather pillow and a feather mattress.

Eleven-year-old Abe went to school again. Years later he wrote of where he grew up, "There were some schools, so called; but no qualification was ever required of a teacher, beyond *'readin'*, *writin'*, *and cipherin'* ' to the Rule of Three. If a straggler supposed to understand latin, happened to sojourn in the neighborhood, he was looked upon as a wizzard." School kept at Pigeon Creek when a schoolmaster happened to drift in, usually in winter, and school was out when he drifted away. Andrew Crawford taught Abe in 1820, James Swaney two years later, and after a year of no school Abe learned from Azel Dorsey. The schoolmasters were paid by the parents in venison, hams, corn, animal skins and other produce. Four miles from home to school and four miles to home again Abe walked for his learning, saying later that "all his schooling did not amount to one year."

Having learned to read Abe read all the books he could lay his hands on. He read many hours in the family Bible, the only book in their cabin. He borrowed and read *Aesop's Fables, Pilgrim's Progress, Robinson Crusoe,* Grimshaw's *History of the United States,* and Weems' *The Life of George Washington.*

Farm boys in evenings at the store in Gentryville, a mile and a half from the Lincoln cabin, talked about how Abe Lincoln was always digging into books, picking a piece of charcoal to write on the fire shovel, shaving off what he wrote, and then writing more. Dennis Hanks said, "There's suthin' peculiarsome about Abe." It seemed that Abe made books tell him more than they told other people. When he sat with the girl, Kate Roby, with their bare feet in the creek, and she spoke of the moon rising, he explained to her it was the earth moving and not the moon—the moon only seemed to rise. Kate was surprised at such knowledge.

The years pass and Abe Lincoln grows up, at seventeen standing six feet, nearly four inches, long-armed with rare strength in his muscles. At eighteen he could take an ax at the end of the handle and hold it out from his shoulders in a straight horizontal line, easy and steady. He could make his ax flash and bite into a sugar maple or a sycamore, one neighbor saying, "He can sink an ax deeper into wood than any man I ever saw." He learned how suddenly life can spring a surprise. One day in the woods, as he was sharpening a wedge on a log, the ax glanced, nearly took his thumb off, and the cut after healing left a white scar for life. "You never cuss a good ax" was a saying then.

Sleep came deep to him after work outdoors, clearing timberland for crops, cutting brush and burning it, splitting rails, pulling cross-cut saw and whipsaw, driving the shovel-plow, harrowing, spading, planting, hoeing, cradling grain, milking cows, helping neighbors at house-raisings, logrollings, cornhuskings, hog killings. He found he was fast and strong against other boys in sports. He earned board, clothes and lodgings, sometimes, working for a neighbor farmer.

Often Abe worked in the timbers, daylong with only the sound of his own ax, or his own voice speaking to himself, or the crackling and swaying of branches in the wind, or the cries and whirrs of animals, of brown and silver-gray squirrels, of partridges, hawks, crows, turkeys, grouse, sparrows and the occasional wildcat. In wilderness loneliness he companioned with trees, with the faces of open sky and weather in changing seasons. As he said later, he "picked up" education. He was the letter writer for the family and for neighbors. This was a kind of training in grammar and English composition. He walked thirty miles to a courthouse to hear lawyers speak and to see how they argued and acted. He heard roaring and ranting political speakers—and mimicked them. He listened to wandering evangelists who flung their arms and tore the air with their voices—and mimicked them. He told droll stories with his face screwed up in different ways. He tried to read people as keenly as he read books. He drank enough drams of whisky to learn he didn't like the taste and it wasn't good for his mind or body. He smoked enough tobacco to learn he wouldn't care for it. He heard rollicking and bawdy verses and songs and kept some of them for their earthy flavor and sometimes meaningful intentions.

His stepmother was a rich silent force in his life. The family and the neighbors spoke of her sagacity and gumption, her sewing and mending, how spick-and-span she kept her house, her pots, pans and kettles. When Abe's sister Sarah, a year after marrying Aaron Grigsby, died in childbirth in 1828, it was Sarah Bush Lincoln who spoke comfort to the 19-year-old son of Nancy Hanks. Her faith in God shone in works more than words, and hard as life was, she was thankful to be alive. She understood Abe's gloomy spells better than anyone else and he named her as a deep influence in him.

In 1829 Tom Lincoln decided to move his family and kinfolk to Illinois. They made three wagons that winter. They loaded the wagons, ready to go early morning of March 1, 1830. Two of the wagons had two yoke of oxen each and one wagon had four horses.

On the wagons were Tom and Sarah Bush Lincoln, her three children, John D. Johnston; Sarah, with her husband Dennis Hanks and their four children; Matilda, with her husband Squire Hall and their son; and Abraham Lincoln on and off an ox wagon with a goad coaxing or prodding the animals. They stopped where night found them, cooked supper, slept, and started at daybreak—a journey, Lincoln said later, "slow and tiresome."

After traveling over two hundred miles to Macon County, Illinois, they found John Hanks, who had picked a location for them on the north bank of the Sangamon River, about ten miles southwest of Decatur, land joining timber and prairie. John Hanks had already cut the logs for their cabin which soon was finished. They built a smoke-house and barn, cleared some fifteen acres, split rails to fence it, planted corn, after which Abraham with John Hanks split three thousand rails for two neighbors, and as "sodbusters" broke thirty acres of virgin prairie for John Hanks' brother Charles.

In December a blizzard filled the sky and piled snow two and a half feet on the ground. Soon another drive of snow made a four-foot depth of it on the level, with high drifts here and there. Rain followed, froze, and more snow covered the icy crust. For days in twelve-below-zero weather, families were cut off, living on parched corn. Some died of cold, lacking wood to burn; some died of hunger, lacking corn. For nine weeks that snow cover held the ground. Spring thaws came and sheets of water spread in wide miles on the prairies.

As the roads became passable, the Lincoln family and kin moved southeast a hundred miles to Coles County. Abraham had other plans and didn't go with them. He had "come of age."

NEW SALEM DAYS

In early 1831, Lincoln with John D. Johnston floated down the Mississippi River in a flatboat of cargo for Denton Offutt, a frontier hustler big with promises and a hard drinker. Stepping off the flat-boat at New Orleans, Lincoln walked nearly a mile, on flatboats, to reach shore. In New Orleans, he could read advertisements of traders. There were sellers advertising, "For sale—several likely girls from 10 to 18 years old, a woman 24, a very valuable woman 25, with three very likely children," while buyers indicated after the

manner of one: "Wanted—I want to purchase twenty-five likely
Negroes, between the ages of 18 and 25 years, male and female, for
which I will pay the highest prices in cash."

Young Abraham could see the narrow cobblestoned streets, the
women with rouged faces and teasing voices at the crib-house
windows on side streets, Negroes shading from black to octoroon,
ragged poor whites, sailors drunk and sober in a dozen different
jargons—the humanly ugly and lovely in a mingling. After a month
or so, with Johnston, he took a steamboat north.

From St. Louis walking overland Lincoln must have wondered
about New Salem and the new life he was moving into in that little
pioneer village on the Sangamon River. There on August 1, 1831, he
cast his first ballot. The polls were in the home of John Camron where
Lincoln was boarding and getting acquainted with Camron's eleven
daughters who teased him about his long legs and arms and heard
him admit he "wasn't much to look at."

Boarding in the Camron house Lincoln could hear at the eating
table or in candlelight before bedtime how young was the village. It
was only in January 1829 that Camron and his partner James Rut-
ledge had permission from the state legislature to build the dam. They
had a survey made the following October, named the place New
Salem, and in December that year they had sold their first lot for
$12.50; on Christmas Day 1829 they had their post office in the new
store of Samuel Hill and John McNeil.

A young and growing country and no one more sure and proud
of New Salem's future than Denton Offutt, promoter, booster and
boomer. He saw Lincoln as honest and able, picked him as a manager,
told people, "He knows more than any man in the United States."
Somehow at this particular time Offutt had an influence on Lincoln
for good, perhaps made Lincoln feel more sure of himself. On a lot
Offutt bought for $10, he and Lincoln built a cabin of logs for a
new store where Lincoln was to be clerk. Offutt's goods arrived and
Lincoln stacked shelves and corners. Soon stories got going about
Lincoln's honesty, how he walked six miles to pay back a few cents a
woman had overpaid for dry goods, and finding he had used a four-
ounce weight instead of an eight, he walked miles to deliver to a
woman the full order of tea she had paid for.

Offutt soon lost interest in his store, let it sink into failure and
skipped out of New Salem not saying where he was going. In April
1832 Lincoln enlisted for thirty days' service in the Black Hawk War

and was elected a captain of his company. He re-enlisted for twenty days and was mustered as a private into a company of mounted Independent Rangers under Captain Elijah Iles, a pioneer trader, land dealer and one of the founders of Springfield. Lincoln on June 16 enlisted for the third time, becoming a thirty-day private in the Independent Spy Corps of Captain Jacob M. Early, a Springfield physician and Methodist preacher who had been a private in the companies of Lincoln and Iles. Six months after his discharge, an army paymaster in Springfield paid Lincoln some $95 for his eighty days in the war. In those days Lincoln had seen deep into the heart of the American volunteer soldier, why men go to war, march in mud, sleep in rain on cold ground, eat pork raw when it can't be boiled, and kill when the killing is good. On a later day an observer was to say he saw Lincoln's eyes misty in his mention of the American volunteer soldier.

Election Day was eighteen days off, on August 6, and after reaching New Salem and washing off the Black Hawk War mud from his boots, Lincoln started electioneering. He traveled over Sangamon County, gave the arguments in his long address issued in the spring, telling the public he was a candidate for the state legislature. Among farmers, he pitched hay and cradled wheat in the fields and showed the farmers he was one of them; at crossroads he threw the crowbar and let the local wrestlers try to get the "crotch hoist" on him. He closed his campaign with a speech in the county courthouse at Springfield. On Election Day Lincoln lost, running eighth in a field of thirteen candidates. But in his own New Salem precinct, he polled 277 of the 300 votes cast.

Later Lincoln wrote of himself after this August election, "He was now without means and out of business, but was anxious to remain with his friends who had treated him with so much generosity, especially as he had nothing elsewhere to go to. He studied what he should do—thought of learning the black-smith trade—thought of trying to study law—rather thought he could not succeed at that without a better education."

He bought a partnership in a store, signing mortgages and notes, got involved in lawsuits and court judgments. On May 7, 1833, as Lincoln told it, he "was appointed Postmaster at New Salem—the office being too insignificant, to make his politics an objection." The pay would run about $50 a year, in commissions on receipts. He had to be in the office at Hill's store only long enough to receive and receipt for the mail which came twice a week first by postrider and later by stage. Letters arrived written on sheets of paper folded and waxed, envelopes not yet in use.

Lincoln was free to read newspapers before delivering them, and he read "the public prints" as never before. The habit deepened in him of watching newspapers for political trends and issues. And he could find excitement at times in reading the speeches made in Congress at Washington as reported in full in the *Congressional Globe* subscribed for by John C. Vance.

Lincoln signed as witness to petitions and deeds, drew and attested mortgages, served as clerk with $1.00 of pay at September and November elections in New Salem, received $2.50 for taking poll books eighteen miles to Springfield. He worked as rail splitter, mill hand, farm hand, helped out at the Hill store. Meanwhile he read or dipped into Volney's *The Ruins of Empire*, Gibbon's *Decline and Fall of the Roman Empire*, Paine's *The Age of Reason*. And his debts haunted him. They added up to more when his former partner, William F. Berry, died on short notice in January 1835, his estate practically nothing, leaving Lincoln responsible for their joint obligations. Thus his debts ran to a total of $1,100—and they wouldn't laugh away. They were little rats, a rat for every dollar, and he could hear them in the night when he wanted to sleep.

Squire Bowling Green, the justice of the peace, proved a friend and counselor, explained to Lincoln what he knew of the Illinois statutes, allowed Lincoln without fee to try small cases, examine witnesses and make arguments. The squire, not yet fifty, weighed 250 pounds and was nicknamed "Pot" for his paunch. He held court wearing only a shirt and pants in the warmer weather.

There were in the fall of 1833 farm sections, roads and towns needing their boundary lines marked clear and beyond doubt on maps—more than the county surveyor, John Calhoun, could handle. On the suggestion of Pollard Simmons, a farmer and Democratic politician living near New Salem, Calhoun, a Jackson Democrat, appointed Lincoln, who went eighteen miles to Springfield to make sure he wasn't tied up politically and could speak as he pleased.

Then for six weeks, daytime and often all of nighttime, he had his head deep in Gibson's *Theory and Practice of Surveying* and Flint's *Treatise on Geometry, Trigonometry and Rectangular Surveying*. From decimal fractions one book ran on into logarithms, the use of mathematical instruments, operating the chain, circumferentor, surveying by intersections, changing the scale of maps, leveling, methods for mensuration of areas. He had sessions with Mentor Graham, the local schoolmaster. Many nights, said Graham's daughter, she woke at midnight to see Lincoln and her father by the fire, figuring and explaining, her mother sometimes bringing fresh firewood for better lighting. On some nights he worked alone till daylight and it wore him down. He was fagged, and friends said he looked like a hard drinker after a two weeks' spree. Good people said, "You're killing yourself."

In six weeks, however, he had mastered his books, and Calhoun put him to work on the north end of Sangamon County. The open air and sun helped as he worked in field and timberland with compass and measurements. He surveyed the towns of Petersburg, Bath, New Boston, Albany, Huron, and others. His surveys became known for care and accuracy and he was called on to settle boundary disputes. Lincoln worked at occasional odd jobs when there was no surveying but he made it a point to find time to keep up his political connections.

In late summer or early fall of 1834 many people in New Salem, Lincoln included, wondered what had become of John McNeil. It was two years since he had left New Salem. Before leaving he had sold his interest in the Hill-McNeil store to Hill, but at thirty-two he was the owner of farms steadily rising in value and was rated one of the shrewdest and richest traders in New Salem. On December 9, 1831, Lincoln with Charles Maltby witnessed two deeds given by John Camron to John McNamar and it was then, if not earlier, that Lincoln learned John McNeil's real name was John McNamar. The one person most anxious about him when he went away from New Salem in 1832 was, in all probability, the nineteen-year-old Ann Rutledge. They were engaged to marry and it was understood he would straighten out affairs of his family in New York State and in not too long a time would come back to her for the marriage. A few months after he left in September 1832, James Rutledge and John M. Camron, the two founders of New Salem, having failed in business affairs, moved with their families into the double-log house of a farm near Sand Ridge that McNamar owned through payment to Camron of $400.

For nearly two years no one in New Salem had heard from the man. And Lincoln, who called McNamar "Mack," who had surveyed the land McNamar owned, and who had lived under the same roof with Ann during the months "Mack" was a boarder at the Rutledge tavern, could hardly have been unaware of what she was going through. Did she talk over with Lincoln the questions, bitter and haunting, that harassed her? Did he tell Ann Rutledge of any dream, daydream or reverie that came to him about love in general or a particular love for her? Or did he shrink from such talk because she might be clinging to some last desperate hope that her betrothed would return? Or did she lean to a belief that John McNamar was gone for all time, then shifting to another awful possibility that he would surely come back to his land and properties, perhaps bringing a wife with him?

Two years of silence could be heavy and wearing. She was twenty-one and Lincoln twenty-five and in the few visits he had time for in this year when surveying and politics pressed him hard, he may have gone no further than to be a comforter. He may have touched and stroked her auburn hair once or more as he looked deep into her blue eyes and said no slightest word as to what hopes lay deep in his heart. Her mother could remember her singing a hymn he liked, with a line, "Vain man, thy fond pursuits forbear." Both were figures of fate—he caught with debts, with surveying "to keep body and soul together" while flinging himself into intense political activities, she the victim of a betrothal that had become a mysterious scandal. They were both young, with hope endless, and it could have been he had moments when the sky was to him a sheaf of blue dreams and the rise of the blood-gold red of a full moon in the evening was almost too much to live, see and remember.

In those New Salem days were some saying Lincoln would be a great man, maybe governor or senator, anyhow a great lawyer, what with his studying of law. Others saw him as an awkward, gangly giant, a homely joker who could go gloomy and show it. It was noticed he had two shifting moods, one of the rollicking, droll story, one when he lapsed silent and solemn beyond any bystander to penetrate.

THE YOUNG LEGISLATOR

On April 19, 1843, Lincoln's name ran again in the *Sangamo Journal* as a candidate for the state legislature. Before that and after, he attended all sorts of political powwows, large and small, and those for whom he surveyed, and those he delivered letters to, did not fail to hear he was in the running. He had become a regular wheel horse of the Whig party backed by John T. Stuart, a Springfield lawyer and county Whig leader. This time Lincoln gave out no long address on issues as two years before. With no presidential ticket in the field, voters were freer in personal choice. Bowling Green, a local Democratic leader, out of his liking for and belief in Lincoln, offered him the support of fellow Democrats. Lincoln hesitated, talked it over with Stuart, then accepted.

So Lincoln played along—speaking little on issues, and showing up, when there was time, any place he could meet voters face to face, shake hands, and let them know what he was like as a man.

In the election for members of the Ninth General Assembly August 4, 1834, Lincoln ran second among thirteen Sangamon County candidates. At twenty-five, Lincoln had won his first important political office, with better pay than ever before in his life, where he would train in the tangled and, to him, fascinating games of lawmaking and parliamentary management amid political labyrinths. After election he ran the post office, made surveys and appraisals, clerked in an October election, made court appearances in connection with his debts, and November 22 was elected a delegate to the State Education Convention to be held in Vandalia December 5. He had drawn closer to Stuart, who in the Black Hawk War had been major of the battalion in which Lincoln was a company captain, had served two years in the legislature, was an able lawyer, a handsome man, six feet tall, of Kentucky ancestry, a shut-mouthed manipulator whose nickname was "Jerry Sly." He deepened Lincoln's feeling about law study and loaned him law books.

Vandalia gave some the impression it had been there a long time and was a little tired though it was only fifteen years old and had been the capital only fourteen years. A town of some 800 people, it overlooked the Kaskaskia River and heavy timber, and to the north and west rolling prairie. Its streets, eighty feet wide, were lined mostly with log cabins, its sidewalks worn paths in grass. Five or six large frame buildings were taverns and boardinghouses, now filling their many empty rooms with legislators and lobbyists. Two weekly newspapers, one Democratic and the other Whig, advertised bedrooms, choice liquors and rewards for fugitive slaves. Main highways crossed the town, stages rolling in regularly, their wheels dusty or mud-coated, with passengers from all directions. The new jail had a "dungeon room" for stubborn birds and a "debtors' room." Into the latter Lincoln could stray for a look at men behind bars because they couldn't pay their debts.

He roomed with Stuart whose leadership made their room a Whig center. Here and in the legislature Lincoln was to meet men, most of them young, who would become governors, Congressmen, U. S. Senators, men of influence and portent. Here he would meet a short and almost dwarfish man, a little giant, thick of body with a massive head, twenty-one years old and absolutely confident of himself— Stephen A. Douglas lobbying for his selection as state's attorney of the First Circuit. Many members had their wives and daughters along and there was a social life new to Lincoln—parties, cotillions, music and flowers, elegant food and liquor, a brilliance of silk gowns and talk that ranged from idle gabble to profound conversation about the state and nation. Around the public square in candlelighted taverns, coffee rooms and hangouts, could be heard the talk and laughter of men eating, smoking, drinking, greeting, getting acquainted, and no lack of office seekers on the hunt.

On December 1, in a two-story ramshackle brick building facing the public square, meeting on the lower floor, the House was called to order, the members sitting in movable chairs, three to a table— cork inkstands, quill pens and writing paper on each table—and on the floor a sandbox as spittoon. A fireplace and stove heated the room. Three tin dippers hung over a pail of drinking water. Evening sessions were lighted by candles in tall holders. Ceiling plaster crashed down occasionally during speeches and roll calls; members got used to it.

Among the fifty-four representatives Lincoln could feel that if he was a greenhorn, so were the other thirty-five first-term members; there were seventeen second-termers, and only one veteran of three previous terms. Three-fourths of them were born in Southern states, only one member a native of Illinois. Seven members had, like Lincoln, been captains in the Black Hawk War; many had been privates. More than half were farmers, one-fourth lawyers, with a sprinkling of merchants and mechanics.

One lobbyist noted Lincoln in this legislature as "raw-boned, angular, features deeply furrowed, ungraceful, almost uncouth . . . and yet there was a magnetism and dash about the man that made him a universal favorite." Before midnight of February 13 the last batch of hacked and amended bills was passed and Lincoln in two days of below-zero weather rode the stage to New Salem.

*

After the fixed programs and schedules of Vandalia, the smoke-filled rooms and hullabaloo, Lincoln now rode lonely country roads and walked in open winter air over fields he was surveying. He had seen lawmaking and politics at a vortex and vague resolves deepened in him. His resolution to study law drove him hard; friends worried about his health. As he wrote later, he "still mixed in the surveying to pay board and clothing bills"; his law books, "dropped" when a legislature met, "were taken up again at the end of the session." The *Sangamo Journal* had announced he was its New Salem agent and would take "Meal, Buckwheat, flour, pork on newspaper accounts."

Before March was over he had completed several surveys. After March he seemed to have little surveying work over the rest of 1835.

There seemed to have been an understanding between Ann Rutledge and Lincoln, with no pledges, that they would take what luck might hand them in whatever was to happen, while they advanced their education. Lincoln had his debts, his law studies, his driving political ambitions, while she had her quandaries related to John McNamar. They would see what time might bring. August came and corn and grass stood stunted for lack of rain. Settlers came down with chills, fever, malaria, Lincoln for his aches taking spoonfuls of Peruvian bark, boneset tea, jalap and calomel.

Soon New Salem heard that Ann Rutledge lay fever-burned, her malady baffling the doctors. Many went out to the Rutledge place, seven miles from New Salem. Days passed. Her cousin, McGrady Rutledge, a year younger than Ann, rode to New Salem and told Lincoln of her sickness growing worse. Lincoln rode out and they let him in for what might be his last hour with her. He saw her pale face and wasted body, the blue eyes and auburn hair perhaps the same as always. Few words were spoken, probably, and he might have gone only so far as to let his bony right hand and gnarled fingers lie softly on a small white hand while he tried for a few monosyllables of bright hope.

A few days later, on August 25, 1835, death came to Ann Rutledge and burial was in nearby Concord cemetery. Whether Lincoln went to her funeral, whether he wept in grief with others at the sight of her face in the burial box, no one later seemed to know. Her cousin, McGrady Rutledge, wrote far later, "Lincoln took her death verry hard." A letter of Matthew Marsh, September 17, had a tone as though the postmaster Lincoln was in good health and cheer. But this tells us nothing of Lincoln's inner feelings. Later when Lincoln was the center of incalculable death and agony and a friend rebuked him for telling funny stories, he cried back, "Don't you see that if I didn't laugh I would have to weep?" He did no doubt take Ann's death "verry hard" yet he was ambulant and doing his work as shown by a timberland survey he completed and dated September 24, 1835.

It was to come to pass that 30 years later New Salem villagers soberly spoke and wrote that Lincoln went out of his mind, wandered in the woods mumbling and crazy, and had to be locked up, all of which was exaggeration and reckless expansion of his taking Ann's death "verry hard." Woven with the recollections of his "insanity" were also the testimonies of what a deep flaming of lyric love there had been between him and Ann. A legend of a shining, deathless, holy and pure passion arose, spread, grew by some inherent vital sheen of its own or the need of those who wanted it, of Ann Rutledge, as a poet wrote, "beloved in life of Abraham Lincoln / wedded to him, / not through union, / but through separation."

The legislature session over in January 1836, Lincoln again worked away as surveyor, law student, politician. He wrote, signed and got other signers to a petition to a county court for an increased allowance for support of Benjamin Elmore, the insane son of widow Jemima Elmore. He wrote wills, located roads, settled boundary disputes, and on March 26 advertised a reward for return of his horse, "a large bay horse, star in his forehead, eight years old, shod all round, and trots and paces." On March 24 the Sangamon Circuit Court recorded him as a person of good moral character, his first step toward admission to the bar and law practice. He advertised that sixty-four persons had uncalled-for letters which unless called for would be sent to the dead-letter office. On May 30 he handed out mail as postmaster for the last time and told his New Salem public that their post office was moved to Petersburg.

The convention system not yet operating, he put himself in the running in June as a candidate for the legislature. He stumped the county, often speaking as one of a string of Whig candidates. In the election August 1 the county gave Lincoln the highest vote of seventeen candidates for the legislature. Sangamon County was taken by the Whigs, having now seven representatives and two senators.

Soon after this sweeping victory Lincoln in stride took his bar examination before two justices of the Supreme Court, passed, gave a dinner to his examiners, and on September 9, 1836, held in his hands a license to practice law in all the courts of Illinois. On October 5 he was in a Springfield court, appearing in a case for John T. Stuart, the beginning of their partnership as a law firm. In October and November he made three more known surveys and said good-by to surveying.

The tall Whigs from Sangamon County averaged six feet in height, Lincoln the longest, and were nicknamed the "Long Nine." Riding the stage to Vandalia two days, they talked about schemes and strategy that would carry through the legislature the one law more important to them than any other, an act to make Springfield the capital of Illinois. Arriving, they saw that Vandalia citizens, scared by the talk of moving the capital, had torn down the old building and were just finishing a new capitol in the center of the public square. Lincoln looked it over, stepping around workmen still on the job, tool sheds and piles of scaffolding lumber, piles of unused sand, brick and stone, perhaps laughing at the building hardly large enough to hold the new legislature, with no look toward future needs. Lincoln had become Whig floor leader and with the Long Nine worked all the time at as many bargains and favors as possible for other members with an eye on the votes that would be needed to change the capital to Springfield.

In the House were sixty-four Democrats to twenty-seven Whigs but in the Senate the roll was twenty-two Democrats to eighteen Whigs. Through Lincoln's strategy the Senate first took up a bill to "permanently locate the seat of government of the State of Illinois." The bill passed and went to the House where maneuver and debate began to rage. A Coles County man who had "been seen" by Lincoln moved an amendment, which passed, that no less than $50,000 and two acres of land must be donated by the new capital when chosen; this would be a mean obstacle to rivals of Springfield. Other amendments, aimed at butchering the bill, came up and failed in the late afternoon as candles were lighted and members could see out of the windows a driving snow. Some members had left the hall as though there would be only more monotonous amendments. Then suddenly a motion was made to table the bill "until next Fourth of July." And the motion passed by 39 to 38! Lincoln and the seven of the Long Nine in the House voted Nay. It looked like the end for their hope of making Springfield the new capital.

That night Lincoln called his Sangamon County colleagues into conference and gave each an assignment. They went out into the driving snow and knocked on doors. They found five members who had voted to table and brought them to change their vote in the morning. They located absentees of the afternoon who favored the bill and got their word to be surely on hand in the morning. Of five members whom they had favored with votes for railroads or canals they asked for a little gratitude. To others they threatened that in the Internal Improvements Bill, not yet passed by the Senate, their two Sangamon senators and others might rub out some of the railroads and canals. To Benjamin Enloe of Johnson County they pointed out that the longest railroad in the state was to run along the west line of his county. Also it seemed they promised to make Enloe warden of the state penitentiary, which promise they kept that very month. From door to door and room to room went Lincoln's colleagues using persuasions and threats.

Next morning, February 18, Enloe moved the bill "be re-considered." A roll call demanded by Douglas showed 42 Yea and 40 Nay. One member shifting from Yea to Nay would have killed the bill. A motion to table "until the 4th of July next" lost by 37 to 46. It was hazardous and delicately shaded politics Lincoln was playing.

Over the next week came more amendments and harassing tactics, including a motion to postpone selection of a new capital till December 1839. On the third reading of the bill February 24, 1837, the House passed it by 46 to 37. The House and Senate then held a joint session on location and the fourth ballot gave Springfield 73, Vandalia 16, Jacksonville 11, Peoria 8, Alton 6, Illiopolis 3—Henry Mills of Edwards voting for Purgatory on the third ballot. The losers charged "bargain and corruption." But it was all over and Springfield put on a jubilee; citizens howled and danced around a big bonfire blazing at the old whipping post on the public square till that relic was ashes.

Robert L. Wilson of the village of Athens and one of the Long Nine wrote of Lincoln as having "a quaint and peculiar way" and "he frequently startled us." He seemed a "born" politician. "We followed his lead; but he followed nobody's lead. It may almost be said that he did our thinking for us. He inspired respect, although he was careless and negligent . . . He was poverty itself, but independent." They had seen much of each other in the legislature and campaigning together, Wilson writing, "He sought company, and indulged in fun without stint . . . still when by himself, he told me that he was so overcome by mental depression, that he never dared carry a knife in his pocket; and as long as I was intimately acquainted with him, he never carried a pocketknife." At a banquet in Athens, Wilson gave the toast: "Abraham Lincoln; one of Nature's Noblemen."

In Springfield, Lincoln read lavish compliments to himself in the press and sat with the Long Nine and sixty guests at a game supper where one toast ran: "Abraham Lincoln: he has fulfilled the expectations of his friends, and disappointed the hopes of his enemies."

In April he packed his saddlebags to leave New Salem where six years before he had arrived, as he said, "a piece of floating driftwood," being now a licensed lawyer, a member of the state legislature and floor leader of the Whig party. The hilltop village, now fading to become a ghost town, had been to him a nourishing mother, a neighborhood of many names and faces that would always be dear and cherished with him, a friendly place with a peculiar equality between man and man, where Bill Greene was nearly correct in saying, "In New Salem every man is a principal citizen." Bitter hours but more sweet than bitter he had had. Here he had groped in darkness and grown toward light. Here newspapers, books, mathematics, law, the ways of people and life, had taken on new and subtle meanings for him.

It was no wilderness that Abraham Lincoln, twenty-eight years old, saw as he rode into Springfield April 15, 1837. Many of its people had come from Kentucky by horse, wagon and boat, across country not yet cleared of wolves, wildcats and horse thieves. A Yankee antislavery element in the Presbyterian Church had seceded to form a Second Presbyterian Church. And there were in Sangamon County seventy-eight free Negroes, twenty registered indentured servants and six slaves.

Lincoln pulled in his horse at the general store of Joshua Speed. He asked the price of bedclothes for a single bedstead, which Speed figured at $17. "Cheap as it is, I have not the money to pay," he told Speed. "But if you will credit me until Christmas, and my experiment here as a lawyer is a success, I will pay you then. If I fail in that I will probably never pay you at all." Speed said afterward: "The tone of his voice was so melancholy that I felt for him . . . I thought I never saw so gloomy and melancholy a face in my life." Speed offered to share his own big double bed upstairs over the store. Lincoln took his saddlebags upstairs, came down with his face lit up and said, "Well, Speed, I'm moved." A friendship, to last long, began, as with William Butler, clerk of the Sangamon Circuit Court, who told Lincoln he could take his meals at the Butler home and there would be no mention of board bills.

The circuit courtroom was in a two-story building in Hoffman's Row, and upstairs over the courtroom was the law office of the new firm of Stuart & Lincoln: a little room with a few loose boards for bookshelves, an old wood stove, a table, a chair, a bench, a buffalo robe and a small bed. Stuart was running for Congress, so Lincoln most of the time handled all of their law practice in range of his ability. Between law cases he kept up his political fences, writing many letters.

Mary Lincoln:
Wife and Widow

WINDING PATHS TO MARRIAGE

When Mary Todd, twenty-one years old, came in 1839 to live with her sister, Mrs. Ninian W. Edwards [Elizabeth Todd], she was counted an addition to the social flourish of Springfield. They spoke in those days of "belles." And Mary was one. Her sister told how she looked. "Mary had clear blue eyes, long lashes, light brown hair with a glint of bronze, and a lovely complexion. Her figure was beautiful and no Old Master ever modeled a more perfect arm and hand." Whatever of excess there may be in this sisterly sketch it seems certain that Mary Todd had gifts, attractions, and was among those always invited to the dances and parties of the dominant social circle. Her sister's husband once remarked as to her style, audacity or wit, "Mary could make a bishop forget his prayers."

Such, in brief, was the woman Lincoln gathered in his arms some time in 1840 when they spoke pledges to marry and take each other for weal or woe through life.

For two years Mary Todd haunted Lincoln, racked him, drove him to despair and philosophy, sent him searching deep into himself as to what manner of man he was. In those two years he first became acquainted with melancholy designated as hypochondriasis, or "hypo," an affliction which so depressed him that he consulted physicians. What happened in those two years?

Some time in 1840, probably toward the end of the year, Lincoln promised to marry Miss Todd and she was pledged to take him. It was a betrothal. They were engaged to stand up and take vows at a wedding. She was to be a bride; he was to be a groom. It was explicit.

Whether a wedding date was fixed, either definitely or approximately, does not appear in Mary Todd's letter to her friend Mercy Levering in December of 1840. Whether or not in that month they were engaged at all also fails to appear. In this letter, however, we

377

learn of Mary Todd, her moods and ways, at that time. She writes from Springfield, giving the news to her friend, mentioning Harriet Campbell who "appears to be enjoying all the sweets of married life." She refers to another acquaintance as ready to perpetrate "the crime of matrimony." This is light humor, banter, for the surmise is offered, "I think she will be much happier." Certain newly married couples, she observes, have lost their "silver tones." She raises the question, "Why is it that married folks always become so serious?"

Lincoln was uneasy, worried. Months of campaigning, traveling in bad weather, eating poorly cooked food and sleeping in rough taverns had made his nerves jumpy. He saw reasons why marriage would not be good for him or for Mary Todd. He wrote a letter to her, begging off. Then he showed the letter to Speed, whose reputation was lively for falling in love and falling out again. Speed threw the letter into the fire, saying in effect that such feelings of the heart shouldn't be put onto paper and made a record that could be brought up later. It was New Year's Day, 1841. Lincoln went to the Edwards house and came back to Speed. He explained that he had told Mary all that was in the letter. And Mary broke into tears, Lincoln took her into his arms, kissed her, and the engagement was on again.

But Lincoln was wretched. He had yielded to tears, had sacrificed a reasoned resolve because he couldn't resist the appeal of a woman's grief. Mary Todd saw his condition, saw that he was not himself, saw further that anything between them was impossible until he should recover. And so, regretfully but without bitterness, she released him from the engagement.

Over Springfield in the circles of these two principal persons the word spread that Mary Todd had jilted Lincoln. After leading him on, encouraging him, she suddenly had decided it was not for the best. So there would be no wedding. And both were content to let the bald fact stand without explanation.

Then Lincoln broke down completely. Two weeks after the night he had tried to tell Mary Todd how he felt and had failed, he took to his bed, miserably sick. Only Speed and Doctor Anson G. Henry saw him. Six days later he was up and around, due, it was said, to the strong brandy which the doctor had prescribed in large quantities. But he was not the old-time Lincoln.

Lincoln wrote two letters to his law partner, Congressman Stuart at Washington, D. C. In one letter he notes, "I have within the last few days, been making a most discreditable exhibition of myself in the way of hypochondriasm." In the second letter: "I am now the most miserable man living. If what I feel were equally distributed to the whole human family, there would not be one cheerful face on the earth. Whether I shall ever be better I cannot tell; I awfully forbode I shall not. To remain as I am is impossible; I must die or be better, it appears to me."

A letter of Mary's written to Mercy Levering in June of the summer of 1841 shows that her heart was not so gay after all. And furthermore, she didn't believe that everything was over and the past all sealed so far as she and Lincoln were concerned.

"The last three months have been of *interminable* length," she confesses. "After my gay companions of last winter departed, I was left much to the solitude of my own thoughts, and some *lingering regrets* over the past, which time can alone overshadow with its healing balm. Thus has my *spring time* passed. Summer in all its beauty has come again. The prairie land looks as beautiful as it did in the olden time, when we strolled together and derived so much of happiness from each other's society—this is past and more than this."

Was she at this time keeping Lincoln in mind and heart for marriage? We can only guess and surmise. It is reasonably certain that Lincoln used with Mary Todd the same words, the same point, he made with Mary Owens three years previous when he wrote Miss Owens to whom he was sort of tentatively engaged, "There is a great deal of flourishing about in carriages here, which it would be your doom to see without sharing it. You would have to be poor, without the means of hiding your poverty. Do you believe you can bear that patiently?"

Was it possible also that Lincoln knew well it was true, as others said, and as he himself said, that he was no ladies' man, that he was, as Mary Owens declared, "deficient in the little links that make for woman's happiness"? Would that explain why his words to Mary Owens in a letter, seemed rather to smack of justice than of passion and affection? Perhaps he was uncannily aware of, and did not care to join in with, the flaming folly of those lovers who out of wild embraces cry, "Love like ours can never die!" Perhaps he was suspicious that the fiercest loves soon burn out; he would rather have plain affection than consuming passion. Possibly he saw eye to eye with Henrik Ibsen declaring, "There is no word that has been soiled with lies like that word love."

Early in 1841 Speed sold his store in Springfield and went to Kentucky. In August Lincoln went to visit him, to rest for weeks in the big Speed home near Louisville. There he met Fanny Henning, the young woman Speed was planning to marry. The wedding date was set. Lincoln went back to Springfield but for months he and Speed were haunted by the approaching wedding. Speed was as shaken and worried about it as Lincoln had been about his affair with Mary Todd. Speed returned to Springfield for a long visit but on leaving for Kentucky again Lincoln handed him a letter to read on the stage to St. Louis and the steamboat for Louisville. The letter was an argument fortifying Speed and giving him reasons and courage for going through with his wedding as planned. "I know what the painful point is with you at all times when you are unhappy: it is an apprehension that you do not love her as you should. What nonsense!"

Speed reached home, found his intended bride sick, the doctors worried. He wrote Lincoln he was in the depths of misery. Lincoln replied, "Why, Speed, if you did not love her, although you might not wish her death, you would most certainly be resigned to it." He asked pardon if he was getting too familiar. "You know the hell I have suffered on that point, and how tender I am upon it."

Speed married Fanny Henning in February of 1842, and Lincoln's letter of congratulation declared, "I tell you, Speed, our forebodings (for which you and I are peculiar) are all the worst sort of nonsense." Speed had written that something indescribably horrible and alarming still haunted him. He implied marriage was no good to him. Lincoln predicted, "You will not say *that* three months from now, I will venture. When your nerves get steady now, the whole trouble will be over forever. Nor should you become impatient at their being very slow in becoming steady." Thus the recovering victim of "nerves" assured one struggling.

Also in this advice to Speed Lincoln includes a little argument that both he and Speed had been dreaming fool dreams about marriage bringing an impossible paradise. They had overrated the benefits and romance of matrimony. "You say, you much fear that the Elysium of which you and I dreamed so much is never to be realized. Well, if it shall not, I dare swear it will not be the fault of her who is now your wife. I now have no doubt, that it is the peculiar misfortune of both you and me to dream dreams of Elysium far exceeding all that anything earthly can realize."

When, a month later, Speed wrote that he was happy and Lincoln's predictions had come true, Lincoln replied, "Your last letter gave me more pleasure than the sum total of all I have enjoyed since that fatal first of January, 1841." Again he refers to Mary Todd. She still haunts him. "Since then it seems to me that I should have been entirely happy, but for the never absent idea that there is *one* still unhappy whom I have contributed to make so. That still kills my soul. I cannot but reproach myself for even wishing to be happy while she is otherwise. She accompanied a large party on the railroad cars to Jacksonville last Monday, and on her return spoke, so that I heard of it, of having enjoyed the trip exceedingly. God be praised for that!"

Speed now sent a warning that Lincoln must either soon make up his mind to marry Miss Todd or put her out of his thoughts completely, forget her. This was correct advice, Lincoln wrote back. "But, before I resolve to do one thing or the other, I must gain my confidence in my own ability to keep my resolves when they are made. In that ability, you know I once prided myself, as the only or chief gem of my character; that gem I lost, how and where you know too well. I have not yet regained it; and, until I do, I cannot trust myself in any matter of much importance."

Perhaps Lincoln used some of these very words to Mary Todd when later in 1842 they were brought together at the home of Mrs. Simeon Francis, wife of Lincoln's friend, the editor of the *Sangamo Journal*. Neither Lincoln nor Mary Todd knew beforehand they were to be brought face to face by Mrs. Francis, so it was said. It was a pleasant surprise. The first meeting was followed by many others.

Early in October Lincoln wrote Speed he knew well that Speed was happier than when first married. He could see in Speed's letters "the returning elasticity of spirits" resulting from marriage. "But," he wrote, "I want to ask you a close question. 'Are you now in *feeling*, as well as *judgment*, glad you are married as you are?' From anybody but me this would be an impudent question, not to be tolerated; but I know you will pardon it in me. Please answer it quickly, as I am impatient to know."

Speed's answer to Lincoln, it seemed, was yes, he was glad both in feeling and judgment that he had married as he did.

A few weeks later, on November 4, 1842, Lincoln and Mary Todd were married at the Ninian W. Edwards home. The Reverend Charles Dresser in canonical robes performed the ring ceremony for the groom, thirty-three years old, and the bride, twenty-three years old.

Mary Todd was now to have fresh light on why newly married couples lose their "silver tones," if they do. She was to know more clearly the reply to her query of two years previous, "Why is it that married folks always become so serious?"

In one of his letters advising Speed to marry, Lincoln had written that his old father used to say, "If you make a bad bargain, hug it all the tighter."

In a letter, five days after his wedding, to a Shawnee-town lawyer regarding two law cases, Lincoln closed with writing, "Nothing new here, except my marrying, which, to me, is a matter of profound wonder."

Abraham Lincoln:
The Prairie Years

LAWYER IN SPRINGFIELD

In the nine, and later fifteen counties of the Eighth Judicial District or "Eighth Circuit," Lincoln traveled and tried cases in most of the counties. He rode a horse or drove in a buggy, at times riding on rough roads an hour or two without passing a farmhouse on the open prairie. Mean was the journey in the mud of spring thaws, in the blowing sleet or snow and icy winds of winter. Heavy clothing, blankets or buffalo robes over knees and body, with shawl over shoulders, couldn't help the face and eyes that had to watch the horse and the road ahead.

The tavern bedrooms had usually a bed, a spittoon, two split-bottom chairs, a washstand with a bowl and a pitcher of water, the guest in colder weather breaking the ice to wash his face. Some taverns had big rooms where a dozen or more lawyers slept of a night. In most of the sleepy little towns "court day" whetted excitement over trials to decide who would have to pay damages or go to jail. Among the lawyers was fellowship with men of rare brains and ability who would be heard from nationally, some of them to be close associates of Lincoln for years. Over the Eighth Circuit area, 120 miles long and 160 miles wide at its limit, ranging from Springfield to the Indiana line, Lincoln met pioneer frontier humanity at its best and worst, from the good and wise to the silly and aimless.

With Stuart away months in Congress, and busy with politics when at home, the heavy routine work fell on Lincoln, who had learned about all he could of law from Stuart. They parted cordially and Lincoln went into partnership with Stephen T. Logan, acknowledged leader of the Springfield bar. Nine years older than Lincoln, he was a former circuit judge, Scotch-Irish and Kentucky-born—a short sliver of a man with tight lips and a thin voice that could rasp, his hair frowsy and red. He wore linsey-woolsey shirts, heavy shoes, and never a necktie, yet he was known as one of the most neat, care-ful, scrupulous, particular, exact and profoundly learned lawyers in Illinois in preparing cases and analyzing principles involved.

After joining Logan, Lincoln had more cases in the higher courts in Springfield. In December 1841 he argued fourteen cases in the Supreme Court, losing only four. Of twenty-four cases in that court during 1842 and 1843 he lost only seven. But Logan was taking a son into partnership, and he saw, too, that Lincoln was about ready to head his own law firm. And Logan, a Whig, elected a member of the legislature in 1842, had an eye on going to Congress, as did Lin-coln. The firm had, on Lincoln's advice, taken in as a law student a young man, William H. Herndon, nine years younger than Lincoln. Shortly after Herndon's admittance to law practice in December 1844, Lincoln and he formed a partnership and opened their office. The younger man had spoken amazement at Lincoln's offer to take him on, Lincoln saying only, "Billy, I can trust you and you can trust me." From then on for years he was "Billy" and called the other man "Mr. Lincoln."

Herndon was intense, sensitive, had hair-trigger emotions. He was of medium height, rawboned, with high cheekbones, dark eyes set far back, his shock of hair blue-black. He knew rough country boy talk and stories, tavern lingo, names of drinks, the slang of men about cards, horse races, chicken fights, women. Yet he was full of book learning, of torches and bonfires, had a flamboyance about freedom, justice, humanity. He liked his liquor, the bars and the topers of the town. He was a Whig, was plain himself and was loved by many plain people. There was a factor of politics as well as law in Lincoln's choosing for a partner the money-honest, highfalutin, whimsical, corn-on-the-cob, temperamental, convivial Bill Herndon.

Lincoln had begun wearing broadcloth, white shirts with white collar and black silk cravat, sideburns down three-fourths the length of his ears. Yet he was still known as carelessly groomed, his trousers mentioned as creeping to the ankles and higher, his hair rumpled, vest wrinkled, and at the end of a story putting his arms around his knees, raising his knees to his chin and rocking to and fro. Standing he loomed six feet four inches; seated he looked no taller than average, except for his knees rising above the chair's seat level.

When at home in Springfield, in the story-and-a-half frame house a few blocks from the city center, he cut wood, tended to the house stoves, curried his horse, milked the cow. Lincoln's words might have a wilderness air and log-cabin smack, the word "idea" more like "idee," and "really" a drawled Kentucky "ra-a-ly." He sang hardly at all but his voice had clear and appealing modulations in his speeches; in rare moments it rose to a startling and unforgettable high treble giving every syllable unmistakable meaning. In stoop of shoulders and a forward bend of his head there was a grace and familiarity making it easy for shorter people to look up into his face and talk with him.

In the small clique of Springfield Whigs who had come to wield party controls, the opposition dubbed Lincoln the "Goliath of the Junto." On streets, in crowds or gatherings, his tall frame stood out. He was noticed, pointed out, questions asked about him. He couldn't slide into any group of standing people without all eyes finding he was there. His head surmounting a group was gaunt and strange, on-lookers remembering the high cheekbones, deep eye sockets, the coarse black hair bushy and tangled, the nose large and well shaped, the wide full-lipped mouth of many subtle changes from straight face to wide beaming smile. He was loose-jointed and comic with appeals in street-corner slang and dialect from the public square hitching posts; yet at moments he was as strange and far-off as the last dark sands of a red sunset, solemn as naked facts of death and hunger. He was a seeker. Among others and deep in his own inner self, he was a seeker.

After eleven years of marriage Lincoln and Mary Todd had stood together at the cradles of four babies, at the grave of one. For these little ones Lincoln was thankful. To handle them, play with them and watch them grow, pleased his sense of the solemn and the ridiculous.

The father and mother had come to understand that each was strong and each was weak. Habits held him that it was useless for her to try to break. If he chose to lie on the front room carpet, on the small of his back, reading, that was his way. If he came to the table in his shirt sleeves and ate his victuals absently, his eyes and thoughts far off, that too was his way. She tried to stop him from answering the front doorbell and leave it to the servant. But he would go to the front door in carpet slippers and shirt sleeves to ask what was wanted. Once two fine ladies came to see Mrs. Lincoln; he looked for her and asked the callers in, drawling, "She'll be down soon as she gets her trotting harness on."

Mary had sewed her own clothes, had sewed clothes for the children; he let her manage the house. In Springfield she was quoted as once saying, "Money! He never gives me any money; he leaves his pocketbook where I can take what I want." Herndon noted: "She wanted to be a leader in society. Realizing that Lincoln's rise in the world would elevate and strengthen her, she strove in every way to promote his fortunes, to keep him moving, and thereby win the world's applause."

Talk about her over Springfield ran that she economized in the kitchen to have fine clothes; she had a terrible temper and tongue. That her husband had married her a thousand dollars in debt, that he charged low fees and had careless habits, that he trusted her and let her have her own way in the household economy, didn't fit well into the gossip. That she was at times a victim of mental disorder, that she was often sorry and full of regrets after a wild burst of temper, didn't make for exciting gossip.

Lincoln, after his one term in Congress, bought a book on logic, studied how to untangle fallacies and derive inexorable conclusions from established facts. On the circuit when with other lawyers, two in a bed, eight or ten in one hotel room, he read Euclid by the light of a candle after others had dropped off to sleep. Herndon once found Lincoln covering sheets of paper with figures, signs, symbols. He told Herndon he was trying to square the circle. After a two days' struggle, worn down, he gave up trying to square the circle.

He penned notes trying to be as absolute as mathematics: "If A. can prove, however conclusively, that he may, of right, enslave B., why may not B. snatch the same argument, and prove equally, that he may enslave A?—You say A. is white, and B. is black. It is *color*, then; the lighter, having the right to enslave the darker? Take care. By this rule, you are to be slave to the first man you meet, with a fairer skin than your own. You do not mean *color* exactly?—You mean the whites are *intellectually* the superiors of the blacks, and, therefore have the right to enslave them? Take care again. By this rule, you are to be slave to the first man you meet, with an intellect superior to your own. But, say you, it is a question of *interest;* and, if you can make it your *interest*, you have the right to enslave another. Very well. And if he can make it his interest, he has the right to enslave you." Thus his private memorandum.

He wrote of the legitimate object of government being "to do for the people what needs to be done, but which they can not, by individual effort, do at all, or do so well, for themselves," such as "Making and maintaining roads, bridges, and the like; providing for the helpless young and afflicted; common schools; and disposing of deceased men's property." Military and civil departments were necessary. "If some men will kill, or beat, or constrain others, or despoil them of property, by force, fraud, or noncompliance with contracts, it is a common object with peaceful and just men to prevent it."

Out of the silent working of his inner life came forces no one outside of himself could know; they were his secret, his personality and purpose. He was in the toils of more than personal ambition.

All other law cases were out when Lincoln threw himself into the defense of William ("Duff") Armstrong, the son of Hannah Armstrong. Before a coroner's jury a house painter named Charles Allen from Petersburg swore that he saw the fight between Armstrong and a man named Metzker, that it was between ten and eleven o'clock at night, and, by the light of a moon shining nearly straight over them, he saw Armstrong hit Metzker with a slung shot and throw away the slung shot which he, Allen, picked up.

In the trial at Beardstown Lincoln aimed to have young men on the jury; young, hot blood would understand his case better; the average age of the jurymen as finally picked, was twenty-three. With each witness Lincoln tried to find some ground of old acquaintance. "Your name?" he asked one. "William Killian." "Bill Killian? Tell me, are you a son of old Jake Killian?" "Yes, sir." "Well, you are a smart boy if you take after your dad."

Again Allen swore he saw Armstrong by the light of a moon nearly overhead, on a clear night, hit Metzker with a slung shot. Nelson Watkins testified that he had been to camp meeting the day after the fight, that he had with him a slung shot, and that he had thrown it away because it was too heavy and bothersome to carry. He had made the slung shot himself, he testified; he had put an eggshell into the ground, filled it with lead, poured melted zinc over the lead, but the two metals wouldn't stick; then he had cut a cover from a calfskin boot leg, sewed it together with a squirrel-skin string, using a crooked awl to make the holes; and he had then cut a strip from a groundhog skin that he had tanned, and fixed it so it would fasten to his wrist.

Lincoln took out his knife, cut the string with which the cover was sewed, showed it to be squirrel-skin, and then took out the inside metals and showed they were of two different sorts that did not stick together—the slung shot Allen testified he had picked up was identical with the one Watkins testified he had made and thrown away. Meantime he had sent out for an almanac, and when the moment came he set the courtroom into a buzz of excitement, laughter, whispering, by showing that, instead of the moon being in the sky at "about where the sun is at ten o'clock in the morning," as the leading witness testified, a popular, well-known family almanac showed that on the night of August 29, 1857, the moon had set and gone down out of sight at three minutes before midnight, or exactly 11:57 P.M. The almanac raised the question whether there was enough light by which a murder could be competently and materially witnessed.

Lincoln told the jury he knew the Armstrongs; the wild boy, Duff Armstrong, he had held in his arms when Duff was a baby at Clary's Grove; he could tell good citizens from bad and if there was anything he was certain of, it was that the Armstrong people were good people; they were plain people; they worked for a living; they made their mistakes; but they were kindly, loving people, the salt of the earth. He had told the mother of Duff, "Aunt Hannah, your son will be free before sundown." And it so happened. As the jury had filed out to vote, one of the jurymen winked an eye at Duff, so he afterwards told it.

Lincoln made safe, moderate investments. Speculations beckoned to others, but not to him. At hotels he took what was offered him with no complaint. He told his fellow lawyer Joe Gillespie he never felt easy when a waiter or a flunky was around. At a meeting of Republican editors in Decatur, he said he was a sort of interloper, and told of a woman on horseback meeting a man on a horse on a narrow trail. The woman stopped her horse, looked the man over: "Well for the land's sake, you are the homeliest man I ever saw!" The man excused himself, "Yes, Ma'am, but I can't help that," and the woman: "No, I suppose not, but you might stay at home."

Before posing for an ambrotype he ran his fingers through his hair to rumple it; on the stump or in jury speeches his hands wandered over his head and put the hair in disorder. Always, it was noticed, the linen he wore was clean; his barbers didn't let the sign of a beard start; he blacked his own boots. As to haircuts, grammar and technicalities, he wasn't so particular. In jury arguments and before a big crowd in Springfield, he wiped sweat from his face with a red silk handkerchief.

For lawyers he would mimic a country justice: "If the court understand *herself* and she think she do." And there was John Moore, driving a yoke of red steers to Bloomington one Saturday, starting home with a jug, and emptying the jug into himself. Driving through timber a wheel hit a stump and threw the pole out of the ring of the yoke. The steers ran away; Moore slept till morning in the cart, and when he awoke and looked around, he said, "If my name is John Moore, I've lost a pair of steers; if my name ain't John Moore, I've found a cart."

And Lincoln had heard a farmer brag about his hay crop one year: "We stacked all we could outdoors, and then we put the rest of it in the barn." On a paper written by a lawyer, with too many words and pages, he remarked, "It's like the lazy preacher that used to write long sermons, and the explanation was, he got to writin' and was too lazy to stop."

Friendship with Leonard Swett, Henry C. Whitney and other lawyers on the circuit grew and deepened for Lincoln, and particularly that with fair-haired and pink-faced Judge David Davis, six years younger, five inches shorter, a hundred pounds heavier. A graduate of Kenyon College, Davis had come west and grown up with Bloomington. He had a keen eye for land deals and owned thousand-acre tracts. On his large farm near Bloomington he had a frame mansion where Lincoln stayed occasionally. In many ways the destinies of Davis and Lincoln were to interweave.

STRANGE FRIEND AND FRIENDLY STRANGER

Lincoln was fifty-one years old. With each year since he had become a grown man, his name and ways, and stories about him, had been spreading among plain people and their children. So tall and so bony, with so peculiar a slouch and so easy a saunter, so sad and so haunted-looking, so quizzical and so comic, as if hiding a lantern that lighted and went out and that he lighted again—he was the Strange Friend and the Friendly Stranger. Like something out of a picture book for children—he was. His form of slumping arches and his face of gaunt sockets were a shape a Great Artist had scrawled from careless clay.

He looked like an original plan for an extra-long horse or a lean tawny buffalo, that a Changer had suddenly whisked into a man-shape. Or he met the eye as a clumsy, mystical giant that had walked out of a Chinese or Russian fairy story, or a bogy who had stumbled out of an ancient Saxon myth with a handkerchief full of presents he wanted to divide among all the children in the world.

He didn't wear clothes. Rather, clothes hung upon him as if on a rack to dry, or on a loose ladder up a windswept chimney. His clothes, to keep the chill or the sun off, seemed to whisper, "He put us on when he was thinking about something else."

He dressed any which way at times, in broadcloth, a silk hat, a silk choker, and a flaming red silk handkerchief, so that one court clerk said Lincoln was "fashionably dressed, as neatly attired as any lawyer at court, except Ward Lamon." Or again, people said Lincoln looked like a huge skeleton with skin over the bones, and clothes covering the skin.

The stovepipe hat he wore sort of whistled softly: "I am not a hat at all; I am the little garret roof where he tucks in little thoughts he writes on pieces of paper." The hat, size seven and one-eighth, had a brim one and three-quarters inches wide. The inside band in which the more important letters and notes were tucked, measured two and three-quarters inches. The cylinder of the stovepipe was 22 inches in circumference. The hat was lined with heavy silk and, measured inside, exactly six inches deep. And people tried to guess what was going on under that hat. Written in pencil on the imitation satin paper that formed part of the lining was the signature "A. Lincoln, Springfield, Ill.," so that any forgetful person who might take the hat by mistake would know where to bring it back. Also the hatmaker, "George Hall, Springfield, Ill.," had printed his name in the hat so that Lincoln would know where to get another one just like it.

The umbrella with the name "Abraham Lincoln" stitched in, faded and drab from many rains and regular travels, looked sleepy and murmuring. "Sometime we shall have all the sleep we want; we shall turn the law office over to the spiders and the cobwebs; and we shall quit politics for keeps."

There could have been times when children and dreamers looked at Abraham Lincoln and lazily drew their eyelids half shut and let their hearts roam about him—and they half-believed him to be a tall horse chestnut tree or a rangy horse or a big wagon or a log barn full of new-mown hay—something else or more than a man, a lawyer, a Republican candidate with principles, a prominent citizen—something spreading, elusive, and mysterious—the Strange Friend and the Friendly Stranger.

In Springfield and other places, something out of the ordinary seemed to connect with Abraham Lincoln's past, his birth, a mystery of where he came from. The wedding certificate of his father and mother was not known to be on record. Whispers floated of his origin as "low-flung," of circumstances so misty and strange that political friends wished they could be cleared up and made respectable. The wedding license of Thomas Lincoln and Nancy Hanks had been moved to a new county courthouse—where no one had thought to search.

The year of the big debates a boy had called out, "There goes old Mr. Lincoln," and Lincoln hearing it, remarked to a friend, "They commenced it when I was scarcely thirty years old." Often when people called him "Old Abe" they meant he had the texture and quaint friendliness of old handmade Bibles, old calfskin law books, weather-beaten oak and walnut planks, or wagon axles always willing in storm or stars.

A neighbor boy, Fred Dubois, joined with a gang who tied a string to knock off Lincoln's hat. "Letters and papers fell out of the hat and scattered over the sidewalk," said Dubois. "He stooped to pick them up and us boys climbed all over him." As a young man he played marbles with boys; as an older man he spun tops with his own boys, Tad and Willie.

When William Plato of Kane County came to his office with the little girl, Ella, he stood Ella on a chair and told her, "And you're not as tall as I am, even now." A girl skipping along a sidewalk stumbled on a brick and fell backward, just as Lincoln came along. He caught her, lifted her up in his arms, put her gently down and asked, "What is your name?" "Mary Tuft." "Well, Mary, when you reach home tell your mother you have rested in Abraham's bosom."

Old Aesop could not have invented a better fable than the one about the snakes in the bed, to show the harm of letting slavery into the new territories. "If there was a bed newly made up, to which the children were to be taken, and it was proposed to take a batch of young snakes and put them there with them, I take it no man would say there was any question how I ought to decide."

When Tad was late bringing home the milk he hunted the boy and came home with Tad on his shoulders and carrying the milk pail himself. Once he chased Tad and brought the little one home, holding him at arm's length; the father chuckled at his son's struggle to kick him in the face. Once as he lugged the howling Willie and Tad, a neighbor asked, "Why, Mr. Lincoln, what's the matter?" The answer: "Just what's the matter with the whole world. I've got three walnuts and each wants two."

In Rushville and towns circling around, they remembered the day he was there. The whole town turned out, among them young women of Rushville society, as such. One of the belles dangled a little Negro doll baby in Lincoln's face. He looked into her face and asked quietly, "Madam, are you the mother of that?" At many a corn shucking and Saturday night shindig, this incident had been told.

Germans and Irishmen had greetings from him. "I know enough German to know that Kaufman means merchant, and Schneider means tailor—am I not a good German scholar?" Or, "That reminds me of what the Irishman said, 'In this country one man is as good as another; and for the matter of that, very often a great deal better.'"

He told of the long-legged boy "sparking" a farmer's daughter when the hostile father came in with a shotgun; the boy jumped through a window, and running across the cabbage patch scared up a rabbit; in about two leaps the boy caught up with the rabbit, kicked it high in the air, and grunted, "Git out of the road and let somebody run that knows how." He told of a Kentucky horse sale where a small boy was riding a fine horse to show off points. A man whispered, "Look here, boy, hain't that horse got the splints?" and the boy, "Mister, I don't know what the splints is, but if it's good for him, he has got it; if it ain't good for him, he ain't got it."

Riding to Lewistown, an old acquaintance, a weather-beaten farmer, spoke of going to law with his next neighbor. "Been a neighbor of yours for long?" "Nigh onto fifteen year." "Part of the time you get along all right, don't you?" "I reckon we do." "Well, see this horse of mine? I sometimes get out of patience with him. But I know his faults; he does fairly well as horses go; it might take me a long time to get used to some other horse's faults; for all horses have faults."

Lincoln told of a balloonist going up in New Orleans, sailing for hours, and dropping his parachute over a cotton field. The gang of Negroes picking cotton saw a man coming down from the sky in blue silk, in silver spangles, wearing golden slippers. They ran—all but one old-timer who had rheumatism and couldn't get away. He waited till the balloonist hit the ground and walked toward him. Then he mumbled: "Howdy, Massa Jesus. How's yo' Pa?"

He liked to tell of the strict judge of whom it was said: "He would hang a man for blowing his nose in the street, but he would quash the indictment if it failed to specify which hand he blew it with."

He could write an angry letter, with hard names and hot epithets —and then throw it in the stove. He advised it was a help sometimes to write a hot letter and then burn it. On being told of a certain man saying, "I can't understand those speeches of Lincoln," he laughed, "There are always some fleas a dog can't reach."

Though the years had passed, he still believed, "Improvement in condition—is the order of things in a society of equals." And he still struggled under the load of that conundrum of history he had written ten years back: "As Labor is the common *burthen* of our race, so the effort of *some* to shift their share of the burthen on to the shoulders of *others*, is the great, durable, curse of the race."

He defended Peachy Harrison who killed Greek Grafton, a law student in the office of Lincoln & Herndon. On the witness stand came old Peter Cartwright, the famous circuit rider, grandfather of the accused murderer. "How long have you known the prisoner?" "I have known him since a babe; he laughed and cried on my knee." And Lincoln led on with more questions, till old Peter Cartwright was telling the last words that slowly choked out from the murdered man, three days after the stabbing: "I am dying; I will soon part with all I love on earth and I want you to say to my slayer that I forgive him. I want to leave this earth with a forgiveness of all who have in any way injured me." Lincoln had then begged the jury to be as forgiving as the murdered man. The handling of the grandfather as a witness cleared Peachy Harrison and set him free.

Over a period of some twenty years Lincoln had signed 20 petitions for pardons for convicted men, the governors of Illinois granting pardons in fourteen cases. He had served as attorney for fourteen of the convicted men and in some cases wrote his opinions and beliefs why the men should be set free. He wrote as to one of his clients that he was of a young family, had lost one arm, and had served five-sixths of his sentence, of another that it was "a miscarriage of justice," of two brothers sentenced to one year for stealing five shoats valued at $10 that the public was "greatly stirred" in their favor.

The name of the man had come to stand for what he was, plus beliefs, conjectures and guesses. He was spoken of as a "politician" in the sense that politics is a trade of cunning, ambitious, devious men. He chose a few issues on which to explain his mind fully. Some of his reticences were not evasions but retirements to cloisters of silence. Questions of life and destiny shook him close to prayers and tears in his own hidden corners and byways; the depths of the issues were too dark, too pitiless, inexorable, for a man to open his mouth and try to tell what he knew.

In the cave of winds in which he saw history in the making he was far more a listener than a talker. The high adventure of great poets, inventors, explorers, facing the unknown and the unknowable, was in his face and breath, and had come to be known, to a few, for the danger and bronze of it.

There was a word: democracy. Tongues of politics played with it. Lincoln had his slant at it. "As I would not be a *slave*, so I would not be a *master*. This expresses my idea of democracy. Whatever differs from this, to the extent of the difference, is no democracy."

He had faced men who had yelled, "I'll fight any man that's goin' to vote for that miserable skunk, Abe Lincoln." And he knew homes where solemn men declared, "I've seen Abe Lincoln when he played mournin' tunes on their heartstrings till they mourned with the mourners." He was taken, in some log cabins, as a helper of men. "When I went over to hear him at Alton," said one, "things looked onsartin. 'Peared like I had more'n I could stand up under. But he hadn't spoken more'n ten minutes afore I felt like I never had no load. I begin to feel ashamed o' bein' weary en complainin'."

He loved trees, was kin somehow to trees, his favorite the hard maple. Pine, cedar, spruce, cypress, had each their pine family ways for him. He had found trees and men alike; on the face of them, the outside, they didn't tell their character. Life, wind, rain, lightning, events, told the fiber, what was clean or rotten.

What he said to a crowd at Lewistown one August afternoon of 1858 had been widely printed and many a reader found it deeply worth reading again and again. His theme was the Declaration of Independence and its phrase, "that all men are created equal," and have unalienable rights to "life, liberty and the pursuit of happiness." That document was a "majestic" interpretation:

> This was their lofty, and wise, and noble understanding of the justice of the creator to His creatures. [Applause.] Yes, gentlemen, to *all* His creatures, to the whole great family of man . . . They grasped not only the whole race of man then living, but they reached forward and seized upon the farthest posterity . . . Wise statesmen as they were, they knew the tendency of prosperity to breed tyrants, and so they established these great self-evident truths, that when in the distant future some man, some faction, some interest, should set up the doctrine that none but rich men, or none but white men, were entitled to life, liberty and the pursuit of happiness, their posterity might look up again to the Declaration of Independence and take courage to renew the battle which their fathers began . . . I charge you to drop every paltry and insignificant thought for any man's success. It is nothing; I am nothing; Judge

Douglas is nothing. *But do not destroy that immortal emblem of Humanity—the Declaration of American Independence.*

Once in 1858 Lincoln wrote a meditation he didn't use in any of the debates. It was a private affair between him and his conscience:

> . . . Yet I have never failed—do not now fail—to remember that in the republican cause there is a higher aim than that of mere office. I have not allowed myself to forget that the abolition of the Slave-trade by Great Brittain was agitated a hundred years before it was a final success; that the measure had it's open fire-eating opponents; it's stealthy "dont-care" opponents; it's dollar and cent opponents; it's inferior race opponents; its negro equality opponents; and its religion and good order opponents; that all these opponents got offices, and their adversaries got none. But I have also remembered that though they blazed, like tallow-candles for a century, at last they flickered in the socket, died out, stank in the dark for a brief season, and were remembered no more, even by the smell . . . I am proud, in my passing speck of time, to contribute an humble mite to that glorious consummation, which my own poor eyes may not last to see.

And that year he read at Bloomington a lecture on "Discoveries and Inventions," repeating it later in Springfield. Scheduled a second time at Bloomington he met so small an audience that he didn't bother to read his paper; he soon dropped the idea of being a "popular lecturer." What he read revealed him as a droll and whimsical humorist, a scholar and thinker, a keen observer and a man of contemplation who, if fate ordained, could have a rich and quiet life entirely free from political ambitions. He touched on man's first discovery or invention of clothes, of speech, of wind power for sailing, of the alphabet, of printing. Rulers and laws in time past had made it a crime to read or to own books. "It is difficult for us, *now* and *here,* to conceive how strong this slavery of the mind was; and how long it did, of necessity, take, to break it's shackles, and to get a habit of freedom of thought, established." A new country, such as America, "is most favorable—almost necessary—to the immancipation of thought, and the consequent advancement of civilization and the arts." Briefly and ironically, in passing, he went political, mentioning "the invention of negroes, or, of the present mode of using them, in 1434." Dominant in the paper he read was love of books, of pure science, of knowledge for its own sake, of a humanity creeping out of dark mist toward clear light.

Somewhere in this period Milton Hay of Springfield heard Lincoln speak offhand a rule or maxim in politics. Hay later passed it on to Joseph Fifer of Bloomington who found it so simple and so nicely singsong that he couldn't forget it: "You can fool some of the people all of the time, and all of the people some of the time, but you can't fool all of the people all of the time."

At a remark in Mayor Sanderson's house in Galesburg that he was "afraid of women," Lincoln laughed, "A woman is the only thing I am afraid of that I know can't hurt me." He told Whitney he hated going through the act of telling a hayrack full of girls in white gowns, each girl one state of the Union, "I also thank you for this beautiful basket of flowers." After a tea party at the home of Mayor Boyden of Urbana, the mayor and Whitney excused themselves for an hour, and left Lincoln alone with Mrs. Boyden, Mrs. Whitney, and her mother. Whitney, on returning, found Lincoln "ill at ease as a bashful country boy," eyes shifting from floor to ceiling and back, arms behind and then in front, then tangled as though he tried to hide them, and his long legs tying and untying themselves. Whitney couldn't understand it unless it was because he was alone in a room with three women.

A woman wrote her admiration of his course in politics, and he thanked her in a letter. "I have never corresponded much with ladies; and hence I postpone writing letters to them, as a business which I do not understand." Men knew of his saying, after giving money or time or a favor in answer to a pathetic but probably bogus appeal, "I thank God I wasn't born a woman."

Herndon believed Lincoln cloaked his ways with women by a rare and fine code, writing, "Mr. Lincoln had a strong, if not terrible passion for women. He could hardly keep his hands off a woman, and yet, much to his credit, he lived a pure and virtuous life. His idea was that a woman had as much right to violate the marriage vow as the man—no more and no less. His sense of right—his sense of justice— his honor forbade his violating his marriage vow. Judge Davis said to me, 'Mr. Lincoln's honor saved many a woman.' This I know. I have seen Lincoln tempted and I have seen him reject the approach of woman!"

A woman charged with keeping a house of ill fame was a client of Lincoln & Herndon; they asked for a change of venue; and Lincoln drove across the prairies from one town to another with the madam of the house and her girls. After the trial the madam was asked about

Lincoln's talk with her. Yes, he told stories, and they were nearly all funny. Yes, but were the stories proper or improper, so to speak? Well—the madam hesitated—they were funny; she and all the girls laughed—but coming to think it over she believed the stories could have been told "with safety in the presence of ladies anywhere." Then she added, as though it ought to be told, "But that is more than I can say for Bill Herndon."

A curious friend and chum of Lincoln was Ward Hill Lamon, his Danville law partner, a young Virginian, dauntless, bull-necked, melodious, tall, commanding, often racy and smutty in talk, aristocratic and, drinking men said, magnificent in the amount of whisky he could carry. The first time he and Lincoln met, Lamon wore a swallow-tailed coat, white neckcloth, and ruffled silk shirt, and Lincoln: "Going to try your hand at law, are you? I don't think you would succeed at splitting rails." As the years passed a strange bond of loyalty between the two men grew. "Sing me a little song," was Lincoln's word to Lamon, who brought out a banjo and struck up the lively "Cousin Sally Downard," or "O Susanna," or the sad "Twenty Years Ago."

Women, music, poetry, art, pure science, all required more time than Lincoln had to give them. He liked to tell of the Indiana boy blurting out, "Abe, I don't s'pose there's anybody on earth likes gingerbread better'n I do—and gets less'n I do."

Herndon told of his partner coming to the office sometimes at seven in the morning when his usual hour to arrive was nine. Or of Lincoln at noon, having brought to the office a package of crackers and cheese, sitting alone eating. Mrs. Lincoln and Herndon hated each other. While Herndon was careless as to where he spat, she was not merely scrupulously neat and immaculate as to linen and baths, she was among the most ambitious women in Springfield in the matter of style and fashion. She knew of such affairs as Herndon getting drunk with two other men and breaking a windowpane that her husband had to hustle the money for so that the sheriff wouldn't lock up his law partner. She didn't like it that her husband had a drinking partner reckless with money, occasionally touching Lincoln for loans. She carried suspicions and nursed misgivings as to this swaggering upstart, radical in politics, transcendentalist in philosophy, antichurch.

At parties, balls, social gatherings, she moved, vital, sparkling, often needlessly insinuating or directly and swiftly insolent. If the music was bad, what was the need of her making unkind remarks about the orchestra? Chills, headaches, creepers of fear came; misunderstandings rose in waves so often around her; she was alone, so all alone, so like a child thrust into the Wrong Room.

At parties, balls, social gatherings, she trod the mazy waltzes in crinoline gowns, the curves of the hoop skirts shading down the plump curves of her figure. Once when talk turned to Lincoln and Douglas, she had said, "Mr. Lincoln may not be as handsome a figure, but people are perhaps not aware that his heart is as large as his arms are long."

She wrote to a sister in September 1857 of a trip east with her husband when he had law business in New York. A moment of happy dreaminess ran through part of her letter. "The summer has so strangely and rapidly passed away. Some portion of it was spent most pleasantly in traveling East. We visited Niagara, Canada, New York and other points of interest."

How often good times shone for them, only they two could tell. They were intense individuals, he having come through hypochondria, and she moving by swirls toward a day when she would cry out that hammers were knocking nails into her head, that hot wires were being drawn through her eyes. Between flare-ups and regrets, his was most often the spirit of accommodation. He was ten years older than she, with a talent for conciliation and adjustment.

There were times when she made herself pretty for him. One picture of her after fifteen years of marriage shows dark ringlets of hair down her temples and about her ears, a little necklace circling her bare neck, three roses at her bosom, and a lily in her shapely hands.

Lincoln in 1857 sent an editor, John E. Rosette, a letter marked "Private":

> Your note about the little paragraph in the Republican was received yesterday, since which time I have been too unwell to notice it. I had not supposed you wrote or approved it. The whole originated in mistake. You know by the conversation with me that I thought the establishment of the paper unfortunate, but I always expected to throw no obstacle in its way, and to patronize it to the extent of taking it and paying for one copy. When the paper was brought to my house, my wife said to me, "Now are you going to take another worthless little paper?" I said to her *evasively*, "I have not directed the paper to be left." From this, in my absence, she sent the message to the carrier. This is the whole story.

A lawyer was talking business to Lincoln once at home and suddenly the door opened. Mrs. Lincoln put her head in and snapped the question whether he had done an errand she told him to do. He looked up quietly, said he had been busy, but would attend to it as soon as he could. The woman wailed; she was neglected, abused, insulted. The door slammed; she was gone. The visiting lawyer, open-eyed, muttered his surprise. Lincoln laughed, "Why, if you knew how much good that little eruption did, what a relief it was to her, and if you knew her as well as I do, you would be glad she had had an opportunity to explode."

She was often anxious about her boys, had mistaken fears about their safety or health, exaggerated evils that might befall them. She gave parties for them and wrote with her own pen, in a smooth and even script, gracious invitations.

Mary Todd had married a genius who made demands; when he wanted to work, it was no time for interruptions or errands. For this brooding and often somber man she was wife, housekeeper, and counselor in personal and political affairs in so far as he permitted. She watched his "browsing" in the pantry and tried to bring him to regular meals. She had kept house years ago, too poor for a hired girl; they burned wood then; now they had a coal cookstove with four lids and a reservoir to warm rain water. She had chosen the beautiful, strong black-walnut cradle, into which she had put, one after the other, four boy babies.

She knew of the money cost in 1858 when he dropped nearly all law cases for months and paid his way at hotels and in 4,200 miles of travel, writing in one letter after the campaign closed, "I am absolutely without money now for even household purposes." At times he did the shopping, Herndon saying that of a winter's morning he might be seen around the market house, a basket on his arm, "his old gray shawl wrapped around his neck."

With their rising income and his taking place as the outstanding leader of his party, Mary Lincoln in the late 1850's enjoyed giving parties occasionally for two or three hundred people. Isaac N. Arnold noted of these evenings "everything orderly and refined," and "every guest perfectly at ease," with a table "famed for the excellence of many rare Kentucky dishes, and in season, loaded with venison, wild turkeys, prairie chickens, quail and other game." She had moved with him from lean years to the comforts of the well-to-do middle class. With ownership of his house and lot, with farm lands, and collectible bills he had out, Lincoln in 1859 had property worth perhaps $15,000 or more.

"MARY, WE'RE ELECTED"

Into the state Republican convention at Decatur on May 9 came John Hanks carrying two fence rails tied with flags and streamers, with the inscription, "Abraham Lincoln, the Rail Candidate for President in 1860: Two rails from a lot of 3,000 made in 1830 by Thos. Hanks and Abe Lincoln—whose father was the first pioneer of Macon County." Shouts followed: "Lincoln! Lincoln! Speech!" He thanked them with a sober face. Cheers: "Three times three for Honest Abe, our next President." Shouts from the convention: "Identify your work!" "It may be that I split these rails," and scrutinizing further, "Well, boys, I can only say that I have split a great many better-looking ones."

Thus the Rail Candidate was brought forth, and the nickname of Rail Splitter. The idea came from Richard Oglesby, a Decatur lawyer, Kentucky-raised, a plain and witty man, who shared Lincoln's belief in the people. Far more important was it that the convention instructed its delegates to the Chicago convention to vote as a unit for Lincoln.

Illinois delegates were outfitting with silk hats and broadcloth suits for the Chicago Republican convention May 16. Lincoln was saying, "I am a little too much a candidate to stay home and not quite enough a candidate to go." Norman B. Judd and others had made a special point of getting the convention for Chicago. They told the national committee that holding the convention in an eastern city would "run a big chance of losing the West." At the corner of Lake and Market Streets the Sauganash Hotel had been torn down, and a huge rambling lumber structure, to hold 10,000 people, had been put up and named the Wigwam.

Judge David Davis had adjourned the Eighth Circuit courts, took over the entire third floor of Chicago's finest hotel, the Tremont House, paying a rental of $300 for spacious Lincoln headquarters and rooms for his staff of Lincoln hustlers, evangelists, salesmen, pleaders, exhorters, schemers. In the parlor of the Lincoln head-quarters were cigars and wine, porter, brandy, whisky, for any delegate or important guest.

Seward victory was in the air; champagne fizzed at the Richmond House. Straw votes on all incoming railroad trains had given William H. Seward of New York overwhelming majorities. Lincoln workers were saying with clenched fists and blazing eyes that the Republicans were beaten at the start if Seward headed the ticket.

Ward Lamon had been to the printers of seat tickets. Young men worked nearly a whole night signing names of convention officers to counterfeit seat tickets so that next day Lincoln men could jam the hall and leave no seats for the Seward shouters. On the first two days of the convention's routine business the Seward men were allowed by the Chicago managers to have free run of the floor. But on May 18, when sunrise saw thousands milling about the Wigwam doors, the Lincoln shouters were shoved through the doors till they filled all seats and standing room; hundreds of New York hurrah boys couldn't squeeze in. Lamon and Jesse Fell got a thousand men recruited for their lung power. They watched their leaders, two men located on opposite sides of the Wigwam. One of them, Dr. Ames of Chicago, it was said, could "on a calm day" be heard clear across Lake Michigan. The other one, brought by Delegate Burton Cook from Ottawa, could give out with a warm monster voice. These two Leather Lungs watched Cook on the platform; when he took out his handkerchief they cut loose with all they had and kept it up till Cook put his handkerchief back. They were joined by the thousand recruits picked for voice noise.

On May 18 Lincoln was talking with two law students when his office door burst open and the *Journal* editor, Baker, told him of the first ballot in Chicago. They walked to the telegraph office, found no later news, and at the *Journal* office met a crowd shouting good news would be coming. Lincoln slouched in a chair but straightened up at the next news of his big gains on the second ballot. And when the wires sang that his nomination had been made unanimous, he knew that a great somber moment had come to him and the firing of one hundred jubilant guns made a shadowed music. He read a flurry of gay telegrams, shook hands all round, then went home to tell the news and see his wife's face beam and glow.

Bonfires of boxes, barrels and brushwood lighted up the Sangamon River country that Friday night. A brass band and a cheering crowd at the Lincoln house surged to the front porch and called for a speech. He saw the honor of the nomination not for him personally but as the representative of a cause; he wished his house big enough so he could ask them all inside. Shouts and yells of hurrah parties broke on the night till the gray dawn of the morning after.

Elements that Lincoln had described as "strange and discordant, gathered from the four winds," had formed a powerful party of youth, wild banners, pilgrims of faith and candlelight philosophers, besides hopeful politicians. Industrial, transportation and financial interests found this party promising. "A Railroad to the Pacific Ocean is imperatively demanded by the interests of the whole country; the Federal Government ought to render immediate and efficient aid in its construction," read the Republican platform plank.

In its platform promises on tariff, on land and homestead laws, on farm and factory legislation to benefit workingmen, industry and business, the Republican party had a sincerity, was attending to issues in degree long neglected or evaded. Before one issue all others shrank, that of union and the wage-labor system as against disunion and slave labor. Carl Schurz had yelled, to a storm of cheers, "We defy the whole slave power and the whole vassalage of hell."

The man in Springfield picked to carry the banner stood at moments as a shy and furtive figure. He wanted the place—and he didn't. His was precisely the clairvoyance that knew terrible days were ahead. He had his hesitations. And he was in the end the dark horse on whom the saddle was put. He could contemplate an old proverb: "The horse thinks one thing, he that saddles him another."

The notification committee at his house formally told Lincoln he was nominated for President. He formally replied, and later, after reading the platform, sent a letter of acceptance. He would co-operate, "imploring the assistance of Divine Providence."

In June the adjourned Democratic national convention met in Baltimore, and after bitter and furious debates, nominated Stephen Douglas of Illinois for President. Douglas stumped the country in what seemed for him a losing fight; he went on tireless, men amazed at the way he wore out, went to bed, and came back fighting.

Lincoln saw the powerful young political party shaping his figure into heroic stature, coloring his personality beyond reality. From hundreds of stump orators and newspapers came praise and outcry for "Abe," "Old Abe," "the Rail Candidate," "the Backwoodsman," "Honest Abe," "the Man of the People," the sagacious, eloquent Man of the Hour, one who starting from a dirt-floor cabin was to move on into the Executive Mansion in Washington.

Letters kept coming to Lincoln—what would he do with slavery if elected? Would he interfere? Would it not be wise now to say plainly he wouldn't interfere? One he had answered, "Those who will not read, or heed, what I have already publicly said, would not read, or heed a repetition of it."

The campaign came to its last week. As the summer and fall drew on Lincoln was to those who met him the same friendly neighbor as always—but with more to think about. He shook hands with Henry C. Whitney in a big crowd, and a half-hour later, seeing Whitney again, he shook hands and called him by name. "He didn't know me the first time," said Whitney.

From nine o'clock on election evening Lincoln sat in the Springfield telegraph office. With friends he stepped across the street to where the Republican Ladies' Club had fixed a supper. Hardly were the men seated when a messenger rushed in waving a telegram. New York had gone Republican. Lincoln's election was clinched.

In the streets, and around the Statehouse, crowds surged, shouting themselves hoarse. The jubilee was still going as Lincoln walked home to say to a happy woman, "Mary, we're elected."

THE HOUSE DIVIDING

Lincoln's election was a signal. "Resistance to Lincoln is Obedience to God" flared a banner at an Alabama mass meeting. Against Southern advice that South Carolina wait till President Buchanan's term ended, Robert Barnwell Rhett and his forces had manipulated the precise dramatic event of secession. Rhett wrote the ordinance of disunion, and in secret session the convention's 169 delegates in St. Andrew's Hall at Charleston, December 16, 1860, passed it without debate in 45 minutes. One by one the six other Cotton States of the lower South joined South Carolina in leaving the Union.

Senators and Representatives from the South spoke sad and bitter farewells to Congress; U.S. postmasters, judges, district attorneys, customs collectors, by the hundreds sent their resignations to Washington. Of the 1,108 officers of the U.S. Regular Army, 387 were preparing resignations, many having already joined the Confederate armed forces. The U.S. mint at New Orleans and two smaller mints were taken over by the Confederate States, as were post offices and customhouses. Governors of seceded states marched in troops and took over U.S. forts that had cost $6,000,000.

Newly organized artillery companies were drilling in Chicago. A thousand Negro slaves were throwing up fortifications in Charleston, South Carolina. Governor Yates notified the legislature, "Illinois counts among her citizens 400,000 who can bear arms." Five million dollars and a hundred thousand troops would be offered by their state, Pennsylvania legislators were saying.

If Lincoln should try to retake the seized forts, he would have to kill in sickening numbers, said John Y. Brown of Kentucky. Lincoln delivered remarks such as, "Please excuse me . . . from making a speech," and, "Let us at all times remember that all American citizens are brothers of a common country." Lincoln told friends privately that the forts seized by the seceded states would have to be retaken. But as to public declarations of policy on this and that, he was waiting.

Delegates at Montgomery, Alabama, on February 4 organized a provisional government named the Confederate States of America, electing Jefferson Davis of Mississippi as President and Alexander Stephens of Georgia as Vice-President. Second to Robert Barnwell Rhett as a torch of revolution was William Lowndes Yancey of Alabama. And yet, in the seats of high power sat neither Yancey nor Rhett. Yancey and other extremists would have liked Rhett to be President. But a moderate element took the power, men who would rather have waited, who would have held a convention and presented demands to the North. In their newly adopted constitution they struck directly at Rhett, Yancey and the slave traders, and bid for international good will by expressly forbidding the African slave trade for all time.

Conventions in North Carolina and Arkansas deliberated, and joined the Confederacy. In Tennessee the voters balloted 105,000 to 47,000 in favor of secession, Union votes coming heavy from the mountaineers. In Virginia, three to one of 130,000 voters were in favor of "the Mother of Presidents" going into the Confederacy, the mountaineers chiefly being Unionist. In Texas, Governor Sam Houston refused to call the legislature and tried to stop secession, but was bowled over.

Henry Adams of Massachusetts was writing a brother, "No man is fit to take hold now who is not as cool as death." It was sunset and dawn, moonrise and noon, dying time and birthing hour, dry leaves of the last of autumn and springtime blossom roots.

"I BID YOU AN AFFECTIONATE FAREWELL"

When a Brooklyn hatter one day in January presented Lincoln with a black silk hat, he turned to say, "Well, wife, if nothing else comes out of this scrape, we are going to have some new clothes." Such attentions pleased Mrs. Lincoln. She had a sprightly manner of saying, "We are pleased with our advancement."

Pressure came on her to give her husband the names of men he should appoint to offices, with reasons why. She spoke of fears about her health, would mention "my racked frame" to other women, and say she hoped the chills she suffered from in earlier years would not return in Washington. She might find Washington a city of tears and shadows. She would go there with new clothes, fresh ribbons, and see. She made a trip in January to New York City, there meeting Robert, who came down from Harvard. She had as good a time as possible for her, choosing and buying gowns, hats, footwear and adornments becoming to one to be called "the First Lady of the Land."

Henry Villard wrote for the New York *Herald* January 26 of the President-elect "delighted" at the return of Mrs. Lincoln and Bob from the east. "Dutiful husband and father that he is, he had proceeded to the railroad depot for three successive nights in his anxiety to receive them, and that in spite of snow and cold. Mrs. Lincoln returned in good health and excellent spirits; whether she got a good scolding from Abraham for unexpectedly prolonging her absence, I am unable to say; but I know she found it rather difficult to part with the winter gayeties of New York." Villard noted, too, that Robert, fresh from Harvard, dressed in an elegance in "striking contrast to the loose, careless, awkward rigging of his Presidential father."

"Lincoln is letting his whiskers grow," men were saying in January, when his upper lip and cheeks were shaved but a stubble left on the chin. Then in February hair had grown over jaws, chin and throat, the upper lip shaven. Why Lincoln took to whiskers at this time nobody seemed to know. Herndon, Whitney, Lamon, Nicolay, heard no explanation from him as to why after 52 years with a smooth face he should now change.

Lincoln rode to Mattoon, missed connections with a passenger train, and took the caboose of a freight train to Charleston. With a shawl over his shoulders, and his boots in slush, mud and ice, he picked his way in the late evening dusk alongside the tracks the length of the freight train to the station, where a buggy was ready. Friends took him to the house where he stayed overnight. Next day he drove eight miles out to an old farm. Sally Bush Lincoln and he put their arms around each other and listened to each other's heartbeats. They held hands and talked, they talked without holding hands. Each looked into eyes thrust back in deep sockets. She was all of a mother to him. He was her boy more than any born to her. He gave her a photograph of her boy, a hungry picture of him standing and wanting, wanting. He stroked her face a last time, kissed good-by and went away. She knew his heart would go roaming back often, that even when he rode in an open carriage in New York or Washington with soldiers, flags and cheering thousands along the streets, he might just as like be thinking of her in the old log farmhouse out in Coles County, Illinois.

A cold drizzle of rain was falling February 11 when Lincoln and his party of fifteen were to leave Springfield on the eight o'clock at the Great Western Railway station. Chilly gray mist hung the circle of the prairie horizon. A short locomotive with a flat-topped smokestack stood puffing with a baggage car and special passenger car coupled on; a railroad president and superintendent were on board. A thousand people crowded in and around the brick station, inside of which Lincoln was standing, and one by one came hundreds of old friends, shaking hands, wishing him luck and Godspeed, all faces solemn. Even the huge Judge Davis, wearing a new white silk hat, was a somber figure.

A path was made for Lincoln from the station to his car; hands stretched out for one last handshake. He hadn't intended to make a speech; but on the platform of the car, as he turned and saw his home people, he took off his hat, stood perfectly still, and raised a hand for silence. They stood, with hats off.

Then he spoke slowly, amid the soft gray drizzle from the sky. Later, on the train he wrote with a pencil about half of his speech, dictating to his secretary John Nicolay the remainder of his good-by words to Springfield: "My friends—No one, not in my situation, can appreciate my feeling of sadness at this parting. To this place, and the kindness of these people, I owe every thing. Here I have lived a quarter of a century, and have passed from a young to an old man. Here my children have been born, and one is buried. I now leave, not knowing when, or whether ever, I may return, with a task before me greater than that which rested upon Washington. Without the assistance of that Divine Being, who ever attended him, I cannot succeed. With that assistance I cannot fail. Trusting in Him, who can go with me, and remain with you and be every where for good, let us confidently hope that all will yet be well. To His care commending you, as I hope in your prayers you will commend me, I bid you an affectionate farewell."

Bells rang, there was a grinding of wheels, the train moved and carried Lincoln away from his home town and folks. The tears were not yet dry on some faces when the train had faded into the gray to the east.

Drawn by Otto J. Schneider from Lincoln's hat and umbrella
in Chicago Historical Society

Abraham Lincoln:
The War Years

AMERICA WHITHER?

"America whither?" was the question, with headache and heartache in several million homes, as Lincoln began his winding journey to Washington. There Congress had not yet, after canvass of electoral results, declared and certified him President-elect. There coming events were yet to unlock a box of secrets. In the hair-trigger suspense General Scott was saying to an aide, "A dog fight now might cause the gutters to run with blood." And he was putting guards at doorways and vantage points to make sure of order when the electoral vote for President would be canvassed February 13.

The high-priced lawyer, Rufus Choate, listening to foreign language opera in New York had told his daughter, "Interpret for me the libretto lest I dilate with the wrong emotion." In the changing chaos of the American scene, people were dilating with a thousand different interpretations. Lincoln was to be, if he could manage it, the supreme interpreter of the violent and contradictory motives swaying the country, the labor pains of the nation.

Only tall stacks of documents recording the steel of fact and the fog of dream could tell the intricate tale of the shaping of a national fate; of many newspapers North and South lying to their readers and pandering to party and special interests; of Southern planters and merchants $200,000,000 in debt to the North, chiefly to the money controllers of New York City; of the jealousy of Virginia and Kentucky slave breeders whose market was interfered with by the African slave traders; of the race question, one thing in the blizzard region of New England, where a Negro on the streets was a rare curiosity, and something else again in the deep drowsy tropical South, where in many areas Negroes outnumbered whites; of Southern slave traders who flouted the Constitutional law prohibiting the delivery of naked cargoes in the Gulf Coast canebrakes and everglades; of the law as to fugitive slaves mocked at by abolitionists stealing slave property and running it North to freedom; of abolitionists South and North hanged, shot, stabbed, mutilated; of the Northern manufacturer able to throw out men or machines no longer profitable while the Southern planter could not so easily scrap his production apparatus of living black men and women; of a new quantity production intricately organized in firearms and watch factories; of automatic machinery slightly guided by human hands producing shoes, fabrics, scissors, pins and imitation jewelry sold by a chain of Dollar Stores; of a wilderness of oil derricks sprung up in western Pennsylvania; of balloons soaring 23,000 feet and predictions of passenger balloons to Europe; of microscopically exact gauges to measure one ten-thousandth of an inch; of the far western State of Iowa having double the white population of South Carolina; of the persistent national vision of a railroad to the Pacific; of covered wagons heading west with signs "Ho for California," "Oregon or Death"; of 500 westbound wagons a day passing through Fort Kearney, Nebraska; of horse stages taking passengers across plains, deserts, mountains, in a regular twenty-three-day run from St. Louis to San Francisco; of the pony express running mail from St. Joseph, Missouri, to San Francisco in eleven days, using 500 horses and eighty riders, each taking the sacks an average of $133\frac{1}{3}$ miles; of farming machinery almost exclusively in the North that doubled and tripled crop land one man could handle; of woman's household work lightened by laborsaving sewing machines, churns, egg-beaters and the like; of Abraham Lincoln reading in his personal copy of *Blackwood's Magazine* that in thirty years the U. S. population would double and in 1940 reach 303,000,000; of immense stretches of the Great Plains where sod might yet be broken for unnumbered millions to come; of new empires of production and trade in the prospects of practical men who had in the past ten years spent $400,000,000 on railroads and canals between the Midwest and the Atlantic seaboard; of lands, homesteads and vast exploits waiting out yonder where the railroad whistle would shatter old solitudes; of backbreaking labor by Irish construction gangs on railroads and canals; of dog-eat-dog rivalries among merchants, manufacturers and other interests battling for customers and trade areas; of customers haggling over retail-store prices and the sensational announcement of A. T. Stewart's big store in New York that goods had one price only, as marked; of the clean and inexplicably mystic dream in many humble hearts of an indissoluble Federal Union of States; of the Mississippi River system draining 1,000,000 square miles of rich farm land, floating $60,000,000 worth of steamboats, hauling from 12 states North and South; of the certainty that the new Republican party power at Washington would aim to limit extension of slavery and put it in the course of "ultimate extinction"; of the 260,000 free Negroes of the South owning property valued at $25,-000,000, one being the wealthiest landowner in Jefferson County, Virginia; of at least one in every hundred free Negroes owning one or two slaves, a few owning fifty or more; of the Southern poor white lacking slaves, land and the decent creature comforts of the Negro house servant, and often clutching as a dear personal possession the fact that he was not born black; of Northern factory hands and garment-trade workers paid a bare subsistence wage, out of which to guard against accident, sickness, old age, unemployment; of the vague hope across the South that Northwestern States might join their confederacy or form a confederacy of their own; of the one-crop Cotton States' heavy dependence on the Border Slave States and the North for food supplies, animal fodder, implements and clothing; of the Cotton States' delusion that New England and Europe were economic dependents of King Cotton; of the American system having densely intricate undergrowth, shot through from the growths of oncoming modern capitalism moderated and offset by an immense domain of cheap land absorbing otherwise disturbing and antagonistic elements.

Thus might run a jagged sketch of the Divided House over which Lincoln was to be Chief Magistrate.

LINCOLN TAKES THE OATH AS PRESIDENT

March 4 dawned with pleasant weather that later turned bleak and chilly for the 25,000 strangers roving Washington. With hotels and rooming houses overcrowded, hundreds had slept on the porches of public buildings and on street sidewalks. Thousands filled the street around Willard's as the forenoon wore away. General Scott and Colonel Stone had arranged for riflemen in squads to be placed in hiding on the roofs of certain commanding houses along Pennsylvania Avenue. From windows of the Capitol wings riflemen were to watch the inauguration platform.

President Buchanan drove with Senator Edward D. Baker of Oregon and Senator Pearce of Maryland from the White House to Willard's in an open carriage. Buchanan stepped out and soon returned arm in arm with Lincoln as police kept a path for them. Then the procession moved down Pennsylvania Avenue with representations from all branches of the Government. A new procession was formed to escort the President-elect to the east portico and the platform outdoors, where a crowd of at least 10,000 that had waited long gave its applause and scattering cheers.

Senator Douglas took a seat and looked over the crowd. One comment ran that rather than a sea of upturned faces it was a sea of silk hats and white shirt bosoms. Lincoln in a new tall hat, new black suit and black boots, expansive white shirt bosom, carrying an ebony cane with a gold head the size of a hen's egg, had the crowd matched.

The silver-bell voice of his close friend, Senator Baker, rang out: "Fellow-citizens, I introduce to you Abraham Lincoln, the President-elect of the United States." The applause was a slight ripple. Then came the inaugural address; Lincoln drew the papers from an inside coat pocket, slowly pulled spectacles from another pocket, put them on, and read deliberately the fateful document.

Then stepped forward Chief Justice Taney, worn, shrunken, odd, with "the face of a galvanized corpse," said Mrs. Clay of Alabama. His hands shook with age, emotion, both, as he held out an open Bible toward the ninth President to be sworn in by him. Lincoln laid his left hand on the Bible, raised his right hand, and repeated after the Chief Justice the oath prescribed by the Constitution: "I do solemnly swear that I will faithfully execute the office of President of the United States, and will, to the best of my ability, preserve, protect, and defend the Constitution of the United States."

The artillery over on the slope boomed with all its guns a salute of thunder to the 16th President of the United States. That was all. The Inauguration was over.

SUMTER—CALL FOR TROOPS

Fort Sumter, three miles out from Charleston, rising almost sheer with the rock walls of its island, was being ringed round with batteries, guns and 5,000 recruits under General P. G. T. Beauregard, constantly in touch with Governor F. W. Pickens of South Carolina and Secretary L. P. Walker of the Confederate War Department at Montgomery. Visitors to the U.S. Army officers or soldiers at Fort Sumter were challenged by Confederate pickets, had to show passes from Governor Pickens.

Week by week the country had watched the emergence of Major Robert Anderson into a national figure. He had kept a cool head and held on amid a thousand invitations to blunder. On April 14th, however, he gave up the fort, after 33 hours of bombardment, their supplies gone.

On that Sunday of April 14, the White House had many visitors in and out all day, Senators and Congressmen came to say their people would stand by the Government, the President. The Cabinet met. A proclamation was framed. It named the States of South Carolina, Georgia, Alabama, Florida, Mississippi, Louisiana and Texas as having "combinations too powerful to be suppressed" by ordinary procedure of government.

"Now therefore, I, Abraham Lincoln, President of the United States, in virtue of the power in me vested by the Constitution and the laws, have thought fit to call forth, and hereby do call forth, the militia of the several States of the Union, to the aggregate number of seventy-five thousand, in order to suppress said combinations, and to cause the laws to be duly executed."

He called on "all loyal citizens" to defend the National Union and popular government, "to redress wrongs already long enough endured." The new army of volunteer soldiers was to retake forts and property "seized from the Union." Also, "in every event, the utmost care will be observed, consistently with the objects aforesaid, to avoid any devastation, any destruction of, or interference with, property, or any disturbance of peaceful citizens."

Also the proclamation called both Houses of Congress to meet at noon on the Fourth of July. The war of words was over and the naked test by steel weapons, so long foretold, was at last to begin.

"MORE HORSES THAN OATS"—OFFICE SEEKERS

As months wore on and the offices were filled, the White House was overrun by young men who wanted commissions in the Army, credentials for raising regiments; officers seeking promotions or new assignments; men seeking contracts for supplies to the Army and Navy.

"Those around him strove from beginning to end to erect barriers to defend him against constant interruption," wrote his secretary John Hay, "but the President himself was always the first to break them down. He disliked anything that kept people from him who wanted to see him." Senator Henry Wilson said he counseled, "You will wear yourself out," at which Lincoln smiled sadly. "They do not want much; they get but little, and I must see them."

The Republicans, new to power, were breezy about their errors in procedure, quick to ask why this or that could not be done. Lincoln usually heard state delegations, Senators and Congressmen, party leaders, before making appointments of importance for their states. Always, too, the governors of the states must have respectful hearing.

George Luther Stearns, Frank Bird and other Boston radicals came away from a session in which they had failed to budge Lincoln, Stearns saying, "There we were, with some able talkers among us, and we had the best position too; but the President held his ground against us." "I think he is the shrewdest man I ever met," said Frank Bird. "But not at all a Kentuckian. He is an old-fashioned Yankee in a western dress."

Donn Piatt, an Ohio journalist, wrote of once hearing William H. Seward, Secretary of State, say that in the ability to manage saying No to office seekers, the President "had a cunning that was genius." In a care-laden hour, according to Carl Schurz, the President pointed out to a friend an eager throng of office seekers and Congressmen in an anteroom and spoke these words: "Do you observe this? The rebellion is hard enough to overcome, but there you see something which, in the course of time, will become a greater danger to the republic than the rebellion itself."

General Egbert L. Viele, while military governor of Norfolk, spent many hours with the President in relaxed moods. He said, as Viele noted, "If I have one vice, and I can call it nothing else, it is not to be able to say 'No.' Thank God for not making me a woman, but if He had, I suppose He would have made me just as ugly as He did, and no one would ever have tempted me."

A young Ohioan, appointed to a South American consulate, came dressed as a dandy, "fit to kill." But he was gloomy. "Mr. President, I can't say I'm so very glad of this appointment after all. Why, I hear they have bugs down there that are liable to eat me up inside of a week." "Well, young man, if they do, they'll leave behind them a mighty good suit of clothes." Cabinet members protesting an appointment of a Democrat once received the reply: "Oh, I can't afford to punish every person who has seen fit to oppose my election. We want a competent man in this office." Simon Cameron, Secretary of War, called in behalf of a young man who had been a pest in applying for

a consulate. "Where do you want to have him sent?" asked the
President. The Pennsylvania leader stepped to a large globe of the
earth, put an arm around it as far as he could reach, and said, "I do
not know what my finger is on, but send him there." And, it was
told, he was accommodated.

From a line of people at an informal reception came a shout:
"Hello, Abe, how are ye? I'm in line and hev come for an orfice
too." Lincoln recognized an old Sangamon County friend and told
him to hang onto himself "and not kick the traces." They shook
hands and after the reception Lincoln had to explain that his old
friend could not handle the transactions in the office he wanted.
With lips trembling, the friend sketched a world of personal history
for Lincoln's understanding in saying, "Martha's dead, the gal is mar-
ried, and I've guv Jim the forty." He moved closer and half whis-
pered, "I knowed I wasn't eddicated enough to get the place but I
kinder want to stay where I ken see Abe Linkern." And for a time
he worked on the White House grounds.

Lincoln had to refuse an office sought by an old friend who was not
fit for it, remarking to Noah Brooks, newspaper correspondent, "I
had rather resign my place and go away from here, if I considered
only my personal feelings, but refuse him I must." The almost for-
gotten Denton Offutt turned up in a letter: "I hope you will Give
me the Pattern office or the office of Agricultural Department or the
Commissary for Purchais of Horses Mules Beef for the Army or Mail
agent . . . I have to be looking out to live . . ."

He remembered good friends of New Salem days—the good-
hearted "Uncle Jimmy" Short and the shrewd Bill Greene—with
offices at nice salaries. He remembered his brother-in-law, Ninian W.
Edwards, no longer well off, with an appointment to quartermaster
at $1,800 a year, and John A. Bailhache, an editor of the *Illinois State
Journal*, with an appointment as a commissary. Illinois party men
brought the President reports of the two men being free with money
beyond salaries and making scandalous appointments of administra-
tion enemies. Lincoln transferred Edwards to Chicago and Bailhache
to New York.

When Lincoln gave his good friend Lamon an appointment, Sena-
tor James Grimes of Iowa arose in the Senate to remark, "The
President of the United States saw fit, in the plenitude of his wisdom,
to import to this District from the State of Illinois Mr. Ward H.
Lamon, and to appoint him the marshal!" Grimes charged that "this
foreign satrap, Mr. Lamon, made a peremptory order, that no person

—not even members of Congress—should be admitted to the [District] jail without first supplicating and securing a written permission to do so from him." Then Grimes went to the White House: "When, for the first time in six months, I attempted to approach the footstool of the power enthroned at the other end of the avenue, I was told that the President was engaged." Thus there was sarcasm, and men of importance played peanut politics. Nevertheless there was the factor that Lamon was not particularly antislavery and there were complaints that jailed Negroes were not really fugitive slaves, but free Negroes kidnaped by white ruffians.

A Senator, on learning from Lincoln that General Henry W. Halleck had negatived proposed military changes, asked the President why he didn't get Halleck out of the way. "Well—the fact is—the man who has no friends—should be taken care of."

A private poured out his complaints one summer afternoon as Provost Marshal Fry came in and heard Lincoln's reply, "That may all be so, but you must go to your officers about it." The private told his story two or three times more as Lincoln sat and gazed out the south window on the Potomac. At last the President turned. "Now, my man, go away, *go away!* I can not meddle in your case. I could as easily bail out the Potomac River with a teaspoon as attend to all the details of the army."

One soldier letter to Lincoln pleaded, "I am near starved if I get much thinner it will take two of us to make one shadder."

One pest of a politician came often asking offices, suggesting removals and creation of new offices, and Lincoln, reviewing his day's routine to a friend, said that at night as the closing act of the day "I look under the bed to see if So-and-So is there, and if not, I thank Heaven and bounce in."

A dispute over a high-salaried Ohio postmastership brought several delegations to the White House, and papers piled high in behalf of two men about equally competent. One day, bored by still another delegation, more arguments, even more petitions, the President called to a clerk: "This matter has got to end somehow. Bring me a pair of scales." They were brought. "Now put in all the petitions and letters in favor of one man and see how much they weigh, and then weigh the other fellow's pile." One bundle weighed three-quarters of a pound more than the other. "Make out an appointment," said the President, "for the man who has the heavier papers."

Senators and Congressmen came with letters begging offices for relatives soon to be married, for friends who were sick and had dependents. "I need the position for a living," wrote one to Charles Sumner, Senator from Massachusetts, "I have been unfortunate and poor." To Salmon P. Chase, Secretary of the Treasury, and other department heads, as to the President, came letters crying personal poverty as a basis for public office, in the tone of one: "God knows no one needs the appointment more than I do." The President liked to tell of a seedy fellow asking Seward for a consulate in Berlin, then Paris, then Liverpool, coming down to a clerkship in the State Department. Hearing these places were all filled, he said, "Well, then, will you lend me 5 dollars?"

The President needed reminders to make sure he would do a thing he was inclined to do. Thus Carl Schurz in a letter to Sumner: "I think he is inclined to send in my nomination tomorrow if he is reminded of it . . . I want to press you to do this reminding. Will you? It will cost you only five minutes."

Lincoln telegraphed S. B. Moody at Springfield, Illinois: "Which do you prefer Commissary or Quarter master? If appointed it must be without conditions." The matter was personal; when a Congressman later wished to name a postmaster in Springfield, Lincoln said, "I think I have promised that to old Mrs. Moody for her husband." The Congressman demurred: "Now, Mr. President, why can't you be liberal?" "Mrs. Moody would get down on me."

Personal sentiments would govern. William Kellogg, Jr., quit West Point under demerit; if he had not resigned he would have been dismissed. His father, an Illinois Congressman, reappointed the boy. A report by General Joseph G. Totten disapproved. Lincoln wrote Edwin M. Stanton, Secretary of War, that the father was a friend of twenty years' standing. "This matter touches him very deeply—the feelings of a father for a child—as he thinks, all the future of his child. I can not be the instrument to crush his heart. According to strict rule he has the right to make the re-nomination. Let the appointment be made. It needs not to become a precedent." Thereafter Lincoln would have the rule that no resignation should be handed in by a cadet without express stipulation in writing that the resigning cadet would not take a re-nomination.

Murat Halstead of the Cincinnati *Commercial* sought men close to the President and tried to land a postmastership for a friend. As a poor loser, Halstead wrote his friend: "I use the mildest phrase when I say Lincoln is a weak, a miserably weak man; the wife is a fool—the laughing stock of the town, her vulgarity only the more conspicuous in consequence of her fine carriage and horses and servants in livery and fine dresses and her damnable airs . . . Lincoln is very busy with trifles, and lets everybody do as they please. He is opposed to stealing, but can't see the stealing that is done." Halstead retailed further information: "The way Chase manages Lincoln is to make him believe that he [Lincoln] is doing all things. The poor silly President sucks flattery as a pig sucks milk."

Chase did not bring to Lincoln a letter of February 19, 1863, from Halstead advising: "Can't you take him [Lincoln] by the throat and knock his head against a wall until he is brought to his senses on the war business? I do not speak wantonly when I say there are persons who feel that it was doing God service to kill him, if it were not feared that Hamlin [Vice-President] is a bigger fool than he is." To John Sherman, Halstead wrote February 8, 1863, "If Lincoln was not a damned fool, we could get along yet. He is an awful, woeful ass."

A woman kept at Lincoln with letter after letter begging her husband's appointment. An extra long letter brought his question, ". . . what is it but an evidence that you intend to importune me for one thing, and another, and another, until, in self-defence, I must drop all and devote myself to find a place, even though I remove somebody else to do it, and thereby turn him & his friends upon me for indefinite future importunity, and hindrance from the legitimate duties for which I am supposed to be placed here?"

David R. Locke, Ohio editor, under the pen name of Petroleum V. Nasby, was writing sketches that had a national audience laughing at issues of the day. He flattened pompous patriots with his comic pot shots:

> 1st. I want a offis.
> 2d. I need a offis.
> 3d. A offis wood suit me; there4
> 4th. I shood like to hev a offis.

Beneath Locke's mockery shone affection, and the President wrote to the satirist: "Why don't you come to Washington and see me? Is there no place you want? Come on and I will give you any place you ask for—that you are capable of filling—and fit to fill." Locke was interested. The President had read some of his writings and was so pleased that in a generous outburst he wrote that Locke could have "any place he asked for." Then, as Locke analyzed it, the President saw he was offering too much to a man he knew only through newspaper sketches, so the saving clause was added, "that you are capable of filling," and, to guard himself entirely, "that you are fit to fill."

Locke did go to see Lincoln, but not to ask for a place. "He gave me an hour of his time," said the humorist, "and a delightful hour it was."

A well-dressed man asked merely that the President allow the use of his name for advertising a project in view. "No!" flashed the President. "No! I'll have nothing to do with this. Do you take the President of the United States to be a commission broker? You have come to the wrong place. There is the door!" The caller slunk away.

How Lincoln could coax, argue and persuade, was in the adroit Thurlow Weed, New York political boss, writing him, "I do not, when with you, say half I intend. Partly because I don't like to be a crank and partly because you talk me out of my convictions and apprehensions, so bear with me please now till I free my mind."

A letter to Postmaster General Blair in the summer of '63 went far in newspaper publication and discussion of it. The Lincoln opposition howled about it from many places; thousands of soldiers read it, forward and backward, for assurance. In two cases of postmasterships sought for widows whose husbands had fallen in battle, the President had endorsed them and now wrote: "These cases occurring on the same day, brought me to reflect more attentively than I had before done, as to what is fairly due from us here, in the dispensing of patronage, towards the men who, by fighting our battles, bear the chief burthen of saving our country. My conclusion is that, other claims and qualifications being equal, they have the better right; and this is especially applicable to the disabled soldier, and the deceased soldier's family."

A man came wearing a colonel's uniform, though no longer a colonel, dismissed for drunkenness on duty. Lincoln knew him. The man had a record for valor in battle. Lincoln heard the story. The man wanted back his old rank and place. Lincoln stood up, too moved and uneasy to stay in his chair. He took the soldier's right hand in both his own. Then slowly, tears in his voice, he told the man: "Colonel, I know your story. But you carry your own condemnation in your face." They were hard words to say, Judgment Day words. Later in referring to the case Lincoln told James M. Scovel, "I dare not restore this man to his rank and give him charge of a thousand men when he 'puts an enemy into his mouth to steal away his brain.'"

A one-legged soldier on crutches asked for some kind of a job; he had lost his leg in battle. "Let me look at your papers," said Lincoln. The man had none; he supposed his word was good. "What! no papers, no credentials, nothing to show how you lost your leg! How am I to know that you lost it in battle, or did not lose it by a trap after getting into somebody's orchard?" The President's face was droll. The honest-looking German workingman, turned soldier, earnestly muttered excuses. Lincoln saw this was no regular place seeker. Most of them came with papers too elaborately prepared. The chances were entirely in favor of any one-legged man having lost his leg in battle. "Well, it is dangerous for an army man to be wandering around without papers to show where he belongs and what he is, but I will see what can be done." Then he wrote a card for the man to take to a quartermaster who would attend to his case.

Once a humble man came asking to be made doorkeeper to the House and Lincoln let him down and out without hurting his feelings. Their conversation, as reported, ran: "So you want to be Doorkeeper to the House, eh?" "Yes, Mr. President." "Well, have you ever been a doorkeeper? Have you ever had any experience in doorkeeping?" "Well, no—no actual experience, sir." "Any theoretical experience? Any instructions in the duties and ethics of doorkeeping?" "Um— no." "Have you ever attended lectures on doorkeeping?" "No, sir." "Have you read any textbooks on the subject?" "No." "Have you conversed with anyone who has read such a book?" "No, sir, I'm afraid not, sir." "Well, then, my friend, don't you see that you haven't a single qualification for this important post?" "Yes, I do." And he took his hat and left humbly, seeming rather grateful to the President.

When Judge Baldwin of California asked for a pass through army lines to visit a brother in Virginia, the President inquired, "Have you applied to General Halleck?" "Yes, and met with a flat refusal." "Then you must see Stanton." "I have, and with the same results." "Well, then," drawled Lincoln, "I can do nothing; for you must know I have very little influence with this administration." In this case it was a pleasantry with Lincoln. The same remark to a soldier's widow, who asked for a sutler's appointment, was a sorry fact.

One day, going over applications and recommendations, Lincoln said he concurred in about all that Stanton proposed. "The only point I make is, there has got to be something done that will be unquestionably in the interest of the Dutch, and to that end I want Schimmelfennig appointed." "Mr. President, perhaps this Schimmel-what's-his-name is not as highly recommended as some other German officers." "No matter about that. His name will make up for any difference there may be, and I'll take the risk of his coming out all right." Then with a laugh he spoke each syllable of the name distinctly, accenting the last: "Schim-mel-fen-*nig* must be appointed."

A speculator pressed for a pass through army lines and a Treasury license to buy cotton. He was steadily refused. "Few things are so troublesome to the government," Lincoln had remarked, "as the fierceness with which the profits in trading are sought." This particular trader brought influence to bear on Lincoln, who signed the permit requested and told the man, "You will have to take it over to Stanton for countersigning." Later the trader came back, in a heat, saying Stanton had torn to pieces and stamped his feet on the paper signed by the President. Lincoln put on a surprised look and asked the man to tell exactly how the Secretary had acted. Then, pausing a moment, he told the speculator, "You go back and tell Stanton that I will tear up a dozen of his papers before Saturday night."

A plan for mingling eastern and western troops was urged on Lincoln by a committee headed by Congressman Owen Lovejoy. Lincoln wrote a note to Stanton suggesting a transfer of regiments. "Did Lincoln give you an order of that kind?" asked the Secretary. "He did, sir," replied Lovejoy. "Then he is a damned fool!" said Stanton. "Do you mean to say the President is a damned fool?" "Yes, sir, if he gave you such an order as that." At the White House Lovejoy told what happened. "Did Stanton say I was a damned fool?" asked Lincoln. "He did, sir, and repeated it." The President was thoughtful. "If Stanton said I was a damned fool then I must be one. For he is nearly always right, and generally says what he means. I will step over and see him."

Thurlow Weed told Leonard Swett that Lincoln kept "a regular account book" of his appointments in New York, "dividing favors so as to give each faction more than it could get from any other source, yet never enough to satisfy its appetite." In giving out offices or favors, the President had one guiding principle, as Swett saw it: "An adhesion of all forces was indispensable to his success and the success of the country; hence he husbanded his means with nicety of calculation . . . He never wasted anything, and would always give more to his enemies than he would to his friends; and the reason was, he never had anything to spare, and in the close calculation of attaching the factions to him, he counted upon the abstract affection of his friends as an element to be offset against some gift with which he must appease his enemies. Hence, there was always some truth in the charge of his friends that he failed to reciprocate their devotion with his favors. The reason was, that he had only just so much to give away. 'He always had *more horses than oats.*' "

Late at night after a long talk on the quarreling political factions in Missouri and Kentucky, Swett was saying good-by and at the door Lincoln said, "I may not have made as great a President as some other man, but I believe I have kept these discordant elements together as well as anyone could."

When Justice McLean of the Supreme Court died late in '61, friends of Davis moved to place him on the high bench. Old Eighth Circuit lawyers became active. Swett spoke for him personally to Lincoln. Months passed, a year, a year and a half—and Judge Davis saw no move of Lincoln to appoint him. On the last day of the October term of court in '62 Davis notified the members of the McLean County bar to meet him in the old courthouse at Bloomington. He spoke to them: "My official connection with the people and bar of this circuit is about to terminate. The President has tendered me an appointment as Associate Justice of the Supreme Court of the United States which I shall accept, although distrustful of my abilities to discharge the duties of the office."

Davis called the roll on the little group of lawyers who during so many years had been boon companions. Three had become judges, two U. S. Senators, one wounded and two killed in battle, one President of the United States. Davis went on to Washington, where he wrote in a letter, "Mr. Lincoln is very kind, but care worn."

THE MAN IN THE WHITE HOUSE

The White House or Executive Mansion gave a feeling of Time. The statue of Thomas Jefferson in front of the main portico stood with green mold and verdigris. The grounds during Lincoln's first year had a smooth outward serenity. Yet hidden in shrubbery were armed men and in a basement room troops with muskets and bayonets. Two riflemen in bushes stood ready to cover the movements of any person walking from the main gate to the building entry.

The Charleston *Mercury* reprinted, October 14, 1862, a New York *Herald* item: "The President's life is considered unsafe by many persons here . . . the personal safety of the commander-in-chief ought to be looked after with the utmost diligence." The President held that the only effective way to avoid all risk was to shut himself up in an iron box, where he could not possibly perform the duties of

President. "Why put up the bars when the fence is down all around? If they kill me, the next man will be just as bad for them . . ." Company K of the 150th Pennsylvania Volunteers went on guard duty the first week in September and in a way became part of the White House family, taking care of Tad's goats and doing other chores.

The main executive office and workroom on the second floor, 25 by 40 feet, had a large white marble fireplace, with brass andirons and a high brass fender, a few chairs, two hair-covered sofas, and a large oak table for Cabinet meetings. Lighting was by gas jets in glass globes, or when needed, by kerosene lamps. Tall windows opened on a sweep of lawn to the south, on the unfinished Washington Monument, the Smithsonian Institution, the Potomac River, Alexandria, and slopes alive with white tents, beef cattle, wagons, men of the army. Between the windows was a large armchair in which the President usually sat at a table for his writing. A pull at a bell cord would bring either of his secretaries, John G. Nicolay or John Hay from the next room. A tall desk with many pigeonholes stood nearby at the south wall. Among books were the *United States Statutes*, the Bible and Shakespeare's plays. At times the table had been littered with treatises on the art and science of war. Two or three frames held maps on which blue and red pins told where the armies were moving, fighting, camping.

The President was at his desk often before seven in the morning, after "sleep light and capricious," noted Hay. His White House bed, nine feet long, nearly nine feet high at the headboard, had bunches of grapes and flying birds carved in its black walnut. Nearby was a marble-topped table with four stork-shaped legs; under its center was a bird's nest of black walnut filled with little wooden bird eggs.

In the earlier days of the administration a digest of the day's news was ready for the President before breakfast at nine o'clock. Then he would usually go over to the War Office, read telegrams, discuss "the situation"; back at the White House, he would take up the morning mail with his secretaries. Tuesday and Friday were usually for Cabinet meetings. On other days a stack of cards from callers would be sifted for old acquaintances and persons on urgent business.

"On other days [than Tuesday and Friday]," wrote Hay, "it was the President's custom at about that hour [noon], to order the doors to be opened and all who were waiting to be admitted. The crowd would rush in, thronging the narrow room, and one by one would make their wants known." Some came merely to shake hands, to wish

Godspeed, others for help or mercy, wailing their woe. Still others lingered, stood at the walls, hanging back in hope of having a private interview.

"Late in the day," wrote Hay, "he usually drove out for an hour's airing; at six o'clock he dined. His breakfast was an egg and a cup of coffee; at luncheon he rarely took more than a biscuit and a glass of milk, a plate of fruit in its season; at dinner he ate sparingly of one or two courses. He drank little or no wine . . . and never used tobacco. He pretended to begin business at ten o'clock in the morning, but in reality the ante-rooms and halls were full long before that hour —people anxious to get the first axe ground. He was extremely unmethodical; it was a struggle on Nicolay's part and mine to get him to adopt some systematic rules. He would break through every regulation as fast as it was made. Anything that kept the people away from him he disapproved. He wrote very few letters and did not read one in fifty that he received . . . He signed, without reading them, the letters I wrote in his name. He wrote, perhaps half a dozen a week himself—not more . . . The house remained full of people nearly all day. Sometimes, though rarely, he would shut himself up and see no one. He scarcely ever looked into a newspaper unless I called his attention to an article on some special subject. He frequently said, 'I know more about it than any of them.' "

Early in the administration Seward wrote his wife, "The President proposes to do all his work." That did not last long. He learned to detail routine and to assign work to others.

A woman demanded a colonel's commission for her son, not as a favor but as a right. "Sir, my grandfather fought at Lexington, my father fought at New Orleans, and my husband was killed at Monterey." She left the office and went down the stairs with a dismissal in her ears: "I guess, Madam, your family has done enough for the country. It is time to give someone else a chance."

A young chiropodist, Isachar Zacharie, an English Jew, was introduced, with the result later that Lincoln wrote a testimonial: "Dr. Zacharie has operated on my feet with great success, and considerable addition to my comfort."

Came a full-bosomed woman of rare face and gleam. "I have three sons in the army, Mr. Lincoln." "You may well be proud of that, madam." "There were four, but my eldest boy—" and that was all she could say as she passed on with his low-spoken "God bless you, madam" in her ear.

A fleshy and dignified man, stern and homely of face, entered one day in swallow-tail coat, ruffled shirt, white cravat, orange gloves. His watch chain had a topaz seal, his cane a gold head. He looked "ominous," said Lamon, and gave the President the impression, "I'm in for it now." The conversation ran on in a chilly way. The visitor, keeping a frozen face, shocked the President with his closing remarks as he was about to leave: "Mr. President, I have no business with you, none whatever. I was at the Chicago convention as a friend of Mr. Seward. I have watched you narrowly ever since your inauguration, and I called merely to pay my respects. What I want to say is this: I think you are doing everything for the good of the country that is in the power of man to do. You are on the right track. As one of your constituents I now say to you, do in the future as you damn please, and I will support you!" Lincoln almost collapsed with glee. He took the visitor's hand: "I thought you came here to tell me how to take Richmond." They looked into each other's faces. "Sit down, my friend," said the President. "Sit down, I am delighted to see you. Lunch with us today. I have not seen enough of you yet."

Congressman A. W. Clark of Watertown, New York, pleaded for a constituent who had one boy killed in battle, another dying in prison and a third son sick at Harpers Ferry—the mother at home having gone insane. The father sat by and wept while the Congressman begged for him to take the sick boy home, as it might help bring back the wandering reason of the mother. Lincoln listened, asked no questions, and wrote "Discharge this man."

Thus ran a few specimens of the stream of thousands who wore the thresholds of the White House, nicked its banisters, smoothed the doorknobs, and spoke their wants and errands. When told this procedure was wearing on him, Lincoln said these were his "public opinion baths."

In a day's clamor and confusion, Nicolay noted the President saying: "I'll do the very best I can, the very best I know how. And I mean to keep doing so till the end. If the end brings me out all right what is said against me won't amount to anything. If the end brings me out wrong, ten angels swearing I was right would make no difference."

An old Springfield friend after an evening in the White House drawled: "How does it feel to be President of the United States?" "You have heard about the man tarred and feathered and ridden out of town on a rail? A man in the crowd asked him how he liked it, and his reply was that if it wasn't for the honor of the thing, he would much rather walk."

"Who has been abusing me in the Senate today?" he asked Senator Lot M. Morrill of Maine in his office one day. The Senator hoped none of them were abusing him knowingly and willfully. "Oh, well," said Lincoln, "I don't mean that. Personally you are all very kind— but I know we do not all agree as to what this administration should do and how it ought to be done . . . I do not know but that God has created some one man great enough to comprehend the whole of this stupendous crisis from beginning to end, and endowed him with sufficient wisdom to manage and direct it. I confess I do not fully understand and foresee it all. But I am placed where I am obliged to the best of my poor ability to deal with it. And that being the case, I can only go just as fast as I can see how to go."

Seward mentioned to his son that he had known people to arrive early and sleep for hours in the hall of the White House waiting to interview the President. Writhing under the grind once, the President told General Robert C. Schenck, "If to be the head of Hell is as hard as what I have to undergo here, I could find it in my heart to pity Satan himself."

The military telegraph office at the War Department was for Lincoln both a refuge and a news source. The bonds were close between Lincoln and David Homer Bates, manager of the office, and the chief of staff, Thomas T. Eckert. The President was more at ease among the telegraph operators than amid the general run of politicians and office seekers. Bates noted that Lincoln carried in his pocket at one time a well-worn copy in small compass of *Macbeth* and *The Merry Wives of Windsor*, from which he read aloud. "On one occasion," said Bates, "I was his only auditor and he recited several passages to me with as much interest apparently as if there had been a full house." Occasionally he questioned the omission of certain passages of a Shakespeare play as acted.

At a large flat-topped desk Lincoln went through flimsies of telegrams received. When he got to the bottom of the new telegrams, and began again reading important ones he had sifted out for second and more careful reading, he often said, "Well, I guess I have got down to the raisins." Operator A. B. Chandler asked what this meant, which brought the story of a little girl who often overate of raisins, and one day followed the raisins with many other goodies. It made her sick; she began vomiting, and after a time the raisins began to come up. She gasped and looked at her mother. "Well, I will be better now, I guess, for I have got down to the raisins."

In this telegraph room Lincoln had first heard of the first and second Bull Run routs, of the Seven Days' battles and McClellan's cry for help at Harrison's Landing, of the *Monitor* crippling the *Merrimac*, of the Antietam shaded victory, of Burnside and Hooker failing at Fredericksburg and Chancellorsville, of blood "up to the bridles of horses," of Lee moving his army far up in Pennsylvania toward Gettysburg. Here Lincoln received a telegram about a skirmish in Virginia where "opposing troops fought the enemy to a standstill," which reminded him of two dogs barking through a fence, continuing their barking until they came to a gate, when both ran off in opposite directions. Here he quoted from Petroleum V. Nasby: "Oil's well that ends well"; and after one of McClellan's peninsular defeats, from humorist Orpheus C. Kerr [Robert H. Newell]: "Victory has once again perched upon the banners of the conquerors."

An official letter on one desk had the signature of John Wintrup, operator at Wilmington, written with extraordinary and sweeping flourishes; Lincoln's eye caught it. "That reminds me of a short-legged man in a big overcoat, the tail of which was so long that it wiped out his footprints in the snow."

A dispatch from General Schenck reported a skirmish in Virginia and 30 prisoners taken, all armed with Colt's revolvers. Lincoln read it and with a twinkle of eye said to the operator that with customary newspaper exaggeration of army news they might be sure in the next day's prints that "all the little Colt's revolvers would have grown into horse-pistols."

A message from a part of McClellan's command once reported that Union pickets still held Ball's Cross Roads and "no firing had been heard *since* sunset." The President asked if any firing had been heard *before* sunset, and the answer being that none was reported, he laughed about the man who spoke of a supposed freak of nature, "The child was *black* from his hips *down*," and on being asked the color from the hips *up*, replied, "Why, *black*, of course."

Mrs. Lincoln had, inevitably, become a topic. Her hand was in squabbles over who should have post offices and West Point cadetships. She had been pleased rather than troubled that the New York *Herald* printed two and three columns a day about her arrival at the Long Branch beach resort, her baggage, accommodations, companions, visits, amusements, toilets, gowns, seclusions. "Mrs. Lincoln, looking like a queen in her long train and magnificent coronet of flowers, stood near the centre of the room, surrounded by a brilliant suite, bowing as the ladies were presented to her . . . Before her, forming a sort of semi-circle, were a number of gentlemen, dressed *en règle*, in all the glory of fine black suits and heavy white neckties."

"Her manner was too animated, her laugh too frequent," wrote a woman. Congressman Washburne, entirely friendly to Lincoln, wrote to his wife, "Mrs. Lincoln came last night; I shall not express my opinion of her until I see you." John Lothrop Motley wrote to Mrs. Motley that he found her "youngish, with very round white arms, well dressed, chatty enough, and if she would not, like all the South and West, say 'Sir' to you every instant, as if you were a royal personage, she would be quite agreeable." Welles wrote in his diary: "Mrs. Lincoln has the credit of excluding Judd of Chicago from the Cabinet."

On New Year's Day, 1863, Browning rode in her carriage. "Mrs. Lincoln told me she had been, the night before, with Old Isaac Newton, out to Georgetown, to see a Mrs. Laury, a spiritualist and she had made wonderful revelations to her about her little son Willy who died last winter, and also about things on the earth. Among other things she revealed that the cabinet were all enemies of the President, working for themselves, and that they would have to be dismissed."

When she took her boys to Niagara Falls and returned, when she stopped at the Metropolitan Hotel in New York and shopped at the big stores, it was chronicled from day to day. *Leslie's Weekly* gave brief items: "Mrs. Lincoln held a brilliant levee at the White House on Saturday evening. She was superbly dressed." Once *Leslie's* had the one-sentence item: "The reports that Mrs. Lincoln was in an interesting condition are untrue."

The run of press items about Southern relatives was steady. One day: "New Orleans papers state that D. H. Todd, brother-in-law of Mr. Lincoln, has been appointed a lieutenant in the Confederate army." Another day: "The Rebel officer who called the roll of our prisoners at Houston is Lieutenant Todd, a brother of the wife of President Lincoln. He is tall, fat, and savage against the 'Yankees.'" Or again: "Eleven second cousins of Mrs. Lincoln are members of the Carolina Light Dragoons of the Confederate forces."

One summer day in '63 Mrs. Lincoln's carriage horse ran away. "She threw herself out of her carriage," reported a newspaper. "Fortunately no bones were broken, and after some restoratives she was taken to her residence." The husband and father telegraphed Robert at Harvard: "Don't be uneasy. Your mother very slightly hurt by fall."

From several dressmakers who applied she had chosen the comely mulatto woman, Mrs. Elizabeth Keckley, who once had been dressmaker to the wife of Jefferson Davis. The first spring and summer fifteen new dresses were made, and as time passed Mrs. Lincoln felt a rare loyalty and spirit of service in Elizabeth Keckley, giving her trust and confidence not offered to others.

Away on frequent shopping trips to New York or Philadelphia, she had telegrams from her husband: "Do not come on the night train. It is too cold. Come in the morning." Or: "Your three despatches received. I am very well, and am glad to hear that you and Tad are so."

In diary and letters John Hay used the nicknames "Tycoon" and "The Ancient" for Lincoln. Mrs. Lincoln was "Madame," and occasionally the "Hellcat" who could become more "Hell-cattical day by day." She questioned whether the Government or the secretaries should pay for the grain of the secretaries' horses in the White House stables. The two secretaries eventually were to find it more comfortable to move from the White House and lodge at Willard's.

The boy Tad meant more to Lincoln than anyone else. They were chums. "Often I sat by Tad's father reporting to him about some important matter that I had been ordered to inquire into," wrote Charles A. Dana, "and he would have this boy on his knee; and, while he would perfectly understand the report, the striking thing about him was his affection for the child." Tad usually slept with him, wrote John Hay. Often late at night the boy came to the President's office: "He would lie around until he fell asleep, and Lincoln would shoulder him and take him off to bed."

"Tad" was short for Tadpole, a wriggler, nervous, active. With a defective palate, his occasional "papa dear" sounded more like "pappy day." He could burst into the President's office and call out what he wanted. Or again Tad would give three sharp raps and two slow thumps on the door, three dots and two dashes he had learned in the war telegraph office. "I've got to let him in," Lincoln would say, "because I promised never to go back on the code."

The boy did things with a rush. "I was once sitting with the President in the library," wrote Noah Brooks, "when Tad tore into the room in search of something, and having found it, he threw himself on his father like a small thunderbolt, gave him one wild, fierce hug, and without a word, fled from the room before his father could put out a hand to detain him." Tutors came and went, Brooks noted.

"None stayed long enough to learn much about the boy; but he knew them before they had been one day in the house." Of this the father would say: "Let him run. There's time enough yet for him to learn his letters and get poky."

A Kentucky delegation was held off, couldn't get in. For political reasons Lincoln did not want to meet them. They were half-cursing among themselves when Tad laughed to them, "Do you want to see Old Abe?" They laughed "Yes," and the boy scooted in to his father. "Papa, may I introduce some friends to you?" "Yes, son." And Tad brought in the men whom the President had carefully avoided for a week, introduced them with formality—and the President reached for the boy, took him on his lap, kissed him and told him it was all right and that he had gone through the introductions like a little gentleman.

Julia Taft, one of Tad's playmates, was small and slight for her sixteen years, wore long curls, flew from one room to another in a ruffled white frock and blue sash. Lincoln called her "Jew-ly," told her she was a "flibbertigibbet." Once he held a handful of small photographs over her head. "Do you want my picture, Jewly?" She danced on her tiptoes, saying, "Please," and heard, "Give me a kiss and you can have it." The shy girl reached up, he leaned over, and she gave him a peck on the cheek. Into his arms he swept her with, "Now we will pick out a good one."

Another girl playing with Lincoln's big heavy watch asked him if it could be broken. "Of course it can't. Why, little girl, you hit it as hard as you can with a bunch of wool and even that won't break it." He asked a little boy some questions the lad enjoyed answering, patted the fellow on the shoulder, and sent him away with the pleasant but puzzling remark in his ears, "Well, you'll be a man before your mother yet."

Charles A. Dana, managing editor of the New York *Tribune*, spoke to Lincoln of his little girl, who wanted to shake hands. Lincoln walked over, took up the girl, kissed her and talked to her. Dana considered it worth mentioning. Important men of high office usually lacked a natural and easy grace in handling a child. With Lincoln, Dana noticed, the child felt easy, as if in the arms of Santa Claus or at home as with some friendly, shaggy big animal dependable in danger.

Robert T. Lincoln, his press nickname "the Prince of Rails," away at Harvard, never saw his father, even during vacations, for more than ten minutes of talk at a time, so he said. Stepping up to his father at one reception and bowing with severe formality, "Good evening, Mr. Lincoln," his father handed Robert a gentle open-handed slap across the face. The two of them in a carriage one day were halted at a street corner by marching troops. "Father was always eager to know which state they came from. And in his eagerness to know from where they hailed, father opened the door and stepping half way out, shouted to a group of workmen standing close by, 'What is that, boys?' meaning where did they come from. One short, little red-haired man fixed him with a withering glance and retorted, 'It's a regiment, you damned old fool.' In a fit of laughter father closed the door, and when his mirth had somewhat subsided, turned to me and said, 'Bob, it does a man good sometimes to hear the truth.' A bit later, somewhat sadly he added, 'And sometimes I think that's just what I am, a damned old fool.' "

Mrs. Lincoln's afternoon receptions and the President's public levees were held regularly during the winters. Usually twice a week, on Tuesday evenings at so-called dress receptions and on Saturday evenings at a less formal function, the President met all who came. "A majority of the visitors went in full dress," wrote Noah Brooks, "the ladies in laces, feathers, silks, and satins, without bonnets; and the gentlemen in evening dress . . . Here and there a day-laborer, looking as though he had just left his work-bench, or a hard-working clerk with ink-stained linen, added to the popular character of the assembly . . . So vast were the crowds, and so affectionate their greetings, that Mr. Lincoln's right hand was often so swollen that he would be unable to use it readily for hours afterward. The white kid glove of his right hand, when the operation of handshaking was over, always looked as if it had been dragged through a dust-bin." Much of the time the President went through the handshaking sort of absent-minded. "His thoughts were apt to be far from the crowds of strangers that passed before him."

The query came, Why not take a vacation and rest? "I sincerely wish war was a pleasanter and easier business than it is, but it does not admit of holidays." At his desk one day his casual word on the hour was, "I wish George Washington or some of the old patriots were here in my place so that I could have a little rest."

Noah Brooks, somewhat scholar and dreamer, a failure as merchant in Illinois and farmer in Kansas, correspondent of the Sacramento *Union*, writing under the pen name of "Castine" news letters widely reprinted on the West Coast, often had close touch with Lincoln, and wrote of one phase: "I have known impressionable women, touched by his sad face and his gentle bearing, to go away in tears. Once I found him sitting in his chair so collapsed and weary that he did not look up or speak when I addressed him. He put out his hand, mechanically, as if to shake hands, when I told him I had come at his bidding. It was several minutes before he was roused enough to say that he 'had had a hard day.' "

Out at Soldiers' Home were trees and cool shade, long sweeps of grassy land. In its 500 acres were drives that overlooked the city, the Potomac and wide landscapes. In the birds and the flowers Lincoln had only a passing interest. But there were trees—oak, chestnut, beech—maple and cypress and cedar—and they gave rest and companionship. He was still a kinsman of these growths that struggled out of the ground and sprawled and spread against the sky and kept their rootholds till storm, disaster, or time and age brought them down.

On the way to Soldiers' Home the Lincoln carriage passed through a city where one traveler had commented that everything worth looking at seemed unfinished. In March '63 the public grounds around the unfinished Washington Monument held droves of cattle, 10,000 beeves on the hoof. Shed hospitals covered acres in the outlying suburbs; one of the better they named the Lincoln Hospital. Into churches, museums, art galleries, public offices and private mansions had arrived from battlefields the wounded and dying. The passing months saw more and more of wooden-legged men, men with empty sleeves, on crutches, wearing slings and bandages.

From a population of 60,000 the city had gone above 200,000. Of the new arrivals of footloose women it was noted they ranged "from dashing courtesans who entertained in brownstone fronts to drunken creatures summarily ejected from army camps." One observer wrote: "Houses of ill fame are scattered all through the city. With rare exceptions, however, they have not yet ventured to intrude into respectable neighborhoods. A few of these houses are superbly furnished, and are conducted in the most magnificent style. The women are either young, or in the prime of life, and are frequently beautiful and accomplished. They come from all parts of the country, and they rarely return more than two seasons in succession, for their life soon breaks down their beauty. The majority of the 'patrons' of the better class houses are men of nominal respectability, men high in public life, officers of the army and navy, Governors of States, lawyers, doctors, and the very best class of the city population. Some come under the influence of liquor, others in cool blood."

Beer, whisky, performances of nude or scantily dressed women, brought many a soldier boy into saloon concert halls to awake later on the streets with empty pockets. Into his drinks someone had slipped "knockout drops." At intervals the lower grade of houses were raided by police or provost marshals. The Washington correspondent of the New York *Independent* wrote in '63: "In broad daylight a few days ago, in front of the Presidential mansion . . . a woman clad in . . . fashionable garments with diamonds flashing from her slender fingers, sat upon the stone balustrade, unable to proceed . . . At last she rose . . . swaying to and fro . . . The carriage of a foreign minister . . . stopped, took in the lady, and carried her to her luxurious home. For the lady is wealthy, occupies a high social position, but she was drunk in the streets of Washington."

The high-class gambling houses, located mostly on Pennsylvania Avenue, were carpeted, gilded, frescoed, garnished with paintings and statuary for the players of faro and poker. At the four leading establishments, where introductions were necessary, could be found governors, members of Congress, department officials, clerks, contractors, paymasters. In one place there was the tradition of a Congressman who broke the bank in a single night's play, winning over $100,000. The gambling places shaded off into all styles, ending at the bottom, where smooth-spoken women plied the young infantrymen with drink and played them out of their last payday greenbacks. Colonel La Fayette C. Baker reported to Stanton in the summer of '63 that 163 gaming houses in full blast required attention.

Of the gaudy and bawdy features of Washington, John Hay wrote, "This miserable sprawling village imagines itself a city because it is wicked, as a boy thinks he is a man when he smokes and swears."

Walt Whitman, author of *Leaves of Grass*, prophet of the Average Man, crier of America as the greatest country in the world—in the making—wrote to the New York *Times* in the summer of '63: "I see the President almost every day, as I happen to live where he passes to or from his lodgings out of town . . . He always has a company of twenty-five or thirty cavalry, with sabres drawn, and held upright over their shoulders . . . Mr. Lincoln generally rides a good-sized easy-going gray horse, is dress'd in plain black, somewhat rusty and dusty; wears a black stiff hat, and looks about as ordinary in attire,

&c., as the commonest man . . . I saw very plainly the President's dark brown face, with the deep cut lines, the eyes, &c., always to me with a deep latent sadness in the expression. Sometimes the President comes and goes in an open barouche. The cavalry always accompany him, with drawn sabres . . . None of the artists have caught the deep, though subtle and indirect expression of this man's face. They have only caught the surface. There is something else there. One of the great portrait painters of two or three centuries ago is needed."

This poet at Fredericksburg saw the mutilated and languishing on blankets laid on the bare frozen ground. Hearing the screams of men lifted into ambulances, among the cases of diarrhea, pneumonia, fever, typhoid, amid the mangled, among "the agonized and damned," he said they had met terrible human tests, and noted: "Here I see, not at intervals, but quite always, how certain man, our American man—how he holds himself cool and unquestioned master above all pains and bloody mutilations."

In soft weather one moonlit February night Whitman sauntered over Washington: "Tonight took a long look at the President's house. The white portico—the palace-like, tall, round, columns, spotless as snow—the tender and soft moonlight, flooding the pale marble —everywhere a hazy, thin, blue moonlace, hanging in the air—the White House of future poems, and of dreams and dramas . . . sentries at the gates, by the portico, silent, pacing there in blue overcoats." Another evening he went to the foot of Sixth Street and saw two boatloads of wounded from Chancellorsville put off during a heavy downpour, to lie in torchlight with the rain on their faces and blankets till ambulances should arrive in an hour or two at the wharves. "The men make little or no ado, whatever their sufferings."

A letter for two boys in New York went from him in March '63. "I think well of the President. He has a face like a Hoosier Michael Angelo, so awful ugly it becomes beautiful, with its strange mouth, its deep cut, criss-cross lines, and its doughnut complexion . . . I do not dwell on the supposed failures of his government; he has shown I sometimes think an almost supernatural tact in keeping the ship afloat at all."

In a thin mist of evening air with willows nearby trembling to a low breeze, amid a cool dew flung out by old oaks above them, Lincoln on the Soldiers' Home grounds stood with others silent over a thoughtful twilight. By and by, as a California woman remembered it and soon wrote home to San Francisco, Lincoln said softly:

" 'How sleep the brave, who sink to rest
By all their country's wishes blest—' "

She was too "easily melted," wrote the California woman. "It made us cry." And she heard him further in the purpling shadows:

" 'And women o'er the graves shall weep,
Where nameless heroes calmly sleep.' "

An English author, Edward Dicey, recorded an anecdote. "At the first council of war, after the President assumed the supreme command-in-chief of the army, in place of McClellan, the General did not attend, and excused himself next day by saying he had forgotten the appointment. 'Ah, now,' remarked Mr. Lincoln, 'I recollect once being engaged in a case for rape, and the counsel for the defence asked the woman why, if, as she said, the rape was committed on a Sunday, she did not tell her husband till the following Wednesday? and when the woman answered, she did not happen to recollect it —the case was dismissed at once.' " Stories like these, added Dicey, "read dull enough in print, unless you could give also the dry chuckle with which they are accompanied, and the gleam in the speaker's eye, as, with the action habitual to him, he rubs his hand down the side of his long leg."

Colonel Gustave Koerner wrote, "Something about the man, the face, is unfathomable." Congressman Henry Laurens Dawes of Massachusetts said early in the administration: "There is something in his face which I cannot understand. He is great. We can safely trust the Union to him." And later he would remember Lincoln's face as "a title-page of anxiety and distress."

A beaming and officious visitor slid into the office one day as Lincoln sat writing and chirruped, "Oh, why should the spirit of mortal be proud?" The President turned a noncommittal face. "My dear sir, I see no reason whatever," and went on writing.

The wearing of gloves for ceremony he regarded as "cruelty to animals," said Lamon, who witnessed Lincoln at a levee trying to give an extra hearty handshake to an old Illinois friend—when his white kids burst with a rip and a snort. The procession of guests heard: "Well, my old friend, this is a general bustification. You and I were never intended to wear these things. They are a failure to shake hands with between old friends like us." And he went on handshaking without gloves. With Mrs. Lincoln he drove to a hotel to get a man and wife, old friends from the West, to take them for a drive. As the man got into the carriage seat alongside Lincoln he was fixed out with brand-new gloves, his wife's doing. So Lincoln began pulling on his gloves—just as the other fellow shed his with the cry, "No! no! no! put up your gloves, Mr. Lincoln," and they rode along and had a good old-time visit. "He disliked gloves," said Brooks, "and once I saw him extract seven or eight pairs of gloves from an overcoat pocket where they had accumulated after having been furnished to him by Mrs. Lincoln."

Meeting a soldier six feet seven, Lincoln surveyed him and asked, "Say, friend, does your head know when your feet get cold?" A strapping cornhusker easily three inches taller than the President had the greeting, "Really, I must look up to you; if you ever get into a deep place you ought to be able to wade out."

In the Patent Office Hospital the President, Mrs. Lincoln, General Abner Doubleday's wife and Noah Brooks visited the patients. Lincoln and Brooks lingered at the cot of a wounded soldier who held with a weak white hand a tract just given him by a well-dressed lady performing good works. The soldier read the title of the tract and began laughing. Lincoln noticed that the lady of good works was still nearby, told the soldier undoubtedly the lady meant well. "It is hardly fair for you to laugh at her gift." The soldier: "Mr. President, how can I help laughing a little? She has given me a tract on the 'Sin of Dancing' and both of my legs are shot off."

Inquiries as to the physical law or mechanical principle that underlay a phenomenon or operation came frequently from Lincoln. "Unless very much preoccupied," wrote Brooks, "he never heard any reference to anything that he did not understand without asking for further information." He would ask, "What do you suppose makes that tree grow that way?" and was not satisfied until he had found out. Or he would take one of his boy's toys to pieces, find out how it was made, and put it together again. Tad had occasion more than once, said Brooks, to bewail his father's curiosity.

The politician, the Executive, the quixotic human being, were inextricable. On board the steamer *Daylight*, which had performed bravely down the Potomac, Lincoln stood where a half-dozen members of the crew brought a tarpaulin to protect him from rain while he insisted on shaking hands with the crew. A fireman in shirt sleeves was the last up, his face and hands sooty and smoked, saying, "My hand isn't fit to give you, sir, but there's not a man aboard loves you more than I do." "Put that hand in mine," cried the President. "It has been blackened by making fires for the Union." Or again on the B. & O. Railroad when a conductor asked him, "Why do you always bother shaking hands with the engineer and fireman, whose hands are always covered with soot and grease?" the answer came, "That will all wash off, but I always want to see and know the men I am riding behind."

When he could not grant a favor, he would generally make an appearance of so doing. A committee requested him to take action in certain claim cases—and he did not want to act. However, it looked like action, and partially satisfied the committee, when he wrote a formal order on Gideon Welles, Secretary of the Navy, to send him the evidence in the cases. He told Welles later there was no other way to get rid of the callers. An old acquaintance in Illinois, having organized a bank under the new National Bank Act, wrote offering some of the stock to Lincoln, who replied with thanks, saying he recognized that stock in a good national bank would be a good thing to hold, but he did not feel that he, as President, ought to profit from a law which had been passed under his administration. "He seemed to wish to avoid even the appearance of evil," said the banker.

John Eaton was thirty-five, had been superintendent of schools in Toledo, Ohio, had become a Presbyterian minister and as chaplain of the 27th Ohio Volunteers had seen active service in Missouri, twice being taken prisoner and more than once preaching to Confederate soldiers on request of their commanders. "The freedom with which he discussed public affairs with me often filled me with amazement," wrote Eaton. The President spoke one day "quite fully" of the opposition, expressing surprise that there should be so much antagonism to his policy in the ranks of the great abolitionists. The criticism of such men as Horace Greeley and Wendell Phillips was "a great grief and trial" to Lincoln, Eaton believed. "Of a well-known abolitionist and orator," wrote Eaton, "the President once exclaimed in one of his rare moments of impatience, 'He's a thistle! I don't see why God lets him live!'"

A report having much useless language lay on his desk, the work of a Congressional committee regarding a newly devised gun. "I should want a new lease of life to read this through," groaned the President. "Why can't an investigating committee show a grain of common sense? If I send a man to buy a horse for me, I expect him to tell me that horse's points—not how many hairs he has in his tail."

A big cavalry raid had filled the newspapers and raised noisy enthusiasm, but failed to cut the enemy's communications. Lincoln remarked to Whitney, "That was good circus riding; it will do to fill a column in the newspapers, but I don't see that it has brought anything else to pass."

A young brigadier with a small cavalry troop strayed into Confederate lines in Virginia and was captured. Receiving the report, Lincoln said he was sorry to lose the horses. "I can make a better brigadier any day, but those horses cost the government $125 a head."

To Thomas L. James of Utica, New York, the President said, "I do not lead; I only follow." When the Prince de Joinville asked what was his policy, he replied: "I have none. I pass my life preventing the storm from blowing down the tent, and I drive in the pegs as fast as they are pulled up."

In company with Judge Jesse L. Williams of Indiana, the Reverend Mr. Livingston discussed Lincoln's letter to General Samuel R. Curtis about the Reverend Dr. McPheeters in St. Louis, charged with disloyalty. Said the Judge, "On the trial of Dr. McPheeters by the general assembly of the Presbyterian Church, your letter to General Curtis was read. But the curious part of the affair was this: One party read a portion of your letter and claimed the President was on their side, and the other party read another portion of the same letter and claimed the President was on their side. So it seems, Mr. President, that it is not so easy to tell where you stand."

Lincoln joined in the laughter and was reminded of an Illinois farmer and his son out in the woods hunting a sow. After a long search they came to a creek branch, where they found hog tracks, and signs of a snout rooting, for some distance on both sides of the branch. The old man said to his boy, "Now, John, you take up on this side of the branch and I'll go up t'other, for I believe the old critter is on both sides."

A sense of speech values in Lincoln registered in such degree that he could say of another, "He can compress the most words into the smallest ideas of any man I ever met." Nicolay heard him tell of a Southwestern orator who "mounted the rostrum, threw back his head, shined his eyes, and left the consequences to God."

Robert B. Nay, released from prison on Lincoln's order, came with a letter of introduction co-signed by Senator Reverdy Johnson, on which Lincoln wrote, "I will not say thee 'Nay.'" On an envelope from Salmon P. Chase he wrote, "Nix." On a note from Seward, "What do you say to sending Bradford R. Wood to the Sandwich Islands?" the President wrote, "It won't do. Must have a tip-top man there next time." On a large envelope holding the documents related to a dispute between an admiral and a general as to their crossed-up authorities, the President wrote neatly, "Submitted to Mars & Neptune." After Shiloh a colonel wrote belittling Grant and Sherman, and Lincoln wrote, "Today I verbally told Col. Worthington that I did not think him fit for a colonel; & now upon his *urgent* request I put it in writing."

When Mrs. Gideon Welles mentioned certain malignant reports in newspapers and someone present said, "The papers are not always reliable," Lincoln interjected, "That is to say, Mrs. Welles, they lie and then they *re-lie*." A woman who had asked the President to use his authority in her behalf at the War Department quoted him: "It's of no use, madam, for me to go. They do things in their own way over there, and I don't amount to pig tracks in the War Department."

He was afraid of long speeches and had a fear of sentiment when fact and reasoning had not laid the way for it. His effort at a flag-raising speech before the south front of the Treasury building was one sentence only: "The part assigned to me is to raise the flag, which, if there be no fault in the machinery, I will do, and when up, it will be for the people to keep it up." Suppose the war ran on three years, four, and seemed at no end, what then? An anxious White House visitor asked that. "Oh, there is no alternative but to keep pegging away."

He could refer to men loyal with "buts" and "ifs" and "ands." The Mississippi Valley was "this Egypt of the West." What was past was past; "broken eggs cannot be mended." To Illinois sponsors of a proposed major general he wrote that "major-generalships are not as plenty as blackberries." The Republican party should not become "a mere sucked egg, all shell and no meat, the principle all sucked out."

A foreign diplomat demurred at Lincoln's condemning a certain Greek history as tedious. "The author of that history, Mr. President, is one of the profoundest scholars of the age. Indeed, it may be doubted whether any man of our generation has plunged more deeply in the sacred fount of learning." "Yes," said Lincoln, "or come up dryer."

Into the White House one day a Congressman brought Jean Louis Rodolphe Agassiz, the world's foremost ichthyologist, authority on fishes, fossils, animal life, glaciers, professor of geology and zoology at Harvard—sometimes referred to as the greatest man of learning in the United States. "Agassiz!" blurted Lincoln to Brooks. "I never met him yet." Brooks started to leave. "Don't go, don't go. Sit down and let us see what we can pick up that's new from this great man."

As Agassiz and Lincoln talked, the conversation did not seem very learned to Brooks: "Each man was simplicity itself. Lincoln asked for the correct pronunciation and derivation of Agassiz's name, and both men prattled on about curious proper names in various languages." Agassiz asked Lincoln if he had ever lectured any, Lincoln having offered some of his speculations on man's discoveries and inventions: "I think I can show, at least in a fanciful way, that all the modern inventions were known centuries ago." Agassiz urged him to finish the lecture. Perhaps sometime he would, Lincoln guessed. The two men shook hands warmly, Agassiz left, and Lincoln smiled quizzically at Brooks: "Well, I wasn't so badly scared after all, were you?" Brooks said it seemed as though Lincoln had expected to be weighed down by the great man's learning. Lincoln admitted to Brooks that he had cross-examined Agassiz on "things not in the books."

At one of many White House functions the British Minister Lord Lyons had, as required by custom, read a long paper one morning, formally notifying the U. S. Government that a prince of the royal family in England had taken unto himself a wife. Lincoln listened gravely throughout, and the ceremony over, took the bachelor Minister by the hand, then quietly, "And now, Lord Lyons, go thou and do likewise."

Did the President vacillate? Was he managed by others? Men and journals shifted in view. The New York *Herald* in May '63 approved Lincoln's reversal of a court-martial order for the hanging as traitors of citizens of loyal states captured wearing uniforms of Confederate officers. Lincoln had declared them to be merely prisoners of war.

In the President's discussions of peace, said the London *Spectator*, "He expresses ideas, which, however quaint, have nevertheless a kind of dreamy vastness not without its attraction. The thoughts of the man are too big for his mouth." He was saying that a nation can be divided but "the earth abideth forever," that a generation could be crushed but geography dictated the Union could not be sundered. As to the rivers and mountains, "all are better than one or either, and all of right belong to this people and their successors forever." No possible severing of the land but would multiply and not mitigate the evils among the American states. "It is an oddly worded argument," said the *Spectator*, "the earth being treated as if it were a living creature, an Estate of the Republic with an equal vote on its destiny."

At home and abroad judgments came oftener that America had at last a President who was All-American. He embodied his country in that he had no precedents to guide his footsteps; he was not one more individual of a continuing tradition, with the dominant lines of the mold already cast for him by Chief Magistrates who had gone before.

The inventive Yankee, the Western frontiersman and pioneer, the Kentuckian of laughter and dreams, had found blend in one man who was the national head. In the "dreamy vastness" noted by the *Spectator*, in the pith of the folk words "the thoughts of the man are too big for his mouth," was the feel of something vague that ran deep in many American hearts, that hovered close to a vision for which men would fight, struggle and die, a grand though blurred chance that Lincoln might be leading them toward something greater than they could have believed might come true.

Also around Lincoln gathered some of the hope that a democracy can choose a man, set him up high with power and honor, and the very act does something to the man himself, raises up new gifts, modulations, controls, outlooks, wisdoms, inside the man, so that he is something else again than he was before they sifted him out and anointed him to take an oath and solemnly sign himself for the hard and terrible, eye-filling and center-staged role of Head of the Nation.

To be alive for the work, he must carry in his breast Cape Cod, the Shenandoah, the Mississippi, the Gulf, the Rocky Mountains, the Sacramento, the Great Plains, the Great Lakes, their dialects and shibboleths. He must be instinct with the regions of corn, textile mills, cotton, tobacco, gold, coal, zinc, iron. He would be written as a Father of his People if his record ran well, one whose heart beat with understanding of the many who came to the Executive Mansion.

In no one of the thirty-one rooms of the White House was Lincoln at home. Back and forth in this house strode phantoms—red platoons of boys vanished into the war—thin white-spoken ghosts of women who would never again hold those boys in their arms—they made a soft moaning the imagination could hear in the dark night and the gray dawn.

To think incessantly of blood and steel, steel and blood, the argument without end by the mouths of brass cannon, of a mystic cause carried aloft and sung on dripping and crimson bayonet points—to think so and thus across nights and months folding up into years, was a wearing and a grinding that brought questions. What is this teaching and who learns from it and where does it lead? "If we could first know where we are and whither we are tending, we could better judge what to do and how to do it."

The dew came on the White House lawn and the moonlight spread lace of white films in the night and the syringa and the bridal wreath blossomed and the birds fluttered in the bushes and nested in the sycamore and the veery thrush fluted with never a weariness. The war drums rolled and the telegraph clicked off mortality lists, now a thousand, now ten thousand in a day. Yet there were moments when the processes of men seemed to be only an evil dream and justice lay in deeper transitions than those wrought by men dedicated to kill or be killed.

Beyond the black smoke lay what salvations and jubilees? Death was in the air. So was birth. What was dying no man was knowing. What was being born no man could say.

THE MAN HAD BECOME THE ISSUE

The Man Lincoln, his person and mind, had come to be the pivotal issue of the 1864 campaign. Some would vote for him with no particular faith, others in a loyalty that had seldom or never swerved. In the chaos of the times he was to these folk a beacon light that in moments almost flickered out into a black despair, yet returned to shine without wavering. His life in the White House, his decisions, speeches and messages issued from there, went out over the country for interpretations, for thanks, curses, doubts. Those interpretations would be told of in the November 8 ballot boxes.

Events moved him to change his policies. Some were baffled by his transitions. Congressman John B. Alley suddenly found the President differed with him on a matter where they had been agreed. "Mr. President, you have changed your mind entirely within a short time." "Yes, I have. And I don't think much of a man who is not wiser today than he was yesterday."

Had the people and events of those tornado years shaped Lincoln more and more into a man paradoxically harder than ever, yet also more delicate and tenuous in human judgments and affairs? Was there more often a phantom touch in what he did? Did certain men and women who studied him either close up or from far away feel that a strange shade and a ghost, having often a healing power, moving toward wider and surer human solidarity, lived and spoke in the White House? For such as there were of these, who knew an intimacy with Lincoln even when he was at his loneliest, who were ready to uphold him when they had no inkling of where his next decision might bring the country—for these one writer tried in *Harper's Weekly* of September 24, 1864, to voice a faith and offer a parable bearing on the election to come in November. This was George William Curtis, signing his paragraphs with his initials.

He could see a ship torn and worn with a long voyage, met by head winds and baffling currents. "A feeling of disappointment and despondency takes possession of the passengers and the crew, and each one attributes to the officer of the ship the inevitable and necessary delays and discouragements . . ." Then the long-wished-for land heaves into view. "Certainty takes the place of disappointed hopes, and they feel with mortification and regret how unjust they have been to the officer whose every hour and thought has been devoted to their welfare, and who has at length brought them with safety, and with a prosperous voyage, to the end of their journey."

A San Francisco woman wrote for a home newspaper of how she quoted for Lincoln a line from Starr King's burial speech for Ned Baker—"Hither in future ages they shall bring . . . the sacred ashes of the advocate and soldier of liberty"—and of how in evening mist among the Soldiers' Home trees Lincoln kindled to the picture of a grand procession in solemn hush winding its way through street crowds of San Francisco on up the heights to the open grave on Lone Mountain. "It seemed to rise before them out of the quiet sea, a vast mausoleum from the hand of God, wherein to lay the dead."

There amid grasses where sea wind and land wind met they had laid for his long sleep the old and treasured friend whose death at Ball's Bluff had meant tears and grief to Lincoln. Now, thought the woman, this weary though lighted and strange man, Lincoln, seemed almost to be dreaming of rest for himself sometime, perhaps in envy of the rest that had come to the bright and daring Ned Baker. He gave a eulogy of his old friend "in a few deep-toned words."

Of November 8, 1864, the day of the national election, John Hay wrote that the White House was "still and almost deserted." The sky hung gray. Rain fell. About noon Noah Brooks called on the President "and to my surprise found him entirely alone, as if by common consent everybody had avoided the White House."

At seven o'clock that evening Lincoln with Hay stepped out of the White House into a night of wild rain and storm. They splashed across the grounds to the War Department telegraph office. At a side door a wet and steaming sentinel huddled in a rubber coat. As Lincoln entered the second-floor telegraph office a dispatch was put in his hands from Forney at Philadelphia claiming 10,000 majority there. "Forney," said Lincoln, "is a little excitable." To Mrs. Lincoln he sent over early reports, saying, "She is more anxious than I."

In Stanton's office later Lincoln saw Gustavus Vasa Fox in glee over two hated opponents beaten. "You have more of that feeling of personal resentment than I," said Lincoln, Hay noted. "Perhaps I may have too little of it, but I never thought it paid. A man has not time to spend half his life in quarrels. If any man ceases to attack me, I never remember the past against him."

The wires worked badly because of the rain-and-wind storm. In a long lull about ten, wrote Brooks, "The President amused the little company in the War Office with entertaining reminiscences and anecdotes." In and out moved Eckert, handing telegrams to Stanton, the President then studying them and commenting. "Presently there came a lull in the returns," wrote Charles A. Dana of the evening, "and Mr. Lincoln called me to a place by his side.

" 'Dana,' said he, 'have you ever read any of the writings of Petroleum V. Nasby?' 'No, sir,' I said: 'I have only looked at some of them, and they seemed to be quite funny.' 'Well,' said he, 'let me read you a specimen'; and, pulling out a thin yellow-covered pamphlet from his breast pocket, he began to read aloud. Mr. Stanton viewed these proceedings with great impatience, as I could see, but Mr. Lincoln paid no attention to that. He would read a page or a story, pause to consider a new election telegram, and then open the book again and go ahead with a new passage . . .

"Mr. Stanton went to the door and beckoned me into the next room. I shall never forget the fire of his indignation . . . that when the safety of the republic was thus at issue . . . the leader, the man most deeply concerned . . . could turn aside to read such balderdash and to laugh at such frivolous jests was, to his mind, repugnant, even damnable. He could not understand, apparently, that . . . this was Mr. Lincoln's prevailing characteristic—that the safety and sanity of his intelligence were maintained and preserved."

Chaos, hate, suspicion, mistrust, vengeance, dark doubts, were in the air. But the marking, handling, counting, of the ballots went on in quiet and good order, fraud or violence showing only in minor incidents. The miscounts and repeaters were only ordinary. Free speech and license to print were so operating that either side would have flared forth about any flagrant departure from the customary election methods.

The American electorate, "the People," spoke on whether a

colossal, heavy, weary war should go on, under the same leadership as it had begun, on whether the same guiding mind and personality should keep the central control and power. On a day of rain and wind that wrecked telegraph systems, the people said Yes to Lincoln.

Brooks directly quoted Lincoln as saying the day after: "I should be the veriest shallow and self-conceited blockhead upon this footstool if, in my discharge of the duties which are put upon me in this place, I should hope to get along without the wisdom which comes from God and not from men."

AN OMINOUS DREAM

The two men who most often warned Lincoln about his personal safety were Stanton and Lamon. To Lamon he had laughing retorts. The envelope on which he had written "Assassination," wherein he filed threat letters, numbered eighty items in latter March of '65. He told Seward, "I know I am in danger; but I am not going to worry over threats like these."

Lamon took no ease about this matter because of a dream Lincoln told him. To Lamon he spoke more than once of his failure to produce again the double image of himself in a looking glass, which he saw in 1860 lying on a lounge in his home in Springfield. One face held glow of life and breath, the other shone ghostly pale white. "It had worried him not a little . . . the mystery had its meaning, which was clear enough to him . . . the lifelike image betokening a safe passage through his first term as President; the ghostly one, that death would overtake him before the close of the second."

Sternly practical and strictly logical man that Lincoln was, using relentless scrutiny of facts and spare derivations of absolutes from those facts, he nevertheless believed in dreams having validity for himself and for others. According to Lamon's study, Lincoln held that any dream had a meaning if you could be wise enough to find it. When a dream came Lincoln sought clues from it. Once when Mrs. Lincoln and Tad were away he telegraphed her to put away a pistol Tad was carrying. "I had an ugly dream about him."

To Lamon it was appropriate that Lincoln held the best dream interpreters were the common people. "This accounts in large measure for the profound respect he always had for the collective wisdom of the plain people,—'the children of Nature,' he called them." The very superstitions of the people had roots of reality in natural occurrences. "He esteemed himself one of their number, having passed the greater part of his life among them."

Of the dream that came to Lincoln the second week of April '65, Lamon wrote that it was "the most startling incident" that had ever come to the man, of "deadly import," "amazingly real." Lincoln kept it to himself for a few days; then one evening at the White House, with Mrs. Lincoln, Lamon and one or two others present, he began talking about dreams and led himself into telling the late one that haunted him. Of his written account of the evening, Lamon said, "I give it as nearly in his own words as I can, from notes which I made immediately after its recital."

Mrs. Lincoln remarked, "Why, you look dreadfully solemn; do *you* believe in dreams?" "I can't say that I do," returned Mr. Lincoln; "but I had one the other night which has haunted me ever since. After it occurred, the first time I opened the Bible, strange as it may appear, it was at the twenty-eighth chapter of Genesis, which relates the wonderful dream Jacob had. I turned to other passages, and seemed to encounter a dream or a vision wherever I looked. I kept on turning the leaves of the old book, and everywhere my eye fell upon passages recording matters strangely in keeping with my own thoughts,—supernatural visitations, dreams, visions, etc."

He now looked so serious and disturbed that Mrs. Lincoln exclaimed: "You frighten me! What is the matter?" "I am afraid," said Mr. Lincoln, seeing the effect his words had upon his wife, "that I have done wrong to mention the subject at all; but somehow the thing has got possession of me, and, like Banquo's ghost, it will not down."

This set on fire Mrs. Lincoln's curiosity. Though saying she didn't believe in dreams, she kept at him to tell what it was he had seen in his sleep that now had such a hold on him. He hesitated, waited a little, slowly began, his face in shadows of melancholy:

"About ten days ago I retired very late. I had been up waiting for important dispatches from the front. I could not have been long in bed when I fell into a slumber, for I was weary. I soon began to dream. There seemed to be a death-like stillness about me. Then I heard subdued sobs, as if a number of people were weeping. I thought I left my bed and wandered downstairs. There the silence was broken by the same pitiful sobbing, but the mourners were invisible. I went from room to room; no living person was in sight, but the same mournful sounds of distress met me as I passed along. It was light in all the rooms; every object was familiar to me; but where were all the people who were grieving as if their hearts would break? I was puzzled and alarmed. What could be the meaning of all this? Determined to find the cause of a state of things so mysterious and so shocking, I kept on until I arrived at the East Room, which I entered. There I met with a sickening surprise. Before me was a catafalque, on which rested a corpse wrapped in funeral vestments. Around it were stationed soldiers who were acting as guards; and there was a throng of people, some gazing mournfully upon the corpse, whose face was covered, others weeping pitifully. 'Who is dead in the White House?' I demanded of one of the soldiers. 'The President,' was his answer; 'he was killed by an assassin!' Then came a loud burst of grief from the crowd, which awoke me from my dream. I slept no more that night; and although it was only a dream, I have been strangely annoyed by it ever since."

"That is horrid!" said Mrs. Lincoln. "I wish you had not told it. I am glad I don't believe in dreams, or I should be in terror from this time forth." "Well," responded Mr. Lincoln, thoughtfully, "it is only a dream, Mary. Let us say no more about it, and try to forget it."

The dream had shaken its dreamer to the depths, noted Lamon. As he had given the secret of it to others he was "grave, gloomy, and at times visibly pale, but perfectly calm." To Lamon afterward, in a reference to it Lincoln quoted from *Hamlet*, "To sleep; perchance to dream! ay, *there's the rub!*"—stressing the last three words.

Once again and with playful touches, bringing his sense of humor into use as though he might laugh off the dream, he said to Lamon: "Hill, your apprehension of harm to me from some hidden enemy is downright foolishness. For a long time you have been trying to keep somebody—the Lord knows who—from killing me. Don't you see how it will turn out? In this dream it was not me, but some other fellow, that was killed. It seems that this ghostly assassin tried his hand on someone else. And this reminds me of an old farmer in Illinois whose family were made sick by eating greens. Some poisonous herb had got into the mess, and members of the family were in danger of dying. There was a half-witted boy in the family called Jake; and always afterward when they had greens the old man would say, 'Now, afore we risk these greens, *let's try 'em on Jake. If he stands 'em, we're all right.'* Just so with me. As long as this imaginary assassin continues to exercise himself on others I can stand it." He then became serious and said: "Well, let it go. I think the Lord in His own good time and way will work this out all right. God knows what is best."

This last he gave with a sigh, and in a way as if talking to himself with no friend Lamon standing by.

BLOOD ON THE MOON

On the calendar it was Holy Week and April 14th was Good Friday. Some were to say they had never before this week seen such a shine of beneficence, such a kindling glow, on Lincoln's face. He was down to lean flesh and bone, thirty pounds underweight, his cheeks haggard, yet the inside of him moved to a music of peace on earth and good will to men. He let it come out in the photograph Gardner made this Holy Week.

The schedule for this Good Friday as outlined beforehand was: office business till eight; breakfast and then interviews till the Cabinet meeting at 11; luncheon, more interviews, a late afternoon drive with Mrs. Lincoln; an informal meeting with old Illinois friends; during the day and evening one or more trips to the War Department; another interview; then to the theater with Mrs. Lincoln and a small party.

At breakfast with Robert the President heard his son tell of life at the front, and he probably did, as one story ran, take up a portrait of Robert E. Lee his son had brought him, and after placing it on the table scan it long, saying: "It is a good face. I am glad the war is over at last."

In the carriage into which the President and his wife stepped were Henry Reed Rathbone, assigned by Stanton to accompany the President, and his fiancée, Miss Clara Harris. The carriage left the White House, coachman Francis Burns holding the reins, and alongside him the footman and valet Charles Forbes. At Ford's Theatre, Burns pulled up his horses. Forbes swung down to the sidewalk and opened the carriage door. The President and his wife stepped out, followed by Major Rathbone and Miss Harris. The guard John F. Parker was at hand. The party walked into the theater at about nine o'clock. An usher led them to their box. The audience in their one thousand seats saw or heard that the President had arrived. They applauded; many rose from their seats; some cheered. The President paused and nodded his acknowledgment of their welcome to him.

On the stage proceeds *Our American Cousin*, a play written fourteen years before by the English dramatist Tom Taylor; on rehearsal he decided it was not for the British public and later had sent it to the New York producer Lester Wallack, who had told Laura Keene it would fit her. She had put it on, but after a fairly good run it has about reached its limit. The play is not unpleasant, often stupid, sprinkled with silly puns, forced humor. The applause and laughter say the audience is having a good time.

From the upholstered rocking armchair in which Lincoln sits he can see only the persons in the box with him, the players on the stage and any persons off stage on the left. The box has two doors. The door forward is locked. The President's party has the roominess and convenience of double space, extra armchairs, side chairs, a small sofa. In the privacy achieved he is in sight only of his chosen companions, the actors he has come to see render a play, and the few people who may be off stage to the left.

This privacy however is not as complete as it seems. A few feet behind the President is the box door, the only entry to the box unless by a climb from the stage. In this door is a small hole, bored that afternoon to serve as a peephole—from the outside. Through this peephole it is the intention of the Outsider who made it with a gimlet to stand and watch the President, then at a chosen moment to enter the box. This door opens from the box on a narrow hallway that leads to another door opening on the balcony of the theater.

Through these two doors the Outsider must pass in order to enter the President's box. Close to the door connecting with the balcony two inches of plaster have been cut from the brick wall of the narrow hallway. The intention of the Outsider is that a bar placed in this cut-away wall niche and then braced against the panel of the door will hold that door against intruders, will serve to stop anyone from interference with the Outsider while making his observations of the President through the gimleted hole in the box door.

At either of these doors, the one to the box or the one from the balcony to the hallway, it is the assigned duty and expected responsibility of John F. Parker to stand or sit constantly, with unfailing vigil. The custom was for a chair to be placed in the narrow hallway for the guard to sit in. The doorkeeper Buckingham told the guard Crook that such a chair was provided this evening. "Whether Parker occupied it at all, I do not know," wrote Crook. "Mr. Buckingham is of the impression that he did. If he did, he left it almost immediately, for he confessed to me the next day that he went to a seat, so that he could see the play." The door to the President's box is shut. It is not kept open so that the box occupants can see the guard on duty.

Either between acts or at some time when the play was not lively enough to suit him or because of an urge for a pony of whisky under his belt, John F. Parker leaves his seat in the balcony and goes down to the street and joins companions in a little whiff of liquor—this on the basis of a statement of the coachman Burns, who declared he stayed outside on the street with his carriage and horses, except for one interlude when "the special police officer [meaning John F. Parker] and the footman of the President [Forbes] came up to him and asked him to take a drink with them; which he did." Thus circumstances favor the lurking and vigilant Outsider.

The play goes on. Out in a main-floor seat is one Julia Adelaide Shephard, writing a letter to her father about this Good Friday evening at the theater. "Cousin Julia has just told me," she reports, "that the President is in yonder upper right hand private box so handsomely decked with silken flags festooned over a picture of George Washington. The young and lovely daughter of Senator Harris is the only one of his party we see as the flags hide the rest. But we know Father Abraham is there like a Father watching what interests his children. The American cousin has just been making love to a young lady who says she'll never marry but for love but when her mother and herself find out that he has lost his property they retreat in disgust at the left hand of the stage while the American cousin goes out at the right. We are waiting for the next scene."

And the next scene? The next scene is to crash and blare and flare as one of the wildest, one of the most inconceivable, fateful and chaotic that ever stunned and shocked a world that heard the story.

The moment of high fate is not seen by the theater audience. Only one man sees that moment. He is the Outsider, the one who waited and lurked and made his preparations. He comes through the outer door into the little hallway, fastens the strong though slender bar into the two-inch niche in the brick wall, and braces it against the door panel. He moves softly to the box door and through the little hole studies the box occupants and his Human Target seated in an upholstered rocking armchair. Softly he opens the door and steps toward his prey, in his right hand a one-shot brass derringer pistol, a little eight-ounce vest-pocket weapon winged for death, in his left hand a steel dagger. He is cool and precise and times his every move. He raises the derringer, lengthens his right arm, runs his eye along the barrel in a line with the head of his victim less than five feet away —and pulls the trigger.

A lead ball somewhat less than a half-inch in diameter crashes into the left side of the head of the Human Target, into the back of the head, in a line with and three inches from the left ear. For Abraham Lincoln it is lights out, good night, farewell—and a long farewell to the good earth and its trees, its enjoyable companions, and the Union of States and the world Family of Man he has loved. He is not dead yet. He is to linger in dying. But the living man can never again speak, see, hear or awaken into conscious being.

The last breath is drawn at 21 minutes and 55 seconds past 7 A.M. and the last heart beat flickered at 22 minutes and 10 seconds past the hour on Saturday, April 15, 1865.

The Pale Horse had come. To a deep river, to a far country, to a by-and-by whence no man returns, had gone the child of Nancy Hanks and Tom Lincoln, the wilderness boy who found far lights and tall rainbows to live by, whose name even before he died had become a legend inwoven with men's struggle for freedom the world over.

The widow was told. She came in and threw herself with uncontrollable moaning on the body. When later she went away the cry broke from her, "O my God, and I have given my husband to die!"

Out on the Illinois prairie of Coles County they went to a farmhouse and told the news to an old woman who answered: "I knowed when he went away he'd never come back alive." This was Sally Bush Lincoln, prepared for her sorrow which came that day.

VAST PAGEANT, THEN GREAT QUIET

In the East Room of the White House lay the body of a man, embalmed and prepared for a journey. On a platform under a canopy of folds and loops of black silk and crape rested the coffin. Tassels, shamrock leaves, silver stars and silver cords could be seen on facings and edges. A shield with a silver plate had the inscription:

Abraham Lincoln
Sixteenth President of the United States
Born Feb. 12, 1809
Died April 15, 1865

It was Tuesday, April 18, and outside surged the largest mass of people that had ever thronged the White House lawn, the estimate 25,000. In two columns they filed through the East Room, moving along the two sides of the coffin, many pale and limping soldiers out of the convalescent wards of the hospitals, many women and children sobbing and weeping aloud as they passed, pausing only the slightest moment for a look.

On Wednesday, April 19, arrived sixty clergymen, the Cabinet members, the Supreme Court Justices, important officials, foreign Ministers, General Grant with white sash across his breast, the new President Andrew Johnson—600 dignitaries in all. Mrs. Lincoln was still too distracted to be present, but Robert Lincoln came.

Bishop Matthew Simpson of the Methodist Episcopal church offered prayer that smitten hearts might endure, might not be called upon for further sacrifices. A bitter cup from the hand of a chastening Divine Father had been given the mourning nation, the Reverend Dr. Phineas D. Gurley, of Washington's New York Avenue Presbyterian Church, said in the funeral address. "His way is in the sea, and His path in the great waters; and His footsteps are not known . . . We bow, we weep, we worship . . . We will wait for His interpretation . . . He may purify us more in the furnace of trial, but He will not consume us."

The closing invocation was spoken by a Baptist clergyman, chaplin of the U. S. Senate, the Reverend Dr. E. H. Gray. The final ceremonial words spoken in the White House over the mute form of the author of the second inaugural and the Louisiana reconstruction speech of April 11 were: "O God, let treason, that has deluged our land with blood, and devastated our country, and bereaved our homes, and filled them with widows and orphans, and has at length culminated in the assassination of the nation's chosen ruler—God of justice, and avenger of the nation's wrong, let the work of treason cease, and let the guilty author of this horrible crime be arrested and brought to justice."

The services were over. The pallbearers took the silver handles. The bong of big bells on cathedrals struck and the little bells of lesser steeples chimed in, as across the spring sunshine came the tolling of all the church bells of Washington and Georgetown, and Alexandria across the river. Counting the minutes with their salutes came the hoarse boom of fort guns encircling the national capital and several batteries sent into the city.

Out of the great front door of the Executive Mansion for the last time went the mortal shape of Abraham Lincoln, sixteenth President of the United States. On the one-mile route to the Capitol, pavements and curbs were packed with onlookers, who also filled every roof, window, doorway, balcony and stairway. Sixty thousand spectators watched a parade of 40,000 mourners. From his sickbed, sore with his dagger wounds, Secretary Seward gazed from the window with mingled grief and thanks.

In the rotunda of the Capitol, under the great white dome that had come to its finished construction while the war raged, twelve sergeants of the Veteran Reserve Corps carried the coffin to a huge catafalque.

In silence during night watches the body of Lincoln lay with eyes never opening to see far above him the arches of the great dome that for him symbolized the Union. In the night watches while the guard mount changed, whispering, quiet on soft feet, into midnight and past into daybreak, midway between House and Senate chambers, midway between those seats and aisles of heartbreak and passion, he lay a horizontal clay tabernacle.

In the morning at ten o'clock the doors opened in special consideration for wounded soldiers from the hospitals, weak and battered men, some with empty sleeves, others on crutches, to file by. Afterward came the public, at times 3,000 to the hour, before midnight 25,000 persons.

Friday morning, April 21, saw the coffin placed aboard a special burial car at the Washington depot. Railroad-yard engine bells tolled and a far-stretching crowd stood with uncovered heads as the train of seven cars moved out of Washington for Baltimore.

This was the start of a funeral journey that was to take the lifeless body on a 1,700-mile route which included practically the same points and stops that the living form had made four years and two months before on the way to the first inauguration. Aboard the coaches were five men who had made that earlier journey: Colonel Ward Hill Lamon, Justice David Davis, General David Hunter, John G. Nicolay and John Hay. A committee of Senate and House members included Elihu B. Washburne, Richard Yates and Isaac N. Arnold of Illinois, James Harlan of Iowa and George W. Julian of Indiana. Mrs. Lincoln, Robert and Tad were to undergo an ordeal; with them was their kinsman Ninian W. Edwards. The Illinois delegation aboard included Lincoln's first law partner John T. Stuart and such Sucker State familiars as Lyman Trumbull, William Bross,

Jesse K. Dubois, Shelby M. Cullom and General John A. McClernand. Among state governors aboard were Oglesby of Illinois, Morton of Indiana, Brough of Ohio, Stone of Iowa.

Baltimore wore mourning everywhere and paid reverence; the human outpouring was unmistakable. More than surface changes had come to Maryland in the four furnace years. As the funeral train moved slowly over Pennsylvania soil, at lonely country crossroads were people and faces, horsemen, farmers with their wives and children, standing where they had stood for hours before, waiting, performing the last little possible act of ceremony and attention and love—with solemn faces and uncovered heads standing and gazing as the funeral car passed. In villages and small towns stood waiting crowds, sometimes with a little silver cornet band, often with flowers in hope the train might stop and they could leave camellias, roses, lilies-of-the-valley, wreaths of color and perfume. At York in a short stop six ladies came aboard and laid a three-foot wreath of red and white roses on the coffin.

Through heavy rains at Harrisburg came 30,000 in the night and morning to see the coffin in circles of white flowering almond. At noon on Saturday, April 22, in Philadelphia a half-million people were on hand for the funeral train. In Independence Hall stood the coffin. Outside the line of mourners ran three miles. "A young lady had her arm broken," said the New York *Herald*, "and a young child, involved in the crush, is said to have been killed. Many females fainted with exhaustion, and had to be carried off by their friends." Besides doors, through two windows in a double column a third of a million people entered and passed by the casket. A venerable Negro woman, her face indented and majestic as a relief map of the continent of Asia, laid evergreens on the coffin and with hot tears filling the dents and furrows, cried, "Oh, Abraham Lincoln, are you dead? Are you dead?" She could not be sure.

At Newark, New Jersey, on the morning of April 24 the train moved slowly amid acres of people, a square mile of them. At Jersey City was a like scene. The Empire State formally received the body from Governor Parker of New Jersey. A hearse moved through street crowds. The ferryboat *Jersey City* moved across the Hudson River, neared the wharf at Desbrosses Street. The Seventh Regiment National Guard formed a hollow square into which moved the funeral cortege. The procession marched to the City Hall through streets packed to capacity.

Never before, so everyone agreed, had New York put on such

garb and completely changed its look so that it seemed another city. On the marble and brownstone fronts, in the ramshackle tenements of "those who live from hand to mouth," came out crape or black folds or drapery or black muslin, rosettes, sable emblems, what the news reporters termed "the habiliments of mourning."

From near noon Monday, April 24, to noon the next day the remains of Abraham Lincoln, horizontal amid white satin, lay in the City Hall. A vast outpouring of people hour by hour passed by to see this effigy and remembrance of his face and form. They came for many and varied reasons. Hundreds who had helped wreck, burn and loot this city, killing scores of policemen and Negroes in the draft and race riots of year before last, came now with curiosity, secret triumph, hate and contempt, a story traveling Manhattan that one entered a saloon hangout of their breed, saying, "I went down to the City Hall to see with my own eyes and be sure he was dead." An overwhelming many came as an act of faith and attestation; they had come to love him and follow him. The few women who sought to kiss his face were hurriedly moved on by the guards. Each might have had some sufficient reason; most of the boys at Malvern Hill and Gettysburg had mothers.

At noon on Tuesday, April 25, a procession moved from the City Hall to Ninth Avenue and the Hudson River Railroad depot. Nearly every race, nationality, religion, political faith, was represented among those who marched, near 100,000. The troops in Union Army blue alone numbered 20,000. The panoramic show took hours. It was massive, bizarre, spectacular, dazzling—yet somber. A hundred thousand strangers had come to New York to see it. The sidewalk, street, curb and window spectators ran perhaps to a million. At the procession's end came a delegation of 2,000 Negroes, some wearing the Union Army service blue. There had been mutterings from a draft-and race-riot element that they would "never let the damned niggers march." This would have interested the man in the hearse, could he have heard it. It was customary and expected. A telegram to General John A. Dix spoke plain that the Secretary of War desired "no discrimination respecting color." And it was so ordered. At the Union Square exercises following the parade the Roman Catholic Archbishop John McCloskey pronounced the benediction, Rabbi Samuel M. Isaacs of the Jewish Synagogue read from their scriptures, the Reverend Stephen H. Syng of St. George's Church offered a prayer, the Reverend J. P. Thompson intoned Lincoln's second inaugural. Evening had come.

An epidemic of verse seized thousands. They sent their rhymed lines to the New York *Herald*, which publicly notified them that if it were all printed there would be no space for news, wherefore none at all would be printed. The Chicago *Tribune* editorially notified them it "suffered" from this "severe attack of poetry," that three days brought 160 pieces beginning either "Toll, toll, ye mourning bells" or "Mourn, mourn, ye tolling bells."

Up the Hudson River east bank the night of April 25 chugged the train of seven cars. On every mile of the route to Albany those on the train could see bonfires and torches, could hear bells and cannon and guns, could see forms of people and white sorry faces. Past midnight of April 25 into the morning hours of April 26 the columns of mourners passed the coffin in Albany.

On this morning of April 26, hunted like a wild beast and cornered like a rat, his broken shinbone betraying him, assassin J. Wilkes Booth met his end. Near Bowling Green, Virginia, in a burning barn set afire from the outside, a bullet drove through his neck bone "perforating both sides of the collar," and he was dragged away from reaching flames and laid under a tree. Water was given him. He revived, to murmur from parched lips, "Tell my mother—I died—for my country." He was carried to a house veranda, there muttering, "I thought I did for the best." He lingered for a time. A doctor came. Wilkes Booth asked that his hands might be raised so that he could look at them. So it was told. And as he looked on his hands, he mumbled hoarsely, "Useless! useless!" And those were his last words.

Across the Empire State that day and night it was mural monotone of mourning, the Erie Canal zone in sober grief with evergreens, flowers, sable emblems. The endless multitudinous effect became colossal. Thirty-six young ladies, gowned in white with black shoulder scarfs and the flag of their country, approached the dazzling when seen for the first time. But when seen and noted the twentieth, thirtieth, fortieth time, they took on a ritualist solemnity smoldering and portentous. Involved was the basis of the stubborn passion that had carried on four years of the bloodiest war known to mankind.

At Buffalo Millard Fillmore, one of the three living ex-Presidents of the United States, attended the funeral, which also was witnessed by the youth Grover Cleveland.

Reports had been published that the face in the coffin was shrunken and decayed to such an extent that perhaps good taste should forbid further exposure of it to public gaze. The embalmer on the train had several times by his craft wrought improvement. However this might be, there came from Toledo an old friend and a valued comforter of Lincoln, David R. Locke, who wrote under the pen name of Petroleum V. Nasby. He wrote now: "I saw him, or what was mortal of him in his coffin. The face had an expression of absolute content, of relief, at throwing off a burden such as few men have been called upon to bear—a burden which few men could have borne. I had seen the same expression on his living face only a few times, when, after a great calamity, he had come to a great victory. It was the look of a worn man suddenly relieved. Wilkes Booth did Abraham Lincoln the greatest service man could possibly do for him—he gave him peace."

At Cleveland the committee on arrangements had a pagoda put up in the city park, with open sides through which two columns could pass the coffin. Over the coffin Bishop Charles Pettit McIlvaine read from the Episcopal burial service. At ten o'clock when the park gates were shut it was said that more than 1,000,000 pilgrims from northern Ohio had paid their homage. A lashing wind drove torrents of rain as the night procession moved escorting the hearse through crowded streets to the depot.

From Cleveland to Crestline the rain kept on in torrents. Nevertheless at all towns and crossroads were the mourners, with uncovered heads, with torches and flags crossed with black. Five miles out from Columbus stood an old woman alone as the slow train came by, tears coursing down her furrowed cheeks. In her right hand she held out a black mourning scarf. With her left hand she stretched imploringly toward the rain-and-storm-bedraggled funeral car, reaching and waving toward it her handful of wild flowers, her bouquet and token.

In the rotunda of Ohio's capitol, on a mound of green moss dotted with white flowers, rested the coffin on April 28, while 8,000 persons passed by each hour from 9:30 in the morning till four in the afternoon. In the changing red-gold of a rolling prairie sunset, to the slow exultation of brasses rendering "Old Hundred" and the muffled booming of minute guns, the coffin was carried out of the rotunda and taken to the funeral train. It was now two weeks since the evening hour that Abraham Lincoln cheery and alive had left the White House in Washington to attend a performance in Ford's Theatre, and from his carriage had taken a final casual glance at the Executive Mansion where he had lived four years and 41 days.

The slow night run from Columbus to Indianapolis saw from the car windows a countryside of people thronging to the route of the coffin. At Pleasant Valley were bonfires. Nearly every town had its arch of evergreens, flags and black drapings. At Urbana ten young women strewed roses on the coffin, one of them breaking down in uncontrollable tears. At Piqua were 10,000 at midnight; at Richmond, Indiana, 10,000 again at three o'clock in the morning.

Tolling bells and falling rain at Indianapolis saw the coffin borne into the State House for a Sabbath to be remembered. On the slow night run to Chicago it was as in Ohio, thousands in Lafayette standing mute and daybreak not yet, thousands more at Michigan City. Now over flat lands ran the slow train, between it and the blue levels of Lake Michigan the long slopes of pine-crept dunes.

The day was Monday, May 1, but in effect the Chicago obsequies had begun the day before when Speaker Schuyler Colfax delivered in Bryant Hall a formal funeral oration. To his portrait of Lincoln as the most forgiving of men Colfax joined allegations of Confederate atrocities: they had at Bull Run buried Union soldiers face down-ward and carved their bones into trinkets; they had wickedly and systematically starved Union prisoners to death. Colfax was for his own purposes still fomenting war hate and metaphorically waving a bloody shirt of incitation.

In the changed tone of the Chicago *Times* could be read the fact that among those who would gaze into the Lincoln coffin with a sincere grief this day would be at least a remnant of Copperheads. "There are not on this day mourners more sincere than the democracy of the Northern States. Widely as they have differed with Mr. Lincoln . . . they saw in the indications of the last few days of his life that he might command their support."

By railway train, by wagon or buggy and on horseback, something like 100,000 people had come into Chicago from all points of the Northwest. The vocal attempts at solemn grief often failed and were overdone. But there was a silent grief—broken only by choked snufflings, by low wailings, by almost inaudible moans—a loss afraid of words. There was a curious dumb sorrow, perhaps deeper than any other.

Slowly at Twelfth Street and Michigan Avenue the funeral train came to a stop. A procession of 50,000 people, witnessed by double as many, escorted the hearse to the courthouse. Not hitherto, however, had any Confederate soldiers marched—though here was a regiment of Confederate prisoners of war who had taken the oath of allegiance and aligned themselves for Union service. In the line of march and looking on, sharing something common, were native-born Yankees and Mayflower descendants, Sons and Daughters of the Revolution, Jews, Negroes, Catholics, Germans, Irishmen, Dutchmen, Swedes, Norwegians, Danes—the so-called "big bugs" and the so-called "ragtag and bobtail" for once in a common front.

A drizzle of rain fell, the streets slushy with a slippery mud. Occasionally planks or supporting two-by-fours of the wooden sidewalks crashed with spectators. Women fainted and two-horse ambulances came. Barkeepers were busy. So were pickpockets. The police-station cells were filled. Considering the extent of the swarming human crush, however, the day was orderly, even sedate.

All night long Monday, and through the early morning hours and all the day hours of Tuesday, the columns moved in and out of the courthouse. An estimated 125,000 people had taken their last glance at the Man from Illinois. A thousand men with blazing torches escorted the coffin to the funeral car for the slow night run to Springfield on the Alton Railroad.

At Joliet were midnight torches, evergreen arches, 12,000 people. Every town and village, many a crossroads and lonely farm, spoke its mournful salutation. Here and there an arch or a depot doorway had the short flash "Come Home."

Then at last home to Springfield. In the state capitol where he had spoken his prophet warnings of the House Divided, stood the casket. Now passed those who had known him long, part of the 75,000 who came. They were awed, subdued, shaken, stony, strange. They came from Salem, Petersburg, Clary's Grove, Alton, Charleston, Mattoon, the old Eighth Circuit towns and villages. There were clients for whom he had won or lost, lawyers who had tried cases with him and against, neighbors who had seen him milk a cow and curry his horse, friends who had heard his stories around a hot stove and listened to his surmises on politics and religion. All day long and through the night the unbroken line moved, the home town having its farewell.

On May 4 of this year 1865 anno Domini a procession moved with its hearse from the state capitol to Oak Ridge Cemetery. There on green banks and hillsides flowing away from a burial vault the crowded thousands of listeners and watchers heard prayers and hymns, heard the second inaugural read aloud. Bishop Matthew Simpson in a moving oration spoke as an interpreter and foreteller: "There are moments which involve in themselves eternities. There are instants which seem to contain germs which shall develop and bloom forever. Such a moment came in the tide of time to our land when a question must be settled, affecting all the powers of the earth.

The contest was for human freedom. Not for this republic merely, not for the Union simply, but to decide whether the people, as a people, in their entire majesty, were destined to be the Governments or whether they were to be subject to tyrants or aristocrats, or to class rule of any kind. This is the great question for which we have been fighting, and its decision is at hand, and the result of this contest will affect the ages to come. If successful, republics will spread in spite of monarchs all over this earth." Came then from the people, noted the *Illinois State Journal*, exclamations of "Amen! thank God!"

Evergreen carpeted the stone floor of the vault. On the coffin set in a receptacle of black walnut they arranged flowers carefully and precisely, they poured flowers as symbols, they lavished heaps of fresh flowers as though there could never be enough to tell either their hearts or his.

And the night came with great quiet.

And there was rest.

The prairie years, the war years, were over.

The burial vault at Springfield

CPSIA information can be obtained at www.ICGtesting.com
Printed in the USA
LVOW051939230812

295668LV00006B/75/A